HEALING
FOODS

MICHAEL VAN STRATEN

HEALING FOODS

NUTRITION FOR THE MIND, BODY, AND SPIRIT

BARNES
&NOBLE
BOOKS
NEW YORK

This edition published by
BARNES & NOBLE, INC.,
by arrangement with The Ivy Press Limited

1997 Barnes & Noble Books

M 10 9 8 7 6 5 4 3 2 1

ISBN 0-7607-0620-4

Note from the Publisher:
Information given in this book is not intended
to be taken as a replacement for medical advice.
Any person with a condition requiring medical
attention should consult a qualified medical
practitioner or therapist.

This book was conceived, designed, and produced by
THE IVY PRESS LIMITED
2/3 St Andrews Place
Lewes, East Sussex
BN7 1UP

Art Director: TERRY JEAVONS
Designer: JANE LANAWAY
Page Make-up: CHRIS LANAWAY
Commissioning Editor: VIV CROOT
Managing Editor: ANNE TOWNLEY
Text Editor: MANDY GREENFIELD
Editors: CAROLINE EARLE, ANDREW KIRK
Picture Research: JAN CROOT
Illustrations: MAINLINE DESIGN
Studio Photography: GUY RYECART, IAN PARSONS

Printed and bound in China

*The publishers wish to thank the following
for the use of pictures:*
Hutchison 8l, 59tl.
Image Bank Dardelet 14tl; De Lossy 21bl; Martin 28tl;
Pragoff 33r; Brown 59b; Bokelberg 63r.
Images 14c; 26bl; 29tr; 54–5.
Rex Features/SIPA 12c.
Science Photo Library Polliack 16tl; Tony Brain 31r; Burgess 52t.
Zefa/Stockmarket 8br; 15bc; 17br; 19tr.
Wartenburg 23bl; /Rossi 35br; 36tr; 43t; 44–5t; 46t; 50t; 53t; 62tl.

Dedication

Without The Ivy Press, this book would not have
happened. I now know why they chose the name;
clinging on with grim tenacity, my editor Viv Croot,
various directors, and the long-suffering Mandy
Greenfield harangued me with gentle persuasion on a
daily, almost hourly basis, until the work was finished.
For all their patience, guidance, and unceasing
cheerful support, I am grateful.

The journalistic input from my partner, Sally Pearce,
greatly enhanced the text; Sally was also purveyor of
food and sustenance throughout the many long nights
during which my secretary and PA Janet Betley and I
worked into the small hours. Janet is the only person
in my office who understands the mysteries of the
computer - without her the book would still be in
there somewhere. Janet's family too have been long-
suffering and now the book is finished, Tony, Louise,
and Kathy must wonder who this strange woman is
they see during the hours of daylight.

It is now scientifically fashionable to talk about the
therapeutic benefits of food, but it was not always so.
When I was a student at the British College of
Naturopathy and Osteopathy in the late fifties and
early sixties, healing through food was regarded as
little short of witchcraft and quackery. I would like to
dedicate this book to those early pioneers of
nutritional therapy whom I knew, respected, and
learnt from – Stanley Lief, Adele Davies, Gaylord
Hauser, Edward, Arthur, and Monty Winer, Dr. Vogel,
Dr. Hugo Brandenberger, Joan Lay, and most
particularly to two eminent medical practitioners who
were the first open-minded enough to have
discussions with me about nutritional therapy: the late
Dr. Sol Cohen and the late Sir Ronnie Raven.

Also Dr. Eric Millstone of the University of Sussex
for his contribution to the section on Food Additives.

Foreword

Alfred Vogel was one of the great pioneers of natural medicine. With centuries of Swiss folklore and tradition to call on, and a vast knowledge of European herbs and plants, he was one of the earliest modern advocates of the use of food as medicine.

"*The Nature Doctor* will show you what an extra-ordinary medicine chest you possess among your household stores. You will be surprised to learn how quite ordinary household foods can in an instant change into healing remedies ... For ten years I had the opportunity of confirming in my own Naturecure clinic at the sick bed the great superiority of natural, biological methods in conjunction with carefully chosen diet. In my experience, Nature is the first and best teacher for the conscientious observer."

Well into his nineties, and still working when he died in 1996, Vogel was the founder of Bioforce – one of the first major companies producing organically grown foods and medicine – which survives him as a testament to his work in the field of natural health. His book, *The Nature Doctor*, was first published in 1952 and is still required reading for any serious student of natural therapeutics. This extract from his introduction to the book has been a guiding principle in my practice for more than 30 years and is the informing spirit of *Healing Foods: Nutrition for the Mind, Body, and Spirit.*

Contents

PART ONE
FOOD FOR LIFE 11

PART TWO
THE FOOD INDEX 61

PART FOUR
USEFUL INFORMATION 209

PART THREE
AILMENTS THAT FOOD CAN
HELP TO HEAL 145

An A–Z of common ailments
and conditions that the right foods
can help prevent or cure

Introduction

Food scientists and nutritionists talk about protein, fats, and carbohydrates. But what real people eat is food. Certainly we need protein, fats, and carbohydrates as fuel for our body, and you will find lots of information about these aspects of nutrition elsewhere in the book. But the truth is that food is far more than fuel and, since man's earliest days as a hunter/gatherer, the acquisition, preparation, and eating of food have formed one of the greatest influences on our social development.

There are inseparable links between food and religion. Whether as offerings to the gods, special meals to celebrate holy days, fasting to purge the body and free the mind, or sustenance for the departed spirit at funerals, food has always been used in religious rites. From the most primitive tribes to the Aztecs, from the Egyptians to the ancient Greeks, from the Druids to the Dalai Lama, in Christianity, Judaism, Buddhism, and Islam, food is enshrined in religious practice.

If food really is so holy, why then, in the dying years of the twentieth century, do we usually treat it with so little respect? Why are we producing generations of junk-food kids? Why are we seeing epidemics of the so-called "diseases of civilization" – high blood pressure, strokes, heart disease, bowel disease, and a rising tide of cancers? Why do so many people seem to live on nothing but burgers, hot dogs, French fries, and other fast-food take-outs, and convenience foods?

Although the World Health Organization and many governments have taken on board the need for healthy-eating messages, it seems that they are all doing too little too late. The money spent on healthy-eating education is a mere drop in the ocean compared to the many tens of millions of dollars and pounds spent by the marketing moguls in the promotion of their latest long-shelf-life, high-profit-margin, low-nutrient-value products. There is,

without doubt, a growing interest in eating more of the foods that nourish and protect mind, body, and spirit, but the general public is confused by conflicting messages.

At every opportunity I poke my nose into other people's carts in the supermarket to see what they are buying. Armed with my tape recorder, I make interviews for my weekly radio program, asking people before they shop what they understand about the "healthy-eating" messages. And the fact is that while many of both sexes and all ages know about healthy eating, they don't understand how to put it into practice. They buy low-sugar foods that contain more salt. They buy low-fat foods that contain more sugar. They buy high-fiber foods made with refined flour and added bran. They buy salami and sausage instead of a fattier-looking meat roast.

It came as no surprise to me that a recent survey of over 800 people living in 500 British households revealed that 93 percent of men and 98 percent of women between the ages of 18 and 54 were deficient in folic acid; 60 percent of women in the same age bracket were not getting enough iron, and 90 percent of both men and women were going short of vitamin B_6; 73 percent of all women had less than the recommended daily amount of calcium; 57 percent of them also had too little zinc, and none of those in the survey actually consumed enough fiber.

You don't need to be a food freak or even a vegetarian to be healthy, although a good vegetarian diet generally means less heart disease, high blood pressure, strokes, and bowel cancer. What you do need is to put some careful thought, a bit more planning, and lots of common sense into your eating. The underlying message of all nutritional advice is that it doesn't matter what you do occasionally – what matters is what you do most of the time. What also matters is the enjoyment you gain from your food, and there is a sensible way of life somewhere between the burger-and-cola addict and the health-food freak.

LEFT *In all societies, food plays a central role. In areas of the world where it is scarce, or hard to come by, it is celebrated with ritual. In the West, we are in danger of taking good food for granted and selling our nutritional birthright for a mess of convenience food pottage.*

BELOW *Bags of health in this well-chosen selection of vitamins, minerals, and fiber (in the form of fresh fruit and vegetables), protein (eggs), and complex carbohydrates (bread, pasta, and potatoes).*

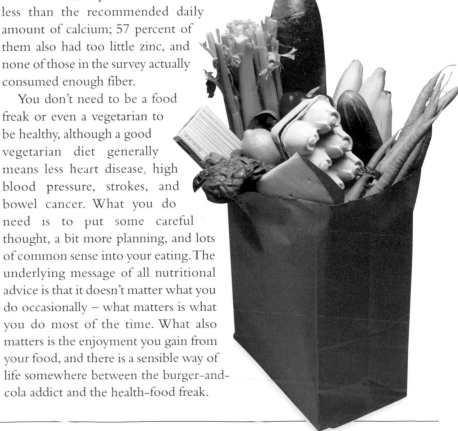

Introduction

More than thirty years as a practitioner have taught me that it is easier to deal with the burger-and-cola addicts – for it is not difficult to point out the error of this lifestyle – than it is to persuade the health-food freaks that they are committed to a disastrous path. Many food fanatics follow diets that simply don't provide enough of the essential nutrients and, worryingly, bring up their children in the same way. There is growing concern among pediatricians that parents are denying their children some vital foods, because they fear the harmful effects of pesticides and other agrochemicals. In the *Journal of Pediatric Health Care,* Wayne Bidlack and Sue Taylor discussed what they label "chemophobia" and maintain that the nutritional health benefits of eating fruit and vegetables far exceed the health risk from trace contaminants. Depriving children of fresh produce puts them at grave risk of malnutrition.

While I would be delighted to see everyone eating organic food, this is not a practical solution, as there is not yet enough supply to meet the demand. Washing food carefully (and peeling it where necessary) minimizes the already small risk, a risk that does not justify withholding the necessary wide variety of foodstuffs from a child's diet.

If all this sounds like doom and gloom, don't despair – the ever-growing phenomenon of ethnic restaurants, grocery stores, and markets throughout Britain and the main population centers of the USA brings us the opportunity to try a vast array of different, and mostly much healthier, foods. Japanese, Indian, Thai, Korean, and Chinese cookery all stem from cultures where meat is used more as a flavoring than a major ingredient – cuisines that historically have depended on plenty of carbohydrates, lots of vegetables, and little or no meat.

But of all the immigrant restaurateurs, none has had more influence on our eating habits than those from the Mediterranean – southern France, Italy, and Spain in particular. Not only does their Mediterranean diet *(see p. 63)* have a positive effect on health, but we can all learn a great deal from their attitude to the social importance of eating. Whole families, often three or even four generations, sit down together for Sunday lunch; animated discussions, heated arguments, and a passionate enjoyment of good food and good wine ensue. This is indeed food for mind and spirit, and fuel for the body.

FIVE EASY STEPS

Eating for mind, body, and spirit is not difficult, it is not cranky, and it is not expensive:

- One-third of your food should consist of raw, fresh produce – fruit, salads, and vegetables. Eat five portions a day for their vitamins, minerals, fiber, and protective phytochemicals.

- Eat whole wheat bread and pasta, brown rice, beans, lentils, and all the other good cereals and legumes for their protein, fiber, calcium, vitamins, and other minerals.

- Get most of your protein from fish, seafood, poultry, and small amounts of red meat, or be even healthier as a careful vegetarian.

- Dairy products and eggs are valuable in any diet, but choose low-fat dairy foods and use them with common sense. Small amounts of pure natural butter are far better for you than lots of chemical margarine, which has the same number of calories but also contains harmful trans fats.

- Avoid expensive processed foods and eat homemade soups, vegetable casseroles, and beans as an occasional alternative to meat. Cut down on all meat products – sausages, hot dogs, burgers, salamis, pâtés, and meat pies – which contain huge amounts of hidden fats.

ABOVE *Rice and pasta are cheap, easy-to-cook sources of carbohydrate energy. For extra nutritional points, choose whole wheat pasta and brown rice.*

◄○►

"Are there protective foods, like raw vegetables, which have cancer-protectors in them? The answer is yes, there are, but how significant are they? I'm still skeptical, but I would advise my own family to switch to the daily five portions of fruit and vegetables as recommended by the Government."

KAROL SIKORA
Professor of Clinical Oncology,
London's Hammersmith
Hospital

◄○►

From the other side of the Mediterranean, in the Middle East and North Africa, there are equally healthy styles of cooking – Turkish, Lebanese, Iranian, Egyptian, and Moroccan – all adapting local produce in their delicious, nutritious, and health-giving dishes. Even the much-maligned Jewish cooking is not all salt beef and pastrami on rye with pickles, or chicken soup and chopped liver.

I have eaten the most wonderful food in the simplest surroundings. The French call it peasant cooking; the Italians village cooking; I call it healthy cooking. From the rain forests of Brazil to the sands of the Kalahari, I have eaten out of the communal village pot. These people have never met a nutritionist in their lives, don't know about microwaves (or want to), don't have to decipher complex food labels – they cook by instinct and they cook their food with love. They welcome a stranger as an honored guest, and for all of them their food is mind, body, and spirit.

PART ONE

FOOD
FOR LIFE

We all need to know what foods will keep us healthy, supple, and strong; and we also need to know how to fine-tune our nutritional program to help us cope with life's major shifts and changes. This part of the book begins by looking at the foods that can protect you, build strength and stamina, and encourage mobility in all ages and both sexes. It then moves onto specifics, looking at

ABOVE *Life can indeed be just a bowl of cherries if you learn the basic rules of good nutrition.*

the varying nutritional needs the body has at different stages in life: puberty and adolescence, young adulthood, prepregnancy, pregnancy and early motherhood, the prime-time years (the thirties to fifties), and the third age. For each stage, a list is given of essential foods to boost vitality and maintain optimum health.

ABOVE *Drink your own health in herbal teas rather than measuring your life out in coffee spoons. Camomile makes a soothing, calming brew.*

The final section recognizes that food is also a major factor in mental and spiritual welfare, that you can indeed "feed your head." It addresses the spiritual, emotional, mental side of life and shows how specific foods can help promote harmony in the soul, regulate sleep, relieve depression and gloom, and keep the brain up to the mark. There is also an essay on safe fasting.

RIGHT *Remember the rule of five; five portions of fresh fruit or vegetables a day, in any combination you like.*

Food to Protect You

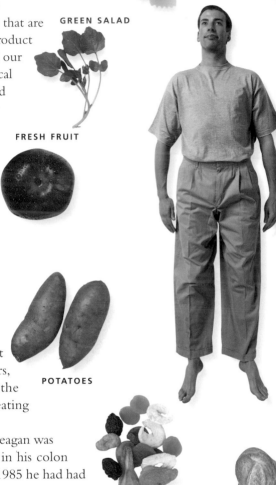

PASTA

GREEN SALAD

FRESH FRUIT

POTATOES

DRIED FRUIT

BREAD

MORE THAN 2,000 years ago Hippocrates said: "Let your food be your medicine, and your medicine be your food." Now scientists are beginning to understand that the food we eat each day can make the difference between life and death. A strong immune system offers protection against the common cold as well as against cancer; fights fatigue as well as fever; promotes resistance as much as recovery. Above all, your natural defenses depend on the state of your nutrition.

The truth is that although an apple a day might keep the doctor away, eating more fresh fruit, salads, and vegetables will keep you out of hospital. Evidence collected from worldwide studies shows that those people whose diets are rich in these simple, inexpensive foods are less likely to suffer from heart disease and cancer. Adding plenty of unrefined carbohydrates increases that protection still further by reducing blood cholesterol and increasing bowel efficiency.

Everyone knows that fruits, salads, and vegetables supply essentials like vitamins and minerals, but even many scientists are unaware of the powerful chemical substances within them that nature produces. These "phytochemicals" play a major part in the protective action of these foods against cancers and other diseases. Without these essential nutrients, individual cells in the human body are unable to function properly.

The antioxidant vitamins A, C, and E, together with selenium and folic acid, are also known to contribute to our ability to fight off cancerous changes, and while pills are not a substitute for good food, there is certainly a place for nutritional supplements as extra insurance against major diseases, but also against aging.

One point on which all the experts agree is that increasing the total amount of fresh produce cannot possibly do any harm; they do not all agree that the evidence for cancer protection is strong enough to make blanket recommendations. But it seems foolhardy to ignore not only eminent scientists such as Gladys Block, Michael Hill, and John Potter, but also the accumulated wisdom of our forebears, who survived against all the odds on a diet of mainly fruit, vegetables, grains, nuts, and seeds.

FREE RADICALS AND ANTIOXIDANTS

Free radicals are unstable molecules that are manufactured by the body as a by-product of normal metabolism. They also fill our environment in the form of chemical pollutants, factory emissions, and exhaust fumes. They are highly destructive, so it is vital that they are removed, otherwise they combine with oxygen, causing severe cell damage.

Antioxidants act as scavengers, cleaning the system of free radicals and protecting against their destructive power. Vitamins C and E, beta-carotene, and other carotenoids are among the most important antioxidants, protecting the body against heart disease and some cancers, and are all present in the foods you should be eating every day.

In 1984 President Reagan was found to have a polyp in his colon and by the summer of 1985 he had had an operation and was on a widely publicized anticancer diet advised by the American Cancer Society. What was the diet? No red meat, no animal fats, lots of fruit and vegetables, plenty of salads, and regular amounts of good cereals – just the sort of diet that alternative practitioners like me have been recommending for half a century. Needless to say Reagan's diet was broadcast across our newspapers and television screens for weeks. But 12 years later, little has changed in the approach of doctors to cancer prevention and food.

There are many causes of cancer, not one single factor. But in the end it is the uncontrolled

ABOVE Ronald Reagan, former president of the US, now a sufferer of the debilitating Alzheimer's disease.

VITAMIN BOOST

A simple regime of extra vitamins and minerals is inexpensive and safe:

Vitamin C	1g
Vitamin A	600µg
Selenium	60µg
Zinc	5mg
Vitamin E	5mg
Beta-carotene	2000µg
Folic acid	200µg

SALAD

FRESH VEGETABLES

CEREALS

EGGS

LEGUMES

GARLIC

ABOVE *By building into your daily menus the appropriate foods, you can help to protect yourself and your family from unnecessary illnesses. All the foods shown in the protective circle have their own special qualities, which are explained in detail in* The Food Index *(pages 60–143).*

multiplication of a group of cells that is "cancer." Free radicals can attack and injure the genes that regulate cell division. So it is important to give the body as much protection as possible, and the antioxidant properties of vitamin C and beta-carotene appear to be vital in this respect.

Increasing the amount of antioxidants in the blood also helps to prevent heart disease. Vitamin E would appear to be the most important of these, in order to reduce damage to the arteries that carry blood to the heart.

BETA-CAROTENE Studies in Europe, Japan, and the US strongly suggest that high levels of beta-carotene consumption, in the form of fruit and vegetables, are linked to a reduced risk of lung cancer and cancers of the digestive system.

VITAMIN C Throughout the world, investigations show that eating plenty of the vitamin C-rich foods offers added protection against cancers of the mouth, throat, cervix, and breast.

VITAMIN E The World Health Organization (WHO) has examined 16 population groups around Europe. They found that the lower the amount of vitamin E in the blood of volunteers, the greater their risk of dying from heart disease.

The American Department of Health, WHO, and Britain's Health Education Authority all recommend a total of five portions of fresh fruit and vegetables each day. Very few people in the UK get anywhere near that amount, despite the evidence that the whole nation would be healthier if we did.

ANTIOXIDANT SOURCE FOODS

Use the following chart to make sure that you are eating enough of the right foods to get your share of the antioxidants. To obtain your daily requirement of vitamins C and E and beta-carotene, simply tot up the percentages of a good selection of the foods listed. If you want optimal health, aim for the magic total of 100 percent for each of these essential nutrients.

VITAMIN C 3½oz/100g of	Percentage of daily requirement	VITAMIN E 3½oz/100g of	Percentage of daily requirement	BETA-CAROTENE 3½oz/100g of	Percentage of daily requirement
blackcurrants	400%	apples	2%	apricots (fresh)	19%
brussels sprouts	80%	asparagus	25%	brussels sprouts	50%
cauliflower	120%	avocado (half)	30%	cantaloup melon	15%
gooseberries	80%	bananas	2%	carrots (new)	75%
green pepper	200%	blackcurrants	10%	carrots (old)	150%
kiwi fruit	196%	broccoli	11%	mango	15%
lemons	160%	carrots	5%	peaches	5%
melon	30%	damsons	6%	spinach	75%
oranges	76%	spinach	20%	tomatoes	7%
potatoes	36%	sweet potatoes	50%		
strawberries	120%	tomatoes	12%	**2oz/50g of**	
tomatoes	40%			lettuce	6%
turnip	34%	**2oz/50g of**		parsley	44%
		hazelnuts	85%		
2oz/50g of		parsley	9%		
lettuce	15%	sunflower seed oil (⅛oz/5g)	30%		
radishes	25%	watercress	5%		
watercress	60%				

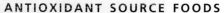

Strength and Stamina

THERE IS A direct relationship between health and fitness. The fitter you are, the better your state of mind, body, and spirit. Fitness encourages better functioning of the body's own immune-defense mechanisms, making it less likely that you will pick up every virus or bacteria that is doing the rounds. Fitness increases the body's own production of endorphins, the "feel-good" chemicals in the brain. Fitness means that you will feel better about yourself, have a more positive self-image, and an enhanced sense of inner peace and calm.

But what is fitness? In simple terms it is a combination of strength, stamina, and mobility. To achieve these three goals in a harmonic balance requires a positive attitude of mind, appropriate regular exercise, and a healthy diet that supplies all the essential nutrients in the proportions that suit your lifestyle. But if you are suddenly overwhelmed with guilt because of your life as a "couch potato," or worried by the extra bulges that weren't there last year and tempted to dash off and join the nearest exercise class – don't, before you have looked at all the options.

If you are going to any exercise class, make sure that the teacher is properly trained (and preferably a member of a recognized professional body). If no one asks you anything about your previous medical history or makes you fill in a medical questionnaire, go elsewhere. Watch a class before you join, to make sure there is adequate supervision – one teacher for a class of 20 or 30 pupils is simply not enough.

True fitness is a combination of strength, stamina, and mobility – it's not much good being able to run a marathon if you can't carry your groceries home from the supermarket, or being a super body-building weight-lifter if you can't pull your sweater off over your head. And you need to get fit in order

BELOW Cycling offers a sociable alternative to solitary hours in the gym. A daily cycle ride of 20 minutes greatly improves stamina and muscle strength.

EXERCISE CAUTION

Sensible exercise is good for your health and improves your shape. But the wrong teacher and the wrong exercise can cause serious problems. Don't get sucked into the latest fad just because it's fashionable. Untrained aerobics teachers are bad enough, but untrained step-and-slide aerobics teachers are even worse. All over Britain and the USA, osteopaths, chiropractors, and other specialists in physical medicine are seeing more and more injuries from this type of ridiculous exercise: back pain and disk problems caused by the exaggerated movements in aerobics; ankle, knee, calf, and hip injuries nowadays from incorrectly taught step classes; ankle, knee, and thigh trauma resulting from the ultimate stupidity of slide aerobics.

to exercise, so if you are overweight, start gently with non-weight-bearing exercise, such as swimming or cycling, or get into the habit of regular walking at a brisk pace.

If you haven't exercised for years, don't start where you left off: 20 years as a "couch potato" is not good preparation for a sudden game of squash with the new office junior – but it is a pretty good prescription for a heart attack. Aim for three sessions of physical activity a week, and make sure that you also exert yourself enough to get out of breath at least once a day. If you get a pain in your chest or feel dizzy, STOP. If it happens more than once, see your doctor. Never exercise if you have a cold, flu, or feel unwell.

Getting into the habit of regular exercise reduces your risk of heart disease, helps to control blood pressure, and is vital to any healthy weight-reduction plan. It improves your sleep, reduces menstrual pain and problems, strengthens your bones, keeps your muscles in good shape, and protects you against injury. Regular exercise also means better general health and fewer days off work. Relief from depression and an improved sex life are additional bonuses.

But take care. You need to speak to your physician before starting any strenuous exercise program, if you are over 40 and habitually inactive; if you suffer from any form of bone or joint disease; if you have high blood pressure or heart problems; if you get chest pain or dizzy spells, or regularly feel faint. If

Strength and Stamina

none of these apply to you, then start exercising now. But remember that it doesn't have to be hell to be healthy – going for the burn is out, and being desperately competitive is unnecessary. Choose activities that you enjoy and make them part of your regular routine. You will be amazed at how quickly you start to feel, and look, better. And, perhaps most surprising of all, even problems like chronic fatigue and tired-all-the-time syndrome (TATT) will improve.

SPORTS NUTRITION

But the key to any healthy exercise program – and even more so if you are seriously involved in sport – is the state of your nutrition. Whether your chosen activity is biased toward strength, stamina, mobility, or a combination of these, your body will need specific foods for specific purposes. If you are a competitive athlete, at any level (no matter whether your chosen sport is golf, tennis, skiing, swimming, karate, American football, or Sumo wrestling) you need the right food, in the right quantities, at the right time. Whether you want to be fit for life or are trying to get fit in order to exercise, the quality of the fuel that you put into your body as food must be your first priority. Regular physical exercise will help build strength and stamina, but to achieve this, especially if you are seriously involved in sport, the right balance of foods in your diet is vital to improve fitness.

Muscle activity needs energy, which is available in two distinctly different forms – aerobic (with oxygen) and anaerobic (without oxygen). Generally speaking, the slow-twitch muscle fibers that are used for endurance, as in cross-country or marathon running, are

FOOD FOR SPORT

Ideally you should be getting 10–15 percent of your calories from protein, 20–30 percent from fats and 50–65 percent from carbohydrates. A healthy "low-fat" diet does not mean "no fat." As well as being a source of vitamins D and E and the essential fatty acids, fats also provide a useful calorie store. Many people still labor under the misconception that to build strong muscles it is necessary to eat large amounts of animal protein – and it was not that long ago that endurance athletes and heavy field athletes, such as rowers, shot-putters, weight-lifters, and hammer-throwers, used to eat vast quantities of steak. In reality, even élite athletes need very little more protein than a sedentary office worker, and some trainers maintain that the normal recommended daily allowance of 0.8g of protein per 2¼lb/kg of body weight is more than enough for both endurance and strength athletes. At most this should be increased to 1.2g of protein per 2¼lb/kg of body weight, but even this amount does not require supplementation with protein powders or high-protein drinks. Over-consumption of protein results in increased levels of the by-product urea, which can cause lethargy and general malaise. It is healthiest to get your protein from fish, poultry, and vegetable sources, modest amounts of dairy products and eggs, but limited amounts of red meat. This keeps your consumption of the harmful saturated fats down to a minimum.

salmon (protein and fish oil)

pasta (carbohydrate, fiber, vitamins, and minerals)

cream cheese (fat and minerals)

aerobic and get their energy by burning glucose and oxygen. Slow-twitch fibers can function for longer periods than fast-twitch fibers, as they produce lactic acid (which interferes with muscle contraction and causes cramp) more slowly. Fast-twitch muscle fibers are those used for explosive effort like sprinting or squash, and they consume energy produced without oxygen. The performance of both groups of fibers can be remarkably improved by training: aerobic exercise for the slow-twitch fibers, and exercise that is isometric (increasing muscle tone without shortening) and isokinetic (opposing one muscle to another) for the fast-twitch ones. A program that includes a comprehensive range of physical activities will increase strength and stamina.

LEFT *If you take up a sport seriously, remember that good nutrition is just as important as training. Running, for example, needs slow-release complex carbohydrates to provide an adequate supply of glycogen for the body to convert into glucose energy.*

Strength and Stamina

ABOVE *Healthy red blood cells, loaded with the oxygen that enables the body to burn food and so release energy. Food rich in iron, folic acid, and vitamin B₁₂ will increase the cells' ability to carry oxygen.*

RIGHT *Cereals such as porridge oats and homemade muesli make a good carbohydrate-based snack. For athletes they are excellent for carbo-loading (building up glycogen stores two hours or so before the event). For everybody, as part of breakfast, they provide all-day stamina.*

When at rest, muscles primarily use fatty acids as their energy source, but as soon as you start exercising, the increased demand for energy is satisfied by using extra glucose in the bloodstream and by breaking down carbohydrate that is stored in the muscle tissue as glycogen – a readily available form of glucose that is also deposited in the liver. With training, it is possible to increase the amount of stored glycogen by 300–400 percent.

If you are unfit, the blood does not carry enough oxygen to sustain prolonged and strenuous activity and your stores of glycogen will run out. With training, oxygenation is improved, along with the body's ability to create energy from fatty acids, so sparing your glycogen stores. This is not only a step to better performance and endurance, but also a great aid in keeping your body weight at the correct level. Slow, long-distance exercise – not exceeding 35 percent of your maximum effort – is the ideal way of stimulating the fat-burning energy process.

Another essential for fitness is a really high level of foods that are rich in iron, vitamin B₁₂, and folic acid, as the ability of the red blood cells to carry oxygen is a key factor in increasing your exercise levels. The ability to do more exercise results in stronger muscles and an effective increase in the performance of your normal metabolism.

Do you need extra vitamins and minerals if you are physically very active? On the whole the answer is no, as your diet should be providing you with all that you need. You are probably consuming 3,000 calories a day or more, and if you are obtaining these from beneficial foods you will be getting more than enough of most nutrients. If you are a vegetarian, it is probably a good idea to take a simple iron and zinc supplement, and if you are consuming fewer than 1,500 calories a day, you will almost certainly need a simple multivitamin and mineral pill. But there is no evidence that taking extra vitamins and minerals has the slightest effect on improving performance. There does appear, though, to be a reduction in the efficiency of the body's natural immune system in athletes who are training intensively and competing regularly, and for this reason I think a supplement of vitamins A, C, and E, with selenium, is a good idea in order to give the immune system an extra boost.

Carbohydrate consumption for the athlete seems to cause a lot of confusion, but it is really quite simple. The great majority of your calories must come from carbohydrates. You have to supply your body with enough carbohydrates before you exercise, and replenish these stores as quickly as possible afterward. If you want to be a serious athlete, what you eat for 365 days of the year is what matters – not just the way you plan your competition days. It is almost certainly best to fit your eating patterns around your training and lifestyle schedules, so you may end up eating five or six small meals a day, rather than stuffing yourself with a huge evening meal just before bedtime. Make sure you get your calories from complex carbohydrates, such as potatoes, whole wheat bread, root vegetables, good cereals, pasta, brown rice, nuts, legumes, and masses of fruit and vegetables. Use dried fruit and seeds as low-bulk, high-calorie snacks.

Strength and Stamina

It is important to keep your fluid intake really high, so drink lots of water, fresh fruit juice, and load up on fluids before training or competition. Don't rely on expensive sports drinks, and avoid salt tablets at all costs. During training and competition drink regular, small amounts of fluids, which should be at room temperature – too much fluid or liquids that are too cold are expelled from the stomach more quickly.

Carbohydrate-loading is the way to make sure that your glycogen stores are up to scratch before you undertake sustained exercise. Because exercising on a full stomach is uncomfortable and inadvisable, you need to eat two to three hours beforehand and to get your carbohydrates from complex starches, not from high-sugar drinks, candies, or chocolate. The muscles are best able to store glycogen during the hour after you have finished exercising, so this is the time to put the carbohydrates back into your system. If it isn't practical to eat a proper meal then, use cereal bars, bananas, and dried fruit for rapid replacement.

One of the benefits of regular weight-bearing exercise is that it helps to build strong bones. Unfortunately this works only when combined with adequate consumption of the correct nutrients – and there are substances that interfere with the body's bone-building ability (see box). Problems arise in some women athletes, especially gymnasts, ballet dancers, distance runners, and obsessive exercisers, in whom body weight can fall so much that they stop having periods and, in effect, undergo an artificial menopause. As their hormone mechanisms switch off, so does their ability to absorb calcium and lay down new bone structure. Over the years I have seen many such women who, at the age of 25 or 30, have a skeleton that could be 20 years older and is already showing signs of arthritis, wear and tear, and osteoporosis. But such unfortunate consequences are all avoidable, just by taking the right precautions.

EATING TO AVOID OSTEOPOROSIS

It is essential to get 10µg of vitamin D and 1,000mg of calcium each day. The body manufactures vitamin D when sunlight falls on the skin, but all the oily fish are rich sources of this nutrient. To guarantee adequate calcium intake, eat a selection of the following every day (in descending order of calcium content): tofu, low-fat cheese, parsley, seaweed, whitebait, tahini, sesame seeds, yogurt, sardines, canned salmon, almonds, figs, molasses, dried beans, Brazil nuts, watercress, all green leafy vegetables, and good bread. These are the top calcium-rich foods and if they are on your regular shopping list, your bones should be fine.

Anticalcium agents – coffee, alcohol, and smoking – all lead to a lower bone-calcium content; uncooked bran contains phytic acid, which interferes with calcium absorption; a high-salt diet increases calcium excretion; and a high consumption of red meat is also linked to lower calcium content in the bones. Your diet should therefore be extremely rich in all fruit and vegetables, fish and shellfish, modest amounts of poultry and low-fat dairy products, and lots of beans, nuts, and seeds.

If calcium supplements are needed, they should contain calcium, magnesium, vitamin D, and boron for the most efficient absorption.

LEFT *Dehydration is a risk during strenuous exercise. Make sure you drink enough before you start your routine, and replenish any lost through perspiration when you finish.*

BELOW *Avoid excess coffee if you suffer from osteoporosis as it inhibits the formation of calcium in the bones.*

BOTTOM *Gentle regular exercise improves oxygenation of the blood and encourages strong bones and supportive muscle.*

Mobility

MOBILITY is one of the key factors in the maintenance of good physical health, as being active stimulates the cardiovascular system, maintains good muscle tone through exercise and good bone strength through weight bearing. Sadly, these important aspects of keeping people mobile are quite often overlooked and the immense psychological importance of mobility nearly always totally ignored, unless you are confined to a wheelchair, when there may be some grasp of the emotional difficulties that this causes. Scant regard is paid to the mental distress resulting from loss of normal mobility; to the lack of independence; to the humiliation of being unable to perform the simplest task, such as putting on your own socks or picking up something you have dropped; or to the despair at not being able to walk your dog or go to the corner store for your newspaper.

PREVENTION

A great deal of immobility is the result of preventable neglect – neglect of sound nutrition, of remedial exercise, and, especially in the elderly, neglect of the encouragement needed to persuade people out of their chairs and onto their feet. There are many reasons for loss of mobility: traumatic injury, temporary illness, chronic joint disease, chronic lung disease, post-operative recovery, severe obesity, ME, and even depression (a more common cause than most people realize). Whatever the reason, eating foods that protect and maintain the integrity of joint surfaces, build up muscle strength, maintain good weight, and nourish the mind and spirit is the first step. And this is true of both prevention and cure.

A normal joint consists of two articulated bony surfaces covered with cartilage and surrounded by a fibrous capsule lined with special tissue called synovium. The space inside the joint is filled with synovial fluid produced by the synovium, which acts as an extremely efficient lubricant. The soft tissues surrounding the joint include muscles, tendons, ligaments, and a bursa, or protective sac.

Arthritis, rheumatoid arthritis, rheumatism, serious joint diseases, and the many other joint problems that crop up in everyday life can be extremely painful and limiting. Some of these problems may be triggered by injury, others by occupation; and hobbies, sport, and unaccustomed overuse of individual joints can all lead to localized difficulties. Medically many of these problems may seem trivial, as are attitudes to their treatment. But they are far from trivial to the unfortunate individual who suffers from them. The general approach to all such joint problems is a combination of ice packs, contrast hot and cold bathing, rest, support, physical therapy, and remedial exercise.

Common to all these problems should be a simple nutritional approach. All the oily fish are beneficial, as they have a positive effect on minimizing atherosclerosis, which affects the circulation. In addition, the omega-3 fatty acids in fish oils stimulate the body's production of prostaglandins, the body's own antiinflammatory hormones. For this reason consume regular amounts of salmon, mackerel, herring, trout, sardines, mussels (especially the New Zealand green-lipped variety), and other shellfish.

There is evidence that a diet low in the specific antioxidants selenium and vitamins A, C, and E increases the likelihood of joint disorders, and for this reason the diet should contain a weekly portion of liver (not for pregnant women), plenty of carrots, broccoli, apricots, sweet potatoes, and cantaloup melon, all rich in vitamin A or beta-carotene. Red and yellow sweet peppers, kiwi fruit, oranges, brussels sprouts, and cabbage should all be eaten in abundance, for their vitamin C. Avocados, fresh nuts,

BELOW *Sardines are round oily fish, an excellent source of omega-3 fatty acids, which help the body manufacture the antiinflammatory hormone prostaglandin. An eating program rich in oily fish will therefore help prevent joint problems.*

Mobility

asparagus, sunflower seeds, and olive oil are rich in vitamin E. Selenium is found in all fish and shellfish, meat, whole grains and cereals, eggs, and brewer's yeast.

Cut down on red meat, red wine, fortified wines like sherry, port, and madeira, large amounts of other alcoholic drinks, game, caffeine, salt, and sodium-based food additives.

Bursitis is an acute inflammation of the bursa, the fluid-containing protective capsule around a joint. The most likely areas affected are the elbow (tennis elbow); the knee (housemaid's knee); and the buttocks (ischial bursitis, otherwise known as weaver's bottom). Avoiding any pressure on the areas involved is essential.

Tenosynovitis, inflammation of the protective sheath around a tendon, most often occurs in the tendons of the fingers, causing trigger finger, and in what is known as the "anatomical snuffbox," where the thumb joins the side of the wrist.

Tennis elbow is not often caused by playing tennis, but is more commonly due to repetitive manual use, such as painting, decorating, sanding, and housework. Golfer's elbow is exactly the same but occurs on the inside of the elbow joint. Plantar fasciitis is a common inflammation of the joint in the bottom of the heel.

Frozen shoulder is excruciatingly painful. Simple tasks like combing the hair, shaving, doing up a bra, getting a wallet from the hip pocket, or putting on a jacket become extremely difficult, if not impossible.

All soft tissue and joint problems require professional treatment. Some of them may result in surgical intervention or the injection of local steroids, but early treatment with physiotherapy, osteopathy, massage, or acupuncture (and often a combination of these) offers the best chance of success. This will be greatly enhanced by following the dietary advice given above.

Even short periods of immobility can lead to rapid weight gain, which can exacerbate the immobility. It is essential to

ABOVE *Melon is rich in vitamin A (beta-carotene), and a delicious way to ensure adequate antioxidant intake.*

BELOW *Mobility is as much a matter of practice as age or genetic inheritance. A craft such as knitting can help prevent fingers from seizing up.*

BACKACHE

Of all the everyday causes of mobility loss, backache is by far the most common. Whatever its cause, good nutrition is as vital to the healing process as taking steps to protect the affected joint, ligament, muscle, tendon, or disk tissues that have triggered the pain in the first place. With the exception of muscle tissue, all the other components involved in back problems have a very poor blood supply, and to ensure rapid healing you must take the right steps to protect and improve this situation. Nicotine, caffeine, and more than a couple of units of alcohol will all constrict the tiniest capillary blood vessels that carry blood to these areas, so they must be avoided. It is also essential to ensure a high intake of the protective foods, such as those high in omega-3 fatty acids, selenium, and vitamins A, C, and E.

make a reduction in your calorie consumption without compromising good nutrition. The easiest way of achieving this is to cut down on all animal fats, except the oily fish. One major pitfall is comfort eating. Because you are immobilized, you may feel miserable, being miserable can lead to depression, and being depressed can lead you to the cookie jar, the sticky bun, and the chocolate cake. You must avoid these temptations.

In the elderly, immobility can become a habit that turns into a self-fulfilling prophecy – the less you do, the less you can do; and the less you can do, the less you do. It is vital to encourage the elderly to take regular exercise – even exercising arms, hands, shoulders, knees, and ankles while sitting is a good start. Studies have shown that even those who have been virtually chairbound for years can soon become active and walking again when encouraged to take up a regular exercise program, combined with good nutrition.

Nutrition for Women

FROM THE fertilized egg right through to old age, health is determined by nutrition. Of course other factors are important too – smoking, alcohol or drug abuse, environmental pollution, accidents, and state of mind all play their part. But, regardless of these, poor nutrition means poor health, and optimum nutrition offers maximum protection from the hostile world that surrounds us.

Good food is essential to both men and women, but the female of the species has a wider variety of specific needs as life progresses from the cradle to the grave.

Glowing health is every woman's birthright. The kind of health that gives you lots of energy, a positive outlook on life, and serenity of mind; the health that makes you look good because you feel good; the health that means a clear skin, bright eyes, and glossy hair; the health that keeps you free from all those problems that women are conditioned to expect – from acne to brittle bones, from morning sickness to postnatal depression, from PMS to menopausal problems.

The Well Woman's Eating Plan described on the following pages will show you how you can secure the birthright of good health for you and your babies. How you can fortify yourself through the seven ages of your life (the teens, the twenties, pre-conception and pregnancy, motherhood, the vital thirties and forties, the menopause, and the golden years) against physical strain and nervous stress.

How you can beef up your natural resistance to infection and disease. How you can kiss goodbye to the traditional woes of womanhood. How you can protect yourself against today's crop of disabling or life-threatening diseases – arthritis, osteoporosis, cancer, and heart disease. And how you can keep your good looks for life – without resorting to the beauty parlor or the plastic surgeon.

This plan does not call for expensive pills or potions. It does not involve complicated diet sheets, expensive meal substitutes, or the latest food-fad regime. The Well Woman's Eating Plan is a positive guide to vitality eating, based on the nutritional Essential Foods that you need at each stage of your life. You will learn to include these in your weekly shopping basket – everyday foods that you can buy in any supermarket, local deli, or street-market stall; wonderful foods that can cost literally a few cents, and yet in terms of your continued good health are worth their weight in gold.

ESSENTIAL FOODS

During each of the seven ages of woman there are specific nutritional needs that are satisfied by the relevant Essential Foods. In each case the seven foods (and one herb) listed should be eaten every week. However, all the Essential Foods are important for every woman. Whatever your age, get to know the entire list and use it as the foundation of your weekly shopping basket. Provided that you are getting a regular intake of all the Essential Foods, there is no need to feel guilty about the odd treat. As long as you are sticking to the spirit of this eating plan, you should not become a food freak. There is nothing more boring than someone who takes their own food to a party, wrapped in a brown paper bag. When your friends all go out, join in, enjoy whatever you eat, and have a good time. A little of what you fancy does you good! There's nothing wrong with the occasional treat, such as a chocolate éclair, doughnut, burger, or French fries, as long as they are not part of your staple diet.

ABOVE *A little of what you fancy can be very good for you – even chocolate éclairs, taken in moderation.*

TOP LEFT *Feeling good from the inside out is an achievable goal for every woman, whatever her age.*

LEFT: *Good nutrition from babyhood onward is the basis for optimum health.*

Nutrition for Women

VITALITY EATING

Vitality means having both physical and mental vigor. These can both be yours if you follow the simple rules of vitality eating.

- Have a mixed diet of as many different foods as possible.
- Eat regular meals, and make sure that you have the time to enjoy and digest them.
- Eat plenty of fresh fruit, salads, and vegetables, particularly the green leafy and yellow ones.
- Cultivate a taste for whole grain cereals.
- Get most of your protein from fish, poultry, and legumes, and rather less from meat, which should be as lean as possible.
- Eat regular but modest amounts of eggs, low-fat cheese, and other dairy products.
- Use plenty of fresh seeds, sprouted seeds, and fresh, unsalted nuts, together with dried fruits. Add them to your meals and eat them as nourishing snacks.
- Drink plenty of fruit and vegetable juices, lots of water, and only sensible quantities of tea, coffee, and alcohol.
- Bread, pasta, rice, and potatoes are very healthy. Eat plenty of them, but watch what you do to them. Lashings of butter, cream sauces, and the fryer are not part of this plan.
- Try to take one-third of your daily diet as fresh and raw foods. For the other two thirds, get into the kitchen. There is nothing as vital as home-cooked food, made from wholesome and nourishing ingredients. It is also a lot less expensive than take-outs, canned food, and TV dinners.

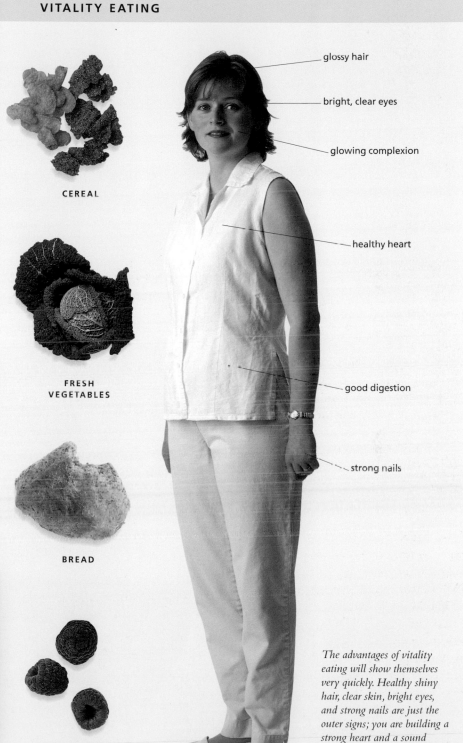

CEREAL

FRESH VEGETABLES

BREAD

FRESH FRUIT

glossy hair

bright, clear eyes

glowing complexion

healthy heart

good digestion

strong nails

The advantages of vitality eating will show themselves very quickly. Healthy shiny hair, clear skin, bright eyes, and strong nails are just the outer signs; you are building a strong heart and a sound digestion, the basis for an ultra-healthy life.

Nutrition for Men

MEN SUFFER more serious illness than women and are much more likely to die prematurely before the age of 65. Between the ages of 55 and 74 a man is more than twice as likely to have a heart attack or stroke than a woman of the same age. Despite the fact that cancer of the prostate is as common in men as breast cancer in women, most men have little idea where it occurs. The commonest malignancy in men between the ages of 20 and 40 is cancer of the testicle, yet they know nothing about self-examination.

At the root of all these problems, and the key to reducing the ravages of premature and largely preventable deaths, is Nutrition with a capital N. Poor nutrition, combined with the type of lifestyle common to so many men, minimal consumption of the protective antioxidants, and overexposure to damaging free radicals, puts men's health at risk.

A recent survey revealed that the majority of men know more about breast cancer and PMS than they do about enlargement of the prostate or cancer of the testicles. This state of blissful ignorance is extremely worrying – there are a thousand new cases of testicular cancer each year and 150 of those affected will die; 8 out of 10 men will have treatment for a prostate problem at some time in their lives, and there are 11,500 new cases each year.

HEART DISEASE, HIGH BLOOD PRESSURE, AND STROKES

This unholy trinity of diseases linking the heart and circulation is the major cause of premature and preventable death in men throughout the UK. In fact, the one league table that Britain consistently comes top of in the Western world is the one that measures deaths from heart disease.

Improved nutrition reduces the risk of heart disease, high blood pressure, and stroke. Increasing the amount of fiber, and particularly soluble fiber from oats, beans, apples, pears, and good cereals, is a great starting point. Eating lots of all fresh fruit, carrots, and dark-green leafy vegetables increases the amount of nutrients that protect your body against heart disease and keep your veins and arteries in good condition. Throwing away the salt cellar – the silent killer on your kitchen table – and cutting down on all foods that contain salt, and on any

additives with the word sodium in their list of ingredients, also helps to reduce blood pressure. Modest exercise (such as a 20-minute walk at least three times a week), sensible alcohol consumption (such as two glasses of red wine a day), together with lots of garlic and good olive oil and a healthy consumption of oily fish will help to keep you out of the league table that no-one wants to win.

MEN'S NUTRITIONAL NEEDS

Men have a greater requirement of some nutrients than women – calories, protein, magnesium, zinc, selenium, thiamin (B1), riboflavin (B2), niacin, vitamin B6, vitamin A, and vitamin E.

ABOVE *Replacing daily doughnuts and Danish with fresh fruit is the first step on a revitalizing nutrition program.*

BELOW *Red wine has a beneficial effect on the circulatory system. If you like it, aim to keep your consumption to two wineglasses a day, best taken with a meal.*

SOME FACTS ABOUT MEN'S HEALTH

- An 18-year-old man has an 80 percent chance of reaching the age of 65, but an 18-year-old woman's chance is 88 percent.
- Life expectancy is 72 for men, 78 for women.
- 80 percent of men need treatment for prostate problems.
- Prostate cancer is as common as breast cancer.
- Testicular cancer is the commonest cancer in men aged 20–40.
- 45 percent of men are overweight.
- 13 percent are obese (double the number just four years ago).
- Only 20 percent of men exercise three times a week.
- 60 percent of middle-aged men are "couch potatoes."
- 7 out of every 8 men has at least one risk factor for heart disease and stroke – high blood pressure, high cholesterol, smoking, lack of exercise, etc.
- Only a quarter of men with high blood pressure have treatment for it.
- Men between 55 and 74 are over twice as likely to have had a heart attack or stroke than women of the same age.
- Almost 90 percent of men never examine their testicles.
- In the last 50 years men's sperm count has halved.

Nutrition for Men

"Strong and convincing evidence from studies carried out around the world shows that a diet rich in fruit and vegetables is associated with a low incidence of heart disease and certain cancers."

DR. KEVIN CHEESEMAN
Epidemiologist at Brunel
University, London

Considering that the US minimum recommended daily allowances (RDAs) are nearly all higher than those in Britain, and that some authorities consider even these to be too low, certain of these deficiencies are definitely linked to disease.

Some of the vitamin and mineral levels that are below, or barely reach, the RDA concern the most protective of nutrients: those responsible for our resistance to heart and circulatory disease and to many forms of cancer. The average British male gets only 2.4mg a day of beta-carotene – there is no UK RDA, but the American National Cancer Institute advises a minimum of 6mg. The average consumption of vitamin C is just under 65mg per day, although it is believed that 6 out of 10 British men fail to reach the 60mg minimum.

Vitamin D is essential for the formation of healthy bones, but the average UK intake is only 3.4µg compared with the RDA of 5µg. Vitamin E, one of the most powerful heart protectors, has an American RDA of 10mg per day, yet the British male's average consumption is only 9.7mg and cardioprotective benefits are seen at much higher intakes than this – especially in the Mediterranean diet.

British men fare badly too in minerals, failing to get enough potassium, consuming on average more than twice the safe level of sodium, and missing out on iron, selenium, and zinc. It is the magical combination of vitamins A, C, and E with zinc and selenium that is fundamental to a super immune system. Every man can give himself the easiest life insurance possible simply by cutting down his consumption of fats, sugars, salt, and refined carbohydrates, consuming modest amounts of alcohol (not more than 21 units a week), and eating abundant quantities of the foods that supply the vital protective vitamins, minerals, soluble fiber, and healthy calories.

Add a little healthy exercise – 20 minutes' brisk walking three times a week is enough to make a difference – take away the risk from nicotine, stir in a little positive thought and relaxation, and you have the recipe for a healthy, happy, and long life.

ABOVE *Life is for living, not simply getting through. Fresh air, relaxation, and regular time out from the stresses of work can all contribute to the sense of perspective necessary to physical and mental health.*

HOW MANY CALORIES DO YOU NEED?

In the past it has been normal to calculate the energy needs of different occupations according to whether they were sedentary, moderately active, or very active. But in our modern society there are very few jobs that could be called "very active," if compared to those 15 or 20 years ago. In our highly mechanized society electric tools, mechanical handling, and lifting equipment have removed much heavy labor.

Today, it is mainly the non-work activities that increase energy needs more than the actual job you do. The following chart will help you calculate your own calorie needs.

CALORIE REQUIREMENTS FOR MEN AT DIFFERENT LEVELS OF ACTIVITY

Age	Activity level	Calories per day
19–29	Inactive	2,400
	Active	3,100
	Very active	3,600
30–59	Inactive	2,400
	Active	3,200
	Very active	3,800
60–70+	Inactive	2,380
	Active	2,500

THE ENERGY EQUATION

Activity	Approximate number of calories used per hour
Sleep	65
Driving, computer tasks, office work	100
Average walking, badminton, table tennis, moderately active dancing	250
Tennis, ice- or roller-skating, fast walking, cycling, slow jogging, hockey	300
Aerobics class, dance class, disco dancing, football	400
Skiing, swimming, heavy DIY (planing, sandpapering, sawing), heavy digging, skipping	500
Weight-lifting, squash, running, aquarobics	650

The Teens: Girls

THESE are years of growth, development, and hormonal change, demanding the best possible nutrition. You will need all the energy you can get, to help you enjoy the fun – and to cope with the problems and stresses – of your busy, exciting, active life.

CALORIES IN ACTION

Whatever you do burns up calories, some activities more than others. Figures are shown as calories burned per hour and are based on the average young girl's routine. See page 27, Calories in Action, for data on energy expenditure on popular sport.

Activity	Calories burned per hour
Sleeping	60
Eating	67
Watching TV	67
Sitting	70
Shopping	120
Normal walking	200
Dancing	300

For growth, development, and energy you need to follow the Vitality Eating rules on p. 21. It's specially important for you to eat a proper breakfast. If you race for the bus every morning after no more than a snatched cup of coffee and half a piece of toast, the temptation to boost nose-diving blood-sugar levels with a sweet mid-morning coffee, a chocolate bar, or a Danish will be almost irresistible. Porridge is a great breakfast – you can make it in just 2–3 minutes. It will give you vital minerals like iron, zinc, and calcium, plus nerve-strengthening B-complex vitamins. Eat it with milk and a little honey. Muesli is equally good, and both cereals are excellent sources of slow-release energy.

If lunch consists of sandwiches, make sure it's whole wheat bread; fill with a hard-cooked egg, cheese, tuna, canned sardines, or chicken for protein.

And add plenty of chopped parsley – just the stuff to give you a glowing, unblemished skin. Cress is a good alternative. Round off your packed lunch with a tub of yogurt (steer clear of those that are high in sugar and additives) and a piece of fruit.

Midday meals are likely to be a rush, so try to sit down to a sensible meal in the evening. Eat it at leisure and make sure it includes a green vegetable; spinach is super for you, and so are celery, carrots, and spring greens. Salad – or at least one raw vegetable – is a must on the menu. It might be a couple of carrots scraped clean and cut into chunks, a crisp stick of celery or slivers of red or yellow sweet peppers. Or try that US favorite: spinach salad with mushrooms thinly sliced into it, and a thick garlicky dressing. If you don't want to be a social outcast, you may find yourself heading for a Big Mac, Coke, and French fries with the rest of the gang. Enjoy yourself. But if there's a salad table – now available in more and more fast-food outlets – help yourself. And why not try vegeburgers or beanburgers as a healthier option once in a while?

COMMON PROBLEMS

EXCESS WEIGHT often worries young girls. But, whatever you do, don't cut down on the sensible food you need for growth and energy. Steer clear of those dangerous lettuce-leaf-and-black-coffee diets – they can seriously damage your health. Instead, remember that the key factors are likely to be excess fat and excess sugar in your diet. There is an awful lot of fat – and the unhealthy, saturated kind, too – in most processed foods. Sausages, burgers, salami, meat

THE TEENS

100 percent of you have teeth.

15 percent of you drink more than 14 units of alcohol a week.

32 percent of you smoke.

20 percent of 16–17-year-olds are on the pill.

40 percent of 18–19-year-olds are on the pill.

Only 12 percent of you use condoms.

25 percent of you will have a baby within eight months of marriage.

Your bones are still growing.

You need 2,110 calories each day.

LEFT *If you like to just have a sandwich for lunch, go for whole wheat bread rather than white; it contains more fiber.*

BELOW *Working hard for exams can take its toll; an ideal mid-revision booster would be a tuna fish and green salad sandwich made with whole wheat bread followed by a piece of fresh fruit.*

pies, French fries, fried foods, ice cream, cheesecake, and milkshakes are some of the worst culprits. Sweet fizzy drinks really pile on the sugar; a 3½oz/100g milk chocolate bar contains a staggering 2oz/56.5g of sugar – that's about a dozen cubes! – and over 500 calories. Watch out for breakfast cereals too, as many of them have added sugar and salt. If your sweet tooth aches for comfort, eat a banana, an apple, some dried fruit, or fresh dates instead for instant energy.

LOW ENERGY should not be a problem for teenagers – but it often is, and girls are specially at risk, because of the monthly drain on their vital iron reserves. Make sure you are getting plenty of iron in your diet – not just from the classic staple, liver, but also from egg yolks, spinach, lentils, nuts, seeds, raisins, and dates. Drinking tea or coffee at the same time hinders your body's ability to absorb that iron. Luckily, vitamin C has the opposite effect, so always have a piece of fruit, a salad, or a glass of orange juice at the same time.

ANOREXIA can sneak up on you, though, if you become too obsessive about your weight and start cutting out mineral-rich foods. The vital mineral here is zinc, lack of which can zap taste-buds and destroy appetite. Good sources of zinc are shrimps, liver, lean meat, the wheatgerm that is present in whole wheat bread (but less so in white bread), sesame and pumpkin seeds, mackerel, cheese, green vegetables, and, best of all, oysters.

ACNE and other skin problems will take care of themselves, if you watch your fat and sugar intake. Your best friend, however, is the color green, which should always be on the menu – even if it's only a sprig of parsley. The green in vegetables and herbs signifies lots of beta-carotene, which your body will process into vitamin A – vital for healthy skin and clear eyes. Green also means lots of chlorophyll, which has a marvelously cleansing, nourishing, and antiseptic action on your skin.

Finally, to keep you feeling streamlined, clear-skinned, and full of energy, you need exercise – pick the exercise you really enjoy and build it into your life. As well as the physical benefits, the endorphins that are released by the brain during exercise will have a positive influence on your mood.

ESSENTIAL FOODS

Dates: To satisfy your sweet tooth. They will supply badly needed iron too, and they are high in potassium.

Eggs: The original low-calorie convenience food. Eggs are a good source of protein, supplying around ¼oz/6g a time.

Lentils: These are rich in protein – supplying over 23g in ³⁄₄oz in 3½oz/100g – and if you eat vitamin-C-rich food at the same meal, this also enables you to absorb their valuable iron and zinc content.

Oranges: Eat a whole fresh orange at the start of a meal – and you will up your intake of iron, calcium, and other useful minerals on the day's menu.

Porridge: You couldn't have a better start to the day than this traditional Scottish breakfast, which supplies iron, zinc, and calcium, as well as the important B-complex vitamins.

Pumpkin seeds: Eat these for their valuable B vitamins, and also for their iron, zinc, and unsaturated fatty acids.

Spinach: This owes its deep, dark green color to its high content of chlorophyll, and it also has a high beta-carotene content.

Parsley: This herb is rich in vitamins A and C, as well as iron.

The Teens: Boys

I T IS DIFFICULT to determine the exact nutritional needs for boys between the ages of 10 and 20. Not only is there a continuous process of growth and development, but this process does not always proceed at a regular pace. Moreover, there is considerable variation in growth patterns between individuals during the teenage years.

Growth spurts come at different times, as does sexual development, and is further complicated by a huge range of activity levels. Throughout this period some boys may spend most of their lives seated in front of a computer screen, exercising little more than a joystick or a keyboard; others may be physically more active, spending some of their time engaged in sport; while a few may become serious, competitive athletes (see sports nutrition on p. 15).

Generally speaking, nutritional recommendations for adolescent boys are based specifically on age, but this is not always the best guide. It makes much more sense to equate these teenagers' food needs with their specific state of development. After all, the dramatic bodily changes that are so obvious across the span of puberty – from the earliest signs of change to the final growth spurt – make it simple to adjust the teenage boy's diet to suit his needs.

Simple in theory, that is. In practice, persuading most teenagers away from the burger and French fries, pizza and milkshake, or hot dog and cola mentality is a different story. Adolescent boys need to eat more food than adult men, relative to their weight and size. They need extra nutrients to support growth and their relatively high levels of physical activity. In order to maintain a healthy diet, at least 50 percent of their calories should come from complex carbohydrates, a maximum of 35 percent from fats, and not more than a total of 15 percent from protein.

The main growth spurt in boys occurs between the ages of 12 and 16, during the time of puberty and sexual maturation, and this is the time of their greatest energy requirement. It is also the time to establish and encourage the healthy eating habits that will stay with them for the rest of their lives. According to the World Health Organization guidelines, recommended by both British and US health authorities, try to aim for six daily servings of starchy foods (rice, whole wheat bread, potatoes, pasta, whole grain cereals), five portions of fruit and vegetables, and two portions each of dairy products and non-dairy proteins (vegetable or animal). The wider the selection of foodstuffs, the broader the spectrum of vitamins and minerals obtained. Teenagers should keep their consumption of fried and high-sugar foods to a minimum – these should be occasional treats, not a staple part of the diet.

In general the US recommended dietary allowances for all age groups are somewhat higher than those in Britain, and although American RDAs exceed the estimated daily requirement by about one-third, even this safety margin can be too little in

NUTRITION FOR BOYS

It is worth noting the US RDAs for adolescent boys, in respect of some key nutritional requirements:

Nutrient	11–14 years	15–18 years
Energy (kcal)	2,500	3,000
Protein	1½oz/45g	3¼oz/95g
Vitamin A	1,000µg	1,000µg
Vitamin D	10µg	10µg
Vitamin C	50mg	60mg
Vitamin B6	1.7mg	2.0mg
Folate	150µg	200µg
Vitamin B12	2µg	2µg
Calcium	1,200mg	1,200mg
Magnesium	270mg	400mg
Iron	12mg	12mg
Zinc	15mg	15mg
Selenium	40µg	50µg
Iodine	150µg	150µg

ABOVE *Strawberries are an irresistible way to get your vitamins and minerals; they are also very good for cleansing the blood, and preventing the joint pains that some teenagers experience as they grow.*

LEFT *Exercise should be a pleasure not a pain; rollerblading is great fun, great exercise, and an environmentally friendly way to get around.*

The Teens: Boys

teenagers on poor-quality diets. The high-calorie, low-nutrient value of many convenience foods pushes aside the consumption of healthier foods containing more of the essential nutrients. US studies have shown that some adolescents get up to 45 percent of their calories from fat, and this makes them prime candidates for heart disease and strokes in later life.

On the other hand, fanatically health-conscious parents are known to reduce their children's fat consumption so much that they become deficient in energy, which can delay puberty and retard growth and mental development. Professor Vincent Marks at the University of Surrey coined the phrase "muesli-belt malnutrition," an accurate description of this over-zealous attitude.

Serious adolescent athletes have very particular problems in respect of their nutrition. To achieve peak performance, they need a top-quality diet that provides sufficient energy and, surprisingly, meets a much higher demand for water.

ACNE

Adolescent boys don't think much about their skin until they develop acne, one of the worst plagues of adolescence. It is caused by an overproduction of the oily substance known as sebum by the sebaceous glands, which in turn is triggered by androgens, the male hormones responsible for sexual maturity. While many doctors deny that nutrition plays any part in either the cause or treatment of acne, the experience of many teenagers and nutritional therapists is quite the reverse. A diet high in fat increases the amount of free fatty acids and triglycerides in sebum, and a diet high in sugar also increases the formation of triglycerides. It is these two fatty substances that are the irritant factors in sebum, and teenagers who reduce their consumption of high-sugar and fatty foods such as chocolates, candies, canned drinks, fried foods, and endless packages of chips nearly always see some improvement in the condition.

Making sure that their diet contains all the beta-carotene-rich foods and lots of vitamin C helps to ensure healthy skin and increased resistance to the bacteria that result in the inflamed pustular eruptions of acne.

ABOVE *The alarming quantity of sugar in the glass on the right is exactly the amount contained in a standard cola drink.*

ABOVE TOP *Chocolate is good in moderation, but should not form the staple diet.*

LEFT *Switching to fresh fruit as a snack rather than chips and candies helps to improve your skin during this time of hormonal upheaval.*

CALORIES IN ACTION

To help you calculate the calorie needs of an adolescent boy, here is a guide to the energy that he will burn up in a variety of different activities. The calories burned per hour are based on the performance of reasonably enthusiastic amateurs, not élite athletes, who use far more.

Activity	Calories burned per hour
Ordinary walking	180
Brisk walking	300
Badminton	340
Gymnastics	420
Tennis	480
Rugby/American football	540
Soccer	540
Squash	600
Jogging	630
Cycling	660
Swimming	720

A Taste of Freedom

ABOVE *Tomatoes are a good source of vitamin C.*

LEFT *Young people usually have things other than nutrition on their minds, but a basic healthy eating plan can make the time of your life even better.*

YOU'RE ON your own now and your life is what you make it. You've already settled into a job, you have left home for a place of your own and have your independence, your own friends, and a hectic social life.

This is the age of romance, when the significant other in your life can swallow up most of your time and attention. It can also be the age of broken hearts … unless you're married already, and are trying to get to grips with running your home as well as your jobs.

But, married or still single, you will find the days are never long enough for all that you want to cram into them. Your diet should be supplying handsome insurance against stress of every kind – trials at work, romance gone awry, too many late nights, and too many skimpy meals eaten in a rush. Turn to the Vitality Eating rules on p. 21, pin up a photocopy of them in the first kitchen you can call your own – and make every effort to stick to them.

These days office lunches can be a healthy treat. Most supermarkets sell a range of ready-prepared salads, starring carrots, coleslaw, apples, celery, nuts, and brown rice. Add a glass of milk or a tub of yogurt and a piece of fruit – and you will be ready for the most taxing afternoon.

Studio apartment cooking can degenerate into endless snacks of bread, cheese, and canned soup. So make sure you don't run out of the staples – potatoes, carrots, onions, a good olive oil, lemons, sliced whole wheat bread, garlic. Stock up on salads – celery, red and yellow sweet peppers, watercress, mustard and cress, scallions – which will last two or three days in the refrigerator. Keep supplies of eggs, low-fat yogurt, cottage cheese, skimmed milk, nuts, and seeds in the refrigerator too. Always have a bowl of fruit containing at least apples, bananas, oranges, and grapes. Make sure your store cupboard has cans of tuna, sardines (preserved in olive oil), tomatoes, kidney beans, sugar-free baked beans, brown rice, pasta, and dried herbs. These staples are far cheaper than buying convenience dinners and you will always be able to whip up a healthy square meal – soup, salad, pasta, or risotto – no matter how tired you are.

Cooking should be a pleasure, as well as a necessity, and it can be a wonderful way to unwind at the end of a stressful day. Master a few survival recipes so that you can rustle up a decent meal in the evening. Everybody – male and female – should know how to make a good, rich vegetable soup. Teach yourself, too, how to use nature's seasonings, instead of lots of salt and bottled sauces. Thyme gives a wonderful flavor and will boost the immune system and help protect you against infections.

BELOW *If you are stressed out, getting fat, losing weight, or in a permanent bad mood, try making a food diary for yourself to pinpoint the problem. Write down every single thing you eat, however small, for a whole week, then examine the results; the example below, drawn up by a 24-year-old computer operator who felt tired and irritable all the time, reveals what's wrong: missed breakfast, sweet snacks instead of filling fruit, and a tendency to eat too late for the digestive system to cope.*

	MON	TUES	WEDS	THURS	FRI
Breakfast	Nothing	3xBlack Coffee + Sugar	Cornflakes and Milk, coffee	Cornflakes and Milk, coffee	Fruit Yogurt; Banana
Morning Snack Drink	7 Chocolate Chip Cookies	1 Cappuccino 1 Danish	Can fizzy drink; doughnut	Coffee	apple
Lunch	Nothing	Chicken Green Salad Mineral Water	2xsandwich white bread, cheese, cucumber	Bagel cream cheese smoked salmon Cheesecake	Sandwich - Granary bread, lettuce, tomato, cucumber, mayonnaise, tuna
Afternoon Snack	2xchocolate bars	chocolate bar	one brownie	candies	grapes
Dinner/ Supper	4 cans beer 2 packs of chips	Pasta with meat sauce; salad, 1 glass of white wine	Nothing	baked beans on toast x2 slices margarine	large pizza - chee... ham, tomatoes 4x glasses of red w... 1 portion tirami... coffee grappa

A Taste of Freedom

PROBLEMS OF THE TOUGH TWENTIES

MENSTRUAL PROBLEMS can be a real drag at this age – cramps, irritability, tension, nausea, and bloating. However, menstrual problems are as much an index of ill health as muddy skin or lank hair, and just as avoidable. Eat plenty of whole grain cereals, nuts, and seeds, particularly almonds, oats, and sesame and sunflower seeds, as they supply the magnesium, B-complex vitamins, vital vitamin E, and iron that will help these problems. Bananas are an Essential Food, rich in B6, iron, and potassium, which helps with water-retention problems.

EMOTIONAL STRESS in your twenties results from romantic involvements, financial worries, work problems, and skimpy fast food meals. Eat lots of B-complex-rich whole grain cereals – whole wheat bread, brown rice, oats – to help you cope. They will supply a rich diet for the nerves and will give you extra stamina too in the shape of calcium, iron, and magnesium. Ration yourself to no more than three cups of coffee a day. Too much caffeine can make you very nervous and irritable. Try one of the many coffee-substitutes, or use decaffeinated coffee instead. Excess caffeine also prevents your body absorbing half the good minerals you may be feeding it. For maximum uptake of these, eat fruit or fresh vitamin-C-rich vegetables and salads at the same meal.

SMOKING AND DRINKING generate free-radical activity *(see p. 135)* and these dangerous chemicals damage your body's cells, increasing your risk of heart disease, cancer, and even wrinkles! Instead of a pack of cigarettes, keep a package of sunflower seeds in your desk drawer to nibble – they are little power-houses of good nutrition. The female liver has a fairly low resistance to alcohol, so don't think you can drink with the boys and get away with it. And don't be browbeaten into drinking for social reasons – these days mineral water is seen on the smartest restaurant tables. Instead of alcohol, drink a non-alcoholic "cooler" of fruit juice with sparkling mineral water, or a vegetable-juice cocktail.

SKIN PROBLEMS like acne can be even more agonizing in your twenties. Try to keep one day a week when you eat nothing but fruit or vegetables, to give your whole system a good clean-out. Vital skin-foods are avocados, cauliflower, broccoli, and cabbage, chlorophyll-rich spinach and watercress, and all brightly colored fruit, especially peaches, nectarines, and apricots. These are loaded with beta-carotene, which is great for your skin.

EXCESS WEIGHT will also respond well to a fruit and vegetable "fast." Keep a food diary of everything you eat or drink for a week, then work out how to "lose" 500 calories daily. Force yourself to exercise briskly – enough to get up a bit of a sweat – at least four times a week. Commit yourself to a regular exercise or dance class with a friend, or walk part of the way to and from work. Brisk exercise "tunes" your metabolism so that you burn up fat faster.

RIGHT However packed your schedule, try to find time for regular, fun exercise.

ESSENTIAL FOODS

Avocados: They're extremely nutritious, highly digestible, and wonderfully filling for their calorie count – around 160 calories for half an avocado.

Bananas: These are high in potassium, which is necessary for healthy hearts, and full of a useful fiber called pectin.

Carrots: A single carrot will supply your vitamin A needs for an entire day.

Cauliflower: Cauliflower supplies silicon – essential for strong bones, healthy hair, and firm skin.

Potatoes: These are good news for the intelligent slimmer. Even a whopper of a baked potato, crispy skin and all, is only around 200 calories.

Sunflower seeds: These are packed with wonderful nutrients – vitamins, minerals, unsaturated fats, and protein.

Tuna: This fish contains omega-3 fats, the beneficial fats that have a strongly protective action on the heart.

Thyme: This has powerful antiviral and antibacterial properties.

Preconception

I F YOU ARE thinking about starting a family, then there is no better time to take stock of your own, and your partner's, eating habits. The impact of poor diet on the reproductive system is dramatic.

For optimum fertility the diet must include a wide variety of foods, especially those that are rich in the vitamins, minerals, and trace elements that are essential for perfect eggs and sperm. Beta-carotene and folic acid are vital, as deficiencies of these are closely linked to birth defects.

Eat plenty of seeds and nuts, the best of which are sesame and pumpkin seeds, Brazil nuts, and walnuts. These are rich in vital vitamin E and zinc. Eat avocados, dates, fresh and dried apricots, citrus fruits, dark green vegetables, pineapples, bananas, olives, carrots, oats, buckwheat, soybeans, free-range eggs, oily fish, cheese, shellfish, free-range poultry, and lean lamb for good protein, beta-carotene and folic acid.

These foods are the ones that provide the best range of all the vitamins, minerals, proteins, and calories that you and your partner need in order to create a healthy baby.

Avocado, for instance, usually high on the weight watcher's list of forbidden fruits, is a must for all women. Rich in potassium, a provider of vitamins A, B, and E, it also contains mono-unsaturated oil – the healthiest sort. Buckwheat contains a chemical called rutin, which has a powerful effect on the circulation, strengthening the tiny superficial vessels and helping in the control of blood pressure.

DIET AND BIRTH DEFECTS

Up to 5 percent of human births produce abnormal babies, and there is overwhelming evidence that this number could be dramatically reduced by an improved diet or by the use of vitamin and mineral supplementation. Although there is little evidence of gross malnutrition in the general Western population, subclinical malnutrition – a problem of very small deficiencies, which can have wide-ranging effects – is now recognized by the scientific community as a matter for serious concern. The nutritional state of women (as well as of their sexual partners) in the three months before conception is the key to the presence or absence of many birth defects, and to the production of healthy babies.

Preconception

LEFT *Creating a baby should be a joyous experience for both partners, particularly when you are both enjoying optimum health.*

Free-range eggs and poultry should be eaten, as they will not have been produced from chicken feed containing hormones, antibiotics, or other additives.

Studies of women attending fertility clinics show that 50 percent of them have been trying to lose weight on unsuitable diets. Substandard nutrition can have catastrophic effects on the body's ability to reproduce and the resulting pregnancies of malnourished mothers produce low-birth-weight babies. It's not just prospective mothers who are what they eat; it's their babies too.

There are some "danger foods" that should be avoided and others that should be taken only in moderation. If you are pregnant or think there is the possibility of being pregnant, do not consume soft, unpasteurized cheese, unpasteurized milk, or any food past its sell by date. This reduces the risk of bacterial infections like *Salmonella* and *Listeria,* which can damage the fetus. E. coli, VTEC, can occur in processed meat products and rare hamburgers. There have now been a number of outbreaks in the UK, most recently in 1996 in Scotland, and major outbreaks in the USA during the last 15 years. This infection can cause serious kidney failure, putting the fetus at risk.

This particular strain of *E. coli* lives in the intestines of cattle, and carcases are often contaminated in the slaughter house. If you're cooking a steak, the intense heat on the outside of the meat is enough to kill the bacteria, even if the middle is rare. But when infected meat is chopped or ground to make hamburgers, the bacteria are distributed throughout the product. Hamburgers should never be eaten until they're thoroughly cooked right through, the juices run clear, and there is not the slightest trace of pink in the middle. The same is true of poultry, to avoid the risk of *Salmonella* infection. Liver, liver sausage, and liver pâté contain extremely high levels of vitamin A, which may cause birth defects, so these should also be avoided.

Foods to be taken in moderation include coffee or tea. When drunk at, or soon after, meals that should be supplying your minerals, they inhibit the body's absorption of these nutrients – including vital zinc. Alcohol is not healthy for the sperm or ovum, so drink no more than an occasional glass of decent wine. And all food that has been highly refined or processed is less nutritious than fresh produce.

FIT FOR FATHERHOOD

Every pregnant woman is bombarded with guidance on modifying her lifestyle but it's just as important for her partner to accept his part of the responsibility for ensuring healthy and speedy conception.

The life story of the sperm is fascinating. It takes about 12 weeks for it to develop from its first cell to maturity, and during this time it is highly sensitive to damage from outside sources. There are three main dangers:

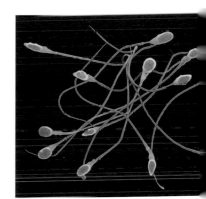

ABOVE *Sperm are produced in their billions, but it is the quality that counts more than the quantity. A healthy sperm produced by a well-nourished father is a great start in life.*

SMOKING – there is growing evidence that cigarettes can reduce the level of male hormones, interfere with sperm development, and even cause genetic changes that could lead to the birth of a malformed child. A German study has shown definite links between congenital defects in babies, and fathers who smoke. Cigarettes are a nasty habit anyway, but prospective parents should stop smoking at least three months before they try for a baby.

ALCOHOL – animal studies have shown that alcohol can also severely damage sperm and lead to genetic abnormalities. If you're planning to become a father, you should make sure that you have no more than two or three drinks a week in the three months leading up to conception.

METAL – sperm can be damaged by a wide range of substances that contain metal. Out-of-date canned foods can be a source of lead, as can old water pipes. Avoid stripping old white paintwork, which may be lead-based. Don't use shampoo containing selenium, aluminum saucepans, kettles, or pressure cookers, or milk substitute that contains aluminum salts.

Preconception

You will also want to ensure sperm are at their healthiest at the time you plan to conceive.

A healthy, balanced diet will give you an adequate intake of all the essential vitamins, minerals, and trace elements. Wherever possible, choose organically grown produce and give yourself extra insurance by taking a good multivitamin and mineral pill.

Body heat is also important. Just as we all feel a bit lazy when we're sitting in the sun, so the sperm cells get less active when they are too hot. Avoid wearing Y-fronts and other tight underpants or jeans. And don't take a hot bath, especially just before intercourse, as it will affect the ability of the sperm to swim up the vagina and then fertilize the egg.

keep a positive mental attitude

keep to a sensible weight

wear loose-fitting underwear and pants

ABOVE *There are many simple things a would-be father can do to improve not only the chances of conception, but to ensure as far as possible that his baby will have a strong, healthy start in life.*

COUNTDOWN TO C(CONCEPTION)-DAY

C-Day minus three months

● Stop all alcoholic drinks: 40 percent of low fertility in men can be laid at the door of even a modest consumption of alcohol. Three months of alcoholic abstinence will raise sperm counts sufficiently, in up to half of all men with fertility problems, for fertilization to occur. Keeping off the booze also improves sperm motility.

● Stop smoking, as this is one of the commonest causes of damaged sperm. Sperm need large amounts of vitamin C to thrive – they contain eight times more vitamin C than blood – and smoking destroys vitamin C.

● Start taking an antioxidant vitamin supplement containing the vital vitamins A, C, and E.

● If you are overweight, now is the time for that healthy, well-balanced, exercise-inclusive, weight-loss program. Obesity upsets the testosterone/estrogen balance and can cause infertility.

● Throw away the Y-fronts and tight jeans and wear boxer shorts and loose-fitting pants. This lowers the temperature of the testicles and increases sperm production.

C-Day minus two months

● Increase vitamin C to 500mg per day to reduce the risk of sperm "clumping" (sticking together in bunches).

● Eat four oranges or two kiwi fruit every day for their vitamin C and bioflavonoids.

● Eat at least two portions a day of beta-carotene-rich foods (carrots, broccoli, apricots, spinach, and other orange or dark-green leafy vegetables or fruit).

● Switch to drinking only bottled water instead of tap water to avoid the risk of environmental estrogen in normal, recirculated domestic water supplies. The estrogens get into the water as a result of women taking the contraceptive pill and HRT, and some environmentalists believe this to be one of the primary causes of a 50 percent decline in sperm counts over the last 30 years.

C-Day minus one month

● Add another 500mg of vitamin C.

● Eat plenty of shellfish and/or a generous handful of pumpkin seeds each day for the extra zinc. This increases the sperm's protection against free-radical damage. Sperm should be rich in zinc, each ejaculation containing 5mg, half the daily requirement for a man.

● Eat at least two avocados a week, plenty of olive oil and sunflower and sesame seeds, all for their vitamin E, another powerful free-radical protector. Also take 400mg of vitamin E each day.

● Cut out all caffeine and caffeine-containing cola drinks – green China or weak Indian tea are acceptable in moderation.

● Avoid all meat and poultry that may have been fed on growth hormones.

● Ease back on your exercise. Sensible activity is a great aid to fertility, as it encourages general fitness, but excessive or obsessive exercise will result in reduced sperm counts.

● Avoid contact with chemical solvents and garden or agricultural insecticides or pesticides. Whenever possible, eat organic foods.

● Keep up this regime until conception is achieved. Then, having made these healthy changes to your diet and lifestyle, why not adopt them for the future for your general health, instead of going back to your bad old ways?

AVOCADO

Pregnancy

YOU ARE what you eat, and your baby is what you eat too. The first rule of being pregnant is to learn to ignore all the friends, mothers-in-law, grannies, and busybodies who keep reminding you that you are "eating for two." You are not. You are eating for one and nourishing one and a bit.

The second rule is to take care of yourself. Don't become obsessed by diet and worry about every bite you take. What you need is a simple common-sense approach for healthy pregnancy, a healthy baby, and the energy to look after it once it is born. This will also make sure that you get back to your pre-pregnancy weight with as little fuss as possible.

EATING HEALTHILY FOR TWO

First, a few don'ts, which may seem obvious but are important. Don't diet to lose weight unless advised by your doctor. Instead take some extra exercise, unless there is a medical reason to contradict this. Don't smoke. It can cause serious harm to

APRICOT

the growing baby. Babies born to smokers are likely to have smaller lungs and are much more likely to suffer from asthma and other chest problems.

You need a minimum of 2,200 calories per day – more if you are physically active – and it is important that you get them from a good mixture of different foods. Your total food intake should increase by around 20 percent, but your body's need for folic acid, vitamins B and C, calcium, zinc, and magnesium increase by far more.

Sardines (with bones), low-fat dairy products, beans, cereals, and nuts provide extra calcium. Meat, garbanzo beans, leafy green vegetables, dried apricots, dates, and raisins will give you extra iron and folic acid. Carrots, spinach, oily fish, eggs, dairy products, and dark green and yellow vegetables all provide vitamin A. Green peppers, citrus fruit, kiwi fruit, and most vegetables, contain vitamin C. And vitamin D is found in oily fish, eggs, fish-liver oil, and margarine.

Vegetarians, and particularly vegans, may be at risk of vitamin B$_{12}$ deficiency and any woman who has been drastically dieting could be missing out on essential nutrients. Talk to your physician about a vitamin and mineral supplement.

You should be getting around 2oz/60g of protein a day. A chicken leg provides about 1oz/30g protein; 1oz/30g of cheese $^1\!/_6$oz/7g protein; 6oz/175g of cod 1$^1\!/_3$oz/35g protein; a two-egg omelet $^1\!/_2$oz/15g protein; 4oz/110g of cooked lentils $^3\!/_4$oz/19g.

To guarantee a healthy balance of nutrients and plenty of good, soluble fiber, aim for five portions of fresh fruit, salad, and vegetables each day. Try to stick to whole grain cereals. During pregnancy food passes through your intestines more slowly to make sure that your body can absorb all the nutrients. Consequently constipation is common, so it is important to drink lots of water.

Weight gain during pregnancy is an important determinant of health for both mother and baby. The rate at which you gain weight will vary and there is usually very little change during the first ten weeks. The healthy average during the second 10–12 weeks is about $^1\!/_2$lb/225g a week, and from then on 1lb/450g a week.

GINGER ROOT

CLOVES

WHAT GOES WHERE

To give you some idea of where the extra weight goes, here is a rough guide:

Baby	7–8lb/3–3.5kg
Placenta	1$^1\!/_2$–2lb/750g–1kg
Amniotic fluid	1$^1\!/_2$–2lb/750g–1kg
Womb	2lb/1kg
Breasts	2lb/1kg
Extra blood	3–4lb/1.5–1.75kg
Fat stores	4–5lb/1.75–2.5kg

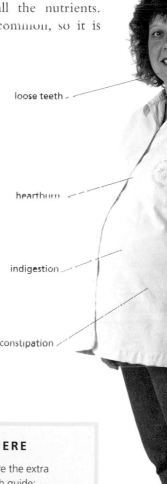

BELOW *Pregnancy is a natural state, and nature has provided many foods to help mothers alleviate the physical inconveniences of pregnancy (constipation, heartburn, flatulence, morning sickness). Ginger and cloves are particularly helpful.*

loose teeth

heartburn

indigestion

constipation

Pregnancy

WHAT NOT TO EAT

There is evidence that the seeds of coronary heart disease are sown in earliest childhood – high saturated fat or sugar consumption by nursing mothers means high-fat milk for babies. Some experts believe they are even sown during pregnancy, so this is a time to avoid foods that are high in animal fats. It is easy to cut out the fat you can see, but much more difficult with hidden fats. Do not eat sausages, salamis, pâtés, meat pies, pasties, Scotch eggs, bacon, ham, burgers, and the dreaded doner kebab (although shish kebab, cubes of lean meat or chicken cooked on a charcoal grill, is one of the lowest-fat fast foods), which all provide around 85 percent of their calories from fat. And cookies, Danish pastries, cream cakes, croissants, ice creams, and chips may all be rich suppliers of unhealthy saturated fats. Also beware of high-fat products labeled "low fat" – they seldom are. They may be "lower" in fat, but they still supply far too much.

Watch out for salt. Too much can cause fluid retention and raised blood pressure, the last thing you want during pregnancy. Too much salt can also increase the amount of calcium that your body excretes and this can be disastrous during pregnancy, not so much for the baby, but because of your own increased risk of osteoporosis in later life. The recommended maximum daily intake of salt is not to exceed 4g a day (about one level teaspoonful), but average consumption in the UK is nearly three times that. Most of the salt we consume does not come from the salt cellar but is hidden in processed foods (even in bread and cereals). So read the labels carefully (see also Salt on p.130).

Alcohol and large amounts of caffeine-containing foods and drinks (coffee, tea, chocolate, and cola drinks) should be avoided. Even decaffeinated diet drinks contain significant amounts of artificial sweeteners, which your baby would be better off without. Even more importantly, caffeine can interfere with the absorption of iron and zinc from your food.

Do not eat liver or liver pâté, as they contain too much vitamin A, which can cause birth defects. Avoid unpasteurized milk and cheese, and any soft or blue cheeses, as they may contain the *Listeria* bug.

All red meat must be cooked thoroughly until there are no traces of pink in the middle, and if you must eat burgers the same applies, as there is a risk of toxoplasmosis and *E. coli* infection. Poultry must be cooked until the juices run clear and there is no trace of pink, and eggs should be cooked until the yolk is hard, in order to protect against *Salmonella*.

All frozen and cook/chill foods must be prepared in accordance with the manufacturer's directions and if you must use a microwave, make sure you know what power it uses, so that you can accurately follow the directions on the package.

Do not drink raspberry-leaf tea (see p.71) during the early stages of pregnancy. It is a great aid during the last ten weeks, however, as it strengthens the uterus muscles and helps with contractions.

ESSENTIAL FOODS

Apples: These neutralize the acidity produced by indigestion. They contain pectin, a fiber that keeps the bowels functioning properly and lowers cholesterol.

Broccoli: This is a rich source of vitamins A and C. It also provides iron, calcium, potassium, and folic acid.

Brown rice: This provides many of the B vitamins, some fiber, iron, potassium, and protein.

Herrings: These are a fine source of vitamins A, B, and D. They also contain iodine, selenium, phosphorus, potassium, iron, and calcium. Most importantly during pregnancy, they supply the omega-3 fatty acids.

Kiwi fruit: These give you twice as much vitamin C as an orange, more fiber than an apple, as much vitamin E as an avocado, and lots of potassium, a lack of which can lead to fatigue and poor digestion.

Onions and garlic: These are good for the heart and circulation.

Walnuts: These nuts are high in protein, B vitamins, calcium, potassium, phosphorus, zinc, and iron.

Cloves: This aromatic spice is a great aid to digestion. It reduces nausea, flatulence, and dyspepsia.

Pregnancy

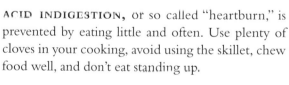

WOOD SHAVINGS

PROBLEMS IN PREGNANCY

Of course there are problems and risks, and you may not feel 100 percent for every single day of the nine months. But you can combat them and see that your growing baby gets the best nourishment, while protecting your own future health.

MORNING SICKNESS can be mastered by most women. Eat a little nourishing snack before bedtime and keep a secret store of food on your bedside table for midnight feasts — oatmeal cookies, crispbreads, walnuts, raisins, sesame seeds, and a bottle of plain mineral water. Have a drink of peppermint tea, lime-flower tea with a little fresh ginger grated into it or weak ordinary tea, with a little honey and no milk, and a plain, unsweetened cracker as soon as you awake. The best anti-morning-sickness medicine of all is ½in/13mm of fresh ginger root, grated into a mug of boiling water, left for five minutes, and strained.

ANEMIA and toxemia are serious complications: iron and protein are the key requirements. Include at least two portions of green leafy vegetables and three protein foods each day. Magnesium is a key mineral and the richest sources are garbanzo beans, kidney beans, cashew nuts, and mackerel.

CONSTIPATION can be tackled by increasing the amount you drink. Have at least 1.7l/3pt of fluid each day, not too much of which is tea or coffee. Keep off the fizzy drinks and watch out for the high natural sugar content of even the pure fruit juices, which should be diluted 50/50 with water. Brown rice, whole wheat bread, dried fruits, vegetables, potatoes cooked with their skins, apples, pears, baked beans, and porridge are great sources of natural fiber, which keep everything on the move. Don't sprinkle spoonfuls of bran over your cereal, as it prevents you from absorbing calcium and iron. Do eat at least three high-fiber foods daily.

VARICOSE VEINS and piles are both linked with constipation, so avoiding that protects you from them. Vitamin E is essential — get it from kiwi fruit, herring, tuna, extra-virgin olive oil, nuts, and canned tomatoes; garlic and onions are also great protectors of your circulatory system. Eat two of these foods daily. Avoid standing, take plenty of walks or other

PICA

Pica is the medical term for strange and unnatural cravings that drive people to eat substances that are not foods. Earth, clay, coal, wood, and chalk are commonly the chosen items.

Pica quite often occurs in pregnancy, but it can also occur in young children and in some serious psychiatric illnesses. This strange abnormality is a sensory malfunction, which seems to be linked to iron deficiency. The symptoms can be induced simply by removing enough blood from volunteers to cause anemia, and reversed by giving iron supplements. So it

seems unlikely that social or behavioral disturbances have much impact on this condition.

The onset of pica should be taken seriously as a sign of potential anemia during pregnancy. Although iron stores in the bodies of anemic babies can be increased by supplements, brain stores do not respond in the same way and this can have long-term effects on the baby's behavior and IQ.

Another serious consequence of pica is the risk of lead poisoning, especially if soil is one of the chosen "foods."

exercise, and if there is a family history of varicose veins, wear good support-pantyhose or stockings.

EXHAUSTION — you will need as much energy as you can muster for the new baby. Complex carbohydrates are much better at providing it than sugars and refined starches. Brown rice, whole wheat bread, lentils, beans, nuts, muesli, porridge, and any salt-free, unsweetened whole wheat cereal are the first choice. Eggs, fish, poultry, lean meat, and low-fat dairy products supply the protein, and a good mixture of cereals and pulses is necessary for vegetarians.

ACID INDIGESTION, or so called "heartburn," is prevented by eating little and often. Use plenty of cloves in your cooking, avoid using the skillet, chew food well, and don't eat standing up.

HIGH BLOOD PRESSURE is the most dreaded of all the problems during pregnancy. Follow the advice given above on weight, anemia, constipation, and varicose veins. Eat lots of herrings, other oily fish, and all seven Essential Foods, especially garlic and onions. Salt is your blood pressure's worst enemy, so throw away the salt cellar. Stress is another key factor in raised blood pressure — relaxation exercises, yoga, meditation, and regular physical exercise are great aids.

BELOW As well as eating properly, expectant mothers should try to put some time aside for relaxation. Simple yoga poses can be very helpful.

Motherhood

THERE'S NOTHING else in life quite like it: the joy of that moment when for the first time you hold your newborn baby in your arms. Suddenly all those long dreary months of waiting seem worth while.

But, as any mother can tell you, motherhood can be tough going – and specially so the first time round. For a start, you will be more tired than you ever imagined possible and you will never get as much sleep as you need.

Even the simplest household chores can suddenly seem overwhelming, a cross word will reduce you to tears, and you will wonder despairingly how on earth other women ever cope with it all. Once the baby is a toddler, you will get a decent night's sleep at last – but you'll need it to cope with an active, demanding two-year-old. And the average mother of four- and five-year-olds will thank you with tears in her eyes, if you can arrange just a couple of hours for her away from it all.

When life is so hectic and demanding, preparing proper meals for yourself may seem a chore you can forget about. Instead, you will probably go for the temporary "lift" of a cup of coffee and a couple of cookies; later on, something out of a can or the remains of the nursery lunch will do. What these substitutes can't and won't do, however, is give you the strength, the nervous resilience, and the sheer stamina that Vitality Eating supplies. Study the rules on p. 21. Don't short-change yourself – your health is vital. Not just for you, but for the whole family.

Your midday meal does not have to involve a lot of fuss: perhaps a tub of low-fat yogurt – just stir in a little honey or some nuts; a baked potato or a whole wheat roll with a piece of cheese; a couple of stalks of celery and an apple. That's a beautifully balanced meal that will keep you going for hours. Between-meal snacks? Dried fruit – especially apricots – will give you a real energy lift. Eat liver once a week; otherwise, cut down on red meat and spend the money on extra fresh fruit and vegetables, especially cabbages, watercress, and spring greens, which will raise your resistance to infection and stress.

PROBLEMS DURING EARLY MOTHERHOOD

"Baby blues" is something most mothers experience. (Postnatal depression is a more serious clinical condition which should be treated by a medical practitioner.) Much of the "blues" is the result of sheer exhaustion, but the right diet can help. Focus on the whole grains – oats, whole wheat, and brown rice – for the stress-proofing that their B-complex vitamins will provide; on yogurt for calcium; and on green leafy vegetables for magnesium, another nutrient badly needed by the stressed nervous system. Zinc is another vital nutrient, and it's specially likely to be deficient in mothers who took iron supplements in pregnancy, as the two minerals need to be in balance. Liver, shrimp, beef, cheese, sardines, and whole wheat bread all supply zinc. For an extra shot of energy, take a daily tablespoon of dried brewer's yeast; blend it with a tub of low-fat yogurt, a banana, and half a glass of orange juice for a delicious drink that's also a complete meal in a glass. Brewer's yeast is loaded with vital B vitamins and minerals, including zinc.

LEFT Good nutrition will deliver the energy you need to get the best out of life with young children, who are at once exhilarating and exhausting.

THE TERRIBLE TWOS

By the time you get to the terrible twos you may be wishing you had never started, but don't despair, they do pass. What you need now is plenty of good energy but not all from carbohydrates (at least not during the daytime). Save the starchy foods, like rice, pasta, potatoes, bread, and honey, for your evening meal to encourage relaxation and better sleep. Mornings should start with a protein breakfast of eggs, fish, cheese, fresh fruit, yogurt, and one slice of good coarse whole wheat bread. If you find yourself flagging during the day, snack on small amounts of high-energy foods like halva, tahini, sesame, sunflower and pumpkin seeds, dried fruit, and fresh unsalted nuts. Eat more protein for lunch – some oily fish would be ideal, but alternate this with poultry, beans, or a meat substitute – with lots of vegetables and/or salads.

LEFT Fresh green leafy vegetables, preferably eaten washed and raw, or with a yogurt dressing, provide magnesium, a key nutrient in the prevention of nervous stress.

Motherhood

STRESS lowers your resistance to infection of any kind, and non-stop demands on your attention can be a particularly exhausting form of stress. To beef up your immune defenses, eat foods rich in vitamins A and C: brightly colored fruits like oranges, grapefruit (especially the pink ones), peaches, nectarines, blackcurrants, and all the beautiful berries. The famous Swiss doctor Max Bircher-Benner, who cured illnesses with a diet high in raw foods, used to tell his patients: "Eat green leaves every day." That's advice you couldn't do better than follow. Cabbage, watercress, spring greens, spinach, and all kinds of lettuce are richly protective, supplying chlorophyll – which is wonderful for your skin, and has anti-bacterial properties – as well as vitamin A and useful minerals such as calcium and magnesium.

EXCESS WEIGHT and **LISTLESSNESS** may be a problem, although you may feel that by rights you should be worn to a shadow. Sweet between-meal snacks that are high in calories, fats, and sugar, but low in real nutritional value and in fiber, such as the classic coffee and doughnut or tea and bun, are one of the commonest reasons. Reach for a healthy snack instead: a piece of fruit, some dried apricots, a handful of raisins, or a tub of yogurt with a little honey stirred in. And remember that excess fat and refined carbohydrates put a heavy workload on your digestive system – while lack of fiber can bring it all to a grinding halt. Poor digestion itself can lead to much more serious health problems in the long run – cancer, arthritis, and heart disease among them. In the short term it will leave you feeling run down and stop you ever feeling on peak form.

FATIGUE is what makes mothers tense and irritable. Fatigue doesn't leave you feeling very sexy, and you won't have much energy to spend on looking attractive, either. At times like these, remember the stores of energy and nutritional wealth packed into tiny seeds. In the traditional medicine of the Middle East, sesame seeds have always been associated with enhanced sexual energy and prowess. Eat them in ready-made purée form, called tahini, available from every health food store and many ethnic grocery stores. Or you can buy hummus, the savory dip made from tahini and garbanzo beans, at any deli, to enjoy with whole wheat pitta (pocket) bread and chunks of

ESSENTIAL FOODS

Apricots: These are rich in beta-carotene, which your body converts into vitamin A. Dried apricots are rich in iron, but wash them thoroughly in warm water to remove the sulfur dioxide used as a preservative.

Cabbage: This can help you cope with stress, anemia, fatigue, and infection.

Grapefruit: This is loaded with vitamins A and C – and the pink kind are even richer in vitamin A.

Liver: This is crammed with vitamin A, B-complex, and so much iron and zinc. Zinc is especially important if you're suffering from postnatal depression.

Sesame seeds: All seeds are regenerating, vital foods, specially useful to help you meet the demands of a rushed and busy life.

Watercress: This contains a natural antibiotic. It's also rich in the vitamin A precursor, beta-carotene, and iron.

Live yogurt: Not only is this twice as easy to digest as milk, but it contains acidophilus bacteria, which recreate a healthy balance in your gut. It's an ideal healthy snack – all you need is a spoon!

Basil: This has a mild calming action. The old herbalists used it to help restore regular periods, and as a remedy for nervous headaches.

raw vegetables. The zinc in sesame seeds will also do wonders for your skin.

The fragrant herb basil is a wonderful tonic for fatigue. Italians would not dream of making a tomato salad without it; and pesto sauce, made with lots of basil and crushed pine nuts, is an extra-delicious ready-made sauce for pasta.

Both fatigue and weight problems will respond to active exercise and being out in the open air. Buggy-pushing may give you the fresh air and sunshine; but you need something just a little more strenuous two or three times a week. Swimming is the ideal exercise for toning the whole body and building stamina – and babies love it too! Make a trip to the pool a family outing that you will all enjoy.

BREAST FEEDING

The average woman between the ages of 19 and 50 has a daily calorie need that is a couple of chocolate cookies short of 2,000 calories. In the first month of breastfeeding, however, she will need 450 more calories each day, increasing to 570 a day by the third month.

Prime Time

THESE are the years of your beautiful prime. You will never have more natural energy than you have now. Your looks have the appeal of maturity as well as the glow of youth, and you exude grown-up confidence and poise.

However, the problem is fitting all the parts of your life together so that you can enjoy the whole. Most people today have to run a household and hold down a job. This can be challenging on good days, exhausting when you are low. The job gets tougher as you climb the promotion ladder. If you have children, you will find they need more and more of your time, love, and attention as they head for the troublesome teens.

And if you're running a home and job and raising a family, then you will sometimes wonder how you got yourself into all this. But don't reach for the quick fix of coffee, a stiff drink, or a cigarette, and don't fall on the sweet snacks for a quick energy lift that will let you down later – as well as aggravating any weight problems you may have. There are much better ways to keep you firing on all cylinders. Above all, don't be tempted to save time by skipping meals; or by lunching on a couple of coffees and a chocolate bar; or by serving up endless microwaved TV dinners, because you feel too tired to cook.

Turn to the Vitality Eating rules on p. 21 to remind yourself what good nutrition is all about. Whole grains, fresh fruits and vegetables, raw salads, and fresh herbs sprouting on the windowsill are basics. So are yogurt, milk, cheese, supplies of fresh nuts, and seeds stored in the refrigerator.

If daily shopping is out of the question, go for vegetables that will happily stay fresh for a few days such as potatoes, carrots, and onions. Store out of the light, in a cool place, in brown paper bags. Go for salad-stuffs such as celery, fennel, sweet peppers, and water-cress that will keep in the refrigerator. In a dark corner of your kitchen devote space to sprouting seeds, organically grown and cheap with it.

BUILD YOUR VITALITY

BEAT PMS – you must do something to overcome this draining and depressing problem. Fight the craving for sugar and chocolate bars. Sweet fruits like grapes and melon will help. So too will dried fruit and almonds. Increase your intake of vitamin B6 from eggs, oily fish like salmon and sardines, whole grain cereals, and bananas. You will also need more zinc and magnesium from pumpkin seeds, liver, shellfish, garbanzo beans, kidney beans, and mackerel. Cut down on tea, coffee, alcohol, and sugar. Evening primrose oil is a natural antiinflammatory which benefits most menstrual problems, particularly PMS, and is equally helpful during the menopause.

TOP *Pumpkin seeds deliver a good supply of zinc, the mineral that works with calcium to keep bones strong, prevents the loss of libido, and helps maintain healthy liver function.*

ABOVE *In your prime, you and your partner have more time and money to spend on yourselves.*

LEFT *Red, green, and yellow peppers keep well for the busy shopper, are super sources of vitamin C, and low in calories: the perfect fast food.*

Prime Time

LOOK AFTER YOUR HEART – now is the time to take a real interest in the affairs of your heart. This is a time of growing responsibility – career, husband, children, or all three. You are likely to be under more stress and pressure, to have less time to look after yourself and your diet. This is not the time to let things slide. Ensure the future health of your heart by eating plenty of high-fiber foods, lots of oily fish like sardines, vegetable proteins such as millet, buckwheat, and beans. Eat foods rich in vitamins A and C, such as cantaloup melon, dark-green leafy vegetables, and as many onions and as much garlic as you can. Use extra-virgin olive oil on salads. Cut down on animal fats, salt, and refined carbohydrates, and drink only modest amounts of alcohol – around 14 glasses of wine, standard measures of spirits or half-pints of beer, as an absolute maximum, per week. Do take some form of regular exercise, which should be weight-bearing.

LET YOUR SKIN BLOOM – all-round good nutrition is the foundation of a good skin. No amount of expensive lotions and potions will compensate for a bad diet. You need lots of vitamin A, from carrots, melon, spinach, nectarines, apricots, kiwi fruit, and liver; chlorophyll, from all green leafy vegetables; vitamin E, from seeds, nuts, cold-pressed seed oils, and avocados. Eat millet for extra silicon. And don't forget dandelion leaves and the green tops of celery, both of which improve the elimination of waste products.

STRESS AND SUPER-RESISTANCE – what can you do to boost your own resistance to infection and disease? Even if you're making the effort to eat well, much of the food you buy is likely to be missing some of the vital ingredients. That's why you need to have a regular daily input of the essential foods that are extra-rich in vitamin C, zinc, vitamin A, and B-complex vitamins. Grapes, citrus fruit, apricots, blackcurrants, pineapple, broccoli, peppers, onions, oats, wheatgerm, almonds, sprouted seeds, yogurt, chicken livers (free-range), eggs, poultry, game, sardines, mackerel, and herring. These should form your staple diet. Stress is a great destroyer of defense mechanisms and needs the same nutritional help, plus lots of celery, which is one of nature's great calming influences. Drink lime-flower tea to help you relax, and try any form of relaxation exercise such as yoga, meditation, and self-hypnosis.

BONES MATTER NOW – the menopause may seem a long way off, but what happens now will determine the state of your bones in thirty years' time. You must start building up your calcium deposits. To do that you need calcium, vitamin D, and sunlight. Each day, you should eat a selection of at least three of the following foods: sardines (eat the bones), spinach, low-fat cheese, yogurt, seeds, nuts, celery, turnips, cabbage, garbanzo beans, herring, tuna, eggs, dried fruit, brown rice, buckwheat, and skimmed milk. You must get as much daylight as you can. That doesn't mean cooking on the shore for two weeks of the year, but getting out into the fresh air and light for a little while each day. It is vital that you start exercising now as well. Weight-bearing makes the bones stronger. Walking and active sports like tennis, squash, badminton, netball, running, or jogging are all good for the bones. Cycling and swimming will not only get your heart working, but will also add to the strength of your bones.

THE THIRTIES AND FORTIES

97 percent of you have teeth.

12 percent of you drink over 14 units of alcohol a week.

34 percent of you smoke.

20 percent of you are on the pill.

20 percent of you use condoms.

12 percent of you will have a baby within 8 months of marriage.

ESSENTIAL FOODS

Almonds: Rich in protein, beneficial fats, zinc, magnesium, potassium, and iron, as well as some B vitamins.

Celery: This is a good nerve tonic, as it contains a lot of calcium. Its diuretic properties have been known for centuries and you can eat it to get rid of fluid retention.

Cheese: This is a rich source of protein, calcium, and phosphorus, as well as the B vitamins, lots of vitamin A, some vitamin D and E.

Grapes: These fruit are easy to digest, and uniquely nourishing.

Melon: Cantaloup melon is a rich source of vitamin A.

Sardines: Rich in protein, vitamins D and B_{12}, calcium, and easily absorbed iron and zinc.

Sprouted seeds: The most pure and nutritious food you can grow on your windowsill.

Sage: This is a powerful healing and antiseptic herb.

The Menopause

THERE is no need to dread the onset of the menopause. It is not a disease, or an abnormality. It is nature's way of preventing pregnancy when it is no longer a good idea.

There are some symptoms of the menopause that can be unpleasant and distressing, some that may lead to medical problems, and others that can be the cause of severe depression. You can improve and control them all. It helps to start your action plan before you reach the critical years *(see Prime Time on p. 38)*, but if you have reached them already, don't despair. It is still possible to make dramatic changes in the way you feel during the menopause. All that's needed is a close look at your eating habits.

Hot flushes, weight gain, headaches, brittle bones, skin problems, depression, sexual difficulties, and an increased risk of heart disease are the most common results of the menopause – and they can all be improved by eating the Essential Foods.

BEAT THE MENOPAUSE MISERIES

HOT FLUSHES are mainly caused by lower levels of the hormone estrogen. Suffering from stress, being very thin, wearing tight-fitting clothes, and too high a room temperature can all make things worse. Vitamin E can help a lot. The best sources are cold-pressed vegetable oils, especially wheatgerm, corn, safflower, sunflower and olive oils, almonds, hazelnuts, sunflower seeds, and pine nuts. There are modest amounts of vitamin E in whole wheat bread, dark-green leafy vegetables, and eggs. Make sure that at least three of these sources are on your daily menu.

This is a time when supplements can be of great help, and a large clinical trial in the UK has shown that a combination of vitamin E, B vitamins, magnesium, manganese, boron, selenium, and chromium is extremely effective. This formula reduced hot flushes, mood swings, headaches, and irritability in the majority of women who took it.

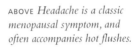

WEIGHT GAIN is a regular cause of anxiety during the menopause. Use all the Essential Foods listed throughout the Well Woman's Eating Plan, together with a lot of those described in this section, to construct your weekly menu. Avoid visible fats as far as you can. Oats, cooked any way you like, are an aid to weight loss, as they help in elimination. They are also a satisfying and filling food. Make sure that you get some exercise each day.

HEADACHES are often related to hot flushes, and to the stress and tension that arise at this time. Beets are an excellent remedy, but don't forget to use the leaves and red stems. Use both root and leaves, raw in salads, dressed with sunflower-seed oil, lemon juice, and sprinkled with sesame seeds. Beets improve the oxygen-carrying ability of the blood, contain iron, and are a good source of folic acid.

BRITTLE BONES – do not believe the experts who tell you it is too late to do anything about your bones once you have reached the menopause. You can still help yourself to have better bones. More calcium, magnesium, zinc, and vitamin D, more sunlight and weight-bearing exercise will all help. So look to your shopping basket. It must contain plenty of spring greens, green, red, and yellow peppers, any dark-green or yellow fruit or vegetables, nectarines, garbanzo beans, pumpkin seeds, sardines, yogurt, and low-fat cheese. Eat at least three of these each day.

DEPRESSION is the commonest menopausal problem after hot flushes. Calcium, magnesium, and the amino acid tryptophan will all do you good. Get these from dairy products, spinach,

ABOVE *Headache is a classic menopausal symptom, and often accompanies hot flushes.*

BELOW LEFT *Unwelcome weight gain is one of the more depressing aspects of the menopausal years. Exercise can help: swimming is particularly good as it strengthens the bones and tones the muscles but does not involve strain or load bearing.*

THE MENOPAUSE

60 percent of you have teeth.

5 percent of you drink more than 14 units of alcohol a week.

29 percent of you smoke.

You need less protein, fewer calories – but much more calcium for your bones.

Now is the time for oily fish and evening primrose oil.

The Menopause

garbanzo beans, sesame seeds, soybeans, cashew nuts, almonds, whole wheat flour, brown rice, bananas, dried fruit, and seafood. The B vitamins are also vital, and you will find these in liver, oily fish, whole grain cereals, eggs, spinach, and yeast extracts. You must have at least two of these foods each day. Exercise stimulates the production of adrenalin, which makes you feel a lot better, so try to make time for physical exertion every day, no matter how low you feel.

SEXUAL DIFFICULTIES – the drop in estrogen affects the secretions of the vagina and the quality of the tissue in the sexual organs. An active, regular sex life will delay these changes considerably. It is likely that many women will spend their later years alone, since most will outlive their husbands. For them, and for other single women, it does not matter whether sexual stimulation is the result of intercourse or masturbation; it's having regular orgasms that counts. Foods rich in vitamin A and E are essential, so make sure of at least two servings daily of oily fish, liver, apricots, spinach, carrots, green and yellow vegetables, vegetable oils, nuts, seeds, eggs, and whole grain cereals. Ginseng is a must here, as for all the menopausal symptoms. It enhances the action of estrogen, so making the most of what your body is producing. It also has an estrogen-like activity of its own. Take some on a regular daily basis.

HEART DISEASE – young women have a much lower risk of heart disease than men, for whom it is the commonest cause of premature death. Once the menopause is reached, however, women are just as likely to suffer this scourge of the Western world. Good nutrition now becomes even more essential. Follow the rules for Vitality Eating on p. 21 and you will be on the right track. Vitamin C is important, as it reduces the risk of blood clots, so eat plenty of red, green, and yellow peppers, kiwi fruit, oranges, and blackcurrants. Onions, garlic, leeks, chives, and scallions are good for reducing cholesterol, as is the lecithin found in eggs, soybeans, and liver.

Of course, the most important single factor in heart disease is smoking, followed by your parents' medical history. Though you can't do anything about the latter, you can give up tobacco, watch your weight, keep physically active, and, almost as important as all of these, control your stress levels.

ESSENTIAL FOODS

Beets: These are traditional medicine for building up the run-down and convalescent. They contain iron and are a good source of folic acid. This makes them a valuable addition to the menopause diet.

Garbanzo beans: They supply protein, vitamins A and C, and some of the B-complex vitamins, as well as calcium, iron, zinc, potassium, magnesium, and phosphorus.

Nectarines: This fruit supplies essential Vitamin A.

Oats: These are a good source of easily digested protein, B-complex vitamins, some vitamin E, calcium, magnesium, potassium, and silica.

Red, green, and yellow peppers: These are an excellent source of vitamin C, but the red and yellow ones also provide a good supply of vitamin A.

Sesame seeds: These are very rich in protein, iron, and zinc.

Spring greens: This vegetable is a real life-saver during the menopause, containing potassium, calcium, and iron, and being a very rich source of vitamins A and C.

Ginseng: This has a powerful tonic and stimulating effect, so is great if you feel a bit down. Take it as a tea in small but regular doses.

SKIN PROBLEMS are also caused by a drop in estrogen levels. Vitamins A and E will both help. Eat plenty of dark-green and yellow vegetables and fruit. Apricots and pumpkins are beneficial. Avocado has a special place here, and you ought to eat two a week. Yogurt, used as a skin cream, is a good idea too. A monthly facial scrub using a tub of yogurt mixed with a heaped teaspoon of coarse sea salt is an excellent, but gentle exfoliant, which removes dead skin.

RIGHT *Skin needs extra care at this time, otherwise it dries out and becomes brittle and flaky.*

The Third Age

TODAY you can expect to live at least until the age of 75. It seems strange that at the beginning of the twentieth century the lifespan of women was no more than 50 years, the menopause was barely acknowledged, and the prospect of another 25 golden years was not even a pipedream. Now, with the help of the Essential Foods, you can enjoy this bonus to the full.

There is no need to suffer in silence with the stiff, aching joints of rheumatism and arthritis. Indigestion and insomnia are not inevitable. Lost concentration and memory can be pushed aside. The specter of heart and circulatory disease need not haunt you. After all, if you have got this far, you can't have got it totally wrong.

loss of brain cells

eyes and ears lose some sharpness

heart and circulatory disease

food intolerance

rheumatism

loss of muscle strength

arthritis

joints lose flexibility

ABOVE The problems of aging are mainly those of degeneration and wear and tear. With sound nutrition, you can slow down the inevitable processes and enjoy a fruitful old age.

ESSENTIAL FOODS

Chicken: This is a great form of low-fat protein, which is also excellent value for money, quick and easy to cook, and high in nutritional value. Use free-range birds if you can as they are free of added growth hormone.

Chicory: This stimulates the gall bladder to produce bile, which makes it an aid to liver function and digestion.

Dried fruits: This is a superb source of energy, fiber and vitamin A (apricots, peaches, and nectarines). Dates and figs are good sources of iron and calcium.

Millet: Rich in protein and low in starch, millet is easy to digest and does not cause wind. It contains silicon, which is needed for the skin, hair, nails, and health of the blood-vessel walls.

Pears: There is some vitamin C in a pear's skin, and lots of fruit sugar for rapid energy in a ripe one. They are also rich in potassium, which is important if you are taking water tablets, extremely easy to digest, and an excellent source of the soluble fiber pectin.

Strawberries: Due to their cleansing and purifying action, they are a great help for all the joint diseases.

Turnips: These are powerful eliminators of uric acid, so they help those suffering from gout and other joint problems. They are also useful for the treatment of chest infections – puréed turnip in a little milk is the traditional European folk remedy for bronchitis.

Garlic: This has to be the great grandpa of all the food plants that have therapeutic properties. No matter what you may think of the smell, put garlic into savory dishes each day and, if you get a cold, you can even eat it on toast.

The brain loses cells as it grows older, the muscles lose some strength, the joints some flexibility, the digestion some tolerance, and the eyes and ears some sharpness. These are the normal processes of living. You're not just what you eat, you're what you absorb from what you eat. You're also what you think and feel. You must have a positive attitude to life, and not let your age prevent you from doing anything you want to do. This is the time for maximum nutrition, and it is geared to foods that supply the most nutrients in the most easily digestible form – high intakes of minerals, A, B-complex, C, and E vitamins, the super-nutrients that protect and nourish each cell.

The Third Age

SURVIVAL DURING THE GOLDEN YEARS

MEMORY AND CONCENTRATION – the B vitamins are essential for the proper working of the entire nervous system, and that includes the brain. A steady level of blood sugar is another factor, and to achieve this you must eat regular meals, which supply enough starches and natural sugars. Liver, chicken, and sardines are most important foods in this respect. Dried fruit such as dates, figs, and apricots should be eaten every day, as they contain the minerals that prevent the body from taking up aluminum – now thought to be a factor in causing senility. Vitamin C is also needed to prevent this, so eat plenty of strawberries and citrus fruit.

JOINT PROBLEMS – to keep rheumatism and arthritis at bay, eat plenty of turnips and their leafy tops. They increase the elimination of uric acid from the system, which aggravates joint problems. Strawberries have a cleansing effect and are also good for the joints. To keep up your muscle strength, you need protein. Chicken is a good source, and you can make a delicious soup from the leftovers. Put in lots of green and root vegetables, so that you have a highly nutritious broth that will keep you warm as well as well fed. All the oily fish are important, so eat them three times a week. Celery, celery leaves, and parsley have a mild diuretic effect (they help the body to eliminate fluids and, with the fluids, uric acid). Eat them in abundance, and also drink a couple of glasses of parsley tea each day – chop up two teaspoons of fresh parsley, add boiling water, and leave the tea to stand, covered, for five minutes. Strain and drink. And cabbage leaves make an amazingly soothing poultice for arthritic joints (see p. 86).

THE DIGESTION – you must eat at regular times, and in sensible quantities. Four small meals a day are better than one or two larger ones. Even if you are alone, lay the table and make mealtimes special. Eat slowly and chew well (look after your teeth, and see a dentist at least once a year if you have your own teeth; every other year if you have dentures). Lentils are an excellent form of protein, easy to digest, without causing wind. Avoid fatty foods, and eat some chicory or globe artichoke each day to stimulate your liver. Pears make a good end to a meal

ABOVE *Gentle exercise, especially in a friendly group, is a great boost for third agers.*

as they contain soluble fiber, vitamin C and, like bananas, lots of potassium, which is important if you are taking "water tablets" (diuretic pills).

CONSTIPATION – less exercise, a poor diet, and too much tea and coffee can soon produce this problem. Don't let it happen to you. Whole grain bread and cereals, dried fruits, millet, greens, and plenty of fresh fruit and salads are needed. Drink lots of water. If you worry about getting up in the night, make sure you take a glassful as soon as you wake up, another during the morning, and at least two more before late afternoon, in addition to your other usual fluids. And add lots of garlic to your cooking. It is a good natural antibiotic and helps keep the bowels regular.

THE HEART AND CIRCULATION – get your protein from fish, millet, poultry, and some low-fat dairy products. Eat meat infrequently. Take plenty of soluble fiber because, together with strawberries, garlic, olive oil, apples, onions, and baked beans, it helps to reduce the cholesterol in your blood. All these measures, alongside a reduction of the caffeine and salt that you consume, will also help to keep your blood pressure down. Exercise is absolutely vital, and these days most communities have exercise classes and swimming sessions specifically for older people. Do what you can, even if it is only some form of regular physical exertion in bed or in your armchair.

THE GOLDEN YEARS

44 percent of you have teeth.

2 percent of you drink more than 14 units of alcohol a week.

20 percent of you smoke.

Take great care of your diet – it's easy to get lazy if you're on your own.

It's never too late to help your bones – so take extra calcium.

The Third Age

OSTEOPOROSIS

Nutritionally this is a key time, as your body's needs change quite dramatically. Appetite tends to decrease, and women become increasingly at risk of osteoporosis, in which the bones become weak and brittle. Physical problems may make shopping more difficult and, for the older woman (who is statistically more likely to be left to cope on her own), there seems to be an inevitable reduction in the variety of foods eaten and in their quality, with more convenience foods, more snacks, less real cooking, and less incentive to take proper care of herself.

The digestion becomes less efficient, leading to a reduction in the amount of nutrients absorbed by the body, even if they are present in the diet to start with. Medication for various ailments may also further reduce the absorption of bone-building substances like calcium, and vitamins C and D.

Vitamin D is essential for the body's use of calcium and is vital in the prevention and treatment of osteoporosis. Antacids containing aluminum and anticoagulants reduce its absorption. Vitamin C is necessary for the production of collagen, an important part of bone structure. Its effectiveness is greatly reduced by aspirin, previous use of the contraceptive pill, tetracycline antibiotics, "sulpha" drugs, mineral oils, and nicotine. If you use any of these, take an extra 500mg of vitamin C daily.

Magnesium deficiency is also a factor in osteoporosis and is commonly linked with a diet high in salt. This is yet another reason for keeping your salt consumption to an absolute minimum. Coffee, large quantities of tea, alcohol, excessive amounts of refined bran, smoking, and lack of weight-bearing exercise all increase the rate of bone loss in osteoporosis. These are simple lifestyle factors that anyone can change. Diets low in calcium, and high in phosphorus and protein, also have an adverse effect on the bones.

Supplements are really important at this time, but they must be taken in the right form. Up to 40 percent of postmenopausal women have been found to have too little acid in their digestive juices, which drastically cuts down on the amount of calcium that can be absorbed from the normal calcium carbonate supplements, to a mere 4 percent – while those with normal stomach acid absorb 22 percent. This problem is overcome by using soluble calcium citrate, which allows a 45 percent uptake of calcium, even in patients with reduced stomach acid.

LEFT *Building up bone strength through exercise and proper diet will help prevent osteoporosis; any hobby involving manual activity can help strengthen the bones of the hand and keep the joints flexible.*

OSTEOPOROSIS DAILY SUPPLEMENT PLAN

Calcium citrate
1000mg

Vitamin C with bioflavonoids
500mg

Vitamin D
5µg

Magnesium
100mg

The Third Age

EATING PLAN

Now is the time to maximize your nutritional input and minimize the antinutrient effect of junk foods, fizzy drinks, and refined carbohydrates. At this time in your life you need foods bursting with nutrients that are easily absorbed, easily digested, and, most importantly, easily prepared.

You certainly don't need the same number of calories as an athletic 25-year-old, but nutritional quality must be your prime consideration. Large-scale surveys have shown alarming deficiencies in the diets of older people in Britain, Australia, and the USA. In 1900 4 percent of Americans were over 65. Today it is 12 percent – amounting to more than 27 million people. Across the board it seems that older women are more at risk from nutritional deficiencies than men – calcium, vitamins A, B6, C, fiber, and

total calories giving the most cause for concern. Up to half of the elderly had low intakes of some of these nutrients and, even worse, more than a quarter of them – both men and women - were taking supplementary bran, which further diminished the minimal amounts of calcium, magnesium, and zinc that they absorbed from their food.

Eat regular amounts of plain bio yogurt, for it is easier to digest than ordinary milk, and lactose intolerance gets worse with age. Adult Orientals and around 70 percent of the adult Jewish and black US populations are most affected by milk intolerance, and it is estimated that a maximum of 12 percent of Caucasian Americans have this problem.

In season you should be enjoying strawberries, raspberries, bilberries, and blackberries for their ability to remove uric acid from the system (celery, cabbage, and leeks do the same). To keep your brain active, the essential fatty acids in oily fish like salmon, sardines, tuna, and anchovies are vital. They are also good sources of zinc and iron, easy to cook, and brilliant convenience food when canned. The fatty acids also help relieve joint pain and stiffness. Eat masses of dark-green leafy vegetables, carrots, pumpkin, and squashes, as they are an important source of beta-carotene, other essential carotenoids, minerals, and vitamins.

At this time in your life you probably don't want to spend much time in the kitchen, but regular meals – no matter how small – are vital. Food does not have to be cooked – a whole wheat roll, a piece of good cheese, some celery, raisins, nuts, and an apple make a nourishing lunch. During the winter months add a bowl of simple homemade vegetable soup to boost the protective antioxidants and help your immune system fight off winter bugs. Oats are one of the most protective foods, rich in fiber, minerals, and protein, so start each day with porridge or muesli.

ANTIOXIDANT SUPPLEMENT PLAN

These days you don't have to mix and match a number of different pills to boost your intake of antioxidants – just buy a good antioxidant formula from your health store or pharmacy. It should contain beta-carotene, vitamins C and E, selenium, and zinc.

LEFT *The reward of healthy eating is a happy and active Third Age; you have the time, so make sure you are physically able to seize it. Stay mobile to enjoy active pleasures such as gardening.*

BELOW *Be kind to yourself in the Third Age; eat well, exercise in moderation, and enjoy life.*

Feeding the Mind and Spirit

IT HAS ALWAYS seemed extraordinary to me that there is universal acceptance of the idea that food is essential to nourish the body, yet the medical establishment does not see the connection between food and the well-nourished mind.

In ancient times things were very different – food was seen as a means of spiritual enrichment, and foods "fit for the gods" were part of our earliest forms of worship. Food deprivation was also known to have a deeply spiritual effect and the great religious leaders, healers, and mystics used fasting as a route to spiritual enlightenment.

From the Pharaohs to the Aztecs and the Mayans, from the native North Americans to the Norsemen of Scandinavia, from the temples of Angkor Wat to Delphi in ancient Greece, foods for the spirit and the soul were buried with the dead. Even in our modern times there are strong links between food, mind, and spirit. The vegetarianism demanded by some religious faiths as the path to self-enlightenment, the spiritual ritual of the tea ceremony in Japan, and the soul-food of Afro-Caribbean communities are typical examples. The pleasure and emotional satisfaction of the expatriate presented with a taste of home by a visitor – the most powerful being the foods of childhood – are evidence of the strong feelings of joy and happiness that foods evoke.

Since the dawn of kitchen medicine, people have used food for nourishment and health – whether physical, mental, or emotional. Herbs added for flavor have other benefits too. Rosemary not only tastes great but aids the digestion of fat, so it is often eaten with fattier meats like lamb; but it also contains volatile oils that stimulate the brain and improve memory – that is why it is planted in gardens of remembrance. Nutmeg enhances the flavor of many different foods, especially rice, but it is also a hallucinogenic and calmative – perhaps that is why British nannies put it into their charges' rice pudding.

Foods do not even have to be eaten to affect the mind and spirit. Their aroma, filled with essential oils from herbs and spices, can transport us instantly back in time to a long-forgotten vacation, a very special meal, a happy event, or a joyous family gathering. Smell is the most primitive of the senses, bypassing the circulatory system and the digestive system and having a direct effect on the brain, with instant repercussions.

If you want to enjoy peace of mind and spirit, there are substances best avoided or taken sparingly, the prime culprits being caffeine and alcohol. Although a glass or two of good wine can be a great mood enhancer, larger quantities of alcohol are extremely depressing, though you may not feel it at the time. As for caffeine, there are those who are extremely sensitive to this complex chemical. One cup of coffee, a couple of cups of strong tea, a can of cola drink, or a chocolate bar is enough to make them mentally hyperactive, although they seldom make the connection. Even those who tolerate caffeine well will be affected by large doses, particularly in terms of mental irritability, poor-quality or loss of sleep, and, most commonly, anxiety states. Be warned, however – if you are an 8–10 cups a day person, giving up coffee suddenly often causes severe headaches.

Substantial quantities of refined carbohydrates, especially sugars and high-fat foods, can play havoc with your state of mind. Wildly fluctuating blood-sugar levels trigger violent mood swings and this is a particular problem for women around period time and for everybody at times of excessive stress.

In this section you will find specific foods and ways of eating that will cheer you up, increase your mental energy, reduce your stress, keep you alert, and get you off to sleep. Sound impossible? Try it for yourself. Whatever your underlying problem, feeding your brain with the appropriate nutrients at the right time, or keeping it free of harmful substances at the wrong time, will make a vast improvement. There is nothing to lose – except perhaps the tranquilizers or antidepressants you may have been prescribed – and everything to gain.

ABOVE *Relaxation techniques such as yoga can help to calm your mind.*

Raising Mental Energy

IS THERE really such a thing as "brain food?" The answer is definitely yes – foods needed for the brain's development while the baby grows in the mother's womb; foods vital for the child, adolescent, and teenager to make sure there is enough energy for brain function; and foods essential to keep the brain active and working correctly well into old age.

There are also foods that are brain antinutrients – those that cause depression, anger, hyperactivity, and violent behavior. Everyone understands the way in which excessive amounts of alcohol can turn the most mild-mannered person into a raging monster, but there are other links between food and behavior that are far more subtle and insidious.

Many old wives' tales contain more than a grain of truth, and grandma's exhortation to her grandchildren, "Eat fish, it's good for your brains," is only just wide of the mark. Research by Professor Michael Crawford at the Institute of Brain Chemistry in London has shown a clear link between fetal brain development and the amount of oily fish consumed by pregnant women. The omega-3 fatty acids found in oily fish make up the greatest proportion of brain tissue during fetal growth and are supplied to the fetus by the mother through the placenta.

FOOD FOR THE BRAIN

Women whose diets are generally poor during pregnancy, and especially those who have a low caloric input (fewer than around 1,500 calories per day), tend to have low birth-weight babies, who lag behind their peers in mental development. Furthermore, children who have been exposed to malnutrition, even when it is successfully treated, show marked delays in their language skills, co-ordination, and social behavior.

In order to function, the brain depends on a constant supply of glucose and oxygen. These are both delivered to the brain by the blood circulating in the body, so for optimum brain function the diet must contain a mixture of foods that provide instant energy, those that give a slower release and some, like proteins, that take a long time to break down. The diet must also be rich in iron-containing foods, which should be in a form that the body can most easily absorb. Meat of all sorts, and particularly liver, are rich sources of haem iron – the iron most easily available to the body. Other forms of iron are more difficult to absorb, but absorption can be increased by eating vitamin C-rich foods at the same time as non-haem iron sources – dark-green leafy vegetables, eggs, dried fruits, and molasses.

A poor diet does not just affect your physical well-being. It can also have a disastrous impact on the way you behave, your ability to think, reason, and concentrate, your memory and coordination, and even your mood at the start of each new day.

In almost every study of essential nutrients, emotional and mental disorders have been among the most prominent symptoms of deficiency. But despite a food-mountain of evidence, there are still many doctors – and psychiatrists in particular – who ignore the very idea of a mood-food connection. What a tragedy this is in terms of human suffering, especially when viewed in the light of the extraordinary and pioneering work of Dr. Carl Pfeiffer, who was for many years Director of the Brain Bio Center in New Jersey, one of the foremost institutions for research into psychiatric illness and nutrition anywhere in the world.

ABOVE *Babies and young children have lots to learn and huge amounts of information to process as they grow up.*

ABOVE *Young adults need to be able to think on their feet and keep their reflexes in good shape as they go into the world.*

ABOVE *The middle aged need mental stamina as they become the responsible adult between children and elderly parents.*

ABOVE *Concentration and memory need support if the Third Age is to be enjoyable.*

LEFT *Learning a new skill in adulthood takes more concentration than in childhood. Playing an instrument requires a great deal from the brain, and is an excellent way to enjoy a cerebral workout. Make sure your diet is rich in the brain foods shown on page 48.*

Raising Mental Energy

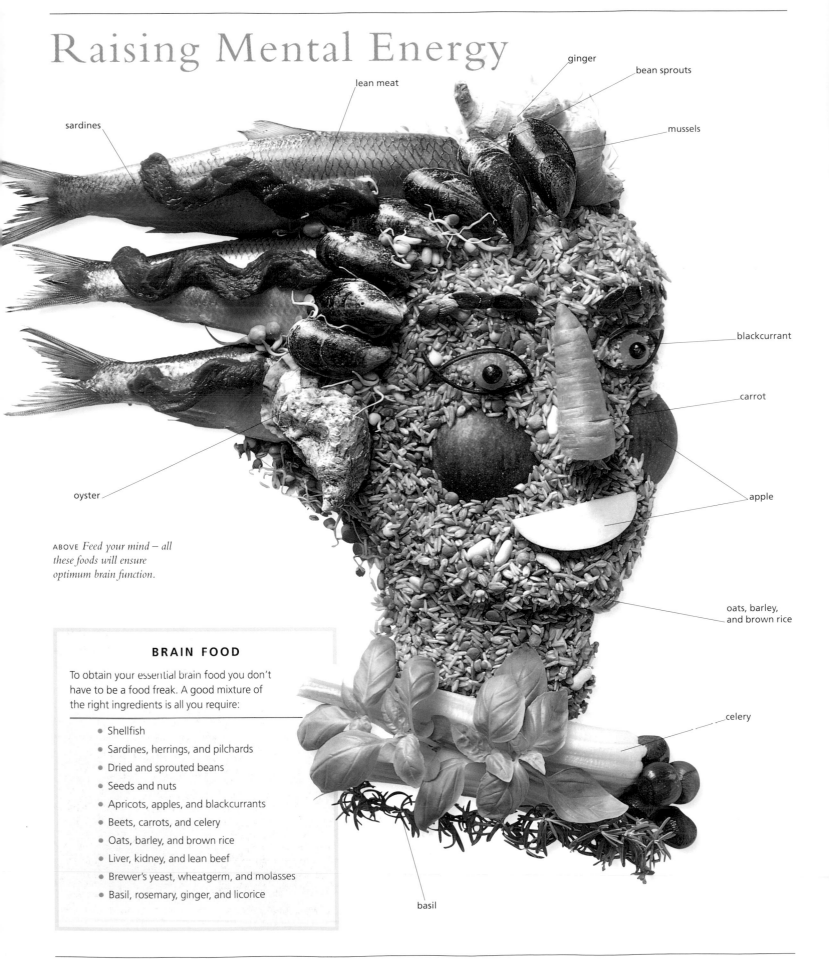

ginger

bean sprouts

lean meat

sardines

mussels

blackcurrant

carrot

apple

oyster

ABOVE *Feed your mind – all these foods will ensure optimum brain function.*

oats, barley, and brown rice

celery

BRAIN FOOD

To obtain your essential brain food you don't have to be a food freak. A good mixture of the right ingredients is all you require:

- Shellfish
- Sardines, herrings, and pilchards
- Dried and sprouted beans
- Seeds and nuts
- Apricots, apples, and blackcurrants
- Beets, carrots, and celery
- Oats, barley, and brown rice
- Liver, kidney, and lean beef
- Brewer's yeast, wheatgerm, and molasses
- Basil, rosemary, ginger, and licorice

basil

Raising Mental Energy

You don't need degrees in medicine and psychiatry to understand the sinking lethargy that smothers you at the end of a long, hard, and much too busy day – when there simply wasn't time for lunch, breakfast vanished in the rush, and the thought of cooking is just too much. And what about the irritability that occurs when you have had more cups of coffee than you could count? All in the mind?

Of course it is easier and quicker to write a prescription for tranquilizers, antidepressants, or sleeping pills than to ask about your eating habits or get you to keep a food diary for a whole week. How many doctors are interested in the number of cups of coffee you have had today? But anxiety, depression, insomnia, irritability, violence, weepiness, exhaustion, panic attacks, mood swings, and all forms of irrational behavior are, more often than not, the direct result of a lack of one, or several, of the essential brain foods.

The vitamin B-complex, folic acid, and vitamins A and E are the most obvious brain requirements, but there are some even more important minerals and trace elements, without which the brain simply will not function as it should – namely, zinc, iron, magnesium, chromium, and selenium. Finally, your brain needs the essential fatty acids. But it is not enough to get all these nutrients in your food; you must also beware the danger foods that deprive you, and your brain, of the nourishment you need.

YOUNG PEOPLE'S MENTAL ENERGY

The major problem for young people and their mental energy is sugar. High-sugar foods – all the things that children like – cause enormous fluctuations in blood-sugar level, which result in peaks and troughs of concentration, application, and mood. To maintain a positive mental state what they need are slow-release energy foods, which also supply the B vitamins essential for brain function: whole grain cereals, beans, oats, starchy fruit like bananas, all dried fruit, and good protein. When Grandma said, "Eat your fish – it's good for your brain," she was close to the truth, especially in relation to oily fish, which contain the omega-3 fatty acids that are essential for brain function.

Foods to avoid are canned drinks – normal or light, as the sweeteners are almost as bad as the sugar – the empty calories in instant desserts, and the junk foods full of additives. If your child loves baked beans on toast, don't worry. As long as the toast is whole wheat and you add a tomato, this is just about perfect brain food.

BELOW *A challenging game of chess; mental energy should be cultivated at all ages.*

Watch your intake of all the refined carbohydrates – white flour, sugar, confectionery, and bakery products – which are severely impoverished in many of the vital substances. Tea, coffee, chocolate, and alcohol either stop the absorption of, or destroy, the same constituents. Too much bran will affect your mineral uptake, and acid fruits cooked in aluminum pans may raise the amount of this toxic metal in your body. This can have severe repercussions in later life: there is a positive link between aluminum and the mental illness Alzheimer's disease.

The missing essential nutrients are often a major factor in problems that may be all in the mind, but which can start in the supermarket. Of course, many psychological and psychiatric illnesses have their roots in more than just bad eating. Sometimes food is the key to the problem, sometimes it is just another piece in the larger jigsaw, but the link between body, mind, spirit, and food is to be ignored at their peril by health-care professionals.

Memory and Concentration

AS WITH ALL brain function, a constant supply of glucose and oxygen is required for brain cells to work at their optimum level. This presupposes the regular consumption of balanced meals to provide a steady, even conversion of food into glucose and an adequate intake of easily absorbed iron, in order to ensure good oxygen-carrying ability in the blood.

In addition, a wide spread of other essential nutrients, especially calories, the B-vitamins, carotene, zinc, and boron, is a prerequisite for concentration and memory. But this is where the controversy starts. It is a widely held belief among the British Department of Health, doctors, and orthodox nutritionists that no-one in the UK, including children, suffers from vitamin or mineral deficiencies, and the same is certainly true of the USA. Yet at the same time our children are bombarded with advertising for junk foods that are high in fats and sugars and often poor-quality sources of nutrients. Week after week anxious parents telephone my radio programs concerned that their children's eating habits result in inadequate nutrition.

Even the food provided in schools is mostly of the burger and French fries variety, and the poorest-quality burgers at that. Most children consume vast quantities of sweet carbonated drinks, chocolate bars, and fatty snacks such as chips. These provide so many of their calories that their appetite is satisfied long before they sit down to eat a balanced meal at home.

We know that the diets of British schoolchildren do in fact show alarming nutritional deficiencies (see box). And these figures are just the tip of the iceberg. To naturopaths like me and my colleagues it came as no surprise at all when a science teacher in Wales announced in 1987 that giving a multivitamin pill to children increased their intelligence. This first small trial was followed up by a second study of 60 children, in a proper double-blind placebo experiment. All the children were given an intelligence test and after eight months on the vitamin pill the tests were repeated. The children on the placebo increased their scores by 1.8 points and those on the multivitamin pill by 9 points.

The medical establishment was galvanized into a frenzy of criticism, denying that this was possible and arguing that British children were not malnourished; even hinting subtly at scientific fraud. But more

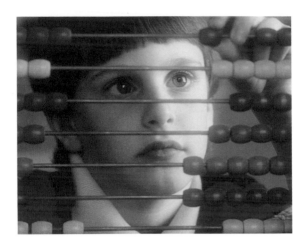

proof was to come. Just before the second results were published I was privileged to spend some time with American criminologist Professor Steven Schoenthaler, at Cal-state University, Turlock. Following the early work by criminologist Alexander Schauss, Director of the American Institute for Biosocial Research in Seattle, and author of *Diet, Crime and Delinquency,* Schoenthaler was already researching the link between nutrition and intelligence with juvenile delinquents. Again, the youngsters who took vitamins showed a dramatic improvement in intelligence in just 13 weeks. After further studies Schoenthaler concluded that a combination of improved diet and simple multivitamin-mineral supplements could change intelligence and behavior in delinquent youngsters (see also *Sugar on p.136*).

Better IQ requires better memory and concentration, and these depend on good nutrition. There is no doubt that the children who benefited most from vitamin supplements in IQ studies were those whose nutritional input was the worst to start with. I am certain that a well-balanced, wide-spectrum vitamin and mineral supplement is a safe insurance policy for those of any age having difficulty with memory or concentration. But I am equally certain that taking a pill does not wholly compensate for living on an appalling diet of junk food.

Brain food must be stimulating and should avoid components that stimulate the brain's release of serotonin (see *Sleep on p. 54*). The worst thing you can do before an important business meeting, an interview, or exam, when you need to be mentally alert and focusing all your concentration, is eat a high-carbohydrate meal. To prevent the post-prandial sleepiness that this type of food causes, go for the protein foods, or at least complex carbohydrates, which combine proteins with starch. Watch out for the animal fats, which also slow down brain function. While one glass of wine may relax your nerves and help you cope better with the mental

ABOVE *Studies suggest that children taking adequate vitamins achieve more academically than those who do not.*

NUTRITIONAL DEFIENCIES

25 percent of 10-year-old boys and 50 percent of 10-year-old girls get less than 70 percent of their daily iron requirements

59 percent of 14-year-old boys and 75 percent of 14-year-old girls get less than 70 percent of their B6 needs

At 15, nearly one-third of boys and over one-fifth of girls get less than 50 percent of their vitamin A needs

Memory and Concentration

ABOVE *A glass of wine can relax the nerves but is not a good idea if focus and concentration is required at work or for academic study.*

BELOW *Following a sensible regimen such as the exam diet (see box) will help make this testing time a rewarding experience rather than a chore.*

stresses of difficult situations, be warned that alcohol is a depressant and at crucial times for memory and concentration it should be avoided.

Zinc is a key factor in both memory and concentration but is commonly lacking in diets that are high in convenience foods. Shellfish is a particularly rich source (and oysters the richest of all), but there is also plenty of zinc in crab, other fish, whole grain cereals, beans and peas, mushrooms, wheatgerm, pumpkin, and sunflower seeds. Of all the culinary herbs, rosemary is the king of the memory enhancers. It stimulates the adrenal cortex and is of great value in loss of memory, nervous tensions, anxiety, and general emotional debility.

Make sure you eat plenty of fresh fruit, particularly grapes, pears, and apples, and a handful each day of fresh unsalted peanuts, walnuts, and almonds to keep your boron levels up. Recent research suggests that boron may play an important part in the transmission of electrical impulses in the brain, and also in calcium levels in postmenopausal women (3mg a day reduced calcium excretion by over 40 percent).

There is no evidence that nutritional changes have any beneficial effect on Alzheimer's disease, but there is a strong link between aluminum and this condition. The link is not proven, but my advice is to avoid aluminum cooking utensils, especially for very acidic foods like soft fruit, rhubarb, jam and pickle-making; also avoid direct contact between acidic foods and aluminum foil, aluminum-based indigestion medicines, and antiperspirants.

Senility and associated short-term memory loss can be helped by improving the diet as outlined above, but it is vital to recognize that many elderly people have poor diets and therefore reduced powers of nutrient absorption. Supplements play a vital role in helping this group of people – a broad-spectrum multivitamin and mineral pill is a must, and regular doses of garlic and *Ginkgo biloba* will help improve blood flow to the brain tissues. Iron, beta-carotene and vitamins B_1 and B_2 are important to memory and mental alertness, especially in older people. Foods such as meat, nuts, wheatgerm, liver, almonds, milk products, dark-green and orange fruit and vegetables, shellfish, and beans should all form part of the staple diet for the elderly.

THE EXAM DIET

For maximum concentration and brain power during the stressful time of exams, it is best to reverse some of your normal eating patterns. The object of the exercise is to be at peak performance for the morning and afternoon, and to unwind, relax, and sleep well during the evening and night. If exams are just around the corner, it is no good trying to sit up until the small hours and cram – if you don't know it now, you never will.

Breakfast (high in protein, low in fat, little carbohydrate)

Large glass of fresh orange juice

Low-fat, bio, live plain yogurt with toasted almonds or pistachios

Poached egg with baked beans

Apple or pear

Mid-morning

Snack of dried apricots, raisins, dates, and plain fresh nuts

Lunch

Mixed salad with cold meat, fish, or low-fat cheese. Add sesame seeds, sunflower seeds, and pumpkin seeds to the salad and include plenty of watercress and tomatoes.

Mid-afternoon

Piece of low-fat cheese or a hard-cooked egg (if you haven't had them already), with an apple, a pear, or a bunch of grapes

Evening meal (now it's time for the carbohydrates)
Fish, meat, or poultry with potatoes and vegetables, **or**

A thick root-vegetable casserole made with potatoes, rutabaga, parsnip, turnip, carrot, onion, celery, shredded cabbage, and kidney beans, rice, or barley, **or**

A generous portion of pasta with your favorite low-fat sauce

A delicious carbohydrate-rich rice pudding

During the evening
Banana and a few dates or figs

During the day drink at least 3½pt/1.7l of fluid, mostly water, but including weak tea, herbal teas, natural fruit and vegetable juices, and no more than two cups of coffee. Sugar is just about your worst enemy, so do try to avoid it in any form (including honey) during the daytime. Save your sugar fix for the evening and keep it as small as possible.

Follow the guidelines for the Exam Diet and your mind will be fully alert when you most need it to be.

Depression

SINCE the earliest civilizations people have understood the link between mental and emotional states and food and drink. For primitive tribes there were no tranquilizers or anti-depressants; instead, they brewed alcohol from fermented foods, chewed on the betel nut or the coca leaf, harvested opium poppies, or hunted for magic mushrooms.

In our modern world, the instant that depression strikes, the answer is the prescription pad, and orthodox medicine seldom considers the role of nutrition as either cause or treatment for depressive illness. As a normal part of everyday life, we are all subject to emotional ups and downs – happiness/sadness, euphoria/despondency, laughing/weeping – all part and parcel of living.

But the awfulness of clinical depression is a different story. It frequently follows some shattering life event – bereavement, serious illness in the family, loss of job, divorce, or bankruptcy – and in these situations all that is usually needed is good support. According to the American Psychiatric Association, there are eight key factors linked to depression: changes in appetite leading to weight gain or loss, insomnia or constant sleeping, hyperactivity or total lethargy, loss of interest and sex drive, reduced energy and fatigue or listlessness, feelings of worthlessness or guilt, lack of concentration, and, finally, dwelling constantly on death or suicide. Any five of these factors occurring at the same time is a certain marker of depression, although someone experiencing four of them is probably depressed, but this state should continue unabated for at least a month for a diagnosis of clinical depression to be made.

Poor diet can have a disastrous impact on memory, coordination, concentration, powers of reason, behavior, and, above all, mood. Mental distress is inevitably linked to a deficiency of iron, magnesium, and B-complex vitamins. Zinc deficiency leads to loss of appetite, subsequent poor nutrition, inevitable chronic fatigue, and finally depression. Antidepressant drugs, which are usually the first line of treatment for chronic fatigue, interfere with zinc absorption, leading to loss of appetite and so on, and so on, into a downward spiral.

ABOVE *The opium poppy, source of opium and heroin. Opiates combat depression by numbing the soul and your responses to the world.*

BELOW *Depression is more than simply feeling down; it can incapacitate sufferers to such a degree that they feel imprisoned and immobilized.*

Since the majority of women and many children have diets deficient in iron, and zinc levels appear to be falling as the consumption of convenience foods rises, it is hardly surprising that depression is becoming more common. Excessive consumption of caffeine, whether in the form of coffee, tea, cola drinks, or chocolate, and large amounts of bran interfere with mineral absorption and can be the first step on the road to depression. Overstimulation of the central nervous system by caffeine can also be responsible for extreme mood swings.

A diet that is high in refined carbohydrates and sugars is a common factor in depressive illness and, contrary to popular belief, alcohol is not a stimulant but a severe depressant – depression being an inevitable consequence of alcohol abuse.

Vitamin deficiencies may have specific effects on mental states as follows:

- Vitamin C – generalized depression, extreme tiredness, outbursts of hysterical behavior.
- Vitamin B12 – general mental deterioration, psychotic behavior, depression, loss of memory, and paranoia.
- Vitamin B1 (thiamin) – depression, irritability, loss of memory, loss of concentration, and exhaustion.
- Vitamin B6 (pyridoxine) – psychosis, mental deterioration, and depression.
- Folic acid – fatigue, irritability, insomnia, forgetfulness, and confusion.
- Niacin – loss of memory, mood swings, depression, and anxiety.
- Biotin – severe lethargy, depression, and constant sleeping.
- Pantothenic acid – insomnia, fatigue, depression, and psychosis.

Commonly prescribed drugs can lead to depression too. The long-term use of steroids, many of the medicines used for the treatment of high blood pressure, and the contraceptive pill are major examples. And despite the fact that many people claim that they smoke in order to relieve tension, nicotine is another chemical which, combined with the raised blood levels of carbon monoxide, has a detrimental effect on mood and brain function.

Depression

Improved nutrition can be used to relieve depression and enhance overall mental health, mental ability, and performance. If you think your problems are all in the mind, don't submit to the belief that you will be forced to limp through the rest of your life on the crutch of tranquilizers, antidepressants, or sleeping pills. Often the solution to your problems lies in your own hands – the hands that purchase, prepare, and put food on your plate.

Fill your shopping basket with all the foods that supply the key nutrients – a wide variety of vegetables, fruit and salads, plenty of whole grain cereals, all types of beans, pasta, and brown rice. Eat regular amounts of oily fish (fresh or canned) and modest amounts of red meat, poultry, and liver.

Traditional "mood foods" have a long-standing place in the folklore of eating, but they are all on this roll of honor for a purpose. They are abundant sources of good energy, and of the vitamins and minerals essential to maintain a positive and happy frame of mind. Grapes, millet, wheatgerm, brewer's yeast, oats, buckwheat, molasses, berries, figs – fresh or dried – unsalted seeds and nuts, shellfish, nutmeg, ginger, basil, and rosemary all have a key role to play in eating to beat depression.

TRYPTOPHAN – A SEROTONIN TRIGGER

One often overlooked nutrient is tryptophan, an essential amino acid component of protein, which the body cannot manufacture for itself. Many of us working in the field of natural medicine are convinced that tryptophan deficiency can be a major trigger of depression. Without sufficient tryptophan, the body does not produce enough of the vital neurotransmitter, serotonin, the brain's passport to the feel-good factor. Foods rich in tryptophan are dried skimmed milk – stir a couple of teaspoons into yogurt, or add it to soups, sauces, milkshakes, and desserts – beef, lamb and pork, vegetarian burger mixes, cheese, pumpkin seeds, poultry, cashew and peanuts, beans, herrings, and eggs.

CHOCOLATE

Chocolate can be a mixed blessing, as its high sugar content can create wild fluctuations in the body's blood-sugar levels. In order to function properly, the brain needs a constant regular supply of sugar, but when the level plunges from hyper to hypo, the effects on mood and behavior can be devastating.

On the other hand, modest amounts of chocolate can give the depressive a real lift, as chocolate contains the chemical theobromine, which triggers the release of endorphins in the brain. It is these brain chemicals that mimic the euphoric feelings of "being in love." It is no accident that chocolate advertisements are nearly always linked to the themes of love, romance, and sex.

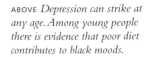

ABOVE *Depression can strike at any age. Among young people there is evidence that poor diet contributes to black moods.*

LEFT *The odd chocolate can cheer a day up but too many can bring you down with a bump, as the high sugar content plays havoc with the blood-sugar levels.*

Sleep

S LEEP IS a great example of the interaction between food, mind, and body. With extra-ordinary perception of the human condition, Shakespeare's words for Macbeth show a remarkable understanding of sleep's importance – the great dispeller of anxiety and stress, the healer of aching limbs, the soother of minds, and certainly a time for nourishing body and spirit. As sleep descends, all the activity hormones are switched off, making way for the growth and repair hormones to get to work. This is when you utilize the nutrients from your food as the body sets about its nightly maintenance work.

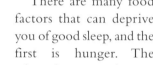

COFFEE

There are many food factors that can deprive you of good sleep, and the first is hunger. The rumbling stomach will surely wake you at three in the morning, when your choice is either to lie there tossing and turning or to mount a midnight raid on the refrigerator. If you are really hungry, then low blood sugar will add still further to your insomnia, as your brain will not be able to produce enough of the sleep-inducing hormones.

On the other hand, taking to your bed after an enormous meal, a couple of bottles of wine and half a pint of caffeine-laden black coffee guarantees a night of little more than fitful dozing. Caffeine in any form, and for some people even in tiny amounts, can drive away sleep for nights on end.

Apart from all the physical causes of insomnia – overwarm bedrooms, a dry, air-conditioned atmosphere, crying babies, noisy neighbors, planes, trucks, police sirens, or snoring partners – one of the most common is dieting.

The scientific link between weight and sleep was first described in a paper published in the *British Medical Journal* in 1976 by Professor Arthur Crisp. He and his researchers conducted a random survey of 1,000 men and women. They were all weighed and asked a selection of questions, with the purpose of determining how they felt about themselves, specifically in relation to anxiety and depression. The result showed that the overweight members of the group

were more satisfied with life and generally of a happier disposition than their thinner counterparts. Happiness is equated with sleeping well, whereas anxiety and depression almost inevitably lead to sleep of lower quality and greater disruption. Overall, the overweight slept for longer and enjoyed proportionately more "paradoxical sleep." It is during this phase of sleep that the greatest degree of muscular relaxation occurs, and more paradoxical sleep means renewed energy the following day. The lack of essential nutrients that results from constant dieting is sufficient to interfere with the workings of the

"Sleep that knits up the ravell'd sleave of care, The death of each day's life, sore labour's bath, Balm of hurt minds, great nature's second course, Chief nourisher in life's feast."

WILLIAM SHAKESPEARE
Macbeth

Sleep

There are many foods that help promote good sleep, especially those that contain the sleep-inducing hormone, serotonin – bananas, pineapples, walnuts, figs, and tomatoes are common examples. Starchy foods contain the essential amino acid tryptophan, which is a precursor of serotonin. That is why malted milk drinks really do help to encourage better sleep. The beneficial effects of these are more apparent in older people and seem to occur during the later stages of sleep, rather than in getting to sleep. If you find that you drop off easily but wake in the small hours, it is certainly worth trying one of these drinks about a half hour before bedtime.

The ancient Romans used wild lettuce as an effective aid to sleep, and herbalists still use it today. Modern varieties are all relatives of the wild plant, so a few lettuce leaves in a sandwich (the bread supplies tryptophan) is a really good bedtime snack. And honey has long been a favorite folk remedy for insomnia. Take it mixed with a little warm milk, in a cup of camomile tea, or in hot water with lemon. Other herbal teas that help you to sleep are lemon balm *(Melissa)*, crushed fennel seeds – especially when sleeplessness is caused by indigestion or wind – lemon verbena, and lime blossom.

There is no denying that we are what we eat, and you cannot expect a good night's sleep if you are constantly consuming large quantities of coffee, tea, chocolate, or cola drinks, all of which supply your brain with a constant stream of irritating caffeine. As far as food is concerned, the watchwords should be: not too little, not too much, but just right. What is just right for you, you will find by trial and error.

ABOVE *Sleeplessness can be a vicious circle: you can't sleep, so you worry about it, and then you can't sleep for worrying about it. It does not help if your partner enjoys blissful nights of slumber.*

RIGHT *Camomile tea is a soothing drink to take before bedtime. It calms the mind and encourages sleep.*

body's biological machine, almost invariably leading to disturbance of sleep.

The message here is clear: if you are already suffering from insomnia, don't go on a weight-loss diet. If you are underweight, then putting on a few pounds will help to improve your sleep patterns. If you are overweight and have a sleep problem, this is not the time to think about reducing your weight by embarking on a strict slimming diet, unless of course there are serious medical reasons why you should – for example, heart disease, severe breathing problems, or if you are awaiting surgery.

Stress and Relaxation

AT MOMENTS of comfort and convenience, stress is not a problem, but when challenge and controversy stare us in the face, the way in which we react – physically, emotionally, and spiritually – is the measure of our success in dealing with stress. Stress is part of everyday life, and our bodies' responses to stressful stimuli have always played a key role in humankind's survival.

The "fight or flight" response, which prepares our bodies for instant reaction at times of danger, and which our bodies produce without conscious effort or command, is the root cause of all the problems associated with our inability to cope with the stresses produced in industrialized Western civilization. This remarkable ability to react instantly to challenge becomes counter-productive when it is impossible to choose either "fight" or "flight;" when the only option is to "grin and bear it," "grit our teeth," or "soldier on" – all expressions that betray the emotions. Many people are ill equipped to deal with excessive stresses, and stress-induced illness is now growing to epidemic proportions. Heart attack, high blood pressure, insomnia, premenstrual syndrome, menopausal problems, sexual disorders, skin complaints, asthma or chest complaints, migraine, and arthritis can all be directly linked to, or caused by, poor ability to cope with stress.

But the way in which stress affects our nutritional status is, in some ways, the most important factor in the whole equation. Overproduction of stomach acid can lead to inflammation of the stomach lining, ulceration, and poor absorption. It often results in gastric reflux and esophagitis, which in turn makes swallowing painful and has an adverse effect on eating. At the other end of the gut, excessive stress can shorten the time it takes for food to pass through the colon, either due to increased motility or inflammatory conditions like colitis. Many nutrients are absorbed in the lower end of the bowel and it is also here that B vitamins are synthesized by the natural flora. The result is a general lowering of nutritional status and a specific reduction in B vitamins, some of the nutrients specifically responsible for the general well-being of the nervous system.

So stress and nutrition are inextricably linked. The negative side is the self-perpetuating downward spiral of poor diet, excessive stress, nutrient deficiency, even worse nutrition, and greater stress.

clear, relaxed mind

controlled breathing

improved digestion

flexible joints

good balance

ABOVE *Yoga is a great help in times of stress. This simple pose is the Vrksasana, or Tree Pose, which is great for stretching and balancing.*

Stress and Relaxation

But there is a positive side too. You can eat to beat stress, and improving your diet should be the first step on the road to recovery. Naturally you have to deal with the other factors too, and yoga, meditation, relaxation techniques, lifestyle changes, self-discipline, and often simply learning to say no without feeling guilty all play a major part.

The idea that stress-related disasters are the exclusive province of the boardroom and high-powered executive is simply not true. No one is immune from this plague. It exists on the factory floor, in the office, at the kitchen sink, in the elderly and the young alike.

While attitudes to the over-stressed patient are thankfully beginning to change, the orthodox medical approach frequently fails to recognize or deal with the root of the problem. The symptoms are treated, but seldom the patient. The physician may not recognize the effects that the patient's mental state is having on his or her body. The psychiatrist may well ignore physical disease altogether. The epidemic of stress disorders is only equaled by the pandemic of prescriptions for antidepressant and tranquilizing drugs – and the consequent dependence on these by millions of people.

> "The ultimate measure of a man is not where he stands in moments of comfort and convenience, but where he stands at times of challenge and controversy."
>
> MARTIN LUTHER KING

RIGHT *The pace of living in developed Western society induces stress in almost all of us.*

THE STRESS-BUSTER'S DIET

Here you need exactly the opposite to the Exam Diet – lots of foods that are calming, soothing, and mood-enhancing, and a minimum intake of those that are stimulating. Top of the list of villains is caffeine. If you are very sensitive to this stimulant, avoid it altogether and stick to decaffeinated tea and coffee. Keep off cola drinks – even the caffeine-free ones contain so much other junk that you are better off without them – and watch out for some of the sports drinks and so-called "energy" drinks, many of which also contain caffeine. If small amounts of caffeine do not upset you, then have no more than one or two cups of caffeine drinks a day.

High-protein diets mean high mental-energy diets, so these are not for you. What you should be eating is lots of the serotonin-containing foods – bananas, pineapple, walnuts, figs, tomatoes, avocados, dates, pawpaw, passion fruit, and eggplants. The basic staple of your diet should be complex carbohydrates like whole wheat bread, pasta, rice, beans, and potatoes. Get your protein from modest amounts of fish, low-fat cheese, eggs, and poultry, but eat very little meat.

This high-carbohydrate diet is rich in tryptophan, which the body converts to serotonin, the mood-enhancing, tranquilizing hormone. Breakfast is a key factor in this stress-busting regime and should comprise predominantly good carbohydrates like porridge, unsweetened muesli, or natural whole grain breakfast cereals. Make the porridge with water and sweeten it with honey and dried fruits, serve the breakfast cereals with pure fruit juices, and prepare your muesli in the traditional Swiss fashion, by soaking it overnight in fruit juice and serving it with a little honey topped with fresh fruit. Finish your stress-busting breakfast with whole wheat toast and honey or good-quality preserves made without additives, and this will set you up for the day.

It is essential to be a grazer – don't go for more than two hours without a carbohydrate snack – in order to keep your blood sugar on an even keel. Avoid all alcohol, but do make use of the natural destressing herbs in your cooking: basil, rosemary, lemon balm, thyme, nutmeg, marjoram, and lemon verbena. Use the appropriate herbal teas to replace ordinary tea and coffee.

Finally, the good news. Although it does contain some caffeine, you could indulge yourself in small quantities of very good-quality chocolate – the darker, the better. Chocolate contains a substance known as theobromine, a chemical that stimulates the release of the body's feel-good hormones, endorphins, from the brain.

Safe Fasting

FASTING has been used as a form of therapeutic treatment for more than 2,000 years. Even Hippocrates used it for a wide range of diseases, as fasting allows the body to concentrate all its resources on dealing with the disease process, rather than with the chemical reactions of digestion.

Although orthodox medicine has ridiculed the use of fasting, certainly for the majority of the twentieth century, enthusiastic supporters have been writing articles about it in journals since the late nineteenth century. In recent years fasting has begun to be more widely accepted as a treatment for obesity, high blood pressure, arthritis, rheumatism, food allergies, eczema, and even psychiatric problems like schizophrenia and depression.

Modern research has demonstrated the effectiveness of fasting as a technique that helps the body deal with highly toxic substances. Just one study makes the point. In 1984 M. Imamura and T. Tung described their efforts to relieve the awful symptoms of poisoning in a large number of Taiwanese patients who had used contaminated rice oil containing toxic polychlorinated-biphenyls (PCBs). All the patients who underwent fasting showed signs of improvement. A few people in this experiment maintained that the relief they got was little short of dramatic.

As a means of boosting the body's immune system, fasting is significantly effective. Studies have shown that after just three days on a supervised fast the white cell count of subjects showed a 25 percent increase – and it is the white cells that act as the body's policemen, attacking, destroying, and mopping up invading pathogens or molecules of foreign protein, which might trigger allergic reactions. It is not certain whether this effect is a direct stimulation or the result of removing immuno-inhibiting toxins.

Fasting is one of the most basic therapies used by traditional British and European naturopaths, and is also widely practiced by natural hygienists in the USA. There are a number of different types of fast, together with "semi-fasts," which are better described as "detoxifying programs." While it is perfectly safe to undertake a fast of three to five days in your own home, anything over three days should be done under medical supervision, and any fast longer than five days should be followed as an in-patient in an establishment where close supervision and skilled professional help are on hand.

If you intend to try a short fast for yourself, it is always advisable to consult your own professional health adviser first, as there are some illnesses and medicines that could be adversely affected by the withdrawal of food. You may choose a total water-only fast for anything between two and five days, a two-day total fast followed by three days of detox., or even a short 24- or 48-hour detoxification program.

FASTING PROGRAMS

However you choose to do it, all fasts should start and finish with a raw food day, the first to prepare your system and the second as a building-bridge back to your normal eating patterns. These days should commence with raw fruit, preferably citrus fruit and/or melon, together with a glass of fresh, unsweetened fruit or vegetable juice. The midday meal should comprise a large selection of vegetable crudités – red and yellow peppers, cucumber, tomato, broccoli florets, cauliflower, celery, carrots, radishes, and a large handful of fresh parsley. Wash all produce thoroughly and eat it raw, drizzled with extra-virgin olive oil. Accompany with a large glass of unsweetened fruit juice or unsalted vegetable juice. The evening meal should consist of a large mixed salad with a dressing of extra-virgin olive oil and lemon juice, and should include lettuce, tomato, a large bunch of watercress, onion, finely chopped

ABOVE *All raw fruit and vegetables used to start and end your fast should be carefully washed; choose organic produce where possible.*

LEFT *A fast of fruit and vegetable juices is a simple way to ensure that you get enough liquid; dehydration must be avoided.*

Safe Fasting

LEFT *Fasting is a ritual duty in many religions. During Ramadan, Muslims fast every day from sunrise to sunset.*

FAST WORK

- A short fast rests your body's physiology and detoxifies the tissues.
- It revitalizes mind and body.
- Fast occasionally, or to speed up the resolution of minor ailments.
- Before you start, check with your health-care professional and seek advice about taking prescribed medication.
- Never fast for more than three days without medical supervision.
- Do not drive when fasting.
- Be prepared for headaches, halitosis, diarrhea, constipation, or a coated tongue.
- Drink a minimum of 3½pt/1.7l of liquid daily.
- Apart from vitamin C and artichoke extract, take no other supplements.

garlic, beets, celeriac, and plenty of fresh, chopped mint. Other herbs can be added to taste. Drink a large glass of unsweetened fruit juice or unsalted vegetable juice. In addition you must drink at least 3½pt/1.7l of fluid, either as water, weak green tea, or any of the herb teas.

In between these two cleansing days, you can follow a total fast on nothing but water – a minimum of 3½pt/1.7l daily – or a mixture of water and unsweetened fruit juices or salt-free vegetable juices. A mono-fast is also possible, which entails eating just one food type throughout the fasting period. The most effective is a grape fast, though you might also choose to eat nothing but apples, which should be peeled, grated, and left to turn brown before eating, in order to reduce their acid content and make them more digestible. Ideally all fruit and juices should be organic, and water should be pure spring water or low in mineral content (especially sodium). Alkaline waters are the most beneficial if these are available.

It is best to undertake your fast days when you are not working, so ideally sandwich a Saturday and Sunday between the Friday and Monday raw-food days. On no account fast for more than three days without medical supervision. You can increase the effectiveness of your body's eliminating functions by taking 1g of vitamin C and an extract of globe artichoke daily during the whole cleansing period. This stimulates and activates the liver and enhances the detox. process.

Be prepared to suffer headaches, light-headedness, bad breath, a coated tongue, and alternating euphoria and exhaustion. A Turkish bath or sauna during the first or last day speeds up the elimination process, but these should not be undertaken on fast days. It is common to feel cold and lethargic while fasting, so stay at home, keep warm, and get plenty of sleep. When you break the fast, take only small mouthfuls, chew the food thoroughly, and take your time.

Fasting is more than just a physical cleansing process. For many thousands of years it has been used

DEHYDRATION

Avoid dehydration – it is vital to maintain your fluid intake at a minimum of 4¾pt/2.25l per day when fasting. Most of this should be taken as water, but you can also drink unsweetened herb teas, green tea, or very weak Indian tea without milk or sugar.

Dehydration causes:
- Dry, cracked lips
- Splits at the corners of the mouth
- Dry, irritable eyes
- Itchy skin
- Headaches
- Halitosis
- Concentrated, strong-smelling urine
- Constipation
- Increased risk of kidney and bladder infections

as a pathway to spiritual enlightenment and holiness. The devout have used it to heighten their awareness, the ancient pagans to appease their gods, the Greeks to bring hallucinatory dreams, and the religious to add a greater depth of meaning to their holy days.

Even a short fast will bring you a sense of physical lightness and well-being, together with feelings of great inner peace and calm. Though the prospect of two or three days without food is not appealing, try it once and you will be a regular adherent.

BELOW *At the end of a fast a sauna or Turkish bath will round off the elimination process and leave you feeling thoroughly cleansed inside and out.*

PART TWO

THE FOOD INDEX

ABOVE *Avocados, rich in potassium and vitamins B₆ and E, are the skin's best friend.*

The Food Index offers an instant guide to the nutritional facts about useful foods. It is introduced by an essay on the nature of nutrition, which makes the valid point that while nutritionists think in terms of protein, fats, carbohydrates, and nutrients, we actually eat food, and goes on to explain how to choose and use food to ensure that our nutritional status is maintained. The pros and cons of lifetime regimes such as vegetarianism and a macrobiotic diet are examined; the principles behind food combining are explained; practical advice is given on an appetizing eating plan for convalescents; and an exclusion diet to test for food intolerance.

The Food Index is simple: divided into thematic food groups, it takes a close look at each of the foods within that group that can offer a positive contribution to health and wellbeing. Each item is given its calorific value (where relevant) and a list of the conditions it can help, as well as those in which it should be avoided. The text expands on the theme. Health Warning boxes alert you to any side effects and Fast Food Aid panels offer tips on how to use the larder as a first-aid kit.

ABOVE *Tomatoes are low in sodium and full of protective beta-carotenes, and vitamins C and E.*

ABOVE *Asparagus is a powerful diuretic and has a mild sedative effect.*

What is Nutrition?

WHAT YOU NEED from any healthy diet is energy, which is obtained from a mixture of foods providing protein, fats, carbohydrates, vitamins, and minerals. The wider the variety of foods that you eat, the less likely you are to be deficient in any of the essential nutrients.

Long before the supermarket, freezer, microwave, and food processor, humans were hunter/gatherers  living largely on nuts, berries, fruit, and roots. We learned to make fire, tools, pots, and weapons, so meat appeared on the menu; we learned to domesticate animals, so dairy products joined the list; we learned to cultivate the ground, so cereals and vegetables followed. Humans thus became omnivores and on this mixed diet survived and developed through the millennia. We did not know about vitamins, minerals, and proteins, yet we thrived and prospered. Why, then, is everyone now obsessed with the topic of nutrition? At the end of the twentieth century Western society is reaping a bitter harvest from the diseases of civilization: heart disease, high blood pressure, cancer, obesity, gallstones, liver failure, and kidney disease are diseases of over-consumption. In the midst of plenty and affluence we are often overfed but undernourished, and the prospects for our children and our children's children seem bleak.

The food we eat has changed more in the past 100 years than in the previous 100,000 and we have been slow to adapt to these changes, most of which have not been for the better. High-fat, high-salt, high-sugar products, storage, processing, intensive farming, growth hormones, and antibiotics have not added to the nutritional value of what we eat today.

But we are nothing if not inventive, and the tide is beginning to turn. In growing numbers the public is turning away from factory-made food, plastic meals and the burger-and-French-fries-with-everything mentality. There is a growing interest in better ways of eating. Health-food stores, ethnic and vegetarian restaurants, and organic farms are booming, and we can all benefit.

VEGETARIANISM

If you are going to be a vegetarian, it is vital that you learn to do it properly. There are endless old wives' tales about the evils that will follow if you don't eat lots of meat. None of them is true, though they are often trotted out by doctors, mothers-in-law, and grannies. You will not become weak if you stop eating meat, nor will you become impotent if you are a man, infertile if you are a woman, or stupid. Billions of people throughout the world are healthy, strong, virile, fertile, intelligent, and active vegetarians.

Just because you remove meat, fish and poultry from your daily meals does not mean there is a reason to worry about your health; in fact, it is likely to be a great deal better without the intake of saturated animal fats. Vegetarians experience less heart disease, less high blood pressure, and less cancer of the stomach and bowel than meat-eaters. Vitamins D and B12 are the only nutrients that may possibly be lacking *(see Macrobiotic Diets on p. 63)* but this is easily overcome *(see Vitamins on p. 212)*.

Vegetarian children and teenagers need a high-energy diet. Make sure that they have plenty of high-energy foods and not too much of the very bulky foods, which may fill them up but leave them short of calories. Dairy products, nuts, seeds, fats, and oils provide more calories and less bulk. For this reason bringing up children on a totally vegan diet (that is, without eggs or any dairy products) can be difficult and I certainly do not recommend it.

Protein has always been the vexed question of vegetarianism. As long as your diet contains a mixture of different vegetable protein sources – a daily combination of cereals and legumes, dairy products, eggs, nuts, seeds, fruit, and vegetables – it will provide you with all the protein you need, and everything else too. Meat-eaters may be surprised that mixing legumes and cereals (for example, baked beans on wholemeal toast, or kidney beans and rice) provides the same quality of protein as a fillet steak.

IRON VEGETABLES

Most doctors seem to worry about their vegetarian patients becoming anemic, as everyone associates the provision of iron with meat and liver. There is plenty of iron in whole wheat bread, good cereals, and dark-green leafy vegetables, which the careful vegetarian will be eating in abundance. Since the absorption of iron is greatly improved in the presence of vitamin C – and again the good vegetarian will be consuming much more fresh fruit than the average meat-eater – anemia is rarely a problem for any but the most careless vegetarians.

TOP LEFT *Intensive farming and the demands of agribusiness mean that quantity often overrides quality.*

ABOVE *Cereals and eggs are good sources of carbohydrate and protein for vegetarians.*

What is Nutrition?

THE MEDITERRANEAN DIET

Why is it that in almost all the countries bordering the Mediterranean, people are healthier than those in northern Europe, Britain, and the US?

The reason is the Mediterranean diet: a diet that results in less heart disease, fewer strokes, and a much lower incidence of a number of different cancers. How can this be possible when you have seen Mediterraneans smoking, feasting on pâté de foie gras, salami, smelly cheese, and vast quantities of wine?

There are two reasons. First, Mediterranean people consume enormous quantities of fruit, vegetables, and salads, which are rich in the protective antioxidants. Second, their diet has been far less influenced by the march of modern food technology, and they eat far less of the highly processed, high-fat, high-sugar foods; olive oil instead of butter and animal or hydrogenated vegetable fats for cooking; masses of garlic, which is both heart-protective and has anti-cancer properties; far more fish and seafood; and considerably smaller quantities of red meat.

The Mediterranean diet is full of wonderful dishes, many of which are prepared without meat – wonderful pasta served with vegetables or seafood; imaginative salads; dishes made with sweet peppers, eggplant, and olives; simply grilled or baked fish, rice dishes containing everything but the kitchen sink; low-fat goat and sheep cheeses; and the delights of coarse country bread with an olive oil and garlic dip to replace high-fat butter.

MACROBIOTIC DIETS

Early in the twentieth century George Ohsawa, an American Japanese living in California, applied the philosophy of Zen to nutrition. He constructed a diet of the most "balanced" foods, based on the yin/yang principle and working through seven stages to the optimum seventh level, which was to be brown rice only – his definition of the perfect food. For the beginner, a period of gradually giving up all meat preceded level one, which comprised 40 percent cereals, 30 percent vegetables, 10 percent soup and 20 percent animal foods (excluding meat). By level three the proportions were 60:30:10, now excluding animal protein. Level seven, the brown rice diet, was to be a periodic ten-day cleansing regime or to be used during illness.

According to macrobiotic philosophy, examples of yang foods are meat, poultry, fish, seafood, eggs, hard cheeses, and salt, whereas yin foods are alcohol, tea, coffee, sugar, milk, cream, yogurt, and most herbs and spices. Foods with a balance of yin and yang are believed to be beans, grains, nuts, seeds, fruit, and vegetables.

Michio Kushi and other Ohsawa disciples spread the word about the supposed benefits of this "macrobiotic" eating. But one worrying aspect of the macrobiotic movement is its disregard of orthodox medicine and its avoidance of all forms of immunization, conventional drugs, or the preventive use of vitamins to supplement the deficiencies that this diet inevitably produces.

While there are certainly some benefits in terms of the macrobiotic diet reducing the risks of obesity, raised cholesterol, high blood pressure, constipation, and some cancers (particularly lung, colon, breast, cervical, and prostate cancer), these do not compensate for the risks attached to such a restricted diet.

This diet is low in protein, almost totally lacking eggs, milk, poultry, and meat, and high in bulk. Consequently the energy supplied by macrobiotic foods is low, which may lead to protein energy malnutrition in children up to the age of weaning, and to slow growth rates right through to adolescence and during pregnancy. Anemia is common, as a result of iron and B12 deficiency, and there is a possible risk of rickets in children right up to school age because of the reduced consumption of vitamin D.

Enthusiasts make many unsubstantiated claims for the benefits of the macrobiotic diet. In reality, it increases the risks of vitamin, mineral, and energy deficiencies just when these nutrients are most needed. The benefits can be obtained, without the risks, by following far less rigid vegetarian principles or by eating a healthy, balanced, omnivorous diet.

ABOVE *Olives, the source of olive oil, one of the staples in Mediterranean cuisine.*

BELOW *The Mediterranean eating style, real food with all the family at the table, is just as important as the ingredients.*

MACROBIOTIC PROS & CONS

Low in protein and high in bulk, the macrobiotic diet has many drawbacks.

- Low in fat, high in fiber.
- Too low in calories.
- Risk of nutritional deficiency, especially in iron, vitamins B12 and D.
- Marginal protein intake.
- Unsuitable for children, pregnant women, or breastfeeding mothers.

ABOVE LEFT *The globe artichoke stimulates the liver, encourages bile production, and helps break down rich, fatty foods.*

What is Nutrition?

FOOD COMBINING

Dr. William Howard Hay was one of the great pioneers of the food reform movement. After suffering severe ill health and getting no relief from his doctors in America in the early 1900s, he decided to treat his condition by making radical changes to his diet. He resolved to eat only such things as he believed were intended by nature as food for man, taking them in natural form and in quantities no greater than seemed necessary for his present need.

This produced dramatic improvements in his health and after three months he had returned to his former vigor. He then applied the same principles to treating his own patients and finally, in his book *A New Health Era*, outlined the principles of the Hay system of eating.

The fundamental principle of the Hay diet is that starch foods and protein foods are not eaten at the same time – so no bread and cheese, fish and French fries, or meat and potatoes. He divided foods into protein, neutral foods, and starch, and allowed his patients to eat neutral foods with starch or protein, but always with a gap of at least four hours between eating foods of different groups. In recent years the Hay diet has become a popular "cure-all" and its success attributed to a variety of pseudoscientific theories.

In practice I have found it unnecessary to apply all Hay's rules too rigidly, and I certainly don't recommend food combining as The Way of Eating for Life. Sticking to the food-combining rules certainly has a dramatic effect on the treatment of people with a wide variety of digestive problems, especially chronic indigestion with no obvious cause. What is more, if you are overweight, following the Hay diet will help you shed a few surplus pounds.

EXCLUSION DIET

People do have allergies to specific foods, like shellfish, eggs, milk, nuts, and strawberries, but most side effects after eating, especially those that occur between one and 24 hours later, are caused by food intolerance. Apart from milk, which is a common problem, foods that may produce adverse effects include coffee, tea, cocoa, chocolate, cheese, beer, sausages, yeast, red wine, wheat, and even tomatoes.

Migraine, asthma, eczema, hives, irritable bowel syndrome, colitis, Crohn's disease, hay fever, rheumatoid arthritis, and menstrual problems are just some of the disorders that may respond to dietary manipulation. Unless the particular food culprits are quite evident – in which case the obvious thing to do is avoid them – an exclusion diet (*see box opposite*) is the best starting point.

FAR LEFT *Plums, like most fruit, belong to the protein group in the Hay eating program.*

LEFT *Fruit, vegetables, rice, and fish: samples of the three food groups, neutral, starch, and protein, that are the basis of the food-combining plan.*

BELOW *Beer counts as a starch in the Hay regime; there is no need to give it up, just make sure you do not drink it with foods from the protein list.*

A GUIDE TO FOOD COMBINING

Eat one starch meal, one protein meal, and one meal of mostly fruit, vegetables, and salads each day. Try to leave four hours between starch and protein meals, but if you have to nibble, try to stick to the neutral food list.

Protein	Neutral	Starch
Meat	All vegetables except potatoes	Potatoes
Poultry		Bread
Game	All nuts except peanuts	Flour, oats, wheat, barley
Fish	Butter	Rice
Shellfish	Cream	Millet
Whole eggs	Egg yolks	Rye
Cheese, milk, yogurt	Sesame, sunflower, olive oils	Buckwheat
All fruit, except those in the starch group	All salads	Bananas, pears, papayas, grapes
All the legumes (lentils, dried beans)	Seeds, sprouted seeds	Dried fruit
Red wine	Herbs	Yogurt
Dry white wine	Honey	Beer
	Maple syrup	
	Gin, whisky	

What is Nutrition?

EXCLUSION DIET

This might look difficult, but you need only follow it rigorously for about two weeks, after which foods may be added back, provided you keep a record of their effect. You will soon be able to list the foods to which you are tolerant and eliminate the others.

After two weeks introduce other foods in this order: tap water, potatoes, cow's milk, yeast, tea, rye, butter, onions, eggs, oats, coffee, chocolate, barley, citrus fruits, corn, cow's cheese, white wine, shellfish, natural cow's milk yogurt, vinegar, wheat, and nuts.

Only try one new food every two days. If there is a reaction, don't try it again for at least a month. Carry on adding foods from the list when any symptoms stop. Any diet that is very restricted puts your health at risk, and although it is alright to experiment on your own for a few weeks, any long-term removal of major food groups should be done only under professional guidance.

Food type	Not allowed	Allowed
Meat	Preserved meat, bacon, sausages, all processed meat	All other meats
Fish	Smoked fish, shellfish	White fish
Vegetables	Potatoes, onions, sweetcorn, eggplant, sweet peppers, chilis, tomatoes	All other vegetables, salads, legumes, rutabaga, parsnip
Fruit	Citrus fruit e.g. oranges, grapefruit	All other fruit (e.g. apples, bananas, pears)
Cereals	Wheat, oats, barley, rye, corn	Rice, ground rice, rice flakes, rice flour, sago, rice breakfast cereals, tapioca, millet, buckwheat, rice cakes
Cooking oils	Corn oil, vegetable oil	Sunflower oil, soy oil, safflower oil, olive oil
Dairy products	Cow's milk, butter, most margarines, cow's milk yoghurt and cheese, eggs	Goat, sheep, and soy milk and products made from them, dairy and transfat-free margarines
Beverages	Tea, coffee (beans, instant, and decaffeinated), fruit cordials, orange juice, grapefruit juice, alcohol, tap water	Herbal tea (e.g. camomile), fresh fruit juices (e.g. apple, pineapple), pure tomato juice (without additives), mineral, distilled or deionized water
Miscellaneous	Chocolates, yeast, yeast extracts, carob, sea salt, herbs, spices, artificial preservatives, colorings, small amounts of sugar or honey, flavorings, monosodium glutamate, all artificial sweeteners	

CONVALESCENT DIET

Convalescence used to be an integral part of all medical treatment. In her famous book, *The Doctor in the Kitchen*, published in the 1930s, English writer Mrs. Arthur Webb wrote: "Food properly prepared and given to the invalid in the right quantities at the right time is of vital importance to build up strength and put the invalid on the road to health." Nutritional needs depend on the type of illness, but the general principles are to include easily digestible, nutrient-rich, and appetizing foods. The antioxidant vitamins A, C, and E, protective minerals such as zinc, and a high intake of iron to ensure good hemoglobin are essential.

ABOVE *Garlic is excellent for convalescents; its natural antiinfection properties support the body's immune system while it is still vulnerable during recovery.*

Eat plenty of blackcurrants, berries, citrus fruit, and kiwi fruit, which are rich in vitamin C and bioflavonoids; dates for their iron and easily converted calories; oats for their protein, B vitamins, calcium, potassium, and magnesium; fish for its easily digested protein and minerals; root vegetables, broccoli, and carrots for their beta-carotene; dried fruits for their energy; garlic, cinnamon, sage, rosemary, and thyme for their antiseptic and circulation-stimulating properties.

Cut down on refined carbohydrates, sugars, alcohol, high-bran foods, animal fats, and red meat.

Breakfasts should include porridge; yogurt with honey and pine kernels; melon; soaked dried fruits with yogurt and cinnamon; whole wheat toast; boiled, poached, or scrambled eggs.

Lunches should comprise white fish; oily fish; broccoli, spinach, carrots; free-range chicken; rosemary, thyme, garlic, and sage.

Evening meals should include light salads; soups made with root vegetables; barley, millet; fruit salads with almonds; low-fat cheese; avocados.

Extras should be fresh fruit, especially grapes, dates, kiwi fruit, citrus fruit, and berries; unsweetened fresh fruit juices; vegetable juices; dried fruit; fresh nuts and seeds.

LEFT *Chocolate, one of the food items not allowed while following an exclusion diet in search of an allergen.*

Fruit

Eating fruit is one of the easiest and most enjoyable ways to boost your nutritional intake. From the seasonal delights of cherries and nectarines to the all-year-round availability of apples and pears, five portions a day of fresh fruit and vegetables will provide you with vital nutrients and fiber.

APPLES

ENERGY PER AVERAGE APPLE 47KCAL

❦ *A good source of vitamin C.*

❦ *A reasonable source of fiber.*

❦ *Good for the heart and circulation.*

❦ *Beneficial for constipation and diarrhea.*

❦ *Eat at least one, but better still two, each day.*

❦ *Best eaten raw, lightly stewed, or grated and left to go brown.*

❦ *Combine well with bananas, rice, and toast in the BRAT diet to relieve diarrhea.*

An apple a day keeps the doctor away, but two apples a day could be a real tonic for the heart and circulation. Apples are rich in a soluble fiber, pectin, which helps the body to eliminate cholesterol and also protects against environmental pollutants. Researchers in France, Italy, and Ireland have found that two apples a day can lower cholesterol levels by up to ten percent. The pectin joins up with heavy metals such as lead and mercury to help the body to

APPLES

get rid of them. Apples also contain malic and tartaric acids, which aid digestion and are especially helpful in dealing with rich, fatty foods. The vitamin C in apples helps to boost the body's own immune defenses.

Traditionally apples have been used to treat stomach upsets, and naturopaths recommend grated apple, which is left to turn brown and mixed with a little honey, as a remedy for diarrhea.

In America, the BRAT diet (that is, bananas, rice, apples, and dry toast) is popular with doctors for the relief of diarrhea. Apples are also an important weapon in the fight against constipation because of their soluble fiber.

Even the smell of apples has a calming effect and helps lower blood pressure. The sugar in apples is mostly fructose, a simple sugar that is broken down slowly and thus helps to keep blood-sugar levels on an even keel.

● **Apples are ideal for people who are suffering from arthritis, rheumatism, gout, diarrhea, gastroenteritis, and colitis. A couple of apples eaten the morning after the night before helps to alleviate some aspects of a hangover.**

PEARS

ENERGY PER STANDARD PORTION 64KCAL

❦ *Good for energy, convalescence, constipation, and cholesterol-lowering.*

❦ *Best eaten ripe and raw, or dried.*

PEAR

The nutritional value of pears is often overlooked, as they are usually considered little more than a pleasant, sweet dessert fruit. In fact, pears are a good source of the soluble fiber pectin. This is not only valuable as a regulator of bowel function, but also has the specific property of helping the body to eliminate cholesterol. Pears are also a reasonable source of vitamin C, supply some vitamin A, a good amount of potassium, and a little vitamin E.

Dried pears are a useful source of protein, iron, vitamin A and vitamin C, and are also an abundant source of potassium and fiber.

● **For people suffering from digestive problems or for convalescents, pears are an extremely easily digested fruit. As they are rich in soluble fiber, they offer a much more appealing alternative to bran.**

HEALTH WARNING

Fresh pears contain a sugar-based alcohol called sorbitol. While this sugar-free sweetener has applications in tooth-friendly foods, in large amounts it may cause diarrhea in a small number of susceptible people.

RHUBARB

ENERGY PER 3½OZ/100G 7KCAL

❦ *Good for constipation.*

❦ *Best eaten lightly stewed.*

This strange-looking plant with giant leaves and pink stems hails originally from China and

Tibet, where it has been used as medicine since long before the start of the Christian era. And medicinal varieties of rhubarb, grown for their roots, not their stalks, were well known to the ancient Greeks, who used the roots of this plant to help treat chronic constipation.

Rhubarb contains small amounts of vitamins A and C, virtually no sodium, a good quantity of potassium and manganese, as well as a surprisingly large amount of calcium. Unfortunately, the edible stems also contain oxalic acid, which interferes with the absorption of the calcium.

● **Rhubarb leaves contain so much oxalic acid that they are seriously poisonous and must never be eaten.**

HEALTH WARNING

Because of the high oxalic acid content of rhubarb, this is not a plant that should be eaten by people with, or prone to, kidney stones, or by anyone suffering from gout.

PLUMS

PLUMS

ENERGY PER STANDARD PORTION 20KCAL

❦ *Good for the heart and circulation and for fluid retention.*

❦ *Best eaten very ripe and raw, or cooked.*

RHUBARB

There are many varieties of plum and most of those found in Britain are hybrids of the sloe or the cherry plum. They probably originated in eastern Europe and have been known and used throughout Europe for over

Fruit

2,000 years. The Japanese plum was introduced to the US in the late seventeenth century by fruit expert Luther Burbank.

Plums contain little vitamin C, modest amounts of vitamin A, and some vitamin E. They are, however, good sources of potassium. Dessert plums have a higher sugar and lower acid content, as well as some useful medicinal value. Sloes, wild plums from the blackthorn bush, are used to make sloe gin, an English country alcoholic drink that is also an excellent remedy for diarrhea.

● **Plums are widely used in Oriental medicine, especially the Japanese Umebushi, which help treat digestive disorders but taste particularly revolting.**

FAST FOOD AID

• Wild plum jelly or jam is a soothing remedy for irritating dry coughs. For instant relief, dissolve 2 teaspoonsful in a mug of hot water with the juice of a lemon and a dash of cinnamon, and drink at bedtime.

CHERRIES

ENERGY PER 3½OZ/100G 48KCAL

❦ *Good for the joints.*

❦ *Beneficial for cancer protection.*

❦ *A useful diuretic.*

❦ *Best eaten fresh (the sweet variety); cooked or bottled (non-dessert types).*

Cherries are one of the few fruits not available for 12 months of the year, so we can delight in this seasonal treat.

Cherries probably originated from the orchards of Mesopotamia in prebiblical times, and they were certainly highly valued by ancient Greek physicians. The wild cherry is pleasantly sweet and is even called the sweet cherry in the US. Sour cherries, like morellos, are wonderful for cooking and bottling, for juice and liqueurs.

Traditionally the bark of the wild cherry was used medicinally, but the dried fruit stalks and the fruit themselves are an extremely effective diuretic – cherries have a reasonable potassium content and virtually no sodium.

● **Cherries contain vitamin C and significant amounts of bioflavonoids, which makes them an excellent antioxidant food. But what adds to their value as a cancer protector is their ellagic acid, which inhibits the carcinogenic cells.**

PEACH

NECTARINES AND PEACHES

NECTARINES:
ENERGY PER STANDARD PORTION 60KCAL
PEACHES:
ENERGY PER STANDARD PORTION 36KCAL

❦ *Good during pregnancy.*

❦ *A very gentle laxative.*

❦ *Useful for those on low-salt diets and those with high cholesterol.*

❦ *Dried peaches are good for anemia, fatigue, and constipation.*

❦ *Best eaten raw, well washed, and ripe.*

NECTARINES

Many food books describe peaches and nectarines as being different varieties of the same fruit. In fact, nectarines are no more than a genetic variation of the peach, and both are part of the *Prunus* family of prunes, plums, and apricots. The botanical name for the species is *persica*, as early botanists thought that peaches originated in Persia. Modern opinion is that the peach started life in China and was taken to Persia by early traders. Peaches and nectarines are now grown commercially in many parts of the world, but the two largest producers, Italy and the US, provide about half of the total world production.

Nutritionally there is little difference between them. They both contain good amounts of vitamin C – nectarines slightly more, one nectarine providing a day's requirement – small amounts of fiber, modest numbers of calories, some beta-carotene and minerals.

Dried peaches contain far more calories but 3½oz/100g will provide almost a day's requirement of iron and one-third of your daily need of potassium. Canned peaches may taste good, but they offer little in the way of health benefits, as nearly all the vitamin C is lost and they are usually canned in heavy syrup and so very high in calories.

● **Peaches and nectarines are virtually fat- and sodium-free, which makes them an ideal food for those with cholesterol and blood-pressure problems.**

PEACH

FAST FOOD AID

• If you are lucky enough to have a peach tree in your garden, the leaves make an excellent poultice for the treatment of boils. Soak them in boiling water until pliable, press out the surplus water, and, when cool enough not to scald, apply them gently to the affected area and cover with a clean cloth.

APRICOTS

DRIED APRICOTS:
ENERGY PER 3½OZ/100G
188KCAL
FRESH APRICOTS:
ENERGY PER 3½OZ/100G 31KCAL

APRICOTS

❦ *Best eaten raw or dried.*

❦ *Fresh and dried apricots are excellent for all skin and respiratory conditions, and useful for those suffering from cancer.*

❦ *Dried apricots are good for constipation, high blood pressure, anemia, and fluid retention.*

❦ *They combine well with rice and other cooked or soaked fruit.*

Apricots contain large amounts of beta-carotene, which the body converts to vitamin A. Ripe, fresh apricots should form a regular part of the diet for anyone with infections or skin problems, or at risk of getting cancer, such as smokers. Dried apricots are a terrific remedy for constipation, due to their high fiber content, but they are also high in sugar, so diabetics should treat them with caution.

Most commercial dried apricots are preserved with sulphur dioxide, which can trigger asthma attacks, so rinse them well before eating.

● **Women of childbearing age benefit from a few dried apricots each day, as they are a good source of iron. Their potassium also stimulates the body to get rid of excessive water and salt.**

Citrus fruit

BERGAMOT, CLEMENTINES, SATSUMAS, GRAPEFRUIT, LEMONS, LIMES, AND ORANGES

*V*irtually unrivaled in the vitamin C stakes, citrus fruit help protect the body against infection and are a particularly good source of insoluble and soluble fiber, as well as potassium. Their tangy taste is just one of the reasons why we should eat more of these health-giving foods.

❦ *Good for resistance, circulatory problems, and varicose veins.*

❦ *Beneficial in the treatment of coughs, colds, and flu.*

❦ *Useful for sore throats and bleeding gums.*

❦ *Good as a cancer-protector, lower cholesterol, and are mildly laxative.*

❦ *Prevent scurvy.*

Best eaten fresh and raw, with some of the pith and membranes around each segment; the juice, although rich in vitamin C and some of the other protective phytochemicals, does not contain the special fiber, pectin.

Of all foods with medicinal properties, citrus fruit are among the most important. They are exceptionally rich in vitamin C, thus preventing the disease scurvy, and are an enormous boost to the body's natural resistance against bacteria and viruses. The US National Cancer Institute has suggested that an increased consumption of citrus fruit and juices is linked to the large reduction in the incidence of cancer of the stomach among Americans.

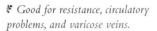

SATSUMA

Tens of millions of tons of citrus fruit are produced worldwide. Most of the actual fruit that we eat is grown in the Mediterranean and the US, but the largest single producer is actually Brazil where, as in the US, a large percentage of the fruit is converted to juice, concentrated,

frozen, and exported to the rest of the world.

Although the ancient Greeks and Romans grew and revered the lemon, bitter or Seville oranges did not find their way to Europe until the twelfth or thirteenth century, and sweet oranges did not appear until the middle of the fifteenth century. A native of northern India, the lemon gets its name from the Hindustani word *limu* and reached Europe via the Middle East; the orange traveled along the same route and its Sanskrit name was *nagaranga*, which became the Arabic word *narang*. Oranges reached the US in the early 1500s and the Portuguese took them to Brazil some time later, but it was not until the 1800s that barrels of oranges started being shipped from Florida to the rapidly growing cities in the north of America.

Why do Americans call Britons "limeys"? The greatest scourge of early seafarers was the risk of scurvy, a disease of bleeding gums, lost teeth, suppurating wounds, wasting muscles, and eventually death. During the eighteenth century it was discovered that taking lime juice prevented scurvy and from that time on all British naval ships going to sea for more than ten days had to carry enough limes in their cargo to ensure that every man had 1fl oz/ 25ml a day of lime juice for the duration of the voyage.

● **Citrus fruit are a treasure trove of nutrients and phytochemicals, which not only protect against disease, but are curative and health-promoting in the most positive sense.**

CLEMENTINE

BERGAMOT

Few people recognize this as a member of the citrus family. It is grown almost exclusively in the coastal area of Calabria in southern Italy, where it is used for its essential oil. This oil is extracted from the peel of the fruit and is highly fragrant, containing limonene, linalol and bergapten.

Bergamot is widely used as a flavoring but is most easily recognizable in the distinctive flavor of Earl Grey tea. Bergamot oil increases the photosensitivity of the skin, which is why it is used in some sun lotions, but it can produce hypersensitivity and very irritating rashes on exposure to sunlight. It should not be taken internally but can be used in aromatherapy.

CLEMENTINES AND SATSUMAS

CLEMENTINES:
ENERGY PER STANDARD PORTION
21KCAL
SATSUMAS:
ENERGY PER STANDARD PORTION
25KCAL

These are both part of the mandarin family, of which satsumas, the Mediterranean mandarin, and the common mandarin are the main hybrids. Common

mandarins include clementines, tangors (a hybrid of the mandarin and orange), and tangelos (a hybrid of the mandarin, grapefruit, and pommelo). Clementines and satsumas are less acidic than lemons, limes, and grapefruit. They are still good sources of vitamin C, although they contain rather less potassium and slightly less of the B vitamins, but they do supply significant amounts of folate.

● **Clementines and satsumas have the advantage of being much easier to peel than oranges and so are often more acceptable to children.**

GRAPEFRUIT

ENERGY PER STANDARD PORTION 24KCAL

Grapefruit contain a high level of vitamin C – it is estimated that one grapefruit supplies nearly 60 percent of the recommended daily allowance in the American diet – and plenty of useful potassium.

They are also well supplied with a number of carotenoids, including beta-carotene, and with pectin and bioflavonoids in the white pith and the cell walls dividing the sections. So make sure that you eat the whole fruit to gain the maximum benefit.

● **Pink or red grapefruit are marginally higher in vitamin C.**

GRAPEFRUIT

LEMON

LEMONS

ENERGY PER STANDARD PORTION 1KCAL

These earned their reputation as a cure for scurvy long before vitamin C was actually identified. They have an abundant supply of this vitamin – 3½oz/100g, providing more than a day's dose – as well as small amounts of some B vitamins, vitamin E, substantial quantities of potassium, magnesium, calcium, and phosphorus, and the important trace minerals copper, zinc, iron, and manganese. They also activate the immune system by stimulating white corpuscle activity. Lemons are rich in bioflavonoids, limonene, and mucilage, the latter being beneficial to the lining of the digestive tract and stomach.

The lemon is thought of as a highly acidic fruit and for this reason it is often forbidden to rheumatism sufferers. In fact its acidity is due to organic acids that are metabolized during digestion to produce potassium carbonate – and this helps to neutralize excess acidity and relieves the pain of both rheumatism and arthritis. Lemon juice is also protective of the mucous membrane lining the digestive tract and can act as a stimulant to the pancreas and liver. Its powerful antibacterial activity makes it first choice as a gargle or mouthwash for sore throats, mouth ulcers, and gingivitis, diluted half-and-half with hot water.

● **Traditionally, lemons have always been used for infections of the respiratory tract. Hot lemon with a teaspoon of honey at bedtime is a classic remedy for coughs and colds.**

FAST FOOD AID

• *Neat lemon juice applied with a cotton bud to pus-filled spots is a powerful bactericide. It is particularly effective for acne.*

• *Lemon juice diluted half-and-half with hot water makes an excellent facial wash.*

• *Lemon juice is antiviral and can be applied directly to cold sores or the rash of shingles, providing that the skin is unbroken.*

• *Chilblains can be relieved by rubbing the surface of the affected area with a slice of lemon dipped in coarse sea salt – but only use this treatment on unbroken skin, unless you're extremely brave.*

LIMES

ENERGY PER STANDARD PORTION 24KCAL

These are the most acid citrus fruit and although they contain more vitamin C than grapefruit, they have slightly less than oranges and lemons. They are grown primarily for their juice, which is used as a flavoring for other foods, particularly drinks. Like other citrus fruits, limes contain high amounts of bioflavonoids.

● **Lime juice** **can be used like lemon juice for its medicinal properties.**

LIME

ORANGES

ENERGY PER STANDARD PORTION 59KCAL

The high vitamin C content of oranges – at least when they have recently been picked or juiced – accounts for much of their benign influence on our health, due to its enormous importance in combating infection and preserving general health. And in a Swedish study of people eating a Western-style breakfast, orange juice, when taken at the same meal, increased iron absorption by up to two-and-a-half times.

Oranges also contain beta-carotene, as well as bioflavonoids in the pith and segment walls. These chemicals, alternatively known as vitamin P factors or C_2 (since they appear to boost the activity of vitamin C), strengthen the walls of the tiny blood capillaries (in scurvy these collapse and the skin shows tiny hemorrhages all over the body).

The nutritional importance of a glass of orange juice is considerable – as a proportion of the US recommended daily allowance, it provides 110 percent vitamin C, 8 percent thiamin, 8 percent folic acid, 4 percent vitamin B6, 4 percent magnesium, 2 percent phosphorus, and just under 2 percent protein, vitamin A, riboflavin, nicotinic acid, calcium, and iron. The high potassium content (250mg) and the minute sodium content (1mg) make orange juice a key nutritional source for sufferers of heart disease, high blood pressure, and fluid-retention problems.

● **The fruit, flowers, and peel of oranges have long been used in herbal medicine. The peel contains hesperidine and limonene, which are used in the treatment of chronic bronchitis. Tea made from the dried flowers is a mild stimulant.**

ORANGE

HEALTH WARNING

Some migraine-sufferers are sensitive to one or other citrus fruit, and sometimes to all of them. Even inhaling the oily zest from the peel can trigger an attack. Before being shipped, many citrus crops are sprayed with antifungal and insecticidal wax, which is toxic. If you can't buy organic or unwaxed fruit, scrub the skin under hot water with a brush before adding the peel to food or drink.

FAST FOOD AID

• *The essential oil neroli, which is made from orange blossom, is widely used in aromatherapy as a mild sedative. Five drops in 1fl oz/25ml of carrier oil can be massaged into the back, neck, and shoulders to relieve tension and encourage sleep.*

• *Neroli is also one of the main constituents in eau-de-cologne. Mopping the brow, and especially the temples, with eau-de-cologne can bring instant relief from a headache.*

Berry fruit

BLACKBERRIES

ENERGY PER 3½OZ/100G 25KCAL

❦ Good for the heart, circulation, and skin problems.

❦ Beneficial for diarrhea.

❦ The leaves are useful for scalds, gum disease, and sore throats.

❦ Best eaten raw or lightly stewed.

❦ Combine well with apples and other berries.

Wild blackberries, or brambles as they are commonly known in British country lore, are extremely ancient fruit. They are mentioned in the Bible, and the ancient Greeks recommended them as a remedy for gout.

Blackberries are extremely rich in vitamin E (although wild berries have a higher concentration than the cultivated varieties). This makes them extremely useful in both the prevention and treatment of heart and circulatory problems.

BLACKBERRIES They are also a good source of vitamin C, which makes them a strong antioxidant, protective against cancers, degenerative diseases, and infections. They contain useful amounts of potassium and enough of the soluble fiber, pectin, to make a significant contribution to the minimum daily requirement.

Blackberry leaves are very astringent, containing large amounts of tannin, which explains many of their traditional uses. Chopped and used as a tea, they make an excellent mouthwash for gum problems and infections like gingivitis, as well as an effective gargle for sore throats; 1oz/25g of dried leaves steeped in 2½ cups/ 600ml of boiling water is also an excellent remedy for diarrhea – two cups per day is usually sufficient.

● **A poultice of leaves macerated in boiling water and left to cool is a traditional remedy for scalds – the tannins in the leaves act as an antiseptic and thereby help prevent secondary infection occurring.**

FAST FOOD AID

• Though blackberry and apple pie is delicious, these wonderful berries that you can gather free from the hedgerows have health benefits, too. Blackberry cordial with nutmeg, cloves, and a little brandy gives a real lift to flagging spirits and relieves those occasional clouds of depression that settle on most of us at some time or another.

• For the treatment of high fevers in adults and children, soak fresh berries in cider vinegar for three days, strain through a sieve, add 1lb/450g of sugar for 2½ cups/600ml of liquid, boil for five minutes, and bottle when cool. One teaspoon of this mixture taken in a glass of water helps to reduce fever and quench thirst. Repeat frequently until the temperature falls.

BLUEBERRIES

THE AMERICAN BLACKBERRY

• Sometimes called the fingerberry or black haw, this is a different species and contains considerably more tannic acid than the English variety. Traditionally it has been used in the US as a fluid extract of dried bark or root, and also as a syrup for the treatment of diarrhea and even dysentery.

BLUEBERRIES

BILBERRIES, WHORTLE-BERRIES, HUCKLEBERRIES, OR WHINBERRIES

ENERGY PER 3½OZ/100G 30KCAL

❦ Good for food poisoning and diarrhea, and as an antibacterial.

❦ Beneficial for cystitis and other urinary infections.

❦ Useful for varicose veins.

❦ Best eaten raw, or cooked in the traditional blueberry muffin.

❦ Dried blueberries are used to make a popular Scandinavian soup.

This delightful shrub is native to both Europe and North America. Blueberries are one of the few fruits of this type that are delicious eaten straight from the bush, though their fruit-sugar content can cause diarrhea, if eaten in excess.

Nutritionally speaking, blueberries are not very exciting, though they do contain reasonable amounts of vitamin C and small amounts of vitamins B_1, beta-carotene, and potassium. It is their natural chemicals, however, that make them valuable in medicinal terms. Blueberries contain the antibacterial anthocyanosides, which have a tonic effect on blood vessels and make them a useful aid in the treatment of varicose veins. Together with the vegetable mucilage that lines the urinary tract and prevents bacteria attaching themselves to the bladder wall, blueberries' antibacterial benefits help in the treatment of cystitis and other urinary infections.

● **When the berries are dried, the concentration of tannins and other antibacterials is substantially increased, which probably explains the effectiveness of Scandinavian dried blueberry soup as a treatment for diarrhea.**

FAST FOOD AID

• An extract of blueberries – made by steeping them for two to three weeks in brandy, then straining them – is a favorite country remedy for food poisoning or diarrhea.

BLUEBERRIES

CRANBERRIES

ENERGY PER STANDARD PORTION 11KCAL

❦ Beneficial for cystitis and other urinary infections.

❦ Good for boosting the immune system.

❦ Best taken as unsweetened juice.

Cranberries are one of the very few fruits native to North America, and for centuries the native North Americans used these extraordinary berries as both food and medicine. They bathed their wounds in cranberry juice, and their medicine men made cranberry poultices to draw out the poison from arrow injuries. Thanks to the vitamin C in cranberries, early American settlers avoided the terrors of scurvy and it was not long before American whalers were carrying barrels of cranberries, just as English ships carried limes. To this day Americans celebrate the fourth

CRANBERRIES

Berry fruit

STRAWBERRIES

Thursday of November with a Thanksgiving meal of turkey, cornbread, sweet potatoes, pumpkin pie, and, of course, cranberry sauce.

For decades American folklore has advocated the use of cranberry juice in both the treatment and prevention of acute and chronic recurring attacks of cystitis, and a number of scientific studies have now confirmed this ancient native wisdom. It has always been thought that the acidity of cranberry juice, together with its hippuric acid, produced its antibacterial effect, but it is now almost certain that this is not its most important constituent. It was not until Dr. Anthony Sobota, Professor of Microbiology at Youngstown State University, Ohio, published the results of his research between 1984 and 1986 that the true explanation began to emerge. Cranberries contain a component that covers the walls of the bladder, kidneys, and interconnecting tubing, which prevents bacteria from attaching themselves to these sensitive tissues, where they would normally live and multiply. Sobota and his colleagues found that a glass of cranberry juice a day was ten times as effective at killing urinary bacteria as conventional antibiotics.

A follow-up study published in March 1994 in the *Journal of the American Medical Association* by Drs. Gerry Avorn, Mark Monane, Gerry Gurwitz, and others, based at various departments of Harvard University Medical School, formed the first placebo-controlled, large-scale clinical trial to test the effects of cranberry juice. Within a month of the trial positive results appeared, with the majority of patients who were taking the real cranberry juice having noninfected urine.

● **Other research has further shown that most sufferers of chronic urinary infection stay infection-free as long as they drink one glass of cranberry juice a day. Overall these results are better than those that are achieved using conventional antibiotic treatment.**

RASPBERRIES

ENERGY PER STANDARD PORTION 15KCAL

✶ *Good for the immune system, cancer protection, and for mouth problems.*

✶ *Best eaten fresh.*

Like grapes, raspberries should be on every hospital menu. This delicious fruit is a rich source of vitamin C – 3½oz/100g provides 75 percent of the UK recommended daily allowance. They are also a useful source of the soluble fiber, pectin, and contain small amounts of calcium, potassium, iron, and magnesium – all vital to the convalescent, as well as to those suffering from heart problems, fatigue, or depression, and all well absorbed, thanks to the vitamin C.

RASPBERRIES

● **Herbalists value raspberries for their cooling effect, which is useful in feverish conditions. Naturally astringent, raspberries can do you good the entire length of your digestive tract, helping to counter spongy, diseased gums, upset stomachs, and diarrhea.**

FAST FOOD AID

• *For centuries herbalists, midwives, and country women have used raspberry-leaf tea as an aid to childbirth. The tea appears to strengthen the muscles of the uterus, making contractions more forceful. It can also be used as a mouthwash for sore gums and mouth ulcers. Add one teaspoon of chopped raspberry leaves, fresh or dried, to a cup of boiling water, cover, let stand for five minutes but no more, then strain and drink. Drink two cups a day during the last two months of pregnancy. Do not take raspberry-leaf tea earlier on in pregnancy.*

STRAWBERRIES

ENERGY PER STANDARD PORTION 27KCAL

✶ *Good for cancer protection, gout, arthritis, and anemia.*

✶ *Best eaten fresh and ripe.*

Until the early 1600s the only strawberries available in Britain and Europe were the tiny but succulent wild strawberries. Originally alpines, these were greatly valued as a delicacy and as a medicine – they even get a mention in one of Ben Jonson's plays of 1603. All the other strawberries that we eat are descended from two American varieties, one of which was introduced to Europe from Virginia in 1629, the other around 1800.

There is a popular myth that anyone with arthritis should avoid strawberries because they are acidic, but nothing could be further from the truth. Linnaeus, the great Swedish botanist, recommended strawberries as a perfect cure for arthritis, gout, and rheumatism. He spoke from personal experience, as he cured himself of gout by eating almost nothing but strawberries, morning and night. This agreeable cure probably works because strawberries help to eliminate the joint-irritating uric acid from the body.

Strawberries are reputed to reduce high blood pressure and are recommended in traditional European medicine for the elimination of kidney stones. They contain modest amounts of iron and, because of their extremely high vitamin C content, the iron is well absorbed, making them useful in both the prevention and treatment of anemia and fatigue – 3½oz/100g of strawberries will give you almost twice your vitamin C requirement for a day.

Strawberries are rich in the soluble fiber, pectin, which helps in the elimination of cholesterol. This, combined with their powerful antioxidant properties, makes them highly effective against heart and circulatory disease. There is also a growing body of evidence which claims that these delicious fruits have antiviral properties, too.

This is one medicine that does not need a spoonful of sugar to help it down. These wonderful berries should be eaten on their own, or at the start of a meal, in order to achieve their best therapeutic value.

● **A few strawberries each day during the season is the cheapest, and most delicious, health insurance you will ever buy.**

HEALTH WARNING

For some people strawberries are a cause of allergic reactions and anyone who knows they are sensitive to these berries should take extreme care to avoid them, as the consequences of a severe reaction can be life-threatening.

REDCURRANTS

ENERGY PER 3½OZ/100G 21KCAL

✶ *Good for strengthening the immune system.*

✶ *The juice is a cooling drink for fevers.*

✶ *Best eaten raw, stewed, as jelly or juice.*

The redcurrant is brother to the blackcurrant, but there are considerable differences in their nutritional value. This plant grows quite happily in most situations and is extremely hardy, surviving the climates of such diverse geographical locations as Britain, northern

REDCURRANTS

Berry fruit

Europe, the US, and Siberia. It is often found growing wild in hedges and ditches, where the fruit is always red, although cultivated varieties may produce whitecurrants (which will not contain any vitamin A).

Although containing only a quarter of the vitamin C of blackcurrants, 3½oz/100g of redcurrants will still supply the UK recommended daily allowance. This makes them valuable for improving the natural function of the immune system. Although when cooked they lose some vitamin C, used as jellies, juices, or stewed with other fruits, redcurrants can make an important contribution to the diet of a recovering invalid. Redcurrants also supply modest amounts of iron and fiber and quite a large amount of potassium, none of which are lost during cooking.

Herbalists have traditionally recommended redcurrant juice as a refreshing and temperature-lowering drink for anyone with a fever.

● **The old British tradition of eating redcurrant jelly with "high" game (game birds that have hung till they begin to putrefy) was thought to protect against harmful bacteria, due to its high acid content.**

FAST FOOD AID

• *Redcurrant jelly is antiseptic and, if applied to a burn after cooling it with plenty of cold water, will ease the pain and prevent blistering.*

REDCURRANTS

BLACKCURRANTS

ENERGY PER 3½OZ/100G 28KCAL

❦ *Beneficial for a strong immune system, for colds, flu, and sore throats.*

❦ *Useful for cancer protection, fluid retention, high blood pressure, stress, and anxiety.*

❦ *Good for diarrhea and food poisoning.*

❦ *Best drunk as juice, eaten as jelly or lightly stewed with other fruits.*

Blackcurrants are an exceptionally rich source of vitamin C, containing four times as much as an equivalent weight of oranges – 2oz/60g gives you 60mg of this vital vitamin, which is particularly stable in blackcurrants. French studies have shown that other substances in the fruit inhibit the oxidation of vitamin C and that a syrup of blackcurrants loses only 15 percent of this vitamin in a whole year.

Pigments called anthocyanosides in their purple-black skins have bactericidal qualities and an antiinflammatory action, both of which are put to good use in the country remedy for sore throats – hot blackcurrant juice sipped very slowly. An easy way to make this is to simmer half a cup of blackcurrants in two cups of hot water for 10 minutes, then strain and add some honey. Or add boiling water to a teaspoon of blackcurrant jelly. This powerful antibacterial effect is valuable in treating and preventing food poisoning, as many of the pathogens that trigger stomach upsets are destroyed by the anthocyanosides.

● **The vitamin C in this tiny berry is a powerful antioxidant, protecting against heart disease, circulatory problems, and all manner of infections. But blackcurrants also contain substantial amounts of potassium but very little sodium, so they help with water retention and are also useful in the treatment of high blood pressure.**

BLACKCURRANTS

FAST FOOD AID

• *Blackcurrant leaves have important medical uses too, containing volatile oils, tannins, and still more vitamin C. Use them as a tea to make a gargle for the relief of mouth ulcers. Drinking this soothing tea can have a direct effect on the adrenal glands, stimulating the sympathetic nervous system and thereby helping to relieve problems of stress and anxiety.*

GOOSEBERRIES

ENERGY PER 3½OZ/100G 40KCAL

❦ *Good for building up natural resistance.*

❦ *Beneficial for constipation.*

❦ *Useful for urinary infections.*

❦ *Best eaten raw (dessert varieties) or lightly stewed (culinary varieties).*

Although this delicious fruit has been cultivated for more than 500 years in Britain and northern Europe, it is hardly grown in the US. In fact, some state legislation forbids its cultivation because it is a host of white pine blister rust and may pose a threat to commercial forestry.

Gooseberries are an excellent source of vitamin C, 3½oz/100g of the fresh berries providing well over half the UK recommended daily allowance. Because of their high acid content, little of the vitamin C is lost in cooking or canning, making them one of the few canned fruits with a significant vitamin C content.

It is a great shame that gooseberries have acquired a rather strange reputation – "playing gooseberry," "babies found under the gooseberry bush" – for they are not only health-giving but delicious, whether eaten raw, cooked in pies, made into sauces, or even turned into traditional English country wine. "Playing gooseberry" actually dates from the middle 1800s, when being asked to "play gooseberry" meant you were going to chaperone a young couple.

Gooseberries are especially popular in Britain and France, and the French name *groseille à maquereau* comes from the delicious gooseberry sauce that the French serve with mackerel. In Britain the same sauce is traditionally served with fatty meats, especially goose. The origin of the name, however, has nothing to do with geese, but comes from the French root *groseille*.

● **Due to their high content of malic acid, gooseberries are useful in the treatment of any urinary infections, as they help acid-ify urine without causing any undue gastric discomfort. They are also a useful source of soluble fiber, which makes them a very palatable remedy for constipation.**

GOOSEBERRIES

FAST FOOD AID

• *For a really bad cold, mix one teaspoon of gooseberry jam, one teaspoon of blackcurrant jam, and the juice of half a lemon in a mug of boiling water and drink three times a day.*

Tropical fruit

PINEAPPLES

ENERGY PER STANDARD PORTION 33KCAL

❦ *Good for digestive problems, fevers, sore throats, and generalized soft-tissue injuries.*

❦ *An excellent heart protector.*

❦ *Best eaten very ripe, or juiced.*

In Hawaii they eat chunks of juicy pineapple as a delicious cure for digestive problems. We now know that the fresh fruit contains an enzyme, bromelain, which can digest many times its own weight of protein in a few minutes and only breaks down food and dead tissue – leaving our intestines undamaged. The juice of fresh pineapples is also an effective folk medicine for sore throats – an instant gargle – and was once a favorite herbal remedy for diphtheria which suggests that it contains compounds with marked antibiotic and antiinflammatory effects.

Some of these compounds, though not the enzyme bromelain, probably survive the processing that produces commercial juice or canned fruit. But, for maximum healing potential, fresh ripe pineapple or freshly extracted juice must be your first choice.

When choosing a pineapple, look for one that feels heavy for its size as this is a good guide to quality. The old wives' tale of being able to tug a leaf easily out of the crown when the pineapple is ripe is meaningless and has no bearing on its potential flavor.

● **Nutritionally, pineapple offers little apart from modest amounts of vitamin C – only half that of oranges. Its fiber content, though, and its ability to break down blood clots make it an excellent heart protector.**

GRAPES

ENERGY PER STANDARD PORTION 60KCAL

❦ *Good for convalescence, weight loss, anemia, and fatigue.*

❦ *Useful for cancer protection.*

❦ *Best eaten raw.*

The origins of the grapevine are lost in the mists of antiquity, but its use for the production of raisins and wine was widespread in the earliest times. *Vitis vinifera* is the species at the root of most modern grape production. It was taken across to the New World by Columbus in 1492 and again by the Spanish and Portuguese who went to both North and South America. For these Catholic invaders, wine was an essential part of the ritual of communion so establishing vineyards was an early priority. The US is now the world's second-largest producer of grapes and raisins.

Grapes are a present that people often take to sick friends in the hospital, and they could do nothing better for them. Grapes are a uniquely nourishing, strengthening, cleansing, and regenerative food, useful in convalescence, for anemia, fatigue, and disorders such as arthritis, gout, and rheumatism, which may result from poor elimination.

Their nutritive powers were confirmed by Mahatma Gandhi, who drank grape juice during his marathon fasts. European natureclinics have since obtained excellent results with a grape mono-fast for a wide range of ailments, including skin problems, disorders of the urinary system, arthritis, and gout.

PINEAPPLE

A two-day mono-fast on grapes every ten days is recommended for those wanting to lose weight. And many naturopaths believe that grapes should be eaten on their own, not as part of a meal, since they ferment rapidly in the stomach. Chewing grapes is also recommended for infected gums.

● **Grapes contain an enormous number of aromatic compounds – far more than all other fruit. The most important of these are the astringent tannins, flavones, red anthocyanins, linalol, geraniol, and nerol. These are believed to provide grapes with their cancer-protective value.**

GRAPES

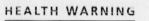

HEALTH WARNING

Since most grapes are sprayed incessantly during cultivation, it is vital to wash them very carefully indeed in warm running water.

GRAPES

MELONS

CANTALOUP MELON:
ENERGY PER STANDARD PORTION 29KCAL
WATERMELON:
ENERGY PER STANDARD PORTION 62KCAL

❦ *Good for mild constipation, urinary problems, gout, and arthritis.*

❦ *Best eaten raw, ripe, and on its own.*

Melons belong to the same group of plants as cucumbers, pumpkins, squashes, and gourds. They have been cultivated in Asia since the most ancient of times and were a valued fruit to the Egyptians, Greeks, and Romans. They were first cultivated in western Europe by the

MELON

French and have been used by herbalists since the latter part of the sixteenth century.

The serpent melon, which is extremely long, is eaten raw or pickled, and is the "cucumber" described by Isaiah, but it is the watermelon, originally native to the East Indies and Africa, that is the great refresher and has long been used medicinally. The seeds were believed to be a good treatment for worms and urinary infections.

Melons are a cooling, delicious treat in hot weather, and a large slice of crunchy pink watermelon beats any canned fizzy drink for refreshment. Watermelon – or a tea made by simmering its seeds in water for 30 minutes – has long been recommended in traditional medicine as a natural remedy for kidney and bladder problems.

● **In fact, all forms of melon are mildly stimulating to the kidneys and gently laxative, making them useful for those with gout or constipation.**

FAST FOOD AID

● *Naturopaths maintain that, like grapes, melons of all kinds should be eaten on their own, or at least at the start of a meal, since they ferment rapidly in the stomach. One of the most traditional naturopathic cleansing regimes is a two-day mono-fast on melons of any kind – a delightful summer break for the whole system.*

Tropical fruit

GUAVAS

BANANAS AND PLANTAINS

BANANAS:
ENERGY PER STANDARD PORTION 95KCAL
PLANTAINS:
ENERGY PER 3½OZ/100G 117KCAL

❦ *Good for physically active people.*

❦ *Beneficial for stomach ulcers.*

❦ *Nutritious convalescent food, specially for chronic fatigue syndrome, exhaustion, and glandular fever.*

❦ *Good for raised cholesterol.*

❦ *Bananas are best eaten ripe (as the skins start to go brown) and raw.*

❦ *Plantains are best eaten underripe and cooked.*

Bananas are one of nature's miracle foods. They are the perfect fast food, which come in their own packaging. They are full of nutrients, especially potassium, vitamin B6, folic acid, and useful amounts of other vitamins and minerals. Slimmers generally avoid bananas in the mistaken belief that they are fattening. But, at only 95 calories per fruit, they represent excellent nutritional value.

The starch in bananas is not easily digested, which is why they should only be eaten ripe when most of the starch has turned to sugar. This happens when the skin turns a speckled brown. The starch in plantains can cause considerable discomfort if they are eaten raw, but this is avoided by cooking them. Because ripe bananas are so easily digestible and the fiber in them is mainly of the soluble type, they are good for the treatment of both constipation and diarrhea, as well as helping to eliminate cho-lesterol from the body. Plantains are very rich in the specific starch that is extremely beneficial in both the treatment and prevention of stomach ulcers.

Plantains contain as much starch as potatoes. They have been used as a prime energy source and staple food in India, South-east Asia, South America, as well as East Africa for centuries.

● **The high content of potassium in bananas helps prevent cramp and, combined with the easily available energy from the ripe fruit, means they are the ideal snack for those engaged in active sport. One banana contains just over a quarter of the daily requirement of vitamin B6, so they should be eaten by women suffering from PMS.**

PLANTAIN

FAST FOOD AID

• *This is an aid not for people, but for plants – a few banana skins buried in the soil around your raspberry canes are a guarantee of succulent, beautifully colored fruit, thanks to the magnesium content of the skins.*

BANANA

GUAVAS

ENERGY PER STANDARD PORTION 23KCAL

❦ *Beneficial for boosting natural immunity.*

❦ *Heart- and cancer-protective.*

❦ *Good for reducing cholesterol.*

❦ *Useful for constipation.*

❦ *Best eaten raw and slightly underripe; wonderful liquidized with natural yogurt.*

Originally a native of Central America, the guava has now spread throughout the tropics and subtropics. It is the most important fruit plant in the large family of Myrtaceae, which also includes cin-namon, cloves, allspice, and nutmeg.

The guava is an extremely rich source of vitamin C – one average fruit supplies five days' worth of the minimum UK requirement. The pink-fleshed varieties are richer in vitamin C than the white-fleshed, and the vitamin C content is at its peak in green mature fruit, but starts to fall the more ripe the fruit becomes. Guavas also contain useful amounts of nicotinic acid, phospho-rus, and calcium, together with plenty of good soluble fiber. Even canned guavas, which can lose up to one-third of their vitamin C content during processing, are an excellent source and retain their fiber content. Unfortunately guavas are nearly always canned in heavy syrup, so don't use the juice.

In recent years guava has become popular as a drink, but unfortu-nately it is usually sold as guava nectar, a mixture of 25 percent fruit purée with 10 percent sugar and 65 percent water.

● **Fresh guava purée added to a tub of natural yogurt makes an exceptionally health-giving and delicious "shake." Rich in calcium, gut-friendly bacteria, vitamins, and fiber, it is a really nutritious addition to breakfast.**

MANGOES

ENERGY PER STANDARD PORTION 86KCAL

❦ *Good for convalescence, skin problems, strengthening the immune system, and cancer protection.*

❦ *Best eaten raw (in the bathtub, they are so juicy!); they are easy to prepare as "hedgehogs" (see below).*

Of all the tropical fruit, the mango is probably the most widely consumed. Eaten and cultivated for over 4,000 years in its native India, it has now spread to south China, the Philippines, South and even parts of North Africa, parts of the Mediterranean, Central and South America, the Caribbean, parts of California, and espe-cially southern Florida and the Keys, as a com-mercial crop.

As a "taste of home," the mango has become an impor-tant commercial export for many countries, supplying expatriates in the colder climes of northern Europe. And what a delicious and health-giving treat it is. Brimful of nutrients, one average mango pro-vides more than a day's requirement of vitamin C, two-thirds of your vitamin A, nearly half your vitamin E, almost a quarter of your fiber, as well as useful contributions of potas-sium, iron, and nicotinic acid. It is this great combination of antioxi-dants, in a very easily digestible form, that should put the mango on everybody's weekly shopping list. There are many varieties, but my favorite is the small, exceptionally sweet mango from Pakistan, which sadly has a short season.

In their native India mangoes are part of the way of life and are eaten throughout the year – in the hot season as drinks made from pulped mangoes, to replace body fluids, especially when strained and mixed with salt, molasses, and cumin to make panna.

Tropical fruit

KIWI FRUIT

When mangoes are cheap and plentiful, use them to make milk-shakes, pie fillings and sauces, or turn them into jam. The easiest way to serve a fresh mango is to slice off the sides as close to the pit as possible. Then, with a sharp pointed knife, score the inside of the flesh in a crisscross pattern. Turn the whole segment inside-out and you are left with small cubes of mango looking like a hedgehog and sticking up from the skin, which can then be chewed off. The middle section containing the pit can be peeled and then either chewed or sliced off.

● **In Ayurvedic medicine the pulp is used to treat high blood pressure and diabetes, the antiseptic twigs to replace toothbrushes for oral hygiene, the bark as a treatment for diarrhea, and even the seed is made into a powder which is used in the treatment of vaginal discharge.**

MANGO

HEALTH WARNING

The mango belongs to the same family, Anacardiaceae, as poison ivy and the peel, especially before it is fully ripe, can be highly irritant. Anyone who has previously been sensitized by mangoes or by contact with poison ivy can suffer a severe reaction. Even using the same knife to cut the flesh that you have used to peel the mango can cause sufficient contamination to represent a hazard. If you have never had a reaction to mango skin, don't be complacent. Preparing 20 or 30 for a party could produce severe blisters. If dealing with large numbers of mangoes, wear gloves.

PAPAYAS

PAWPAWS

ENERGY PER STANDARD PORTION 50KCAL

❦ *Good for digestive problems.*

❦ *Beneficial for the skin and for an improved immune system.*

❦ *Best eaten raw and ripe.*

This delicious, nutritious tropical fruit was originally a native of southern Mexico and Costa Rica. Thanks to the Spaniards, who introduced papayas to Manila in the middle part of the sixteenth century, it is now grown throughout the tropics. The world's biggest producer by far is the US, where most of the fruit is grown in Hawaii.

Nutritionally this is a very important plant food in developing countries, as the papaya produces fruit throughout the year and is an excellent source of vitamin C. Like most other orange-colored fruit and vegetables, it is also an excellent source of beta-carotene, which is important in its own right as an antioxidant and is also converted by the body into vitamin A. An average papaya fruit supplies twice the minimum daily need of vitamin C and well over a quarter of the vitamin A. Papayas are excellent for treating skin problems because of their high beta-carotene content, and their generous provision of

PAPAYA

---

vitamin C helps boost the body's immune defense mechanisms. They are also a useful food for invalids, the flesh being soft and easy to chew.

With 3g of fiber in an average fruit, papaya also help reduce cholesterol levels as well as maintaining regular bowel function, but this is only part of their value as a digestive aid. Their most important constituent is an enzyme called papain, which is a great aid to digestion, although present in larger quantities in the unripe fruit. Commercially, papain is extracted as a white latex from the unripe fruit and dried to produce a powder for use as a commercial meat tenderizer. In traditional medicine, the ancient South American Mayans used the latex, the juice, and the fruit in their herbal medicines. In South American cooking, meat is often wrapped in papaya leaves to produce tender and succulent dishes.

Next time you eat papaya, save the seeds, as they make an unusual spicy flavoring when added to pickles, vinegars, and oils.

Canned papaya is widely available but nutritionally poor compared to the fresh fruit. Most of the vitamin C content and more than half the beta-carotene are lost during the canning process.

● **The leaves have been used to encourage the rapid healing of wounds, boils, and leg ulcers, and the seeds as a traditional remedy for worms.**

KIWI FRUIT

ENERGY PER STANDARD PORTION 29KCAL

❦ *Good for the immune system, skin, and digestive problems.*

❦ *Best eaten raw – slice the top off like a boiled egg and eat with a teaspoon.*

The kiwi is not just a pretty face in a *nouvelle cuisine* dish. This little fruit with its shabby fur coat is a treasury of nutritional riches. The kiwi originally came from China,

---

and then growers in New Zealand popularized the fruit. Hence it became known as the kiwi fruit after the country's national emblem – the kiwi bird.

The kiwi fruit contains almost twice as much vitamin C as an orange and more fiber than an apple. One kiwi fruit gives you twice as much vitamin C as you need for a day. Compared with other fruit it is unusual in that its vitamin C content remains very stable and, although there are some losses soon after harvesting, 90 percent of it is still present after six months in store.

The kiwi fruit is also particularly rich in potassium, of which Western diets, which are high in sodium from processed foods, can be dangerously short. Deficiency of this mineral, which is vital to every single cell in our body, can lead to high blood pressure, depression, fatigue, and poor digestion. The average kiwi fruit supplies about 250mg of potassium, but only about 4mg of sodium.

When buying kiwi fruit, choose those that are soft enough to yield to gentle pressure. They can be stored in the refrigerator – and should be peeled just before eating.

● **The fiber content of kiwis and their particular type of mucilage make them an excellent, but extremely gentle, laxative. This makes kiwi fruit ideal for the elderly, who are frequently deficient in vitamin C and suffer from chronic constipation. Kiwis also contain an enzyme called actinidin, an efficient aid to digestion which is similar in action to the papain found in papaya.**

Dried fruit

DATES

FRESH AND DRIED

FRESH DATES:
ENERGY PER 3½OZ/100G 96KCAL
DRIED DATES:
ENERGY PER 3½OZ/100G 248KCAL

❦ *Excellent for anemia, postviral fatigue syndrome, and CFS.*

❦ *Useful for exhaustion following prolonged physical exertion.*

❦ *Beneficial for constipation.*

❦ *Best eaten as a snack or as an appetizer before meals. Fresh dates are much lower in calories than dried ones.*

DRIED DATES

Dates have been cultivated throughout the Middle East for at least 5,000 years and form an extremely important food crop in this region of the world. They can be used as substitutes for sugar, as a staple food, and even for making fermented alcoholic drinks. Dried dates can even be ground into flour. Although traditionally most of the dates eaten in Britain and the US are semidried, it is now possible to get fresh dates with comparative ease. The dates traditionally eaten in Britain at Christmas time are nutritionally the worst of all, being coated in sugar syrup.

Fresh dates provide 96 calories per 3½oz/100g, but the same amount of dried dates provides around 250 calories. Fresh dates also contain modest amounts of vitamin C, but there is virtually none in the dried variety. However, it is the minerals in dates that are most interesting, especially their iron content, which seems to be little appreciated beyond the East. The amount of iron is totally dependent on the variety of date, irrespective of the amount of iron there is in the soil. It only requires 14 dates (3½oz/ 100g) of the Khidri variety from Riyadh to provide more than the total daily iron requirement for men and women. Gondela dates from

the Sudan are even richer, with just 10 dates (1¾oz/ 50g) exceeding the daily requirement. One or two date varieties are very poor sources of iron, but the vast majority make highly significant contributions. All dates are a reasonable source of fiber and a rich source of potassium. Though they contain only small amounts of the B vitamins, they do, however, provide reasonable amounts of folate.

Arabs traditionally eat dried dates with tea or coffee, but they also mix them with buttermilk or thick yogurt, making a dish of excellent nutritional value. A dessert made with compressed dried dates sprinkled with sesame seeds adds polyunsaturated fatty acids and proteins, making this delicious snack into a virtual meal.

Bearing in mind that the desert-roaming Bedouin often traveled for days with little more to eat than a store of dates, figs, and flour, why not add a few to the lunchbox of any child or adult?

● **The high iron content of dates, together with their easily available energy, makes them an excellent nutrient for those suffering from anemia and illnesses that produce chronic fatigue.**

FRESH DATES

FAST FOOD AID

• *Suffering from a lack-luster love life? Throughout the Middle East dates are considered a highly potent sexual stimulant.*

PRUNES

ENERGY PER STANDARD PORTION 160KCAL

❦ *Good for constipation, high blood pressure, fatigue, and lethargy.*

❦ *Best eaten as they are, soaked, or used in cooking; prune juice is highly nutritious.*

Prunes are the dried fruit of a specific variety of plum tree, which most famously grows around the small French town of Agen below Bordeaux, close to the convergence of the great rivers Lot and Garonne. Prunes have an ancient heritage, dating back to the Crusaders, who brought them to Britain from the Middle East. But in this famous area of France, the Arabs held sway for more than 800 years and it was almost certainly they who planted the first *pruneaux d'Agen* – a label with as much history as the *Appelation Contrôlée* of any fine wine.

Today California produces twice as many prunes as the rest of the world put together – 70 percent of the total supply. Production there started when Californian nurseryman Louis Pellier persuaded his brother to bring cuttings of the prune plums with him when he returned from France with his new bride in 1856. Prunes are rich in potassium, making them valuable for those with high blood pressure, rich in fiber and iron, and also contain useful amounts of niacin, vitamin B6, and vitamin A. They are an excellent source of energy, being easily digested and producing 160 calories per 3½oz/100g.

● **Prunes also contain a chemical (hydroxyphenylisatin) that stimulates the smooth muscle of the large bowel, making prunes a very gentle laxative without any purgative action.**

FAST FOOD AID

• *If you are seriously trying to reduce your fat intake, use puréed prunes as a substitute for fat when baking. This can be used as a direct replacement for butter, margarine, or oil. Because of its natural sweetness, you can reduce the sugar content of most cake recipes too.*

PRUNES

HEALTH WARNING

Commercially produced prunes may be treated with sulfur and coated with mineral oil to keep them soft, glossy, and prevent them sticking together. Remove these additives by cleaning in several washes of warm water. Mineral oils can interfere with the body's absorption of fat-soluble vitamins and can be harmful to the lining of the bowel.

Dried fruit

FIGS

FRESH AND DRIED

FRESH FIGS:
ENERGY PER 3½OZ/100G 43KCAL
DRIED FIGS:
ENERGY PER 3½OZ/100G 213KCAL

❦ *Good for energy, constipation, digestive problems, anemia, and cancer protection.*

❦ *Best eaten ripe and raw when fresh; dried figs can be eaten as they are, or soaked as part of a dried fruit compote.*

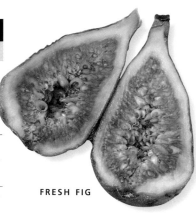

FRESH FIG

Figs have been valued by humans since the earliest recorded times. Adam and Eve used fig leaves and there are many other biblical references to this delicious fruit, testifying to its value as food, medicine, and symbol of plenty. Isaiah advised a poultice of figs to treat a life threatening tumor on the Israelite King Hezekiah. In Ancient Greece, Olympic athletes were fed vast quantities of figs to build up their strength and stamina. The Romans believed the fig tree to be sacred – the wolf that saved Romulus and Remus having rested under one – and it was traditional to give presents of fresh figs at New Year.

The common fig is a member of a large family containing around 800 species and growing throughout India, the Middle East, Turkey, Greece, and the rest of the Mediterranean. The Indian species *Ficus religiosa* is known as the Sacred Fig and Hindus believe that its wood was used for the original sacred fire with which the gods gave knowledge to humans. To this day devout believers sit encircling this Tree of Life to meditate and create

FIGS

FAST FOOD AID

• *Fresh and dried figs, as well as the traditional syrup of figs, are excellent laxatives.*

• *You can also use figs to treat boils, abscesses, and gumboils – bake a fresh fig in the oven for half an hour, cut it in half, and apply the warm, soothing paste over the inflamed area. This rapidly draws the boil to a head.*

• *For a wart cure that works, if you have a fig tree in the garden or a pot plant indoors, you can squeeze a milky, latex-like substance out of a broken leaf or stem and paint it onto your wart. Cover the surrounding skin with Vaseline first to avoid irritation, and wear rubber gloves to squeeze out the latex. Within a few hours a slightly inflamed ring of skin will appear around the wart which should gradually shrivel and drop off. Repeat after a few days if necessary.*

inner spirituality, peace, and mental harmony. Another fig variety, the banyan tree, is also sacred to the Hindus and is widely used in Ayurvedic medicine.

Modern science shows that figs are a rich source of benzaldehyde, an anticancer agent. They also contain healing enzymes, flavonoids, and an enzyme known as ficin, which aids the digestion by tenderizing protein foods.

● **All in all, figs are a wonderful source of easily digested nutrients, including iron, potassium, beta-carotene, both soluble and insoluble fiber, and energy. In many parts of the East and Asia figs have the added bonus of being regarded as a powerful aphrodisiac.**

RAISINS

ENERGY PER STANDARD PORTION 82KCAL

❦ *Good for high blood pressure, fluid retention, low energy, anemia, and constipation.*

❦ *Best eaten well washed as a snack, or added to salads or fruit dishes.*

Raisins are dried grapes, the very best of which are allowed to dry naturally on the vine. Traditionally raisins are laid out on earth floors and the bunches turned every 7–10 days for about three weeks. Modern production methods in Australia and California use

HEALTH WARNING

Commercially produced raisins may be treated with sulfur and coated with mineral oil to keep them soft, glossy, and to prevent them sticking together. Remove these additives by cleaning in several washes of warm water. Mineral oils can interfere with the body's absorption of fat-soluble vitamins and can be harmful to the lining of the bowel.

covered, open-sided sheds and mechanized harvesting to cut the vines below the clusters of grapes so that the fruit begins to dehydrate in the vineyard.

People have been drying fruit in the sun as a way of preservation for at least 5,000 years, and the Romans in particular included raisins in many of their medical prescriptions. When early settlers first crossed the Atlantic they took their dried fruits with them, and raisins are now firmly established as an American favorite. Many of the finest, especially the natural Thompson seedless raisins, are now produced in California.

All the nutritional benefits of grapes are concentrated into raisins, making them a wonderful store of instant energy – 3½oz/100g of raisins contains almost 2½oz/70g of natural sugars, glucose, and fructose. They are therefore an ideal high-energy food for athletes, hikers, mountaineers, and anyone suffering from chronic fatigue.

Unlike high-sugar confectionery, raisins are rich in other nutrients: fiber (to help reduce cholesterol and improve bowel function); iron (3½oz/100g providing more than 25 percent of the recommended daily allowance for women); selenium, and a huge amount of potassium (which prevents fluid retention and helps reduce blood pressure). Raisins also contain small amounts of vitamin A and small but significant quantities of the B vitamins.

● **The combination of good, quickly available calories and B vitamins make raisins the perfect snack for all those suffering from depression, anxiety, and nervous irritability.**

RAISINS

Root vegetables

SWEET POTATOES

Root vegetables – ranging from the humble potato and turnip to the more exotic yam and globe artichoke – have long been undervalued and received rather an indifferent press, but they are now undergoing something of a renaissance for their high fiber content and the exciting cancer-protective properties of the Cruciferae family.

FAST FOOD AID

• *Potato-peel tea – containing high doses of potassium – is recommended in traditional medicine for high blood pressure.*

POTATOES

OLD POTATOES:
ENERGY PER 3½OZ/100G 75KCAL

FRENCH FRIES:
ENERGY PER 3½OZ/100G 239KCAL

❦ *Beneficial for digestive problems, especially constipation and ulcers, for chronic fatigue, and anemia.*

❦ *Best eaten baked in their skins, steamed, or boiled in minimal water.*

POTATOES

POTATOES

It was the native South Americans who first cultivated potatoes and this humble plant was destined to become worth more than all the gold and silver that the Spanish plundered from the mines of the Incas, who gave the world corn as well as the potato. It is certain that the Spanish took potatoes to southern Europe, but it was Sir Frances Drake who introduced them to both Ireland and Britain.

Potatoes are an extraordinary nutritional package and for generations they were the staple food of Irish agricultural workers. Potatoes supply fiber, B-complex vitamins, useful minerals, and enough vitamin C to keep scurvy at bay, even when boiled or baked. Baked potatoes are nutritionally superior, since many important nutrients, including potassium, are to be found in the skin.

For years doctors have crossed potatoes off the menu for would-be slimmers but, contrary to popular belief, they are in fact good news as part of a weight-loss regime. Boiled or baked, they contain fewer than 100 calories per 3½oz/100g. Eat them with low-fat cottage or soft cheese instead of high-calorie butter or sour cream, and add a carrot, a tomato, and a bunch of watercress to make a well-balanced, very low-calorie meal.

Not surprisingly, it is what you do to your potatoes that makes them healthy or otherwise. Roasting them in the bottom of the pan with your meat adds ⅛oz/5g of fat per 3½oz/100g of potatoes; homemade deep-fried chips produce ½oz/15g of fat per 3½oz/100g – and this goes up even more if they're crinkle-cut or exceedingly thin. Chips provide almost 1½oz/36g of fat per 3½oz/100g (around ¾oz/26g for low-fat varieties!). Compare this with the 0.1g of fat per 3½oz/100g of boiled or baked potatoes, which are just as delicious.

Although its full nutritional value depends on the variety and the type of soil in which it is grown, the potato is a better supplier of energy and protein than almost any other food crop.

When cooked, potato starch is very easy to digest, making it suitable for invalids, anyone with digestive problems, and particularly as a weaning food for infants. The biological value of potato protein is just as good as that of the soy bean – one large baked potato provides a quarter of your daily need – making it an ideal food for children, invalids,

and vegetarians. It also provides more than one-third the US recommended daily allowance of vitamin C (one half of the UK).

● **Throughout northern and eastern Europe, naturopaths have used raw potato juice as a highly successful treatment for stomach ulcers and osteoarthritis. The treatment is simple – half a small glass of the raw juice, four times a day, for a month. The taste is vile, but you can camouflage it by adding apple and carrot juice, or even some honey. Alternatively, you can add the fresh juice to any soup just before you eat it, but not during cooking.**

HEALTH WARNING

Potatoes that are damaged, have turned green, or are sprouting contain a toxic chemical called solanine. The amount increases if potatoes are exposed to light. At best, even small amounts of solanine will make you feel unwell, while larger quantities can be fatal. Together with tomatoes, bell peppers, chilis and eggplants, potatoes are part of the "nightshade" family Solanaceae. All these can be aggravating to the pain and inflammation of rheumatoid arthritis, although they are not a problem in osteoarthritis.

SWEET POTATOES

ENERGY PER 3½OZ/100G 87KCAL

❦ *Beneficial for visual problems and night vision.*

❦ *Good for skin problems and cancer protection.*

❦ *Best eaten boiled, mashed, or baked.*

The sweet potato is often confused with the yam (see opposite), and many books describe them as alternative names for the same plant, but in fact they are separate species, with the yam being nutritionally inferior.

The sweet potato is a traditional lowland root crop in many tropical climates and was first brought to Europe by Columbus, who took it back to Spain, from where it spread and enjoyed considerable popularity. But the taste for sweet potatoes waned and they were not to become a popular vegetable in Britain until the influx of immigrants during the 1950s from the Caribbean islands. This created a new demand for this vegetable and for many other delicious foods from the Caribbean. They are now available at most supermarkets and street markets.

YAM

Root vegetables

Sweet potatoes are an excellent source of starch, and therefore of energy. They provide some protein, vitamins C and E, and a huge amount of carotenoids, including beta-carotene.

● **It is these and the other phytochemicals in the tubers that make sweet potatoes such a powerful anticancer food. A mere 3½oz/100g a day can dramatically reduce your risk of lung cancer. This is even more important if you are a smoker or ex-smoker.**

YAMS

ENERGY PER 3½OZ/100G 114KCAL

❦ *Good for energy.*

❦ *Best eaten boiled, baked, or mashed.*

Yams are very rich in carbohydrate and are used as a staple food, especially in Africa. They contain some protein and reasonable amounts of vitamin C, but virtually no vitamin A or E, and far less fiber than sweet potatoes.

Yams are, however, a source of phytoestrogens and may help to protect against hormone-linked cancers, as well as helping women going through the menopause.

● **Although a better source of energy than sweet potatoes, they contain slightly less protein, but this is believed to be of better nutritional quality. Ideally, eat plenty of both.**

CARROTS

ENERGY PER STANDARD PORTION 21KCAL

❦ *Valuable for cancer protection.*

❦ *Good for the heart, circulation, and eyesight.*

❦ *A useful aid to liver function and helpful in jaundice.*

❦ *Beneficial for the skin and mucous membranes.*

❦ *Good for diarrhea in babies.*

❦ *Best eaten old and cooked – baby new carrots taste delicious raw but contain far fewer of the vital carotenoids than the much darker-colored, old, cooked carrots.*

Carrots contain so much beta-carotene that a single carrot provides enough for your body to convert to a whole day's dose of vitamin A. This is vital for healthy skin and disease-resistant mucous membranes, which is why carrots are so important for the protection of the lungs and the function of the entire respiratory system. Vitamin A is also essential for proper night vision. Although British pilots were fed carrots during the war to help them see better in the dark, the publicity for this story was put out as a cover for the development of radar.

Beta-carotene is much better absorbed from cooked carrots – even more so if there is some fat or oil in the same meal to aid absorption. Until recently beta-carotene was seen only as a precursor to vitamin A, but it is now becoming apparent that beta-carotene, like other carotenoids, performs many vital functions of its own, notably as a cancer-protective agent.

In more than 40 published studies of the relationship between the occurrence of cancers and a high consumption of carrots, 75 percent of them revealed a definite reduction in cancer risk. There is even experimental evidence that eating carrots can reverse malignant

CARROTS

changes in cells. A lower risk of lung and breast cancer is closely associated with a high consumption of carrots.

Traditional folklore has long advised the use of carrots in the treatment of diarrhea, particularly for small children and infants, for whom carrot purée is both a healthy food and good form of medicine. Naturopaths recommend a two-day fast on nothing but fresh carrot juice and plenty of mineral water to help stimulate the liver and relieve the symptoms of jaundice.

In Britain there was a recent scare about the high levels of pesticide residue in carrots, and the government recommended that they should be peeled and the top and bottom parts discarded. Organophosphate pesticides are extremely toxic, so whenever possible choose organically grown carrots. This is even more important if you are feeding them to babies and small children, but there are now excellent varieties of commercially available, organic baby foods.

● **As an antiaging food, carrots are believed to offer some protection against ultraviolet radiation, helping to protect the skin against damage and wrinkles. Their other antioxidant vitamins, C and E, make them a must for anyone with arterial disease, and research in Russia has demonstrated that carrots have a particular ability to improve blood flow in the coronary arteries of the heart.**

RUTABAGA

ENERGY PER 3½OZ/100G 24KCAL

❦ *Good for cancer protection.*

❦ *Useful for skin problems and weaning.*

❦ *Best eaten boiled or in stews, casseroles, and soups.*

Another of the large and health-giving Cruciferae family, rutabaga is often thought of as no more than cattle fodder. But it is an excellent vegetable with a delicate flavor and all the anticancer properties of this group of plants. It contains significant amounts of vitamin C – 3½oz/100g providing 75 percent of the recommended daily allowance – useful amounts of vitamin A, almost no sodium, a little fiber and small amounts of trace minerals, depending on the soil quality. 3½oz/100g of rutabaga supplies only 24 calories and lots of satisfying, filling bulk, making this vegetable a real bonus for those watching their weight.

● **Mashed together with potato, rutabaga produces a most interesting and flavorsome variation. This combination also makes an excellent early weaning food for babies.**

HEALTH WARNING

Like other Cruciferae, rutabagas contain goitrogens and should be eaten in moderation by anyone with thyroid problems or taking long-term thyroxine treatment.

RUTABAGA

Root vegetables

PARSNIPS

ENERGY PER 3½OZ/100G 64KCAL

❦ Good for fatigue and constipation.

❦ Best eaten boiled, mashed, or roasted (in vegetable oil, not in the fat that comes out of your meat).

This frequently ignored and much maligned vegetable deserves better treatment. It has a unique and delicious flavor and is worthy of more interesting applications than ending its life as a few cubes thrown into a stew.

The wild parsnip has long been known in most of Europe, where it grows on chalky soil along the roadsides and around the edge of cultivated fields. Parsnips, like carrots, have been cultivated since ancient times – the Roman emperor Tiberius had fresh parsnips brought all the way from the banks of the River Rhine to Rome. In Germany they are often eaten with salted fish during Lent; in Holland they are used to make soup; in Ireland they were boiled with water and hops to make beer; and in the English countryside tradition, they were made into jam and parsnip wine.

The great herbalists Culpeper, Gerard, Tournefort, and even John Wesley, had nothing but good to say of parsnips as a highly nutritious food – for cattle and pigs as well as humans. And they weren't wrong.

The parsnip is a prime example of food that should be eaten when in season. The modern

PARSNIP

supermarket trend to have all foods available from the four corners of the earth throughout the year means that overcultivated, forced, and artificially fed produce ends up on the plate, containing very little flavor and almost certainly diminished nutritional value.

● Parsnips are a good source of healthy calories, fiber, potassium, folic acid, vitamin E, and traces of minerals and other B vitamins. They taste at their best and sweetest after the first hard frosts of winter.

TURNIPS

ENERGY PER 3½OZ/100G 23KCAL

❦ Good for gout, arthritis, and chest infections.

❦ A useful cancer-protector.

❦ Best eaten raw in salads, lightly boiled, or added to soups and stews.

Turnips are another member of the Cruciferae, with all the healing properties of this amazing family of plants. They almost certainly started life in Eurasia and were probably the genetic origin of the Chinese cabbage. Spreading to Siberia, then to eastern Europe, and finally to northern Europe, the turnip has been a food crop for over 4,000 years.

Those who grow their own turnips know the delights of eating the green, leafy tops as a succulent early spring vegetable. These have long been used as a treatment for gout and arthritis in traditional medicine, as they eliminate uric acid from the body.

A thin purée of turnips, cooked in milk, is an old country remedy for bronchitis – it is the sulfur compound, raphanol, that helps kill off the bacteria responsible for this complaint. It is not surprising that this member of the Cruciferae family has such strong healing powers, as well as the anticancer activity of its relatives.

● Turnips are a good source of fiber, as well as containing small but useful amounts of calcium, phosphorus, potassium, and some B vitamins. They are also a good source of vitamin C.

BEETS

ENERGY PER 3½OZ/100G 36KCAL

❦ Good for anemia and leukemia.

❦ Valuable for all the chronic fatigue syndromes.

❦ Beneficial for women of childbearing age; and beet leaves are especially good for osteoporosis.

❦ Good for convalescents.

❦ Best eaten raw and grated as a salad; boiled as a vegetable, with the leaves cooked like spinach; baked in the oven, or as soup (borscht).

❦ Most commonly eaten pickled – though not quite so nutritious, not too many nutrients are lost during the pickling process.

The ancient Greeks so revered the beet as a medicinal plant that it was regularly offered up on a silver platter as a tribute to the god Apollo in the temple at Delphi. Although there is not yet a great deal of scientific evidence to support its medicinal value, there is more than enough folklore and herbalists' knowledge to recommend this humble plant strongly. It should be eaten in some form at least once a week – and more frequently for specific therapeutic benefits.

BEET

In Romany (Gypsy) medicine, beet juice was used as a blood-builder for patients who were pale and run-down. In Russia and eastern Europe it is used both to build up resistance and to treat convalescents after serious illness. And the Swiss pioneer of organic horticulture, Dr. Hugo Brandenberger,

developed a technique of lacto-fermentation to preserve organic beet juice in its most nutritious form to treat leukemia.

Beet has for many years been used in the treatment of cancer in central Europe and now scientific research is beginning to explain its action. It is now known that specific anticarcinogens are bound to the red coloring matter, and beet also increases the cellular uptake of oxygen by as much as 400 percent.

Beet greens are equally valuable, containing beta-carotene and other carotenoids, lots of folate, potassium, some iron, and vitamin C. All of this makes the roots and greens excellent for women in general and especially for those planning pregnancy.

An excellent treatment for TATT (tired-all-the-time syndrome), chronic fatigue syndrome, mononucleosis, or recovery from other debilitating illnesses is a mixture of beet, carrot, apple, and celery juice. Take a small wine glass of this delicious drink before each meal. But don't panic if it looks as though you are passing blood in your urine or stool – it's only the beet showing up!

● Fresh juice made from raw beet makes a powerful blood-cleanser and tonic. It has also been valued for centuries as an effective digestive aid and liver stimulant.

HEALTH WARNING

Some people may have a digestive system that is sensitive to the strong, peppery compounds in radishes, so they should not be eaten by anyone suffering from ulcers or gastric inflammation. Like most of the Cruciferae, radishes can affect the functioning of the thyroid gland and so should not be eaten by anyone with thyroid problems.

Root vegetables

GLOBE ARTICHOKE

ARTICHOKES

GLOBE ARTICHOKES:
ENERGY PER 3½OZ/100G 18KCAL
JERUSALEM ARTICHOKES:
ENERGY PER 3½OZ/100G 41KCAL

❦ *Good for both liver and gall bladder problems.*

❦ *Help to lower cholesterol.*

❦ *Have a good diuretic effect.*

❦ *Useful for gout, arthritis, and rheumatism.*

❦ *Best eaten raw, if very small; large globe artichokes should be boiled and may be eaten hot or cold, with an olive oil and lemon dressing.*

❦ *Anyone with liver or gall bladder disease should eat three a week; otherwise they are an excellent regular part of a healthy diet.*

Every French housewife knows that the globe artichoke is a boon to the digestion and a powerful stimulant of the gall bladder and liver. Rich in a bitter chemical called cynarine, they traditionally form the first course of any over-rich meal because they stimulate the production of bile, which makes the digestion of fats much easier. Bile works in the same way as dishwashing liquid on greasy dishes – it breaks the fat down into minute globules, dramatically increasing the surface area that is exposed to the stomach's digestive juices.

Herbalists have traditionally used extracts of the artichoke to treat high blood pressure, and it is also known to help the body get rid of cholesterol.

If you're lucky enough to find fresh baby artichokes, eat them raw with a little olive oil for maximum healing benefits. They can also be lightly sautéed and mixed with pasta. If, like the Italians, you manage to buy them with their leaves on, cook these together with the peeled, chopped stalks in order to increase your intake of cynarine.

The globe artichoke is a type of thistle, originating from the Mediterranean part of Europe. It is not to be confused with the Jerusalem artichoke, a North American plant that found its way to France during the 1600s and is rich in potassium, but not much else. Both types of artichoke, however, contain a chemical called inulin, instead of starch. Like fiber, inulin does not get broken down during digestion but is fermented by the action of bacteria in the large bowel (colon), so it can be an embarrassing source of flatulence. Jerusalem artichokes are best eaten as soup.

● **Together with its diuretic properties, the artichoke is a cleanser and detoxifier, which makes it useful for people suffering from gout, arthritis, or rheumatism.**

RADISHES

ENERGY PER STANDARD PORTION 1KCAL

❦ *Good for cancer protection.*

❦ *Beneficial for liver and gall bladder problems, indigestion, and chest problems.*

❦ *Best eaten raw.*

The ancient Pharaohs cultivated radishes and thought them a valuable food source – so much so that workers building the pyramids were paid in garlic, onions, and radishes. And in traditional Chinese medicine radishes were listed in the medical texts toward the middle of the seventh century. Although originally native to southern Asia, they are now widely cultivated throughout Europe, Britain, China, and Japan. Surprisingly, they did not reach Britain until the mid-1500s, appearing in an early herbal in 1597.

Like cabbage, broccoli, and brussels sprouts, radishes are part of the Cruciferae family and as such contain glucosilinates and other sulfurous compounds, which are valuable for those at risk from cancer. But it is for gall bladder and liver problems that the herbalists have found this delicious vegetable most useful. Radish juice acts powerfully on the gall bladder, stimulating the discharge of bile, as French studies have demonstrated.

Radishes contain many other nutritional goodies as well – plenty of potassium, a little calcium, lots of sulfur, a reasonable amount of vitamin C, and some folic acid and selenium. But an excess of the hot, stinging radish can be too much of a good thing, irritating rather than stimulating the liver, kidneys, and gall bladder.

● **Radishes should be eaten as fresh as possible, while still young and crisp – their tops should be eaten at the same time, aiding their digestion.**

FLORENCE FENNEL

ENERGY PER 3½OZ/100G 50KCAL

❦ *Useful for digestive problems, especially excessive flatulence.*

❦ *A mild diuretic.*

❦ *Good for slimmers.*

❦ *Best eaten raw in salads, braised, or boiled.*

For more than 2,000 years varieties of fennel have been grown for the delicate flavor of their pale-green fronds, which go ideally with fish. The seeds have also been used medicinally for hundreds of years (*see Herbs and Spices, pp.124–9*). But the Florence fennel variety is grown as much for its large, greenish-white bulb, with its definite taste and distinctive smell of anise.

It is the volatile oils, such as anisic acid, limonine, fenchone, and anethole, that impart the unique flavor as well as the medicinal properties.

● **Although nutritionally not a powerhouse of vitamins and minerals, the fennel bulb has the great advantage of providing only 50 calories per 3½oz/100g as well as helping to eliminate surplus fluids from the body.**

RADISHES

FAST FOOD AID

• *Add a few slices of fennel to any salad or pop some in your sandwiches for an extra boost.*

FLORENCE FENNEL

CHILI PEPPERS

Soft vegetables

AVOCADO

AVOCADOS

ENERGY PER STANDARD PORTION 276KCAL

❦ *Good for the heart and circulation.*

❦ *Excellent for the skin.*

❦ *Help in the relief of PMS.*

❦ *An excellent invalid food.*

❦ *Cancer-protective.*

❦ *Best eaten raw and ripe.*

Avocados probably started life in Peru, where it is believed they were originally cultivated 8,000–9,000 years ago. In Guatemala the fruit, dried leaves, fresh leaves, rind, bark, and even the seed are used medicinally by the indigenous natives.

The avocado is rich in potassium, lack of which can lead to depression and exhaustion. It also contains vitamin B6, which helps iron out the mood-swings in women suffering from premenstrual syndrome. Thanks to their vitamin E and B content, they also aid in the relief of stress and sexual problems such as infertility and impotence.

Every slimmer thinks that avocados are fattening, but calorie for calorie they offer super nutritional value. Their high content of mono-unsaturated fats – especially oleic acid, like olive oil – makes avocados one of the most powerful antioxidant foods. It is this property that offers protection against heart disease, strokes, and cancer.

The avocado's flesh and oil have long been popular with traditional practitioners as a skin treatment and it is now known that chemicals in the avocado stimulate the production of collagen, which helps to smooth out wrinkles and give skin that wonderful young fresh look – cheaper and safer than either injections or dermabrasion. It is also a good source of vitamins A and E, which are excellent for the skin, whether the avocado is eaten, or pulverized and used as a face mask.

Because the fats in avocado are easily digestible and it contains antifungal and antibacterial chemicals too, puréed avocado is an excellent food for invalids, convalescents, and sick children.

● **Guacamole is not just something you eat with tacos, but a high-protein, high-energy, high-protection-factor food.**

PEPPERS

ENERGY PER STANDARD PORTION 2–3KCAL

❦ *Good for skin problems and the mucous membranes.*

❦ *Beneficial for night and color vision.*

❦ *Useful for natural resistance.*

❦ *Best eaten raw or chargrilled.*

BELL PEPPERS

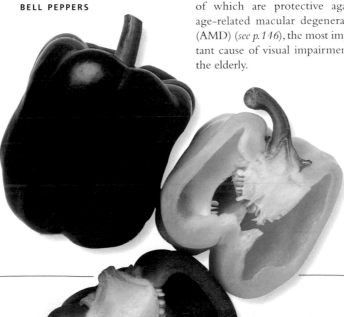

Bell peppers, together with pimento and chili peppers, are all members of the Capsicum genus and belong to the Solanaceae family, which also includes potatoes, eggplants, and tomatoes. Bell peppers are green, and as they ripen they become red or yellow.

The entire Capsicum family was native to the Americas and it was Columbus who introduced them to Europe, from where they soon spread to Africa and Asia. Native North Americans have used peppers for over 5,000 years as both food and medicine (*see Cayenne in Spices, p. 128*).

Bell peppers are an important source of vital nutrients. They are low in calories (15–32 per 3½oz/100g), very rich in vitamin C (120–40mg per 3½oz/100g), and an important source of vitamin A, particularly red peppers – 3½oz/100g of which provide almost a whole day's requirements. They also supply useful amounts of folic acid, some fiber, and potassium. Because of the waxy chemicals in the skin of bell peppers, they are protected against oxidation and their vitamin C content remains high, even some weeks after harvesting, especially if they are kept in a refrigerator. Peppers are also an important source of other carotenoids, apart from beta-carotene, most importantly lutein and zeaxanthin, both of which are protective against age-related macular degeneration (AMD) (*see p. 146*), the most important cause of visual impairment in the elderly.

● **Also nutritionally important are the bioflavonoids in peppers, which are valuable for their powerful antioxidant properties. This makes peppers protective against heart and circulatory disease, as well as some forms of cancer.**

CORN

CORN

CORN ON THE COB

ENERGY PER 3½OZ/100G 54KCAL

❦ *Good for vegetarian diets, for providing energy and fiber.*

❦ *Best eaten boiled whole or as separate grains, especially in salads.*

Corn, or corn on the cob, is a variety of maize bred for eating as a vegetable, rather than conversion into flour or meal. These hybrids are designed to slow down the conversion of sugar to starch, both during the ripening process and after harvesting, and taste much sweeter than maize, although the sweetest corn on the cob is one picked from your garden, cooked and eaten within the hour.

Corn is a good source of protein and also contains significant amounts of fiber, some vitamins A and E, and small amounts of the B vitamins, including folic acid.

● **Canned corn contains only one-third of the starch, and five times as much natural sugar as fresh corn. But beware – it contains a great deal of salt, whereas a fresh cob contains virtually none.**

Soft vegetables

ZUCCHINI AND SQUASH

ZUCCHINI:
ENERGY PER STANDARD PORTION 18KCAL
SQUASH:
ENERGY PER STANDARD PORTION 12KCAL

❦ *Good for slimmers.*

❦ *Zucchini are beneficial for skin problems.*

❦ *Zucchini are best eaten raw or slightly steamed, but always with the skin on; squash, steamed, or stuffed with savory ingredients and baked in the oven.*

Zucchini and squash belong to the same family as melons, pumpkins, and cucumbers. Zucchini are more nutritious than squash because the skin, which is rich in beta-carotene, can be eaten.

This delicious and versatile vegetable is not a baby squash but a specific variety of its own, although left to grow it will end up looking like a squash. Hugely popular throughout Italy for centuries, zucchini remained a well-kept secret until the 1950s or 1960s when they gained increasing popularity in both the UK and northern Europe. Thanks to southern Italians migrating to the US, the seeds also found their way across the Atlantic, where the zucchini flourished.

Squash has very little flavor and even less nutritional value, but it can be a healthy way of presenting other foods – stuffed, baked, or steamed.

For a cheap and instant vitamin A boost, put some pasta on to cook, then wash, top and tail, and coarsely grate two or three zucchini (with the skin on). When the pasta is cooked, strain and return it to the saucepan, add the zucchini, then a generous drizzle of extra-virgin olive oil, some black pepper, and a sprinkle of fresh parsley (since zucchini are so low in calories, you can afford to be a bit liberal with the olive oil). Mix together thoroughly. The heat of the pasta will gently warm the zucchini. Sprinkle on a little cheese and accompany the dish with a glass of red wine and a fresh tomato and basil salad – enjoy and be healthy.

You can serve zucchini flowers raw in salads or, for a delicious treat, fill them with ricotta cheese, dip them in batter, and deep-fry for one minute. Use olive oil or pure sun- or safflower oil – the taste is delicious and the extra calories worth it for the occasional pleasure.

● **Zucchini and squash also contain folic acid – 3½oz/100g supplying more than a quarter of our daily need – and are a rich source of potassium while being low in calories.**

ZUCCHINI

FAST FOOD AID

• *If your suffer from blackheads or similar skin problems, a slice or two of squash or zucchini gently rubbed over the affected area will help to combat these stubborn spots by drying out the skin and blotting up any excess oils.*

PUMPKINS

ENERGY PER STANDARD PORTION 11KCAL

❦ *Good for cancer protection.*

❦ *Useful for skin and breathing problems.*

❦ *Best eaten cooked as a vegetable, sweet as a pie, or as soup.*

As you might expect from their wonderful deep-orange hue, pumpkins are full of beta-carotene, the vitamin A precursor that helps protect against cancer, heart troubles, and respiratory disease. In population studies, people eating plenty of pumpkin, or other orange-yellow members of the squash family, ran a lower risk of getting lung cancer. And because of their vitamin A content, pumpkins are also a useful food for vegetarians.

Pumpkin, along with all the edible squashes, is extremely popular in the US, but in Britain it is most familiar in the form of the Hallowe'en lanterns made out of pumpkins once a year. Thanks to African and Caribbean influences, however, pumpkin and squashes are now becoming more popular, and the wonderful red pumpkin is often to be found on the menus of better Indian restaurants in Britain.

● **Don't throw away the seeds, as they are a very good source of protein and zinc (*see p.99*).**

FAST FOOD AID

• *There are many traditional and herbal remedies for parasites, but this extremely safe treatment for tapeworm does work. After fasting for 12 hours, take 2oz/60g of fresh pumpkin seeds, remove the outer skins by scalding them, and grind the remaining green pulp to a paste with a little milk. Take the mixture at the end of the fast, and two hours later take 4 teaspoons of castor oil, mixed with some fruit juice. Wait for the tapeworm to be passed, usually within three hours. Do not use castor oil on a regular or long-term basis, as a laxative or for any other reason – it can be harmful.*

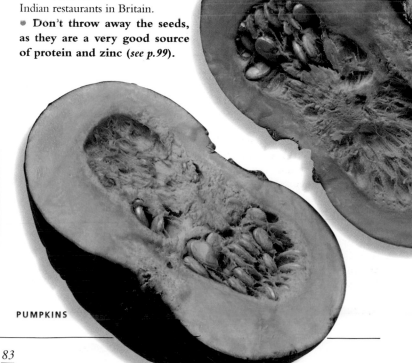

PUMPKINS

Onions, leeks, and garlic

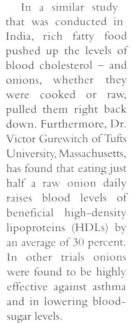

LEEK

ONIONS

ENERGY PER STANDARD PORTION 22KCAL

❦ *Good for reducing cholesterol and preventing blood clots.*

❦ *Useful for bronchitis, asthma, arthritis, gout, respiratory problems, and chilblains.*

❦ *Best eaten raw, baked in their skins, or in traditional recipes like onion soup.*

Onions are impressive country medicine for a huge range of ailments – among them anemia, bronchitis and asthma, genito-urinary infections, arthritis and rheumatism, gout, and premature aging. They star in hundreds of old wives' remedies, most deliciously as the famous onion soup at the end of a night on the tiles, which is part of Parisian mythology.

Originally natives of the northern hemisphere, onions have been cultivated for many thousands of years, as much for their medicinal value as for their flavor. In medieval times they were hung in bunches on door posts as a protection against the plague. The wild onion is a traditional medicine of the native North Americans, who use them in the treatment of colds and and to soothe insect stings. Traditional Chinese herbalists use scallions as a poultice to treat boils and as medicine to relieve nasal congestion. Onion is even reputed to be both an aphrodisiac and a remedy that stimulates the growth of new hair.

Onions contain the enzyme allinase, which is released when you slice the bulb. The action of allinase on sulfur compounds results in the chemicals that not only give onions their flavor but also make you cry. Onions are very low in calories, but scallions especially are a good source of vitamin C, as well as small amounts of some B vitamins and traces of minerals.

Onions belong to the same family as garlic, leeks, scallions, chives, and shallots – and, like garlic, they are currently the subject of extensive medical research. Science now confirms the age-old reputation of the onion as a cure-all, especially their protective action on the circulatory system.

In a trial which was carried out in the UK at Newcastle's Royal Victoria Infirmary, 22 volunteers were first fasted and then fed fatty fried British breakfasts consisting of bacon and eggs. Half the volunteers also had a helping of fried onions. When post-breakfast blood samples from both groups were analyzed, they showed a startling difference. The blood samples of those who ate no onions showed an increased tendency to clot – a state that could eventually lead to life-threatening thrombosis. The blood of the onion-eaters, however – despite all the bacon and egg they had consumed – showed a reduced tendency to clot. The results speak for themselves.

In a similar study that was conducted in India, rich fatty food pushed up the levels of blood cholesterol – and onions, whether they were cooked or raw, pulled them right back down. Furthermore, Dr. Victor Gurewitch of Tufts University, Massachusetts, has found that eating just half a raw onion daily raises blood levels of beneficial high-density lipoproteins (HDLs) by an average of 30 percent. In other trials onions were found to be highly effective against asthma and in lowering blood-sugar levels.

● **Onions are also powerfully diuretic, dissolving and eliminating urea, thus making them useful in the treatment of rheumatism, arthritis, and gout. Their traditional value in the treatment of chest infections is due to their powerful antibacterial activity.**

FAST FOOD AIDS

• *For colic in babies, slice an onion, infuse it in hot water for a few minutes, leave to cool, then give the baby a teaspoonful.*

• *For the treatment of chilblains, rub the affected area with slices of raw onion.*

• *To reduce a moderately high temperature, bake a large onion in a hot oven for 40 minutes, then crush to extract the juice, which should be mixed with an equal amount of honey. Take two teaspoons of the mixture every two to three hours until the temperature falls.*

ONIONS

LEEKS

ENERGY PER STANDARD PORTION 18KCAL

❦ *Beneficial for all chest and voice problems and for sore throats.*

❦ *Useful for reducing high blood pressure and cholesterol levels, and for cancer protection.*

❦ *Good for gout and arthritis.*

❦ *Best eaten lightly steamed, hot or cold with a vinaigrette dressing.*

Leeks have 4,000 years of history as both food and medicine. One writer describes prebiblical Egypt as a country in which "onions are adored and leeks are gods." The Greeks and Romans held them in the highest esteem, especially for the treatment of throat and voice problems. The infamous Emperor Nero ate leeks every day to improve the quality of his singing voice. They became the national emblem of the Welsh and are worn by Welshmen throughout the world on St. David's Day to celebrate the historic triumph of their King Cadwaller when the Welsh defeated the Saxons in AD 690. During the conflict the Celtic soldiers wore leeks so that they could recognize friend from foe.

Leeks are a member of the all-powerful Allium family – garlic, onions, chives – and, though not as rich in the anticarcinogenic chemicals, they too are important in the detoxification process. They are also antibacterial and, as such, contribute to protecting against stomach cancer, destroying some of the bacteria in the gut that change harmless nitrates into cancer-causing nitrites.

When preparing leeks, most people discard the dark-green leafy parts that normally grow above ground, and eat only the white

Onions, leeks, and garlic

stem. This is a great mistake because the dark-green bits at the top of the leek are a good source of beta-carotene, which the body converts into vitamin A.

● **Although leeks contain only small amounts of vitamins, minerals, and fiber, they are a reasonable source of folic acid and vitamin C and a good source of potassium. They are diuretic and have the ability to eliminate uric acid, so they make an excellent food for anyone who may be suffering from gout or arthritis.**

GARLIC

ENERGY PER STANDARD PORTION 3KCAL

❦ *Good for cancer protection, lowering cholesterol levels, reducing blood pressure, improving circulation, coughs, stomach upsets, and fungal infections.*

❦ *Best eaten raw in salads, baked in the oven as a whole bulb, or, if fried, not allowed to go brown.*

The first herb planted by Roman doctors on arriving in a new country was garlic, even then the most valued of medicinal herbs. It was brought to Britain by Roman centurions, who wedged pieces of fresh garlic between their toes to prevent the inevitable fungal infections that resulted from their long, arduous marches.

From ancient Egypt through the civilizations of ancient Greece and Rome, England in the Middle Ages to the end of the nineteenth century, garlic was the most widely used medicinal plant in the world.

It has long been known that garlic has a broad antibacterial effect – first proved scientifically by Louis Pasteur in 1858. It can destroy fungal infections and is a useful antidote to some poisons, especially alcohol and heavy metals.

A few years ago, within the space of one week, three separate patients told me that their doctors were puzzled by changes in the behavior of their blood samples. They had all consulted me for different reasons, but all had heart or circulatory problems and were taking anti-coagulant drugs to "thin" their blood – and all had had their doses of medication reduced. Why did I find this news so exciting? Because the only treatment that I had prescribed that was identical for all of them was large doses of garlic.

The latest research into the powerful effect of garlic on the heart and circulation shows that it has the unique ability both to prevent and treat some of the factors that are linked to heart disease. Scientists who study the distribution of illnesses in different populations know that in those countries where large quantities of garlic are eaten there is a lower rate of death from heart attacks, despite the fact that in many of these countries there is just as much smoking and drinking as there is in the UK. Britain has the lowest consumption of garlic in Europe and the highest rate of premature death from heart disease, although this has declined considerably in the US, following a successful health-education campaign mounted by the US government.

The sulfur compound, allicin, which is released when garlic is crushed, both encourages the elimination of cholesterol from the body and reduces the quantity of unhealthy fats produced by the liver. In healthy volunteers on fatty diets it has been shown to reduce the level of cholesterol in the blood by up to 15 percent.

At a recent International Garlic Symposium in Berlin some of the most exciting work concerned the reduction of blood cholesterol, high blood pressure, and blood clots, the three most important factors involved in heart disease and strokes. In a study of patients with raised cholesterol, half were given a placebo and half garlic, in the form of standardized tablets (no dietary advice was included). After 16 weeks the placebo group remained the same but in the garlic-eating group cholesterol levels went down by an average of 12 percent.

A report in the *British Medical Journal* confirms the benefits of garlic in heart disease, but emphasizes the importance of using preparations containing adequate amounts of the active sustance, allicin, which may not be present in extracts or oils made by steam distillation. Meanwhile, work in the eye hospital at Aachen University, in the Transfusion Institute at the University of Saarland, and at the University of Munich has provided clear evidence that garlic dilates the blood vessels and reduces the stickiness of blood.

Garlic also has cancer-protective properties. Professor Kourounakis from Greece and Professor Wargovich from the University of Texas are both working in this field. The Greeks have investigated the way in which garlic can destroy the highly destructive chemicals known as free radicals, which can initiate the production of cancerous cells in the body. Wargovich is investigating a wide range of natural compounds and studying their protective effect against cancer.

GARLIC

Both before and after exposure to the toxic compounds, garlic reduced and, in some cases, prevented the development of some artificially induced cancers in laboratory tests.

● **Bronchitis, catarrh, sore throats, asthma, indigestion, constipation, diarrhea, and even athlete's foot can all be helped by eating this powerful bulb.**

A BULB A DAY...

• *So what is the best way to get your garlic? The quality varies, depending on the soil in which it is grown. The best garlic is grown organically in China, the US, and southern France and gives a rich yield of the vital allicin compound, which is released by crushing but may be destroyed by cooking at high temperatures, especially frying.*

• *If you don't fancy munching a raw garlic clove each day, you can take a garlic supplement. Look for whole, dried garlic powder in tablets, which retain the goodness of the fresh clove. There must be a high proportion of allicin and the product should be standardized – each pill in each batch containing an exact dose, equivalent to a medium, fresh, high-quality clove.*

FAST FOOD AID

• *As a home remedy, try a crushed clove mixed with a dessertspoon of honey, and a squeeze of lemon juice dissolved in a cup of hot water. It is just the thing to take, three times a day, for catarrh, bronchitis, and sinus problems*

• *For indigestion, constipation, and mild stomach upsets, crush a clove of garlic into a cup of warm milk and drink after meals.*

• *If you suffer from cystitis or other urinary infections, crush a clove into a small tub of natural yogurt and make sure that you eat one pot each morning and evening.*

Brassicas

RED CABBAGE

The brassica family – of which cabbage, cauliflower, and brussels sprouts are but the best known – is prized for its useful vitamin C and beta-carotene content and, increasingly, for its protective powers against cancer. So include more of these versatile foods in your daily diet.

🌾 *Excellent for cancer protection.*

🌾 *Useful for the prevention and treatment of stomach ulcers.*

🌾 *Good for anemia, respiratory diseases, and acne.*

🌾 *Best eaten raw (white and red cabbage), slightly steamed, or boiled as quickly as possible in minimal water in a pan with a tight-fitting lid.*

CABBAGE

RED CABBAGE:
ENERGY PER STANDARD
PORTION 19KCAL
WHITE CABBAGE:
ENERGY PER STANDARD
PORTION 24KCAL

Cabbage has rightfully earned its reputation as "the medicine of the poor." The ancient Romans valued it; herbalists in the Middle Ages used it; and nineteenth- and early twentieth-century Europeans cooked it, juiced it, and made poultices out of it. But recent British methods of cooking have ruined this king of vegetables.

Cabbage contains healing mucilaginous substances, which are similar to those produced by the mucous membrane of the gut and stomach for their own protection. Traditionally European naturopaths have used it to treat stomach ulcers, prescribing 2pt/1 liter of fresh cabbage juice to be taken daily, in divided doses, for ten days. Modern research has shown that this regime results in complete healing. Cabbage is also rich in sulfur compounds – these cause the smell of overcooked cabbage – making it valuable for chest infections and skin complaints.

Dark-green leafy cabbage is rich in iron and its high content of vitamin C makes for better absorption by the body. It should be eaten in abundance by anyone suffering from anemia and by all women of childbearing age, especially because it is extremely rich in folate. It is also an excellent source of beta-carotene, another aid to healthy skin.

WHITE CABBAGE

By far the most exciting development in the history of cabbage is the discovery of its enormous cancer-protecting value – even the Romans used it for treating tumors. Population studies have shown that where people eat large quantities of cabbage (and its relatives), some cancers – particularly cancer of the lung, colon, breast, and uterus – are far less common. This effect is attributed to the presence of phytochemicals (protective plant chemicals), especially glucosinolates, which are present in all plants of the brassica family. As soon as the leaves are chopped, crushed, juiced, or cooked, enzymes are released in the plant, which convert the glucosinolates into anticarcinogenic indoles.

Overcooking cabbage in boiling water not only leads to major nutrient losses into the water, but also to the disappearance or deactivation of many of its healing compounds. Cooked cabbage may also be indigestible, so steam or boil it in its own juices, in a sealed pan, for as short a time as possible. The majority of the nutrients are found in the dark outer leaves, so do not discard them.

● **Surprisingly, animal studies have also shown that cabbage can have a mild protective effect against radiation, which may be useful for those working with VDU screens, having radiation treatment, or lots of X-rays. Centuries of use have also given the cabbage a traditional role as a vegetable stress-buster.**

DERMATITIS ALERT

People with sensitive skins should be careful when handling brassicas, which can cause contact dermatitis. Chopping a cabbage once or twice a week should not be a problem, but if you're preparing sprouts for 20 people or shredding enough cabbage to make coleslaw for a party, wear rubber gloves.

FAST FOOD AID

• *Cabbage can be used as a poultice for arthritic joints. Remove two or three of the largest outer leaves. Cut out the stalks and the central veins and bruise the leaves all over with a rolling pin or knife handle. Wrap them around a hot-water pipe, steam them for a few minutes, or put them in a microwave until they are comfortably warm – but not scalding hot. Wrap the leaves around the affected joint and secure in place with a crêpe bandage or thin towel. Leave for 15 minutes and repeat several times a day. This treatment is great for osteoarthritis, rheumatoid arthritis, sports injuries, strains, and sprains.*

HEALTH WARNING

All members of the brassica family – cabbage, cauliflower, brussels sprouts, broccoli, kale, watercress, mustard, and particularly rutabaga and turnips – should be eaten in modest amounts by people who are taking the thyroid medication thyroxine, or iodine for an underactive thyroid. All the brassicas contain a goitrogenic factor, which interferes with the ability of the thyroid gland to absorb iodine, but you would have to eat very large amounts each day to be at risk.

Brassicas

**BRUSSELS
SPROUTS**

SAUERKRAUT

ENERGY PER STANDARD PORTION 3KCAL

❦ *Good for cancer protection and immunity.*

❦ *Beneficial for digestive problems.*

❦ *Best eaten pickled, though it can be heated.*

Sauerkraut is an ingenious method of preserving cabbage. While still raw, the cabbage is finely shredded and layered in a stone crock, with sea salt and spices such as juniper berries. Each layer is pressed firmly down. By the time the crock is full, the cabbage juices have fermented to produce that soured taste, which you either love or loathe. Large-scale commercial production is done in oak barrels or stainless-steel vats.

For many centuries sauerkraut was a dietary staple of the poor peasantry all over Europe, a good way to preserve the fall glut of cabbages so that they could go on being eaten through the lean months of winter.

Sauerkraut can truly be called a wonder-food, since the

SAUERKRAUT

enzymes and vitamin C of the cabbage are well preserved, and it must have saved millions from death or debility due to scurvy. It was sauerkraut that made possible the long voyages of Captain Cook and the astonishing empire-building feats of the Dutch during the seventeenth century. The Dutch merchant ships were well supplied with sauerkraut for their long voyages to the Far East and the Americas, while the crews of Holland's commercial rivals at sea were dying of scurvy.

Apart from its vitamin C content – 3½oz/100g supplying a quarter of the recommended daily allowance – it also contains calcium and potassium. Traditionally used as much for medicine as for food, sauerkraut is useful for the relief of indigestion, stomach ulcers, skin problems, arthritis, and colds.

● **The lactic acid that forms in the cabbage during the long process of fermentation does a wonderful clean-up job in the digestive tract. This allows the beneficial gut bacteria to multiply, kill off the harmful bacteria, and produce a healthy, well-functioning digestive tract.**

KOHLRABI

ENERGY PER 3½OZ/100G 23KCAL

Sometimes called the turnip cabbage, this is similar in taste to turnip. Although it is a cruciferous vegetable – a descendant of the original wild cabbage – it arrived in Germany from Italy in the mid 1500s. It is most popular in Germany, though health-conscious folk in other parts of the world have always valued this interesting member of the brassica family.

● **The food value and health benefits of kohlrabi are almost identical to those of cabbage. It is rich in potassium, a very good source of folic acid and vitamin C, but does not contain any beta-carotene.**

**BRUSSELS
SPROUTS**

BRUSSELS SPROUTS

ENERGY PER 3½OZ/100G 42KCAL

❦ *Good for cancer protection and improved general resistance.*

❦ *Useful for skin problems.*

❦ *Beneficial for constipation.*

❦ *Best eaten steamed, to preserve their vitamin C and folate content.*

Brussels sprouts are members of the cabbage family (brassicas) and have most of the same health benefits. They are particularly rich in glucosinolates, one of the powerful anticancer chemicals (see cabbage on opposite page for further details). Their high vitamin C content also helps to promote improved natural resistance to disease.

Sprouts are also a very good source of beta-carotene, which is a great aid to all skin problems. Their high fiber content makes them an excellent remedy for constipation and useful in the treatment of raised cholesterol and high blood pressure.

Sprouts can cause flatulence, but this may be lessened by adding a few caraway or dill seeds when cooking.

● **3½oz/100g of brussels sprouts provides more than half the daily requirement of folate, which makes them great food for women planning pregnancy.**

KOHLRABI

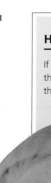

**SAVOY
CABBAGE**

HEALTH WARNING

If you have thyroid problems, see the health warning for cabbage on the opposite page.

Brassicas

SPINACH

ENERGY PER STANDARD PORTION 23KCAL

☙ *Good for cancer protection and sight protection.*

☙ *Beneficial for pregnant women.*

☙ *Best eaten raw or cooked in the minutest possible amount of water.*

As every Popeye fan knows, spinach is rich in iron. Sadly, in this respect, generations of mothers who have tried forcing spinach down their children's throats have largely been wasting their time. The large amounts of iron and calcium in spinach are not easily available to the body, since spinach has high levels of oxalic acid. These combine with the minerals and are then excreted as insoluble salts. Spinach also contains considerable amounts of uric acid, so this vegetable is best avoided by those with gout and arthritis.

But spinach is also very rich in the dark-green plant "blood" chlorophyll, so anemia patients, or those suffering from fatigue and mental strain, should eat plenty of it, preferably raw in salads. It is also exceptionally rich in folic acid, which is easily absorbed, 3½oz/100g providing three-quarters of the daily need. This should put spinach firmly on the shopping list of any woman who is planning pregnancy or who is already expecting.

Cancer patients, or those at risk from cancer, such as heavy smokers, should include plenty of spinach in their diet. Cancer research is increasingly focusing on the whole spectrum of carotenoids – not just beta-carotene – in dark-green or brightly colored fruits and vegetables, and spinach is even more highly endowed with these potential cancer-fighters than carrots. In population studies, dark-green vegetables, with spinach heading the list, were found to be strongly protective against cancer.

SPINACH

One of the great unknown virtues of spinach is its ability to protect against the eye disease AMD (age-related macular degeneration). A recent large-scale study in the US compared patients with AMD – the commonest cause of visual impairment in the elderly – with a similar group without the disease. The one major difference between them was that the majority of those with AMD did not like, and had never eaten, substantial quantities of spinach or collard greens. Most of those who were lucky enough not to suffer from AMD had consistently eaten substantial amounts of both these vegetables, which are exceptionally rich in a number of carotenoids.

● **Scientists suggest that this protective effect of spinach is not due to its beta-carotene content but to two other compounds, which are known as lutein and zeaxanthin, neither of which is substantially present in vegetables such as carrots, bell peppers, and pumpkins.**

COLLARD GREENS

ENERGY PER 3½OZ/100G 26KCAL

More popular in the US than Europe, collard greens are another variety of these great health-promoting foods, rich in anticancer phytochemicals.

● **Like other Cruciferae, they are rich in the indoles that specifically protect against hormone-mediated cancers like breast, ovary, prostate, and testicular cancer.**

KALE

ENERGY PER 3½OZ/100G 33KCAL

Another brassica that is a member of the Cruciferae family, kale is grown specifically for its shoots and yellow leaves. It almost certainly started life like other varieties of its family in western Europe, particularly in the eastern Mediterranean area, but is now distributed throughout the world.

With all the anticancer properties of the brassica family and a huge amount of beta-carotene – 3½oz/100g provides almost a whole day's dose for the average woman – kale deserves to be more popular. It has the advantage of being extremely hardy and can survive winter temperatures down to 5°F/-15°C, but it can also cope with high summer temperatures.

● **One of the great traditional dishes of the hardy Dutch is** *stampot,* **which is a delicious and heart-warming combination of mashed potato mixed with lightly steamed, chopped kale.**

KALE

Brassicas

PAK CHOI

ENERGY PER 3½OZ/100G
12KCAL

One of the most famous of all the Oriental brassicas, pak choi is the general name for several members of this group. There are records of the Chinese cultivating these vegetables for both food and medicine since the fifth century.

The Chinese cabbage is the most important and the most widely grown vegetable throughout eastern Asia, Korea, and Taiwan. Pak choi is best eaten raw or very lightly cooked by stir-frying.

• **Pak choi is an extremely nutritious vegetable, providing potassium, calcium, beta-carotene, folic acid, and vitamin C as well as small amounts of the B vitamins.**

BROCCOLI

ENERGY PER 3½OZ/100G 33KCAL

☞ *Good for chronic fatigue syndrome, anemia, stress-related problems, and for women planning pregnancy.*

☞ *Valuable for cancer protection.*

☞ *Useful for skin problems, recurrent infections, and lowered immunity.*

☞ *Best eaten very lightly steamed.*

Ever since the scare over President Reagan's bowel cancer, broccoli has rapidly become a four-star vegetable. The American National Cancer Institute advised a special diet for the President, and this eating plan included eating copious amounts of broccoli.

Like other members of the cruciferous family of vegetables, broccoli has been shown to have protective powers against cancer. (Other crucifers include cauliflower, kale, radishes, horseradish, cabbage, spring greens, turnips, brussels

BROCCOLI

sprouts, and kale.) According to an analysis made at the National Cancer Institute in 1987, six out of seven major population studies showed that the more cruciferous vegetables you eat, the lower your chances of developing cancer of the colon, while other cancers appear to slow down as well.

A number of chemical compounds in cruciferous vegetables have been identified as being responsible for this beneficial effect. In response to cell damage, the major glucosinolates in cruciferous vegetables are converted into indoles – nitrogen components that may offer some protection against cancer. In Japan, where the incidence of colon cancer is extremely low, the average intake of glucosinolates is 100mg a day. In Britain, where there is a high incidence of colon cancer, it comprises less than a quarter of this amount.

Broccoli is also rich in carotenoids, including the vitamin A precursor beta-carotene, which is known to inhibit the activation of cancer cells. It is the presence of these carotenoids that make broccoli such a favorite in the treatment of skin problems.

The combined presence of iron, vitamin C, and folate also helps with the improvement of anemia, protects against birth defects and raises energy levels in the chronically fatigued.

• Since 3½oz/100g of broccoli provides almost one-third of the daily requirement of vitamin E, this delicious vegetable is equally at home as a guardian of good heart health and circulatory efficiency. Compounds produced during the digestion of cruciferous vegetables also suppress free-radical formation, making crucifers especially valuable for those with joint problems.

CAULIFLOWER

ENERGY PER 3½OZ/100G 34KCAL

☞ *Good for cancer protection and general immunity.*

☞ *Best eaten raw, slightly steamed, or boiled as quickly as possible, with some of its leaves, in minimal water in a pan with a tight-fitting lid.*

Like cabbage, cauliflower is a member of the brassica family but, although it contains the same cancer-fighting compounds, it provides less beta-carotene, riboflavin, and folic acid. These essential constituents are easily destroyed by cooking, so cut cauliflower into small florets, wash well, and eat as a *crudité* with dips made from flavored live yogurt or fromage frais. The white part of the cauliflower is, in fact, the immature flowering head. Eating some of the tender green leaves which grow closest to the flower increases its beta-carotene and folic-acid content.

• **Cauliflower is a good source of vitamin C, which makes it useful as a booster food for the immune system.**

FAST FOOD AID

People always imagine that cauliflower is a "windy" vegetable. In fact, raw cauliflower florets eaten with a dip made of live yogurt, a drizzle of olive oil, two tablespoons of cider vinegar, and a crushed clove of garlic are a great remedy for flatulence, constipation, and general digestive discomfort.

CAULIFLOWER

Salad vegetables

CELERY

CHICORY ROOT, CHICORY, AND ENDIVE

CHICORY:

ENERGY PER 3½OZ/100G 11KCAL

❦ *Good for cleansing and detoxifying the digestive system.*

❦ *A therapeutic tonic in the spring.*

❦ *Useful as a mild diuretic, in jaundice, and as a liver stimulant.*

❦ *Best eaten raw or cooked; the root can be ground and used as a coffee substitute.*

Wild chicory, also known as wild succory, has an ancient history as both a food and a medicine. The Egyptians, the Arabians, the Greeks, and the Romans all used it for both purposes. It appears in the writings of Ovid and Virgil, and even Charles Dickens writes about chicory being cultivated for its roots.

The most widely cultivated modern varieties are Witloof (broad-leaved, often blanched with yellow/green tips) and the curly endive, Ruffic. Chicory made its first appearance in the US in the early nineteenth century and it is now an important horticultural crop in Florida, where some of the red varieties are especially popular.

Both chicory and cultivated endive are excellent sources of vitamins A (if not blanched) and C. They also contain some B vitamins and bitter terpenoids, which account for their stimulant effect on the liver and gall bladder. Both the leaves and roots have a gentle diuretic action as well as a mild therapeutic tonic effect.

The coffee substitute made from ground chicory root has the benefit of not containing caffeine. Although there is little scientific proof of its value, it is known to be a mild diuretic, to be slightly sedative, and to stimulate the functioning of the glands in the digestive tract. Those who have difficulty digesting milk and milk products can benefit from drinking it, as the dried chicory-root powder helps to break down milk into much smaller particles, which means that they are more easily digested in the stomach.

The Greek physician Galen called chicory "the friend of the liver" – "so people with jaundice should eat quantities of chicory," declares the French herbalist Maurice Mességué.

● **Chicory has an equally beneficial effect on the kidneys and is useful in urinary infections. Such an efficient eliminator of toxic wastes has obvious uses for those with skin problems and for sufferers from arthritis, rheumatism, and gout. Another study has shown chicory to have an antiinflammatory action.**

FAST FOOD AID

● *Bruised chicory leaves make a good poultice for swollen joints and inflamed skin eruptions.*

CELERIAC AND CELERY

CELERIAC:

ENERGY PER 3½OZ/100G 18KCAL

CELERY:

ENERGY PER STANDARD PORTION 2KCAL

❦ *Good for rheumatism, arthritis, and gout.*

❦ *Beneficial in reducing fluid retention.*

❦ *Useful for reducing blood pressure.*

❦ *A good calming and antistress food.*

❦ *Best eaten raw or juiced, but the strongest medicinal benefits come from the seeds.*

Wild celery was highly valued by the Romans for its medicinal value, and cultivated varieties were developed by Italian gardeners in the Po Valley during the Middle Ages. It was introduced to Britain as a vegetable only toward the end of the seventeenth century, since when both wild and cultivated varieties have been popular with herbalists.

Celeriac is a turnip-rooted variety of celery, but it is the bulbous round stem that is eaten rather than the stalks. Its smell is similar to that of celery but it has a less pronounced flavor. It may be eaten grated into fine matchsticks, either raw or parboiled, and served as salad with your favorite dressing. Nutritionally and chemically celery and celeriac are similar, but the white bulb of celeriac and the blanched white celery stems do not contain beta-carotene, whereas dark-green celery stalks do. Celeriac is a rich source of folate, which makes it an excellent addition to salads for women planning pregnancy, and both vegetables supply vitamin C, potassium, and fiber.

Hippocrates used celery in the treatment of nervous patients and modern research now confirms just how right he was. Research in both China and Germany has demonstrated that essential oils extracted from celery seed have a powerful calming effect on the central nervous system. These same oils have also been shown to reduce high blood pressure.

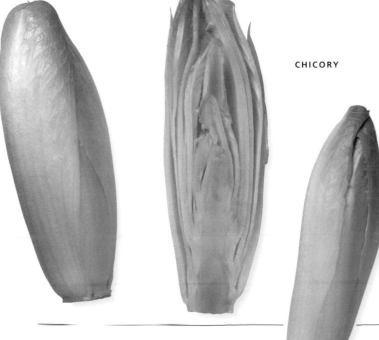

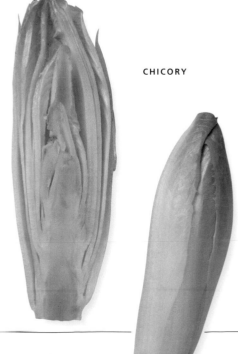

CHICORY

Salad vegetables

The most traditional and still widely used benefit of celery is in the treatment of rheumatism, gout, and arthritis. A celery and celery-juice fast is used by the Japanese as a treatment for rheumatism, and celery cooked in milk and celery-seed tea are traditional Romany (Gypsy) remedies for joint disorders. Its diuretic effect helps the body to get rid of excess fluid, together with uric acid, which aggravates the pain of all these joint disorders.

● **The seeds are also an effective antiseptic and this, combined with their diuretic effect, makes them helpful in the treatment of cystitis and other urinary infections.**

HEALTH WARNING

Do not take celery-seed tea if you are pregnant or have kidney disease. Only use culinary celery seed to make infusions – seeds for planting may be dressed with toxic chemicals.

FAST FOOD AIDS

• *One glass of mixed carrot and celery juice each day makes a good diuretic remedy.*

• *For gout and arthritis put half a teaspoon of celery seeds in a cup, fill with boiling water, cover, and leave for ten minutes. Pour through a fine tea strainer, add a little honey, and drink one cup three times a day.*

ASPARAGUS

ENERGY PER STANDARD PORTION 33KCAL

❦ *Good for cystitis, fluid retention, and constipation.*

❦ *Helps arthritis and rheumatism.*

❦ *Best eaten steamed, with a little olive oil or melted butter.*

❦ *Use woody parts of the stem to add flavor and medicinal value to soups.*

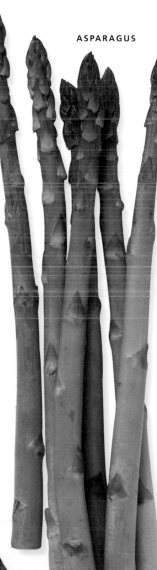

ASPARAGUS

CELERIAC

You may imagine that asparagus is just a gourmet treat, but it has been cultivated for over 2,000 years and used medicinally since the sixteenth century. Once you have eaten a portion of asparagus you will know that its major effect is that of a diuretic. Not only does it increase the amount of urine passed, but the smell of its active compound, asparagine, is noticeable in the urine within minutes of it being eaten. Because of this effect, asparagus has long been used by herbalists as a treatment for rheumatism and arthritis, though it is not recommended for the treatment of gout because it contains purines, which may aggravate this condition.

In the first century AD the Greek physician Dioscorides was using this plant for kidney and liver problems. Asparagus contains some fiber, which gives it a gentle laxative action, and it is also mildly sedative.

Don't throw away the water in which you have cooked your asparagus – either drink it, or add it to soups or stocks for its diuretic value.

● **Asparagus is an excellent plant for women to eat around the time of their period, because it is helpful in reducing the discomfort of swollen breasts, fingers, and ankles.**

CUCUMBER

ENERGY PER 3½OZ/100G 10KCAL

❦ *Therapeutic for the skin and eyes, and for dieters.*

❦ *Best eaten with the skin on, well washed in warm water to remove the wax.*

CUCUMBER

It is quite extraordinary that this strange plant is so popular.

Nutritionally, it is devoid of virtually everything, save a tiny amount of vitamin A (10µg per 3½oz/100g) and a minute amount of iodine (3µg). It has a particularly high water content – 96.4 percent – so cucumber is both refreshing and low in calories.

Cucumbers started life in southern Asia and became popular in Egypt, Greece, and ancient Rome, possibly for their refreshing, clean, and slightly astringent flavor.

● **There is a long Indian, Middle Eastern, and Eastern European tradition of pickling cucumbers to preserve them. Such pickles are delicious but, apart from the tiny amount of nutrients already listed, are of little nutritional value.**

FAST FOOD AIDS

• *Thin slices of cucumber placed over each eye are an extremely soothing treat after a day of staring at a computer screen, long-distance driving, irritating sunshine, dust, or hay fever.*

• *Cucumber also makes an excellent astringent facial cleanser for oily skin.*

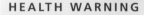
LETTUCE

Salad vegetables

LITTLE GEM
LETTUCE

LETTUCE

ENERGY PER STANDARD
PORTION 7KCAL

❦ Good for insomnia,
agitation, and bronchitis.

❦ Best eaten fresh and raw, as warm
salad, or in soup.

LOLLO
ROSSO

Considering that lettuce is 95 percent water and contains only 7 calories in an average portion, it is not surprising that it is the weight-watcher's favorite (or sometimes least favorite) food. But lettuce is more than just water. It contains vitamin C, beta-carotene, folic acid, some calcium, lots of potassium, a little iodine, and even a modest amount of iron.

There are many varieties of lettuce and its nutritional value not only varies from type to type, but also depends on the time of the year and whether you eat the dark outer leaves or the very pale inner heart. As a general rule of thumb, the darker the leaf, the higher its beta-carotene content.

All modern lettuces are descendants of the wild lettuce, much prized by the ancient Romans, from whom it gets its botanical name *Lactuca virosa* — *virosa* meaning slimy

or rank and referring to the milky juice from the broken stem and the fact that this is poisonous in large amounts. The juice has the same properties as a very mild form of opium and, though cultivated lettuces are less potent, they still possess some of the sedative effects of their wild ancestor.

Herbalists still use extracts from lettuce leaves to make sunburn lotion. Lettuce also contains a number of significant phytochemicals, including lactucin, flavonoids, and coumarins. Herbal medicines are made from the dried extracted "milk" and it is highly probable that lettuce was used as a medicine long before the Romans discovered its properties, as lettuce seeds have been excavated from some of the oldest Egyptian tombs.

As well as being a nutritious and delicious addition to any meal, a lettuce sandwich at bedtime is a far healthier alternative to sleeping pills. The combined sedative effects of the lettuce and the tryptophan released by the digestion of carbohydrates ensures a good night's sleep.

● **Any woman considering pregnancy should bear in mind that 3½oz/100g of lettuce provides more than a quarter of the daily need for folic acid.**

FAST FOOD AID

• *Whole large lettuce leaves boiled for a couple of minutes in water make an excellent poultice for boils, stings, and insect bites — apply them as hot as is comfortable, but not hot enough to scald.*

HEALTH WARNING

Where possible, choose organic lettuce or grow your own as, like celery, lettuce has the ability to accumulate synthetic nitrates from fertilizer. And the milky sap that oozes from the cut end of a lettuce, or sometimes from the broken stems, can be extremely irritant to the eyes – so take care.

WATERCRESS

ENERGY PER STANDARD PORTION 4KCAL

❦ Good for stomach infections, food poisoning, and anemia.

❦ Useful for cancer protection.

❦ Best eaten raw and well washed.

Watercress is another member of the health-promoting Cruciferae family, together with cabbages, broccoli, brussels sprouts, kale, turnips, and horseradish. And, like them, it should figure prominently in the diet of those at risk from cancer. Watercress is rich in vitamins A, C, and E, the powerful antioxidants that protect against cardiovascular disease as well as cancers.

Hippocrates described watercress and its medicinal values in 460 BC, and built the world's first hospital next to a stream flowing with pure spring water so that he could grow fresh watercress for his patients. The Greeks and the Romans believed that watercress was a cure for madness, though taking it as a purée mixed with vinegar did not do much for Nero. Both Sir Thomas More in the early 1500s and the

WATERCRESS

great English herbalist Nicolas Culpeper believed that watercress was good at protecting against scurvy. And during the 1920s the British Admiralty gave sailors tablets made from watercress to protect them against this awful disease.

But there is even more to this nasturtium branch of the cruciferous family. Both watercress and nasturtium contain a benzyl mustard oil – similar compounds give "bite" to the related horseradish and radish – which research has shown to be powerfully antibiotic. But, unlike conventional antibiotics, those found in watercress – and in the leaves and flowers of the attractive nasturtium – are not only harmless to our intestinal flora, but are positively beneficial to the health of our gut. So eat plenty of watercress, add an attractive nasturtium leaf or flower to your salad and you will greatly enhance your natural resistance. Respiratory and urinary infections in particular will benefit from a regular consumption of watercress.

Dr. Stephen Hecht, Professor of Cancer Prevention at the University of Minnesota, has recently published a dramatic report on the importance of watercress as a preventer of lung cancer in smokers. For those who cannot give up smoking, chemoprevention in the form of 1¾oz/50g of watercress, eaten at three meals each day for three days, produced enough of the chemical phenethyl isothiocyanate to neutralize the important tobacco-specific lung-carcinogen NNK. This extraordinary protective chemical, also known as gluconasturtin, is released from watercress only when it is chewed or chopped.

● **Add to this the fact that watercress is also a useful source of iodine – essential for the proper functioning of the thyroid gland – and you will understand why it should not just be used as a garnish but should be eaten in generous quantities by all.**

WAKAME

Edible seaweed

*N*ext time you pick up an armful of seaweed on the shore, it might surprise you to know that this is in fact an algae, in spite of the fact that it looks like a land plant, with roots, stems, and leaves.

❦ *Good for anemia, boosting the immune system, lowering cholesterol, the treatment and prevention of osteoporosis, and weight loss.*

❦ *Best bought dried and soaked before use, unless it is added to soups or stews.*

Most edible seaweeds are made up of the green, brown, and red varieties and, although often described as kelp, this term properly describes members of the *Fucus* species, most varieties of which occur only in northern seas, and which have traditionally been used in agriculture and medicine for hundreds of years. From Cornwall to the west coast of Ireland, from the Channel Islands to the Hebrides, kelp has been prepared by drying, burning, and reconstituting.

NORI

Other varieties of seaweed, especially in China and Japan, have long been highly regarded as both food and medicine, and as we now know of its nutritional value, I find it extraordinary that people aren't rushing to put it on their shopping list.

Although there are slight variations in the make-up of different varieties, the importance of adding seaweeds to the diet cannot be overstated. They are an excellent source of protein, but low in calories. They are full of soluble fiber, extremely rich in calcium and magnesium, a tremendous source of beta-carotene, rich in potassium, and exceptionally well supplied with iron and zinc. Seaweed is by far the richest source of natural iodine of all foods, a mineral which is essential for the normal functioning of the thyroid gland. For vegetarians and vegans, seaweeds are a real must, because of their vitamin B12 content – 3½oz/100g providing many times the minimum daily requirement (alfalfa, comfrey, and fermented soybeans are also plant sources of B12).

As the influence of Oriental cooking spreads in both Britain and the US, many seaweeds can now be purchased in your local store. They are widely used in Japanese recipes and although the soaking and cooking waters can be high in salt, this can be discarded and the dishes flavored with traditional Japanese condiments like rice vinegar, soy sauce, tamari, or shoyu.

● **Folklore tells us that seaweeds lower blood pressure, cure stomach ulcers, prevent goiter and protect against some forms of cancer. In nutritional terms, these ancient remedies certainly work.**

HEALTH WARNING

Kombu contains a large amount of sodium, so it is unsuitable for people who have high blood pressure or those on a low-salt diet.

KOMBU

ENERGY PER 3½OZ/100G 43KCAL

This seaweed is often used to make nutritious soups and savory dishes as it is a good source of calcium and vitamins A and C. It is a strongly flavored seaweed and one strip is normally enough to make 1pt/500ml of stock.

NORI

ENERGY PER 3½OZ/100G 136KCAL

Very rich in protein and minerals, nori is normally used as a garnish sprinkled onto savory dishes or cooked vegetables. It is often used in Japanese cooking to wrap up tasty morsels of savory ingredients

WAKAME

ENERGY PER 3½OZ/100G 71KCAL

This is similar to kombu and is high in protein, iron, and calcium. Another good seaweed for beginners, as its taste is not dissimilar to that of green vegetables, it is used in Japanese cooking to make the nourishing and popular miso soup.

FRESH KELP

OTHER SEAWEEDS

• *Arame* This is a good seaweed for beginners, as it has a sweet flavor and is excellent in salads and soups.

• *Dulse* This seaweed is more familiar in parts of Britain and the US. It grows along the seaboard of Canada and North America, Iceland, and Ireland, and is definitely not a beginner's seaweed. No matter how long you cook it, it is always tough and has a strong, salty taste. The Irish make a traditional dulse soup which is, I believe, an acquired taste.

• *Hiziki* Sun-dried and shredded, with a sweet, delicate flavor, hiziki is immensely rich in calcium and iron – 1¾oz/50g supplies enough for an adult's daily requirement of both these essential minerals.

• *Laver* One of the red seaweeds that grows off the coast of south Wales and Ireland, this can be gathered on the beach and for this reason has been a popular food in Wales for many hundreds of years. As a traditional Welsh breakfast it is rolled in oatmeal, fried, and served with eggs and bacon, however, be prepared for a very strong taste of the sea. The Welsh also use this seaweed to make laver bread – again, I am told, this is definitely an acquired taste and not for seaweed novices.

HEALTH WARNING

Some seaweed, such as laver, grows off the British coast. If you do gather seaweed on the beach, do first make sure that the shore is not polluted.

Mediterranean vegetables and fungi

TOMATOES

TOMATOES

ENERGY PER STANDARD PORTION 14KCAL

❦ *Good for cancer protection.*

❦ *Useful for skin problems and fertility.*

❦ *Best eaten fresh and ripe, as purée, juice, or even canned.*

Tomatoes are probably one of the world's most important food crops and worldwide production is measured in tens of millions of ton(ne)s each year. Sadly, ever-increasing commercial pressures, more sophisticated production methods, and genetic engineering do a disservice to this wonderful fruit. It is, by the way, really a fruit and not a vegetable.

In the US tomatoes are consumed to such an extent that they have now become an important source of nutrients.

The ancestral home of the tomato is the western coastal region of South America, stretching from Ecuador to Peru and Chile. Even in the high mountains, wild varieties abound – these are cherry tomatoes, the forerunners of all modern varieties. The first domestication probably occurred in Mexico, and tomatoes were subsequently introduced to Europe by the Spanish during the sixteenth century, after which they rapidly rampaged across southern Europe. As members of the Solanaceae family, which includes the deadly nightshade, tomatoes were at first treated with suspicion, but they soon became popular and achieved their rightful place as a delicious and health-giving food.

Tomatoes are extremely rich in antioxidants, especially carotenoids like beta-carotene and lycopene, as well as vitamins C and E, making them good protectors of the cardio-vascular system and against some forms of cancer. They are also extremely low in sodium and quite rich in potassium, so they are helpful in conditions like high blood pressure and fluid retention.

Canned tomatoes lose very few of their nutrients but do gain some extra salt. If you are buying tomato juice or the traditional Italian passatta, be sure to choose low-salt varieties. But nothing tastes quite like tomatoes grown in your own garden or greenhouse, where you can select varieties for their flavor rather than for their long shelf-life and tough skins.

A ripe tomato contains more than 200 volatile compounds that give it its unique aroma and flavor. But the one chemical that may cause problems is tomatine. All the Solanaceae contain alkaloids (like the poisonous solanine found in green potatoes); tomatine, however, does not appear to be toxic and is present in only small quantities in ripe tomatoes, although green tomatoes contain about double the quantity. For this reason green tomatoes may trigger migraines in some susceptible people.

● **Tomatine does not normally present a problem in cooked green-tomato chutney, but it may be more of a concern in the US, where these pickled green tomatoes are a highly popular snack.**

HEALTH WARNING

Tomatoes, like all the Solanaceae, may aggravate the pain and discomfort of rheumatoid arthritis. Certain people find that they have allergic reactions to tomatoes. If you find that recurrent mouth ulcers and eczema are a problem, then you should significantly reduce your consumption of tomatoes.

OLIVES

ENERGY PER STANDARD PORTION 3KCAL

❦ *Good for the skin, circulation, and the heart.*

❦ *Best eaten thoroughly rinsed to remove the high salt content.*

The olive tree is remarkable, since it can continue to bear fruit for a thousand years or more. It has been cultivated since prehistoric times in some Mediterranean areas and has always been intimately related to the nutritional, medicinal, religious, and cultural aspects of every civilization,

As well as being grown for their fruit, olive trees are the source of the most nutritious of all vegetable oils – olive oil. Medicinally, olive leaves are extremely important and they can be gathered at any time of the year.

Crete was probably the home of cultivated olives 5,500 years ago and their religious symbolism is still with us today – the olive branch signifying peace, the olive wreath given to the victors in the original Olympic games and still used to adorn racing drivers. Since ancient times olive oil has been used in religious ceremonies and the leaves to heal wounds, and the Bible is strewn with references to the olive tree.

Olives straight from the tree are not edible, but are hard and extremely bitter. For this reason they have to be processed by pickling in heavily salted water. Consequently most table olives have a very high sodium content, up to 2,250mg per 3½oz/100g. The Greek method of treating olives differs in that it does not use an intermediate treatment with lye, a strong alkaline solution,

but relies solely on brine. But whichever olives you choose, wash them thoroughly under running water for at least 15 minutes to remove as much salt as possible, then steep them in olive oil prior to eating – the oil may be flavored with garlic, herbs, or spices.

Olives do provide a reasonable amount of vitamin E, a little fiber, and some mono-unsaturated oil, but little else of nutritional significance.

● **It is the antioxidant compounds in the olive that give it, and its oil, such enormous health benefits. Oleaesterol is the most important of these protective substances.**

HEALTH WARNING

The olives in a dish on the bar, at a cocktail party, and in most restaurants are straight out of the jar, can, or package and are saturated in salt. If you have high blood pressure, don't eat a single one – not even the one in your Martini. And if you don't have high blood pressure, these olives are a pretty good way of getting it.

FAST FOOD AID

● *Olive leaves are known to contain oleuropein, which is powerfully antibacterial and antiviral. This same chemical is present throughout the olive tree and the fruit. Strong, bitter tea brewed from olive leaves can reduce blood pressure and increase natural immunity, and has been used in the treatment of chronic fatigue syndrome.*

OLIVES

EGGPLANTS

ENERGY PER STANDARD PORTION 20KCAL

❦ *Helps lower cholesterol levels and high blood pressure.*

❦ *May be cancer-protective.*

❦ *Best eaten when small, baked in the oven; larger fruit are best used for ratatouille.*

❦ *Often eaten fried, which dramatically increases the calorie count.*

These beautiful, deep purple fruit (probably originally egg-shaped, hence its name) are part of the Solanaceae family of plants, which includes potatoes, tomatoes, and deadly nightshade. All foods in this family are best avoided by people with rheumatoid arthritis.

Originally from India and parts of Southeast Asia, eggplants have been grown for food and medicine for thousands of years. It is possible that their traditional use as a cancer treatment may have some real value after all, as they contain protease inhibitors, which are known to be anticancer chemicals.

● **This plant has been shown to reduce the amount of fat deposited in the arteries of animals fed on a high-fat diet, and eggplants should always be included in the normal dietary program for blood pressure reduction.**

FAST FOOD AID

• *If you grow your own eggplants, the leaves can be used as a poultice to treat boils, burns, and abrasions. Take care, though, for the leaves are toxic and should only be used externally.*

MUSHROOMS

ENERGY PER STANDARD PORTION 5KCAL

❦ *Good for vegetarians and vegans (mushrooms contain vitamin B12), weight-loss programs, depression, and anxiety.*

❦ *Best eaten fresh (raw in salads, lightly sautéed, or added to soups, stews, and casseroles) or dried (well washed, soaked, then used as fresh).*

SHIITAKE MUSHROOMS

Mushrooms, like truffles, are the edible portions of fungi – mushrooms appearing above ground, truffles below. Of course not all mushrooms are edible, some of them being highly poisonous and others unpalatable.

Our relationship with mushrooms is long and fascinating. The Egyptians believed they were a gift from the god Osiris, while the ancient Romans thought they resulted from the lightning thrown to earth by Jupiter during storms –

which explained their sudden appearance, as if by magic. But there are written records going back to the Chinese Chow Dynasty, which reveal that mushrooms were already in use 3,000 years ago as both food and medicine. And researchers believe that this use can be traced back for at least another 3,000–4,000 years. In some parts of South America "magic mushrooms" have long been used as part of religious ceremonies because of their recognized hallucinogenic effects.

Whatever their history, we should all be eating more mushrooms than we do. They are a good source of easily absorbed, high-quality protein, containing more than most other vegetables, and are extremely low in calories, a scant 55 per 3½oz/100g, unless you choose to dip them in batter and deep-fry them, which is a different story altogether. Mushrooms also contain some B vitamins, lots of phosphorus, and a large amount of potassium.

But it is their B12 content that is extraordinary. Most textbooks state that mushrooms do not contain this vital vitamin, but the most up-to-date research reveals that mushrooms contain 0.32–0.65µg per gram of fresh mushroom. Two or three button mushrooms, or one reasonable-sized field mushroom, will therefore supply all the B12 you need for an entire day, which is vital for vegetarians and

even more so for vegans, as other plant sources of B12 are very limited. The same is true for vitamin E, which is listed as zero in mushrooms in most textbooks. Again, modern research reveals that most mushrooms are a rich source of this essential nutrient, 3½oz/100g providing more than the minimum daily requirement.

Dried mushrooms generally have a much fuller flavor and, although expensive, Italian, Japanese/Chinese, and French varieties are now widely available. For modern food researchers it is the Oriental mushrooms that are extremely interesting, with Shiitake, reishi, and maitake mushrooms commonly used medicinally in Japan and China. Shiitake are the source of traditional Chinese medicines for the treatment of depressed immune function.

● **Reishi are believed to promote longevity and help treat liver diseases, high blood pressure, and asthma. Maitake are also used for high blood pressure, cancer, liver disease, and the immune system.**

HEALTH WARNING

On the continent of Europe wild mushroom-gathering is a national pastime and interest is now growing in the US and Britain. If you decide to join the hunt for mushrooms yourself, make sure that you have an excellent reference book and that you check with an expert before eating any edible fungi.

Nuts and seeds

From the diet of Australopithecus, the ape-man of prehistory, to the ancient Greeks, the Roman cookery of Apicius, and the biblical lands of the Middle East, the food of medieval Europe, the rain-forest tribes of South America, the Native North Americans, and the mountain-dwelling Hunzas, nuts have been a staple food.

❧ *Good for lowering cholesterol – rich in beneficial polyunsaturated and mono-unsaturated oils.*

❧ *Beneficial for constipation, hemorrhoids, and varicose veins.*

❧ *Protective against some forms of cancer, especially breast and prostate cancer.*

❧ *Good for male fertility.*

In the late twentieth century nuts have largely been relegated to the position of high-salt, high-fat nibbles accompanying alcoholic drinks. What a tragic waste of one of nature's most abundant store-houses of energy and nutrients!

Nuts can make a vital contribution to a healthy balanced diet, but avoid salted nuts and particularly commercially produced nut snacks, which may be roasted in saturated or hydrogenated fats.

The total fat in nuts often exceeds even that in fatty meat. With the exception of coconuts, this is nearly all a mixture of unsaturated fats. However, all nuts are good sources of protein, with peanuts being the best, containing as much as the same weight of cheese, followed by almonds, while walnuts and Brazil nuts contain as much as the equivalent weight in eggs. However, nut protein is not "complete," as most nuts lack some amino acids, but in a mixed diet this does not matter as the deficiencies will be made up from other sources.

Nuts are all deficient in vitamin B_{12}, but in respect of the rest of the vitamin B-complex, nuts are the equal of any meat. Although lots of minerals are present, all nuts contain phytic acid, and peanuts oxalic acid, making it more difficult for your body to absorb the minerals from nuts. Roasting them or using them in cooking breaks down these acids. And eating good sources of vitamin C at the same time as nuts improves the absorption of their iron.

Nuts and nut oils become rancid very quickly – and rancid fats are harmful as they interfere with vitamin E activity and may trigger bloodclots. There have been links between a high consumption of rancid oily foods and an increase in stomach cancer.

● **Most nuts (except coconut and pine nuts) contain linoleic acid, which counteracts cholesterol deposits and is thought to protect against heart disease.**

HEALTH WARNING

Severe allergic reactions to nuts and seeds can be fatal. Although such reactions are still comparatively rare, peanut allergy in particular is growing at an alarming rate and 25 percent of all children have the possibility of developing allergies. Early exposure to nuts as a child, or a history of allergic illness in your family, seems to increase the risk. Peanut products occur in all sorts of baby goods, including foods, milks, and even nipple creams for breastfeeding mothers, but some manufacturers are now removing nut extracts from their baby products. The best solution is to give your baby homemade food and to keep everything as pure as possible. The same reaction can occur with sesame seeds, poppy seeds, and all other seeds and nuts.

ALMONDS

ENERGY PER 3½OZ/100G 612KCAL

The two varieties are sweet almonds and bitter almonds, but those most commonly eaten are the sweet ones. Bitter almonds contain toxic prussic acid and should never be eaten raw as this poison is destroyed only by heating – they are primarily used to make almond oil. Almonds are rich in protein, fat, and vital minerals like zinc, magnesium, potassium, and iron, as well as some B vitamins. Since they are also high in oxalic and phytic acids, which combine with these minerals to carry them out of your body, you should eat them at the same time as vitamin C-rich foods for maximum absorption. Of all nuts, almonds contain the most calcium, and 20 percent protein – weight for weight, they have one-third more protein than eggs. Almond oil is especially soothing to the skin.

FAST FOOD AID

• *Almond milk is a classic sickroom drink, both sustaining and soothing. Soak ½ cup of whole almonds in tepid water, then skin them. Pound them (you can do this in a food processor) with part of 2pt/1 liter of water. Add the paste to the remaining water, stir in a tablespoon of honey, strain through cheesecloth, and drink.*

MACADAMIAS

ENERGY PER 3½OZ/100G 748KCAL

Although originally an Australian plant, this is now a major cultivated crop in Hawaii. It is rare to find macadamias as fresh nuts, since they are nearly always roasted and salted. They are very high in fat, so they go rancid quickly. They are a reasonable source of fiber, protein, iron, and zinc, but very high in salt.

SUNFLOWER SEEDS

ENERGY PER 3½OZ/100G 581 KCAL

When you see a vast Mediterranean field of sunflowers turning their faces to the midday sun, it seems hardly surprising that the ancient Incas worshipped this plant. The seeds are extremely nutritious, as well as tasting good. They provide large amounts of protein, B vitamins, iron, zinc, potassium, and selenium, and are one of the best sources of vitamin E.

PECANS

ENERGY PER 3½OZ/100G 689KCAL

These originated as part of the staple diet of the native North Americans. They are traditionally used in many American recipes, both sweet and savory. They are a good source of protein, very high in unsaturated fats, and contain a reasonable quantity of fiber. They also provide modest amounts of calcium, magnesium, iron, and zinc, and although they contain very little vitamin A, 3½oz/100g provide more than the recommended daily allowance of vitamin E.

BRAZIL NUTS

ENERGY PER 3½OZ/100G 682 KCAL

These grow in tropical South America, most famously in the Brazilian rain forest, where I have stood under trees that can grow up to 200ft/60m tall. Brazil nuts are high in fat and go rancid very quickly. Buy only the amount you need for current use, and only from a reputable supplier with a rapid turnover. They are one of the richest of all sources of the essential mineral selenium – a few Brazil nuts each day should give you all you need, enough to protect you against heart disease and cancer.

Nuts and seeds

CHESTNUTS

ENERGY PER 3½OZ/100G 170KCAL

You can buy these wonderful nuts with or without their shells, fresh or dried, ground into meal, and even canned or frozen. Chestnuts are native to southern Europe, parts of Asia and North Africa, and also grow well in the US. When grown in Britain they produce poor crops and must not be confused with the poisonous horse chestnut, which is used in herbal medicine. Chestnuts must be cooked before eating – in the UK traditionally being roasted on an open fire – but can also be used in sweet and savory dishes, cooked with vegetables, in soups, or as traditional turkey stuffing. Dried and ground into flour, they are excellent for people suffering from celiac disease or indeed any form of gluten intolerance, as they are gluten-free. Chestnuts are much lower in calories than other nuts because they contain far less fat, but they are also low in protein. They do supply some vitamin E, potassium and vitamin B6.

SESAME SEEDS

ENERGY PER 3½OZ/100G 598KCAL

These have been popular for centuries in the Middle East and the Far East, where they have a reputation as an aphrodisiac, which may well be due to their vitamin E and iron content. They are an exceptional source of calcium and a very good source of protein and magnesium. They are also rich in B vitamins, especially niacin and folate. In the Middle East they are used to make a popular spread called tahini, a thick paste similar in texture to peanut butter, but without the lumps. Sprinkled on top of, or added to, cakes and especially wholewheat bread, they add lots of nutrients and a distinctive nutty flavor. They are an essential ingredient in Asian cooking, being added to stir-fries, and sesame-seed oil is excellent both for salads and wok cooking.

COCONUTS

ENERGY PER 3½OZ/100G 351KCAL

The coconut palm is abundant all over the tropics and plays an important part in many native cuisines. Coconuts are delicious eaten fresh and the "milk" is refreshing, although not very nutritious. When shredded (dried), coconut can be used in cooking, but is often compressed into hard slabs of coconut cream. This cream can also be bought in cans and is widely used in curries. However, coconut – fresh or shredded – is much higher in saturated fats than other nuts. It is a good source of fiber and provides useful quantities of other nutrients, but should be eaten in moderation.

HAZELNUTS

ENERGY PER 3½OZ/100G 650KCAL

These grow widely all around the Mediterranean and particularly well in the English county of Kent. An excellent source of protein, fiber, and magnesium, they also contain iron, zinc, and lots of vitamin E – 3½oz/100g provide nearly a week's worth. Hazelnuts are very low in salt, so they make a healthy and nutritious snack for anyone suffering from high blood pressure or heart disease. They are good eaten on their own, used in cooking, salads, breakfast cereals, or turned into hazelnut butter.

PINE NUTS

ENERGY PER 3½OZ/100G 688KCAL

These are a great Mediterranean delicacy, being the seeds of several varieties of pine trees. They are a key ingredient of traditional Italian pesto sauce, in which they are ground and combined with garlic, basil, and olive oil. They make a very good addition to salad dishes, and in the Middle East they are frequently mixed in with rice. They are an excellent source of protein although quite high in fats, the vast majority of which are unsaturated. They supply a little fiber but important amounts of magnesium, iron, and zinc and large quantities of vitamin E and potassium.

PISTACHIOS

ENERGY PER 3½OZ/100G 601KCAL

It is almost impossible to buy these delicious and very moreish nuts unsalted, although some health-food stores do stock pistachios that have been soaked in lemon juice and sun-dried without salt – a delicacy for which it is really worth hunting. Salted pistachios contain far too much sodium and, because it is so difficult to eat just a few, they are best not left sitting around as a temptation. Pistachios are a good protein source, contain valuable amounts of fiber, with some quantities of iron, zinc, and vitamin A, as well as significant amounts of vitamin E and potassium. Avoid eating too many as pistachio ice cream – it's simply fat and more fat.

PUMPKIN SEEDS

ENERGY PER 3½OZ/100G 569KCAL

In spite of their 569 calories per 3½oz/100g, these seeds are very nutritious, almost a quarter of their weight being protein. They are also lower in fats

than most other nuts or seeds, a good source of fiber, magnesium, and potassium, an excellent source of iron, phosphorus, and zinc, and contain a little vitamin A. Pumpkin seeds make much healthier nibbles than the usual dish of salted nuts, and because of their high zinc content they are particularly valuable for men. Zinc is essential for the production of fertile sperm, as well as being a specifically protective substance for the prostate gland, so a handful of pumpkin seeds a day is good health insurance.

PEANUTS

ENERGY PER 3½OZ/100G 564KCAL

This is really a legume, rather than a nut, which started life in South America. Peanuts are extremely nutritious whether eaten raw or roasted, but not as healthy when salted. You can eat them straight from the shell and use them in both sweet and savory recipes. They are extremely high in protein, 3½oz/100g providing nearly half a day's requirements, and comparatively low in fat. They are a good source of fiber, magnesium, iron, and zinc, an excellent source of vitamin

D, and a valuable source of iodine. Commercially they are used to make peanut butter (which is better for you without salt) and peanut (groundnut) oil.

CASHEW NUTS

ENERGY PER 3½OZ/100G 573KCAL

Delicious though these are, salted cashew nuts are a real danger food in terms of high blood pressure and heart disease, 3½oz/100g providing more than half your recommended daily intake of salt. Plain roasted cashews, however, are delicious and rich in heart-protecting mono-unsaturated fat. They are also a good source of potassium, nicotinic acid, and folate. Cashew-nut butter, though high in calories, is a very good source of nutrients. These trees also grow in Brazil, and the nuts hang underneath the fruit of the cashew tree – the rain-forest-dwelling Brazilians preferring the fruit to the nuts. Cashews are always sold shelled and roasted, as the roasting destroys the highly caustic oil between the two layers of its shell.

WALNUTS

ENERGY PER 3½OZ/100G 688KCAL

With varieties indigenous to North America and the Middle East, and introduced to Europe by the Romans, walnuts have been a nutritious delicacy for many centuries. Wet walnuts, eaten immediately after picking and before the shells have dried out, are a great delicacy. But whether eaten fresh, chopped into cakes or cookies, pickled or pressed into oil (terrific with salads), walnuts are a healthy food. Low in saturated fat, high in polyunsaturated and mono unsaturated fats, they provide protein, a small quantity of zinc, vitamin E, and useful amounts of folate. Walnuts are also very low in sodium.

Legumes

L egumes – including the whole range of dried and green beans, as well as sprouting beans and soy products – are a marvelous source of soluble fiber and, in combination with wholegrains, can offer an excellent and inexpensive alternative to meat. So whether you enjoy good old baked beans or tofu with rice, you can afford to make more of this nutritious food group.

GREEN BEANS

RUNNER/STRING, FRENCH, BROAD/FAVA

BROAD BEANS:
ENERGY PER 3½OZ/100G 58KCAL

FRENCH BEANS:
ENERGY PER 3½OZ/100G 24KCAL

RUNNER BEANS:
ENERGY PER 3½OZ/100G 22KCAL

❦ *Good for constipation and digestive problems.*

❦ *Useful for skin disorders.*

❦ *Beneficial for male sexual potency.*

❦ *Runner and French beans are best eaten lightly steamed and eaten hot as vegetables, or left to cool and served with a good quality olive-oil dressing in salad.*

❦ *Broad beans can be eaten raw when small and tender, steamed, or puréed with garlic.*

B oth runner and French beans are eaten when the pods are young and before large beans have formed inside them. Nutritionally they are almost identical and contain vitamins A and C, which are not present in dried beans. Like the dried beans, however, both runner and French beans contain some of the chemical group known as lectins. These can cause stomach upsets if eaten raw, so it is always best to cook the pods. Their vitamin A content makes them useful in the treatment of all skin disorders and they contain sufficient fiber to help with constipation.

BROAD BEANS

Broad beans do not contain any lectins and are delicious eaten raw, as long as they are young and no thick skin has yet formed around them. They are a good source of protein and, if served as a purée with olive oil and garlic, nutritious food for those convalescing.

In addition they are an excellent source of pantothenic acid (one of the B-complex vitamins), which is important in maintaining the right level of cholesterol to enable proper functioning of the pituitary, adrenal, and sex hormones. Broad beans have traditionally been advocated as an aid to male potency.

An alternative name for the broad bean is the fava bean, so called after a serious form of anemia known as favism. Up to 35 percent of some Mediterranean populations and 10 percent of Chinese, Indians, and Africans are deficient in a specific enzyme, which means that they could develop this disease after eating broad beans, or even after

inhaling the pollen from the sweetly scented flowers.

● **Beans are rich in potassium, very low in sodium, and have a mild diuretic effect. They are also rich in folate, so they make good food for women who are planning pregnancy.**

HEALTH WARNING

In common with foods such as cheese, pickled herrings, wine, banana skins, and yeast extracts, broad bean pods are on the "forbidden food" list for people who are taking monoamine oxidase inhibitors (MAOIs), a group of antidepressant drugs.

DRIED BEANS

ADUKI BEANS:
ENERGY PER 3½OZ/100G 123KCAL

BAKED BEANS:
ENERGY PER STANDARD PORTION 109KCAL

BLACK-EYED PEAS:
ENERGY PER 3½OZ/100G 116KCAL

BUTTER BEANS:
ENERGY PER STANDARD PORTION 62KCAL

GARBANZO BEANS:
ENERGY PER 3½OZ/100G 42KCAL

KIDNEY BEANS:
ENERGY PER 3½OZ/100G 123KCAL

MUNG BEANS:
ENERGY PER STANDARD PORTION 55KCAL

NAVY BEANS:
ENERGY PER STANDARD PORTION 57KCAL

PINTO BEANS:
ENERGY PER STANDARD PORTION 82KCAL

SOYBEANS:
ENERGY PER 3½OZ/100G 141KCAL

❦ *Good for the heart and circulation – they lower cholesterol levels.*

❦ *Beneficial as cancer-protective foods.*

❦ *Good for healthy bowel function.*

❦ *Ideal food for high blood pressure.*

❦ *Best eaten cooked or canned, but watch out for added salt.*

D ried beans have been a staple survival food since time immemorial. Excluding fruit and vegetables, there are only about 50 species of plant that make a major contribution to people's diet worldwide. Most of them are cereals, but second come the legumes – the family that contains all the beans, or pulses as they are also known. Cereals contain only about one-third of the protein that is found in beans, so in many ways bean cultivation is far more important than cereal cultivation.

Apart from the obviously oily members of the bean family, like the groundnut and the peanut, beans are low in fat and salt, contain no cholesterol, but are a rich source of proteins, starches, vitamins, minerals, and fiber. They have two other great advantages – they are extremely cheap and can be stored for far longer than nearly any other food. They are some of the most nutritious, satisfying, versatile, healthy, and, with a little imagination, delicious foods that money can buy.

KIDNEY BEANS

Legumes

Beans are a great source of the best sort of fiber, the soluble kind – two tablespoons of cooked kidney beans give you four times as much as one slice of wholewheat bread. Many studies in Britain and the US have shown the important benefits, in terms of the heart and circulation, of eating beans. Their soluble fiber combines with cholesterol and helps to eliminate it from the body. Professor Vincent Marks of Surrey University fed baked beans to pigs and found that the cholesterol in their blood went down. He then gave 1lb/450g of baked beans to the whole university rugby team each day – with the same good effect on their cholesterol

At the same time, eating beans as a major source of protein means that you can avoid eating so much animal protein, which is inevitably rich in the most dangerous types of saturated fat. Pound for pound, beans contain nearly as much protein as steak, but at a fraction of the cost. It is interesting to compare the amount of protein in beans with what most people consider to be the main protein foods, like beef and chicken. An average broiled rump steak contains around 27 percent protein, roast chicken 24 percent, beefburgers 20 percent and a hot dog 9.5 percent, whereas beans range from 19 to 26 percent.

None of the beans contains all the essential amino acids that make up protein, but this doesn't matter if they are eaten as part of a mixed diet. Strict vegetarians have to remember to combine beans with one or more of the other main food groups – dairy products, nuts, and seeds or cereals – at the same meal. It is particularly important that vegetarians do eat beans as a source of protein, because they also contain such substantial amounts of folic acid. This is one of the B vitamins that nonvegetarians get from meat, and a lack of it may cause birth defects as well as anemia, so it is essential for women to make sure they get plenty of folic acid.

Beans are an excellent source of the minerals calcium, iron, copper, zinc, phosphorus, potassium, and magnesium. Because of their high potassium and low sodium content, they are an ideal food for anyone with high blood pressure or for people needing a low-sodium diet for other reasons. For diabetics beans comprise an excellent form of starch, as they are easily but slowly digestible and they convert to relatively small amounts of sugar.

Beans are generally cancer-protective, as they contain protease inhibitors, which help prevent the development of cancerous cells.

BLACK-EYED PEAS

But what about wind? There is no getting away from this rather antisocial and embarrassing side effect, but you can reduce the flatulence factor by proper cooking.

Lentils, mung beans, black-eyed peas, and split peas do not need to be soaked, but all other beans should be soaked for at least six to eight hours before cooking. Kidney beans must be boiled hard for ten minutes, strained, then simmered until tender. This destroys a toxin called lectin, which can cause stomach upsets.

If you cook beans with salt, the skins become tougher, less digestible, and more available to gut bacteria, which cause fermentation. Not putting a lid on the saucepan keeps the skins soft and digestible. If you must have salt, add it after cooking.

Canned beans are great for quick, healthy meals, but make sure that you strain and rinse them very well under running water before you eat them, as they are always preserved in brine and it is much healthier to remove the excess salt.

MAKING A WIND BREAK

• The German name for the herb summer savory is the "bean herb" and adding some of this herb when cooking beans reduces flatulence (adding fennel or caraway seeds will have the same effect).

If you happen to have a traditional American cookbook, you will know just how versatile beans are, from the chuck-wagon dishes of the West to the hot, spicy meals of Mexico.

● **Aduki beans are good for fiber, magnesium, potassium, and zinc.**
● **Baked beans, or navy beans, are a rich source of fiber and a reasonable source of iron, selenium, and iodine – but watch out for added salt.**
● **Black-eyed peas are good for fiber and selenium and excellent for folate.**
● **Butter beans are useful for fiber, potassium, and iron.**
● **Garbanzo beans are good for fiber, calcium, iron, and zinc.**
● **Haricot beans are good for fiber and iron.**
● **Kidney beans are excellent for fiber, potassium, and zinc.**
● **Mung beans are slightly lower in starch, but good for folate.**
● **Pinto beans are rich in potassium, fiber, and folate.**

BEAN SPROUTS

ENERGY PER STANDARD PORTION 5KCAL

❧ *Excellent for cancer and cancer protection.*

❧ *Good for anyone with a compromised immune system.*

❧ *Beneficial for all chronic fatigue states.*

❧ *Best eaten fresh and raw, in salads or sandwiches; combine well with other vegetables for stir-frying.*

BEAN SPROUTS

Bean sprouts – not just traditional mung beans, but many other types of sprouted bean too – are a wonderful source of vitamins and minerals. They have been described as "the most live, pure, nutritious food imaginable." They are also cheap and easy to grow – even if you don't own so much as a window box. I always think of sprouted beans, and seeds too for that matter, as "future foods": inside the bean are all the nutrients that are needed to trigger the growth of the next generation of plants.

When you sprout beans, what you produce is an enormously enhanced package of the nutrients already there. In one study, only small amounts of vitamin C were found in wheat grains, but this increased by 600 percent over the next few days.

Legumes

The traditional mung beans of Chinese cooking have been part of the Oriental diet for centuries and a whole folklore of medicinal properties has grown up around them. Early twentieth-century research in the UK suggested that bean sprouts were extremely rich in vitamin C, and how accurate that research proved to be – 3 1/2oz/100g of bean sprouts provide all the vitamin C necessary for two days.

Bean sprouts are very cheap food and, if you grow your own, guaranteed free of pesticides, insecticides, fungicides, and accidental atmospheric pollution. For some people who suffer from systemic *Lupus erythematosus,* however, they may produce an allergic reaction.

You can plant bean sprouts any day of the year (but only buy organic beans and seeds) and harvest them fresh for instant consumption, so that you avoid processing, storage, and packaging. They do not need cooking, cleaning, or preparing; aduki, mung and soybeans, alfalfa, sesame and fenugreek seeds, barley and wheat grains, and garbanzo beans are all easy to sprout. You can buy special sprouting equipment or simply use an empty jam jar with a large opening.

Sort the seeds, removing any obviously damaged ones. Soak them in ample tepid water for 12 hours, then drain. Put them in the jam jar and cover with cheesecloth kept in place with an elastic band. Put your jar in a warm, dark place. Rinse the seeds with fresh water at least a couple of times a day, and make sure you dry them well. You will be ready to harvest this powerhouse of nutrition in two to six days.

● **Bean sprouts are an ideal food for cancer patients and are used extensively at many clinics practising the natural approach to cancer by those anxious to boost their immune defenses, and for all conditions needing first-class nutrition.**

SOYBEANS

SOYBEANS

ENERGY PER 3 1/2OZ/100G 141KCAL

❦ *Useful cancer-protective food.*

❦ *Good for heart and circulatory disease.*

❦ *Best eaten as tofu, soy milk, soy cheese, soy sauce, or miso.*

Soybeans contain the most complete protein and lend themselves to the production of a range of nutritious products (see next section) – tofu (fermented beancurd), soy milk, soy cheese, soy sauce, miso (soybean paste). But it is the anti-cancer activity of the soybean that makes it so valuable. Its antioxidant content protects against free-radical damage, which can lead to heart and circulatory disease as well as to cancer. Japanese studies have shown a risk reduction of around one-third for stomach cancer simply by eating a daily portion of miso soup.

However, soybeans are a common food allergen and may cause indigestion or headaches in some people.

● **Soybeans also offer protection against the hormone-linked cancers – breast, ovarian, and cervical – due to their phyto-estrogen chemicals, known as isoflavones. The most recent of these to be isolated is genistein, which is known to limit the growth of cancer cells.**

BEANCURD

TOFU, SOY MILK, SOY CHEESE, AND MISO

TOFU:

ENERGY PER 3 1/2OZ/100G 261KCAL

❦ *Good for cancer and cancer protection.*

❦ *An excellent substitute for those with a milk allergy.*

❦ *Invaluable for vegetarians.*

❦ *Good for diabetics.*

❦ *Beneficial for heart disease, high blood pressure, and high cholesterol.*

❦ *Good for those with a family history of gallstones.*

❦ *Useful for constipation.*

Although soybeans themselves are not widely consumed as beans, soy foods have been eaten for centuries in Asia. Over the last 20 years there has been a growing interest in the medical value of consuming soy products, which have also found wide acceptance as a substitute for meat for the ever-growing number of vegetarians in the Western world.

In this form they are usually presented as meat-like products – soy sausages, soy chicken nuggets, soy cubes that resemble ground beef and soy. At the height of "mad cow disease" (BSE) in Britain, sales of these products rocketed. Hopefully, some nonvegetarian families who switched to these alternatives may continue to incorporate them into their normal meat-eating diets. There is ample evidence that the combined effects of eating less meat and more soybean reduces the risk of stomach cancer, raised cholesterol, and heart disease.

Miso (fermented soybean paste) is produced from cooked soybeans mixed with rice, barley, or more soybeans that have been fermented. The mixture is left to ferment further, producing a thick, dark, and highly nutritious paste.

Soy milk for drinking is made by soaking, pulverizing, cooking, then filtering the beans. It is further refined and then has sweeteners, oil, flavorings, and salt added. Extra calcium is often added so that soy milk more closely approximates to the nutritional value of cow's milk. It may then be turned into soya cheese. Soy milk and cheese are excellent substitutes for anyone allergic to dairy products.

Tofu (soybean curd) is made from soy milk, which is coagulated, the whey discarded, and the curds pressed to form the tofu. Cubes of tofu can be used in many ways, as it is highly absorbent and takes on the flavor of other ingredients with which it is cooked.

As Japanese food becomes more popular, the use of all these soy derivatives is becoming increasingly common in home cooking. It is worth bearing in mind that the Japanese do not eat tofu in huge quantities, but use small amounts with rice as their staple energy source together with a wide range of vegetables, especially seaweed (kelp). This is important, as it is believed that soy may contain certain substances that reduce the function of the thyroid gland, while seaweed is rich in iodine, which stimulates the thyroid.

● **Overall the benefits of soy and its products are enormous. So, if you haven't tried them already, now is the time to be adventurous.**

TOFU

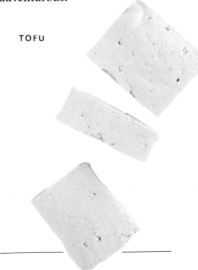

Legumes

PEAS

ENERGY PER 3½OZ/100G 83KCAL

❦ *Good for stress, tension, and the digestion.*

❦ *Best eaten very fresh or frozen.*

Peas are undoubtedly the most popular of all vegetables eaten in Britain, although sadly, from a nutritional point of view, canned peas take the lion's share of the market. Because the sugars in peas start to convert into starches as soon as the pods are picked from the vine, many people prefer the sweeter taste of frozen peas, though nothing matches the wonderful flavor of home-grown peas straight from the garden.

Modern technology allows peas to be frozen almost instantly after harvesting, conserving both their sweetness and their vitamin C content, and they can be kept frozen for up to a year without nutritional losses. Green peas provide an excellent source of thiamin (vitamin B₁), with 5oz/150g supplying more than a day's need. They are also a valuable source of folic acid, supply useful amounts of vitamins A and C, and are a good source of protein, although they need to be combined with cereals like rice, pasta, or bread to make complete protein.

Dried peas and garbanzo beans are also nutritionally valuable but contain no vitamin C. The now popular snow peas are similar in composition to green peas, but by eating the entire pod, the amounts of vitamins A and C that you consume increase considerably.

● **All forms of peas (together with garbanzo beans, which are also a legume and are used in a similar way to peas by different peoples) are excellent sources of dietary fiber.**

HEALTH WARNING

Peas contain quite large amounts of phytate, which can reduce the bio-availability of minerals like iron, calcium, and zinc. Don't make peas the only green vegetable you ever eat.

FAST FOOD AID

• *A large bag of frozen peas makes the cheapest reusable ice pack for the treatment of strains, sprains, bruises, frozen shoulder, tennis elbow, etc. Always put a thin layer of cloth between your skin and the frozen peas. Make sure you mark the peas in indelible ink so that they don't get eaten by mistake.*

PEAS IN PODS

PEAS

LENTILS

ENERGY PER STANDARD PORTION 41KCAL

❦ *Useful for vegetarians and diabetics.*

❦ *Good for reducing cholesterol, stress, and nervous exhaustion.*

❦ *Best eaten cooked on their own or combined with oil, onion, and spices, to make traditional Indian dahl.*

Lentils have been used as food by man since prehistory – evidence of them having been found in excavated prehistoric sites in Switzerland. Like all legumes, lentils supply abundant amounts of protein and starch and are a good source of the B vitamins. They also contain significant amounts of iron, zinc, and calcium. The downside is their phytic acid content, which makes it more difficult to absorb these minerals. Eating a good source of vitamin C together with lentils increases the amount of iron absorbed.

Although lentils are rich in protein, this protein does not contain all of the essential amino acids. Combining lentils with cereals like rice or whole-grain bread provides the body with complete protein – and vegetarian Indians always eat rice or bread as an accompaniment to their dahl.

The most usual forms of lentils are red, yellow, green, or brown and there is little nutritional difference between them. Unique among legumes, lentils do not need to be soaked before cooking.

● **Their high fiber content makes lentils an excellent protector against bowel cancer, and their abundant supply of B vitamins, especially niacin, makes them the perfect food for anyone who is suffering from excessive stress or severe mental exhaustion.**

HEALTH WARNING

Lentils are high in the group of organic compounds known as purines, which can cause uric acid salts to be deposited in the joints, so they are best avoided by those with gout (*see p.180*).

GREEN AND RED LENTILS

Meat

Despite the bad press received by the meat industry in recent years, meat (whether beef, pork, lamb, or offal) remains an excellent source of protein, B vitamins, and easily absorbed iron and zinc. If raised and cooked correctly and eaten occasionally or in small amounts, there is no reason why meat should not form part of a nutritious mixed diet.

T-BONE STEAK

BEEF

CORNED BEEF:
ENERGY PER 3½OZ/100G 217KCAL
STEWED GROUND:
ENERGY PER 3½OZ/100G 229KCAL
BROILED, LEAN RUMP STEAK:
ENERGY PER 3½OZ/100G 168KCAL

❈ Contains a broad variety of essential nutrients, especially iron and zinc.

❈ Good for anemia, stress, and other nervous disorders.

Beef has traditionally been one of the most highly sought of all meats. Defined by the *Oxford English Dictionary* as the flesh of ox, bull, or cow, it gets its name from the Latin *bos, bovis*. In early English history beef was reserved for the ruling Normans and it was not available to the Anglo-Saxons until after the thirteenth century.

Throughout the world some 237 million head of beef and calves and 11 million head of buffalo are produced annually, and beef is, without doubt, the universal meat.

There is no denying its nutritional benefit: it supplies most nutritional needs apart from fiber, although some constituents like calcium, vitamin C, and folate are present only in small amounts. Beef is a good source of trace elements such as iodine, manganese, zinc, cobalt, selenium, nickel, chromium, molybdenum, fluorine, vanadium, and silicon. The presence of these is dependent on the soil on which the animals graze, or on the components of manufactured feed.

In recent years the growing trend toward vegetarianism, and concerns about the nutritional effects of eating beef, have led to white meats replacing beef, to a certain extent, as the major source of animal protein in both America and Great Britain. All but the very leanest cuts of beef can contain up to 20 percent by weight of saturated fat and there is a certainly growing awareness of the connection between high levels of meat consumption and raised blood cholesterol levels. Furthermore, the link between cancer of the large bowel (colon) and copious amounts of red meat in the diet is good reason to make the consumption of beef an occasional treat, rather than a daily occurrence.

The nutritional composition of different sorts of beef varies widely. For example, 3½oz/100g of corned beef contains 950mg of sodium, compared with 320mg in stewed ground and only 56mg in broiled, lean rump steak. The total fat in corned beef is 12.1g, in ground beef 15.2g, but in steak only a meager 6g.

The way beef is cooked is an important factor in nutritional terms. Trimming excessive visible fat before cooking reduces the total fat in the finished dish. Joints should be roasted on a trivet, so that the fat drips into the pan below. Steaks and chops should be cooked in the same way. Overcooking meat on the barbecue leads to the greatest production of carcinogens, the highest levels of all being found in combination with the highest fat content. Take especial care with lower-cost sausages and burgers, which contain more fat.

The undercooked burger can also harbor harmful bacteria. One strain, *E. coli* 0157:H7, VTEC, can

E. COLI

• E. coli *0157:H7, VTEC is believed to affect more than 20,000 Americans each year and it is estimated that some die, or are permanently affected, as a result. Over 500 people became ill throughout California, Idaho, Nevada, and Washington State in 1993 and several of the affected children died as the result of eating contaminated burgers. But it is not just in the US that this virulent bacterium has left its mark. A major outbreak in Scotland in 1996, followed by a second in early 1997, left at least 20 people dead and many seriously ill.*

BSE

• BSE (otherwise known as "mad cow disease," but properly called bovine spongiform encephalopathy) is a slow, and inevitably fatal, illness that affects cattle, usually between the ages of three and five. It is believed that the current UK outbreak started because cattle were fed processed offal (organ meats) from sheep suffering from a similar illness called scrapie. It is also thought that BSE is not passed on by eating the meat, but only through infected offal, especially the brain and spinal cord, though this has not been proven. The nearest human disease that also affects the central nervous system is Creutzfeldt-Jakob disease (CJD). It is known that CJD, which kills around 50 people a year in the UK, can take up to 20 years to develop and, despite assurances that it is not possible for humans to catch BSE, experts such as Professor Richard Lacey are not convinced.

• The British government insists that the recent outbreak of BSE (1996) is under control and actually declining, but neighboring European countries are not so sure. The European Parliament recently commissioned a report on BSE, which is highly critical and represents an indictment of intensive farming. There have since been two more deaths in the dairy industry and a significant increase in the number of young people with CJD. The government is slaughtering infected cattle and their calves, and Europe has banned the import of all British beef and live animals until further notice. As a result British cattle farmers are going bankrupt every week.

GELATIN

Meat

get into meat at the time of slaughtering. When infected meat is ground, the bacteria are distributed throughout the finished product and if the resulting burger is rare, some of the bacteria may survive.

There have been a number of scares regarding beef in recent years, the most alarming being BSE (see box opposite). Rather more insidious is the risk of contamination of beef by the illegal use of chemicals, and although antibiotics have long been banned as an animal-feed additive, there are now signs that illegal hormones are being used on a wide scale all over Europe.

Growth hormones were banned by the EU in 1988 because of the possible risk to humans consuming treated meat. In the US some laboratory-produced "natural" hormones are allowed as growth promoters, but although their use is controlled, it is virtually impossible to tell whether animals have been given extra doses because the hormones are undetectable.

There is a link between eating large amounts of red meat and higher rates of both colon and prostate cancer, which are estimated to have killed 27,800 and 38,000 American men respectively in 1994, while 28,200 American women died from colon and rectal cancer.

• **In small quantities beef is a perfectly acceptable part of a normal mixed diet, although general nutritional advice, both from the World Health Organization (WHO) and the Harvard School of Public Health, suggests that it should only be eaten a few times a month.**

GELATIN

ENERGY PER STANDARD PORTION 10KCAL

Gelatin is the result of prolonged boiling of animal skin, tendons, and ligaments. All these are largely made up of a substance called collagen – so beloved of the cosmetics industry – which is mostly protein. But it is a form of protein that is very difficult for the human system to digest. The gelatin that is produced by boiling is more easily digested but is of only limited nutritional value.

It is gelatin that makes a stew thick and "hearty," and in the presence of other forms of protein, like beans, split peas, barley, or lentils, gelatin can provide reasonable protein. The main commercial use for it is as a setting agent in many preprepared products such as trifles, mousses, and similar desserts (vegetarians beware!), and as the main ingredient of jellies and aspic. Because it is so cheap to produce, more gelatin is used by the food industry than any other form of setting agent.

Calf's-foot jelly was a traditional Victorian sickroom food made by prolonged boiling of a calf's foot. Unfortunately all meat jellies are very easily contaminated by bacteria, so they need to be handled and kept with great care.

• **Gelatin is the subject of two old wives' tales: eating cubes of raw jelly does not give you worms, nor does it strengthen your fingernails.**

VEAL

ENERGY PER 3½OZ/100G 109KCAL

❦ *Good for high-protein, low-fat diets.*

❦ *Best eaten roast or pan-fried, in minimal quantities of vegetable oil.*

Veal has become a highly controversial meat in recent years, mainly due to the way in which calves are reared and transported. They are taken from their mothers early and kept immobile in crates, then fed on milk to produce white flesh. Particularly distressing is the practice of shipping live calves in trucks to Europe without adequate provision for their comfort, feeding, and general well-being.

Happily, rearing calves in this way is now illegal in the UK, though still commonplace in much of Europe. For those without qualms about eating three-month-old baby cattle, veal does provide a good source of nutrients. It contains less than half the fat and fewer calories than lean beef, though it is an excellent source of protein, zinc, potassium, and B vitamins. Milk-fed veal supplies only half the iron present in ordinary beef, though this is not the case in calves that have been naturally reared on their mothers' milk and allowed to graze normally. This produces much darker meat, which is only slightly less rich in iron than mature beef.

Hugely popular in Italy, Holland, and most of northern Europe, veal is commonly served coated with egg and bread crumbs, then fried, which increases its fat content dramatically.

• **Vegetarian or not, veal is one meat that we can all live happily and healthily without.**

RACK OF LAMB

LAMB

ENERGY PER 3½OZ/100G 156KCAL

❦ *Good for anemia, those on high-protein diets, and for loss of appetite.*

❦ *Best eaten broiled, roasted on a rack or, best of all, dry-roasted in the Greek/Middle Eastern style (see below).*

Like all meat, lamb is an excellent source of protein, easily absorbed iron and zinc and B vitamins. Of all the farmed animals, lamb is least likely to be contaminated with antibiotic residues or to have been fed on reconstituted animal protein.

The amount of fat that you get with your lamb depends on the cut, how it is cooked, and what you actually eat of it. Ideally, most of the fat should be removed before cooking and any that is left on the meat should be avoided.

FAT CONTENT

Broiled chops
Eaten without fat: 12.3g fat/3½oz
Eaten with fat: 29g fat/3½oz

Roast leg
Eaten without fat: 8.1g fat/3½oz
Eaten with fat: 18g fat/3½oz

Roast shoulder
Eaten without fat: 11.2g fat/3½oz
Eaten with fat: 26g fat/3½oz

To dry-roast lamb, seal the meat all over in hot oil and remove from the pan. Sweat garlic, bay leaves, peppercorns, and rosemary together in a pan. Add a little red wine and return the lamb to the pan. Cover, and cook slowly, checking the fluid level regularly. When almost done, remove the lid and turn up the heat. Serve with green lentils.

• **New-season spring lamb is always the most tender and has the lowest fat content, but modern breeds are all generally lower in fat.**

Meat

PORK

ENERGY PER 3½OZ/100G 122KCAL

☙ *Good for anemia, stress, and other nervous disorders.*

☙ *Useful for PMS and male fertility.*

☙ *Best eaten thoroughly cooked.*

Pigs have been domesticated in China for almost 7,000 years and were first introduced to North America by Columbus, who transported them from the Canary Islands in 1493. Throughout the seventeenth century colonists from Britain took their own livestock with them and it was not long before a thriving industry grew up centered around pig production – there was a large slaughtering plant at Cincinnati by the early 1800s, and locals called the city Porkopolis.

There is a popular misconception that pork is a "fatty" meat, whereas in fact modern breeds produce meat that contains less fat than beef or lamb, and very little more than chicken if eaten without skin. Naturally the type of cut and the way it is cooked can make an enormous difference. The total fat in 3½oz/100g of lean broiled chops is ¼oz/10.7g, in lean roast leg only 6.9g and in broiled belly of pork a massive 1¼oz/34.8g. The amount of cholesterol is the same for all three cuts, 110mg – one-third of the total daily cholesterol intake that is currently recommended by the American Heart Association.

PORK

There is no doubt that pork is an extremely good source of nutrients, containing large amounts of thiamin (B₁), niacin, riboflavin (B₂) and zinc. It is also a reasonably good source of vitamin B₆, phosphorus, and iron, the latter being haem iron, which is much more easily absorbed and used by the body.

The abundance of B vitamins makes pork a good food for all stress and nervous problems, while the B₆ and zinc certainly help with PMS and the zinc is particularly useful for the maintenance of healthy sperm. The beneficial levels of iron are useful in the prevention and treatment of anemia, and in addition to all this pork is an excellent source of complete protein – a 3½oz/100g serving of lean pork providing more than half the daily requirement.

Although tapeworm is now rare in pork produced in Britain and the US, it is still quite common in less developed countries, and for this reason pork should always be thoroughly cooked, with no traces of pink in the middle and with clear running juices when it is cut or pierced. Delicious though crackling is, it is nothing more than crispy fat and it is far healthier to remove as much fat as possible before cooking any cut of pork.

Some of the chemicals used in producing ham and bacon are known to be carcinogenic if consumed in excess, particularly the nitrites, which not only prevent bacteria infection but also maintain the red/pink color of ham and bacon. Both products are also extremely high in salt, and for this reason should be eaten sparingly. They are best avoided by anyone with high blood pressure.

● **Some of the by-products of pork are interesting medically, especially the hormones such as pig insulin and heparin; the heart valves, which are used as replacements in human surgery; and even the pig's skin, which can be used in the treatment of severe burns.**

OFFAL

ORGAN MEATS

LAMB, OX, AND PIG KIDNEYS:
ENERGY PER 3½OZ/100G 86–91KCAL
CALF, CHICKEN, LAMB, AND OX LIVER:
ENERGY PER 3½OZ/100G 92–155KCAL

☙ *Good for anemia, skin, and eye problems (especially poor night vision).*

☙ *Beneficial for general fatigue, male fertility and potency.*

☙ *Best eaten in stews or casseroles (lamb, ox, or pig liver), or lightly sautéed (calf liver, chicken liver, or kidneys).*

Some people are a bit squeamish when it comes to eating offal, which are known in the US as organ meats. On the whole this is a pity, because they are delicious as well as being extremely rich sources of some nutrients. They can be high in cholesterol and many people confuse health problems associated with cholesterol-rich foods with blood cholesterol levels *(see Fish on p.111)*. But unless you have very high cholesterol levels it is perfectly safe to enjoy both liver and kidneys from time to time.

Kidneys are extremely rich sources of vitamin B₁₂ – 3½oz/100g supplies 40 times more than you need for a day. They also have a high content of biotin, folic acid, and a significant amount of vitamin C. Liver is a major source of easily absorbed iron (essential for blood formation) and zinc (vital for healthy sperm and potency). A lack of zinc is one of the common causes of exhaustion and poor appetite.

Liver also contains a huge amount of vitamin A, lots of the B vitamins (especially B₁₂), and significant amounts of vitamin C. Ox liver contains the most B₁₂ and at one time was the medical treatment for

LIVER

pernicious anemia. There are variations of nutrients between calf, chicken, lamb, ox, and pig livers, but they are all rich in the vitamin A, which is so essential for healthy skin and good night vision. Vitamin A is fat-soluble and is stored in the liver, not excreted by the body.

The ancient Persian writings in the *Ebers Papyrus*, the oldest surviving prescription book, have a recipe for night blindness, which involves roasting an ox liver, grinding it to a paste, and giving it to the patient who is blind at night. This would certainly have been a huge success, as night blindness is caused by deficiency of vitamin A, though I am sure the ancient Persians were unaware of this.

● **Polar bear liver is known to be dangerously poisonous because it contains such enormous amounts of vitamin A that it is toxic to humans.**

KIDNEYS

HEALTH WARNING

Pregnant women, or those attempting to get pregnant, should not eat liver, liver pâté, or liver sausage. Although sufficient vitamin A is essential for the proper development of a baby, excessive amounts of liver, or liver products, eaten by a mother during pregnancy can cause serious birth defects.

Poultry

CHICKEN, DUCK, GOOSE, TURKEY

*D*omestic fowl or poultry – whether the inexpensive forms of chicken and turkey or the more luxury duck and goose – are all excellent sources of protein, vitamins, and minerals. While chicken in particular requires careful cooking, all poultry offers a succulent and nutritious feast.

DUCK

- *Good for convalescence and anemia.*
- *Helpful for building general resistance.*
- *Beneficial for pregnancy (free-range and organic poultry only).*
- *Good for PMS.*
- *Best eaten broiled, roast, barbecued, as chicken and turkey burgers or kebabs – hot or cold, all without skin; excellent as soup.*

CHICKEN

ENERGY PER 3½OZ/100G 153KCAL

The domestic chicken, a native of northern India, is a direct descendant of the wild jungle fowl and was certainly being eaten by the ancient Egyptians by the fourteenth century BC. Until the advent of intensively reared poultry, chicken and turkey were luxury meats. Chicken was normally reserved for special occasions and turkey for Christmas and Thanksgiving. They are now so cheap that they are everyday foods for most people, but the price we pay is lack of flavor and texture, a higher saturated fat content, and the risk of unwanted chemical residues such as antibiotics and growth-promoting hormones. It is far better therefore to spend more money on free-range organic poultry and to eat it less frequently.

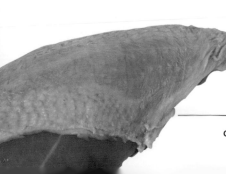

Chicken meat contains far less fat than other red meats and, as most of this is contained in the skin, it is easily removed. As well as protein, chicken provides easily absorbed iron and zinc (twice as much in the dark meat as in the white). This makes it an excellent food during pregnancy and beneficial as a blood- and resistance-builder.

Roast chicken should have all the fat removed from inside the body cavity. It should then be roasted on a rack so that all the fat drips into the bottom of the pan – but don't cook the potatoes there and don't eat the skin.

- **Chicken breast contains double the dark meat's quantity of vitamin B6, so it is useful to help women overcome the symptoms of PMS.**

DUCK

ENERGY PER STANDARD PORTION 361KCAL

This is also an excellent source of protein, iron, zinc, and nearly all the B vitamins. Delicious though the crispy skin is, you will get 29g of fat if you eat 3½oz/100g of meat and skin, but only 9.7g if you stick to the meat. It is even more important to cook duck on a rack, and it helps to prick the skin all over with a sharp fork or skewer, so the fat layer under the duck's skin can trickle out as it melts.

- **Served with traditional apple sauce, duck not only tastes wonderful, but the pectins in the apple help the body to eliminate much of the cholesterol eaten with the duck.**

GOOSE

ENERGY PER 3½OZ/100G 319KCAl

The Romans regarded geese as sacred and thought goose liver a great delicacy, and the modern French *foie gras* is considered by chefs and gourmets to be one of the world's most highly prized foods, although the geese are force-fed in order to produce this fatty, degenerate, and vastly enlarged liver.

Goose is enormously fatty, containing almost as much fat as protein, although this is easily reduced by placing the bird on a rack over a large pan of water, then covering the bird in foil, and tucking the edges of the foil inside the pan. Heat on top of the stove until the water boils, then leave the goose to steam for half an hour. Discard the fat-laden water, then roast the goose on the rack as normal, deducting half an hour from the cooking time. When cooked, don't eat the skin.

- **Goose is tremendously rich in iron and zinc, a good source of phosphorus and potassium, and 3½oz/100g provides more than a day's recommended dose of vitamin B12.**

TURKEY

ENERGY PER 3½OZ/100G 319KCAL

Unlike other poultry, turkey is extremely low in fat, containing only 2.7g per 3½oz/100g. It is rich in protein and supplies easily absorbed iron and zinc (more in the dark meat than in the white). Its low fat content tends to make it a dry, insipid bird unless great care is taken when cooking it. Generally speaking, the larger the bird, the less it dries out and the better the flavor. You can even enjoy some of the skin

as a crispy treat. Leftover turkey is delicious cold and can also be used in curries and hashes.

All poultry can be used to make soup, though it is important to remove as much fat as possible, either by skimming, blotting with absorbent paper, or refrigerating overnight so that the hardened fat can be removed in the morning. The traditional "Jewish penicillin," so beloved of European and American Jewish mothers, is in fact a piece of folklore with more than anecdotal value. Researchers have found that a special sulfur compound in chicken soup really does protect against throat and chest infections.

- **The protein content of poultry soup is very easily absorbed, making it perfect invalid food, and it may also be beneficial for a poor immune system, chronic fatigue, and sexual dysfunction.**

HEALTH WARNING

The vast majority of the intensively reared British chicken flock is infected with the *Salmonella* bacterium. While this does not present a health hazard when chicken is properly cooked, undercooked chicken is an extremely common cause of food poisoning (*see p.176*). When cooking chicken at home, make sure that frozen birds are thoroughly defrosted first, for 24 hours in a refrigerator. If roasting, ensure that the oven is hot before placing the bird inside. Prick the thickest part of the chicken thigh to check that the juices run clear before serving. If barbecuing, it is best to part-cook the chicken first before finishing it on the barbecue. Any chicken or turkey that is still pink when you cut it, or whose juices still appear blood-stained is not sufficiently cooked.

Game and game birds

As we approach the twenty-first century, there is a growing interest in the consumption of game — both feathered and furred. The deep full flavors of a crisply roasted pheasant, a venison hotpot, a wild turkey, a wood pigeon, or a game pie exemplify the greatest traditions of English and American cookery.

❦ *Unlikely to contain growth hormones or antibiotic residues, unless intensively farmed.*

❦ *Extremely low in saturated fat.*

❦ *A super source of proteins.*

❦ *An excellent source of iron and B vitamins.*

Most game is high in protein and low in fat compared to other meats: 3½oz/100g of venison has 2–3g of fat, compared with 15g in roast beef; 4g in rabbit, compared with 15g in shoulder of pork; 5g in pheasant, compared with 9g in chicken. Fat-watchers will be astounded to learn that the king of game birds, the British red grouse, contains only 0.9g of fat per 3½oz/100g.

Although there has always been a demand for game in Britain, it is surprising that the increasing use of game in the US should be thought of as a "new trend," because game probably has the longest tradition in the whole American food culture. After decades of bland burgers, tasteless factory-farmed chicken, and convenience meals, the tide is turning. As the mounting toll of heart disease makes the American public increasingly cholesterol-conscious, questions of diet and health are leading them back to their culinary traditions.

According to John Ash and Sid Goldstein in their wonderful book, *American Game Cooking*, the farmed game of America is the perfect compromise. The animals range freely over huge areas without restraint, are raised without hormones, antibiotics, or steroids, and are inspected for quality, health, and lack of parasites.

Their all-year-round availability means that they are to be found constantly on supermarket shelves. Much of the game sold in Britain is wild, but some game animals, such as venison, are now being farmed in the UK, too.

The best way to cook all young game birds is to roast them with a slice of bacon over the breast. A hot oven gives the bird a crispy brown skin, but game should never be overcooked. Older game birds are best served as a casserole.

● **Game birds also provide considerably more potassium, calcium, phosphorus, iron, thiamin, vitamins B$_6$ and B$_{12}$, and folate than other meats.**

GROUSE

ENERGY PER 3½OZ/100G 59KCAL

The British red grouse is regarded as the ultimate game bird. Almost impossible to rear commercially, it is highly prized by shooters on the Scottish grouse moors and by the diners in restaurants throughout Britain, which compete to offer the first grouse of the season. Allow one bird per person.

HEALTH WARNING

Although much of the game available in Europe is wild and therefore free of artificial growth hormones, pesticides, and antibiotics, those preparing game must be aware that, in some cases, the lead shot might still be present. Take utmost care to remove the pellets before cooking.

PHEASANT

QUAIL

ENERGY PER 3½OZ/100G 100KCAL

One of the smallest and most delicately flavored of game birds, quail are mostly raised, rather than shot. Allow two per person and roast them with herbs, broil, or even barbecue them. The only way to eat quail is by using your fingers.

PARTRIDGE

ENERGY PER 3½OZ/100G 127KCAL

Succulent and strongly flavored, wild partridges have much less fat than farmed, so they need extra lard and frequent basting. Partridge and grouse both make wonderfully delicious casseroles. Allow one average bird per person.

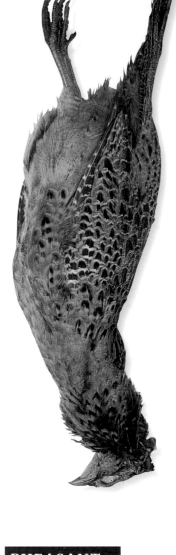

PHEASANT

ENERGY PER 3½OZ/100G 114KCAL

Shot pheasant is usually allowed to hang for several days, producing a stronger, gamey flavor. Supermarket birds are normally not hung, so they are not so gamey. An average pheasant serves two people.

QUAIL

Game and game birds

PIGEON

ENERGY PER 3½OZ/100G 88KCAL

The English wood pigeon is a very lean bird, and only wild ones are available. They roast well, but the best part is the breast, which can often be found smoked and thinly sliced. The American equivalent, squab, is commercially raised and contains a small amount of fat.

● **Squab is slightly larger than the wild pigeon and should be roasted quickly and never overcooked. It is delicious de-boned and either sautéed or broiled with fresh thyme.**

PIGEON

VENISON

RABBIT

ENERGY PER 3½OZ/100G 68KCAL

Farmed or wild, rabbit makes a delicious and delicately flavored dish – high in protein, low in fat, and, in terms of calories/weight ratio, it contains the fewest calories of all. Joints of rabbit can be broiled or sautéed, but rabbit stew is the traditional and best method of cooking. The wild hare is more difficult to come by, although its numbers have increased in recent years. The jackrabbit, as it is called in the US, is fine when marinated and roasted while young, but otherwise this animal can be a bit on the tough side and hard to chew, so for this reason is best served in a stew.

● **To compensate for the rabbit's lack of many nutrients, apart from protein, use plenty of root vegetables in the stew and serve with a large salad.**

VENISON

ENERGY PER 3½OZ/100G 165KCAL

Though usually farmed rather than wild, venison is now making a comeback. When properly dressed and hung, the flavors and texture are superb. Delivering only one-third of the calories and half the fat of beef, and considerably less than chicken, venison is a healthy option. Prime cuts should be cooked at a very hot temperature and for just enough time to be medium-rare. Otherwise, marinate the venison before cooking. Red wine, oil, and herbs are common marinades in Europe and the UK, while buttermilk is a favorite in the US.

● **English venison hotpot with vegetables and the American hunter's campfire recipe cooked in coffee and cider vinegar are both wonderful.**

WILD TURKEY

ENERGY PER 3½OZ/100G 114KCAL

The traditional wild turkey of North America bears little resemblance to the white-fleshed variety that is eaten on Christmas Day and Thanksgiving. Wild turkey has a wonderful flavor, a firm texture, and very little fat, as well as being rich in protein, iron, and zinc. You can roast your wild bird in the same way as its domestic cousin.

● **John Ash and Sid Goldstein have several traditional recipes in their cookbook and my favorite combines the American wild turkey with plenty of onions, spices, chilis, and that other great Mexican contribution to food – chocolate – resulting in Turkey Molé.**

If you are prepared to be a bit more adventurous, try adding wild boar to your culinary repertoire. Or for more exotic flavors still, how about scallopini of alligator or grilled rattlesnake? Thanks to the ever-growing interest in game, herds of buffalo are once more roaming the prairies of America, and 3½oz/100g of buffalo tenderloin provides 36g of protein – far more than beef – and only 1g of fat, compared with 15g in beef.

RABBIT

Fish and shellfish

*A*lthough we have moved on a long way from the days of hunter-gathering, fish is the one component of our diet that is still largely hunted. Though some fish, such as salmon and trout, are now farmed, the majority of fish landed on our shores have been hunted and caught.

❦ *Good for everyone (apart from those allergic to fish and shellfish, and gout sufferers – see health warning opposite).*

❦ *Low in saturated fat, high in protein.*

❦ *There are essential fatty acids in oily fish and a powerhouse of vitamins and minerals not easily obtained from other food sources.*

❦ *Good for weight control.*

❦ *Oily fish are beneficial for rheumatism, osteoarthritis, rheumatoid arthritis, eczema, psoriasis, cyclic breast pain, and most inflammatory diseases.*

❦ *Useful for heart protection.*

Since the beginning of the 1960s the fish-processing industry has accounted for a considerable proportion of the fish that we eat, much of it in the form of fish fingers, ready-prepared supermarket dishes, and canned fish. Sadly, although Britain is surrounded by waters containing some of the finest fish in the world, fish consumption is still extremely low. The traditional fishvendor has all but died out, although more and more supermarkets are now stocking fresh fish (even though much of it has been previously frozen) and are gradually introducing new generations of consumers to the glories of eating different varieties.

It appears that many home cooks are afraid of fish, being unsure how to prepare and cook it and how long it will keep. Recent generations have not grown up with their mothers buying fresh fish, which is indeed highly perishable (especially the oily fish). But common sense is all that is needed and good health dictates that we should be eating far

more fish than we do. The average Briton consumes around 42lb/19kg per person per year, not much compared with the Japanese, who eat their way through a vast 154lb/70kg per person per year.

Stories of marine pollution (and occasionally of chemical pollution of rivers) and the consequent contamination of fish may have put some people off. And contamination with heavy metals has been a problem in some parts of the world for very long-lived fish like tuna. But all canned tuna is now routinely monitored for mercury contamination. Pollution of shellfish with sewage has been another major concern, but environmental agencies and legislation now exert stringent controls over the untreated sewage that is released into the sea.

In Victorian times the average Londoner consumed 15½lb/7kg of herrings a year and an average of four oysters a week, these being foods for the poor, just like the cockles and whelks that they also ate in huge quantities. But by the start of the twentieth century most Britons preferred the flavor of white fish, and the bone disease, rickets, consequently became a major scourge, though Jewish children in London's East End seldom got this crippling disease – their immigrant parents having brought their taste for pickled, salted, and fresh herrings with them from Eastern Europe.

● **Fish remain an exceptional source of protein and minerals, and sea fish are particularly valuable for their high iodine content. B vitamins are found in all types of fish, and oily fish are valuable sources of vitamins A, D, and E, together with the omega-3 essential fatty acids.**

WHITE FISH

COD (WHITE FISH):
ENERGY PER 7OZ/200G 160KCAL

White fish are all very similar from a nutritional standpoint, whether they are sea fish – like cod, haddock, whiting, monkfish, sea bream, catfish, red and grey mullet, snappers, plaice, sole, and halibut – or freshwater fish, like pike, perch, bream, and carp. They contain virtually no fat, few calories, and plenty of protein. They all contain B vitamins but little iron, and although halibut (which is slightly oily) may contribute a little vitamin A, white fish do not in general supply fat-soluble vitamins. Cod and halibut liver are very rich in vitamins A, D, and E, but these are used solely for the production of oil. White fish roe is an excellent source of B vitamins and as good a source of iron as some meat. Fish roe contains cholesterol, so it may pose a health risk for people with genetic fat-metabolism disorders or high blood-cholesterol. ● **There is no disputing the health benefits of consuming less red meat, and what better substitute could there be than lots more fish? The World Health Organization's food pyramid advises eating fish a few times each week.**

OILY FISH

HERRING (OILY FISH):
ENERGY PER STANDARD PORTION 171KCAL
TUNA (CANNED):
ENERGY PER STANDARD PORTION 85KCAL

Mackerel, salmon, trout, tuna, herrings, anchovy, sardine, whitebait, sprats, and eels are now known to contain high levels of eicosapen-tanoeic acid, one of a group of fatty acids belonging to the omega-3 family, which are essential to healthy cell function. A number of studies have demonstrated their value in such diverse conditions as

atherosclerosis, arthritis and rheumatoid arthritis, cyclic breast pain, and skin diseases like eczema and psoriasis.

As well as being exceptionally rich in vitamin D, small oily fish – like sprats, whitebait, and canned sardines – are excellent sources of calcium. Canned tuna, however, contains less than half the vitamin D of fresh tuna, the rest being lost during the processing. As well as the fat-soluble vitamins, oily fish provide energy and minerals – sprats supply

CASANOVA'S SECRET

• *What did Casanova know that you don't? To the poet, music may be "the food of love," but in reality it is oysters. Casanova, the greatest lover of all time, used to eat 70 a day, which he claimed were the reason for his super-stud performance. Oysters have been a favorite aphrodisiac food for centuries, dating right back to Roman times. What the Romans did not know, as they ate vast quantities of native Colchester oysters – the best in the world – was that they contained substantial quantities of zinc, an essential mineral for the production of sperm and the maintenance of male potency. A dozen of these magnificent molluscs provide more zinc than you require for a whole week.*

the same quantity of iron, weight for weight, as beef; sardines the same as lamb; and 3½oz/100g of broiled fresh herring or canned salmon, or a broiled bloater, supplies more than a week's worth of vitamin D.

When buying fish canned in oil, avoid those marked "vegetable oil." Instead, choose fish canned in olive, sunflower, or soybean oil. Drain off all surplus oil before consumption.

• **Oily fish are often smoked to preserve them. Eating large amounts of smoked food has been linked to a higher incidence of cancer, so these should be regarded as occasional treats.**

SHELLFISH

OYSTERS (MOLLUSCS):
ENERGY PER STANDARD PORTION 78KCAL

SHRIMP (CRUSTACEANS):
ENERGY PER STANDARD PORTION 59KCAL

These can be divided conveniently into crustaceans – crabs, lobsters, shrimp, crayfish, langoustine – and molluscs – mussels, oysters, cockles, whelks, winkles, clams, and scallops. All shellfish contain the same amount of protein and other nutrients as white fish, although they are much saltier. The vitamin and mineral content of crustaceans is the same as that of white fish, while molluscs contain far more iron and vitamin A. They are also good sources of zinc, especially oysters, cockles, whelks, and winkles.

There has been a lot of controversy about the high cholesterol content of some shellfish, but most experts now agree that this is a hazard only for those suffering from genetic lipid-metabolism diseases, which cause their bodies to produce excessive quantities of cholesterol. A regular intake of shellfish has been shown to reduce the level of the LDL fats that are most dangerous to the heart (*see Fats and oils, p. 132*). Shellfish also contain small amounts of the essential omega-3 fatty acids – though nowhere near as much as oily fish – which are cardio-protective.

• **Another good reason for eating shellfish is their high selenium content, an important mineral that can be deficient in the US diet. Selenium deficiency has been closely linked with heart disease and a greater risk of cancer of the esophagus and prostate.**

111

Bread

Good bread really is "the staff of life" but, in spite of all the evidence to the contrary, most people still believe that bread is fattening. It is one of the first foods to be cut out of a slimming diet. In fact, bread is a vital part of a healthy, balanced diet, and can be an aid to weight loss. "How?" I hear you shouting. "We've always been told to cut down on starch if we want to lose weight."

WHOLE WHEAT BREAD

BROWN BREAD:
ENERGY PER STANDARD PORTION 78KCAL

WHITE BREAD:
ENERGY PER STANDARD PORTION 85KCAL

WHOLE WHEAT BREAD:
ENERGY PER STANDARD PORTION 77KCAL

* *Good for weight loss.*

* *A useful source of healthy calories for the physically active.*

* *Beneficial for constipation, diverticulitis, and hemorrhoids.*

* *Good for stress.*

* *Best eaten as whole wheat bread – either fresh or toasted.*

* *Combines well with almost anything.*

The first thing to understand is the difference between the complex and refined carbohydrates. Refined carbohydrates are those such as sugars and highly processed starches which provide large quantities of empty calories. Complex carbohydrates are found in whole grain cereals such as brown rice, pasta, oats, barley, and whole grain wheat. These supply many other essential nutrients, and are also a rich source of vital fiber.

All of the "good" complex carbohydrates help to fill you up, and displace the high-fat, high-sugar foods that are every slimmer's enemy. So, is it better to eat whole wheat or white bread? Is white bread actually bad for you? And how much bread should you eat anyway?

The answers are quite simple. Whole wheat bread is better for you. White bread is not in itself bad for

---

FAST FOOD AID

• *A bread poultice is the best way to draw an erupting boil. Put some slices of bread in a strainer and pour boiling water over them. Use a wooden spoon to stir the bread around until it forms a moist hot ball. Turn this out into a clean cloth and squeeze out the surplus moisture. When cool enough for comfort, apply to the affected area and leave until it gets cold. Repeat the process until the boil comes to a head and bursts. Keep it covered with a sterile dressing until the skin has healed.*

---

you, but not eating whole wheat bread is unhealthy. Six slices of whole wheat bread each day will supply just over half of the total amount of fiber that you should consume and a good proportion of the minimum 50 percent of your calories that should come from complex carbohydrates.

The importance of fiber in the diet has been a cornerstone of alternative health since the turn of the century (Dr. John Kellogg advocated it at his Battle Creek sanatorium) and the medical establishment has finally come to realize its value. Regular helpings of whole grain bread help to reverse the downward trend in the quality of the Western diet, which is now richer in fat, sugar, salt, and refined foods. In the UK an average bread consumption used to be five-and-a-half large slices per day, but now is under three.

If your diet includes plenty of whole wheat bread, then you can also eat some of the more exotic breads as well without a guilty conscience. Do avoid the so-called "starch-reduced" varieties, though, which contain around 80 percent more calories in the same weight of bread. Some white loaves made for toasting contain added sugar, so that they go a golden brown under the broiler. If children are not keen on eating whole wheat bread, try making sandwiches with one slice of whole wheat and one of white.

Six million loaves of processed, sliced, wrapped white bread come off the factory production lines each day. We are encouraged to believe that this tasteless product is just as good for us as an old-fashioned, whole wheat loaf. The real comparisons are worth a closer look.

Whole wheat bread contains five times as much fiber as white bread, significant amounts of vitamin E, which is not present at all in white

---

bread, more potassium, iron, zinc, copper, magnesium, thiamin, riboflavin, pantothenic acid, folic acid, pyridoxine, and biotin. It provides

---

HEALTH WARNING

Watch out for the amount of salt in commercially produced bread. Just to confuse you, most manufacturers put it on the label as "mg of sodium per 3½oz [100g] of bread." The label that says "530mg of sodium per 100g of bread" actually means that 3½oz (100g) of bread has a salt content of 1.3g – more than a quarter of the total recommended salt intake per day.

People suffering from celiac disease (*see p. 180*) are not able to eat food containing gluten – one of the proteins present in cereals like wheat, rye, and, to a lesser extent, barley and oats. Sadly, conventional bread can make them extremely ill and must be avoided.

---

ten times as much manganese, twice as much chromium, and one-and-a-half times as much selenium. However, you should not rely on whole wheat bread as a good dietary source of calcium, magnesium, or zinc as it contains much more of the chemical phytic acid than white bread, which interferes with the body's absorption of these minerals.

Nowhere are the influences of other cultures more obvious than in the breads they produce – using different processes, different mixtures of grains, with and without yeast, with the addition of herbs, spices, and toppings. What follows is a nutritional comparison of some of the most popular variations (quoted per 3½oz/100g of bread).

● **The key to getting the best out of your daily bread is what you put on it. A thick layer of butter or margarine, or a large dollop of strawberry jelly will do more harm than good.**

Bread

BREAD FACTS

Type of bread	calories	fiber
White bread: refined flour with a host of additives. Often fortified with vitamins and minerals, including calcium.	235	1.5
Brown bread: sometimes white-flour colored, but may contain some less refined flour. May be fortified like white bread.	218	3.5
Whole wheat bread: made from 100 percent flour with all the bran, fiber, and vitamins. Contains more of almost everything, especially vitamins B and E, iron, zinc, and selenium.	215	5.8
Chapati: classic Indian bread.	328	2.5
French bread: delicious with cheese or salami, but low in fiber, high in salt, with a bonus of high iron.	270	1.5
Granary: better than brown bread, as made with malt flour and whole wheat kernels – mind your teeth.	235	4.3
Matzos: traditional Jewish unleavened bread, eaten to celebrate Passover, but now available all year round. Virtually salt-free (about 5 percent in other breads).	384	3.0
Milk bread: higher in calcium, but also fat.	296	1.9
Naan: another traditional Indian bread.	336	1.9
Pitta (pocket), whole wheat: traditional Greek bread with less salt, more fiber, iron, and zinc.	265	5.2
Pumpernickel, traditional German bread made from a mixture of whole grains, including rye. Valuable for its low-fat, high-fiber content, vitamin E, and iron.	219	7.5
Rye bread: another traditional European bread, which is high in fiber, low in fat, high in vitamin E, and a good source of iron and zinc.	219	4.4
Soda bread: traditional non-yeast bread from the remote parts of Scotland, Wales, and Ireland. Originally made with bicarbonate of soda and cream of tartar, and cooked on a bakestone.	258	2.1

SODA BREAD

YEAST

DRIED YEAST
ENERGY PER 3½OZ/100G 169KCAL

❦ Baker's and brewer's yeast are good sources of B vitamins and folic acid.

❦ A very small percentage of people are yeast-sensitive and need to avoid yeast-containing foods.

❦ Candida albicans is the yeast that causes thrush.

Yeast, as used in baking and brewing, has been a friend to humanity since time immemorial, but in recent years it has been getting a bad press. There are many strains of yeast, but only one actually causes health problems in humans – Candida albicans, the yeast present in the gut and mouth that is responsible for thrush. Almost any organ of the body can be attacked by Candida, but oral and vaginal thrush are probably the most common infections, followed by skin infections and anal thrush in babies, as a sequel to severe nappy rash.

In general terms, severe infections with Candida are seen in the very young, the elderly, as a result of antibiotic treatment, and frequently in patients whose immune system is compromised by disease (HIV), chemotherapy, radiotherapy, or the long-term use of some drugs, especially corticosteroids and oral contraceptives.

There is a current vogue, mostly in the complementary medical field but also popular with doctors involved in clinical ecology, to blame Candida for a number of vaguely defined, multiple-symptom illnesses – multiple allergies, chronic fatigue, depression, memory loss, mood swings, recurrent urinary infections, recurrent ear infections, diarrhea,

FRENCH STICK

constipation, swollen joints, spots in front of the eyes, blurred vision, or simply feeling lousy.

Proponents of this theory prescribe long-term treatment with antifungal drugs, together with rigid dietary programs which exclude foods that have a link with any form of yeast. Such diets also generally exclude high-sugar foods, refined and processed foods, and foods containing a range of colorings, flavorings, preservatives, and other chemicals.

There is a general acceptance that reducing sugar consumption helps in the treatment of proven Candida infections, but the concept of generalized and systemic candidiasis has not been widely accepted by the medical profession. Anyone seeking this type of nutritional advice would be well advised to consult a qualified medical practitioner working in the field, for there are many dubious "clinics" and testing laboratories offering nutritionally ill-conceived advice and expensive tests.

Some 10–15 percent of normal individuals are known to be sensitive to yeast. In 100 patients suffering from urticaria (nettle rash), 36 were sensitive to Candida albicans. In a separate study, in which only 14 percent of the patients tested were yeast-sensitive, their urticaria responded to a low yeast diet.

Take particular care that children are not forced to endure dietary programs which may be seriously nutritionally deficient. In my experience, the side effects of this form of treatment are often worse than the original problem.

● **Whether yeast-free diets work because they exclude many types of yeast, or simply because they encourage better general nutrition, has yet to be proven, so it is advisable to approach this type of treatment with an open, but skeptical mind.**

Cereals

Cereal is the name given to the seeds of a group of plants from the grass family. The most important cereals grown throughout the world are barley, maize, millet, oats, rice, rye, and wheat. Their nutritional value is much the same and their main constituent is starch.

MIXED GRAINS

All of the unrefined whole grain cereals are richer in fiber, B vitamins, and minerals than refined cereals. With the exception of yellow maize, none of them provides beta-carotene. Cereals also lack vitamins C and B12, so that in spite of their being the staple food for many indigenous populations, unless they are combined with other vegetables and some animal protein sources,

---

FAST FOOD AID

• For stomach acidity, chronic indigestion, ulcers, and irritable bowel syndrome, mix half a teaspoon of arrowroot powder to a paste with a little cold water, add a cupful of boiling water and a dash of nutmeg, stir well and leave to stand till cool enough to drink. Take this remedy morning and evening between meals.

---

deficiency diseases follow. Some whole grain cereals contain significant amounts of phytic acid, a substance which interferes with the body's absorption of iron, calcium, and zinc.

Although medical evidence shows indisputably that whole grain cereals are healthier, the modern palate seems to prefer the highly refined varieties, which can be stored for much longer periods without spoiling and can more easily be turned into aggressively marketed, high-profit products. It is comparatively simple to remove the outer coverings of bran and germ from wheat and rice, which lose 80 percent of their vitamin B1, most of their vitamin B6 and fiber, and the valuable vitamin E-containing oils in the germ.

In Britain and the US most bread is made from refined wheat flour, as its high gluten content adds elasticity to the dough and causes the bread to rise better (see p. 112–113).

Cereals are only as nutritious as the soil in which they grow. Most British bread used to be made from Canadian and North American wheat, grown in soil rich in selenium. Today, thanks to the EC, British bread is made mostly from European wheat that is grown in low-selenium soil. As a result, the average daily consumption of selenium in the UK (at 30µg) is approximately half what it was 20 years ago and only half the minimum daily requirement for women. Even in the US there are areas with selenium-poor soil and people living in these regions, especially those on low

incomes and poor-quality diets, may be deficient. All the evidence now shows a striking link between low selenium consumption and an increased risk of cancers of the lung, prostate, and colon. Research carried out in China also confirms that low selenium intake can lead to higher rates of heart disease.

Sago, tapioca, and arrowroot are frequently called cereals, but they are not seeds so they do not contain the germ layer that is rich in B vitamins, and they are very low in protein. In some emerging countries these starchy foods still form a staple part of the diet and provide very poor nutrition. The consequent lack of other nutrients can lead to severe deficiency diseases.

● **People suffering from celiac disease, however, must avoid wheat flour, barley, oats, and rye, all of these cereals contain gluten, which can cause them serious malabsorption problems and illness.**

ARROWROOT

• *This is not actually a cereal, but a refined starch made from the roots of the maranta plant, which was first discovered on the island of Dominica in the late 1600s. From there it was taken to Jamaica, India, Europe, and the southern states of North America. Although it is used as an energy-providing food – 3½oz/100g containing 355 calories – arrowroot is virtually devoid of all essential nutrients and of poor nutritional value. Its medicinal effects are, however, important, as it contains demulcents, which are soothing to the stomach and the intestines. It has traditionally been used by herbalists in the treatment of diarrhea. It is also useful as a thickening agent in cooking and, because it contains no gluten, is valuable for those suffering from Celiac disease.*

BARLEY

BARLEY

ENERGY PER STANDARD PORTION 72KCAL

❦ *Good for urinary infections.*

❦ *Good for constipation.*

❦ *Beneficial for inflammations of the throat, esophagus, and digestive tract.*

❦ *Helps lower cholesterol levels.*

❦ *Makes milk more easily digestible, especially for babies.*

❦ *Cancer-protective.*

❦ *Best eaten as pot barley (more nutritious than the polished pearl barley).*

❦ *Combines well with all vegetables to make soups.*

❦ *Good boiled in water to make drinks, and baked with milk to make puddings.*

The botanical name for barley is *Hordeum* and in Roman times it was so highly thought of as a strengthening food that some of the greatest gladiators were called *Hordearii*, as barley was their staple food. The great Roman gastronome Apicius included a number of barley recipes in his writings, including *Tisanam* and *Tisanam sic facies*. These were both soups based on the Roman doctor's concept of *tisanam* – a variety of barley waters used as medicine, hence the modern word "tisane." Barley has been cultivated

Cereals

for longer than any other cereal, and barley bread was a staple food during the Middle Ages.

Now is your chance to benefit from this wonderful grain. Use lots of barley in your cooking: as flour added to recipes for cookies, muffins, and cakes; as grits in cereal and vegetable mixtures; and added to soups. All forms of barley contain soluble fiber and beta glucans, which help the body to get rid of excess cholesterol. They also contain some of the protease inhibitors, which have a definite cancer-protective action.

Herbalists have traditionally used lemon barley water for the treatment of cystitis and all other urinary infections. To make your own, put ½oz/15g of washed pot barley in a pan with 2pt/500ml of water and two washed, quartered, unwaxed lemons. Bring to a boil, cover, and simmer gently for 30 minutes. Strain through a sieve, keep in the refrigerator, and drink several glasses a day.

● **The soothing demulcents in barley make it an ideal food for the relief of sore throats, esophagitis, gastritis, and colitis and, like other grains, barley is mineral-rich. Containing calcium, potassium, and plenty of the B-complex vitamins, it is useful for people suffering from stress or fatigue, and a nourishing food for convalescents.**

BUCKWHEAT

ENERGY PER STANDARD PORTION 73KCAL

This cereal was either brought to Europe from Asia by the Crusaders or to Spain by the Arabs some centuries earlier – no one knows for certain. It is now widely grown in temperate regions, especially in the US, and it is a staple of the daily diet in Russia and Poland. Although it is popularly considered a grain, buckwheat is in reality a seed, rich in the flavonoid

glycoside known as rutin. This strengthens and tones the walls of the tiniest blood vessels, the capillaries, making buckwheat useful in cases of frostbite or chilblains, as well as for capillary fragility in general. It is also recommended by herbalists for treating varicose veins. Rutin is a great aid in the treatment of high blood pressure and hardening of the arteries.

● **Buckwheat flour makes delicious and nourishing crêpes and is widely used in Oriental cooking. But for a real flavor treat combined with good nutrition it is hard to beat the traditional Russian crêpes known as blinis – delicious, especially eaten with lemon tea.**

BULGAR
BURGHUL
CRACKED WHEAT

ENERGY PER STANDARD PORTION 353KCAL

In the Middle East cracked wheat is often used instead of rice. It is made by soaking whole wheat grains in water, then putting them into a very hot oven until they crack. These delicious, nutritious, and nutty-flavored grains make a great addition to salads and are particularly good as the Lebanese recipe, tabbouleh. This is made from soaked, dried cracked wheat, mixed with onions, mint, parsley, lemon juice, and extra-virgin olive oil.

COUS COUS

ENERGY PER 3½OZ/100G 227KCAL

This is one of the most popular dishes from North Africa. It is prepared from the inner part of the wheat grain and is normally cooked by steaming it in a couscousier, though you can improvize by lining the top of an ordinary steamer with a piece of cheesecloth. It can be used to make sweet or savory dishes.

MAIZE

FLOUR:
ENERGY PER 3½OZ/100G 353KCAL
GRITS:
ENERGY PER 3½OZ/100G 262KCAL
CORNFLOUR:
ENERGY PER 3½OZ/100G 354KCAL

Originally native to South America, maize has become a staple food in many poor areas of the world. It is not so long ago that the deficiency disease pellagra was common in the southern states of the US, where maize provided the bulk of food for poor communities. Pellagra causes itchy, scaly red skin, sores in the mouth, brain lesions, damage to the nervous system, and difficulty in walking.

Ground maize and popcorn provide the nutrients from the whole grain, while grits are made from milled corn and lose nutrients like white flour. Maize flour is gluten-free, so it is ideal for people with celiac disease.

● **The Italians use it to make polenta, and in Mexico it is used to make tortillas.**

MILLET

ENERGY PER 3½OZ/100G 282KCAL

This is another cereal suitable for sufferers of celiac disease as it contains no gluten. It is highly regarded by naturopaths, and US natural healer Paavo Airola describes it as "the most nutritious cereal in the world – a truly wonderful complete food, high in protein and low in starches – very easily digested and never causes gas and fermentation in the stomach."

Millet is rich in silicon, which is vital for the health of hair, skin, teeth, eyes, and nails. Lack of this mineral can result in a sagging of the body's connective tissue. And, because millet is never highly refined, it retains all its essential nutrients. It can be used as a thickener in soups, stews, and vegetable casseroles, or it can be ground into a coarse flour to make bread.

● **There are different varieties of millet, the best-known of which is sorghum. This is a much-ignored cereal in Britain and the US, although it is popular with "food reformers." It should be used much more widely.**

OATS

ENERGY PER 3½OZ/100G 401KCAL

Oats must surely rank as a prince among cereals. They are richly nutritious, containing over 12g of protein in 3½oz/100g of oats; also polyunsaturated fats, a little vitamin E, and plenty of the B-complex vitamins (see also *Bran* on p.117 and *Breakfast Cereals* on p.116). They are also spectacularly high in calcium, potassium, and magnesium.

MILLET

OATS

Oats have played an important part in traditional herbal practice: possets and caudles made from oatmeal with water, lemon juice, sugar, spices, and perhaps ale or wine have long been a standard remedy.

Dr. James Anderson of the Veterans Administration Hospital in Kentucky has shown that the cholesterol levels of patients fed a daily dose of oat-bran have declined (and that oat-bran is also beneficial for diabetics). Research into the benefits of eating oats has finally persuaded the Food and Drug Administration (FDA) in the US to take the unprecedented step of approving a food-specific health claim.

● **After reviewing nearly 40 published papers, the FDA stated: "The beta-glucan soluble fiber of whole oats is the primary component responsible for the total and LDL [low-density lipoprotein] blood cholesterol-lowering effects of diets that contain these whole oat-containing foods." I am certain that this will be the first of many proven claims for "functional foods."**

SAGO

• *Like arrowroot, this is not a cereal but a virtually pure starch extracted from the pith of the sago palm tree. It produces a high-calorie food – 355 calories per 3½oz/100g – but virtually no other important nutrients. Its nutritional value is, however, greatly increased when cooked with milk to make the traditional sago pudding. Sago starch is widely used commercially in confectionery, desserts, noodles, and biscuits, as well as in the manufacture of sweeteners and monosodium glutamate. It is also the basic ingredient of the prawn crackers served in every Chinese restaurant.*

RYE

ENERGY PER 3½OZ/100G 379KCAL

The nutritional value of rye is similar to that of wheat, with two important exceptions. It contains considerably more fiber and far less gluten, so that rye bread does not rise a great deal and tends to be much heavier than wheat bread, but for people who do not have celiac disease but have an adverse reaction to gluten, rye is often well tolerated. Rye grows well in cold climates, so rye breads are popular in Scandinavia, Russia, and northern Germany.

● **Most rye breads are a mixture of rye and wheat flours, but pumpernickel and black bread should be made exclusively from rye. If you have gluten problems, check the labels carefully – it is quite common for rye breads to be colored with caramel to make them darker, so you can't judge by the color alone.**

SEMOLINA

ENERGY PER STANDARD PORTION 70KCAL

This is produced by extracting the coarse particles of the wheat endosperm. In India and the Middle East it is used to make wonderful sweet desserts, often flavored with rose water or other perfumed extracts.

● **In Italy it forms the basic ingredient of that wonderful dish, gnocchi, which is prepared with milk, semolina, egg, Parmesan, and nutmeg – a rich combination of essential nutrients.**

TAPIOCA

TAPIOCA

ENERGY PER STANDARD PORTION 72KCAL

This is not a real cereal as it is prepared from the root of the manioc (cassava), a 6½ft/2m-high shrub native to Central and South America. It grows mostly in Brazil, but is cultivated throughout the tropical world as a major energy food, served with fish and meat dishes. Manioc contains highly toxic glycosides (more in the bitter variety than in the sweet) so the rainforest tribes prepare it by careful soaking and cooking. The native Brazilians gave the name tapioca to the grain-like finished product that is their prime source of starch. Because tapioca is easily digestible it is a good high-energy food for convalescents.

● **Unfortunately manioc contains little but starch and, unless it is part of a more mixed diet together with other sources of protein, it may cause the protein-deficiency disease known as kwashiorkor.**

WHEAT

ENERGY PER 3½OZ/100G 386KCAL

This cereal is a vitally important staple food in the Western diet. The majority of wheat ends up as flour and finally as bread. Although bread consumption is declining, it still accounts for a quarter of all the protein in the British diet (*see Bread, p.112*). Although refined wheat flour is fortified with some of the nutrients that are lost in the manufacturing process, zinc, magnesium, vitamin B6, pyridoxine, vitamin E,

SEMOLINA

and fiber are not replaced. The wheat germ left over when white flour is made is a rich source of the B-complex vitamins and vitamin E. It is rich in unsaturated fatty acids and an excellent food supplement, especially for invalids and convalescents. Sprouted wheat is also very rich in nutrients (*see p. 102*). Because of its high gluten content, people with celiac disease cannot eat wheat flour.

● **A centuries-old British dish called frumenty – whole wheat grains baked overnight in the ashes of the fire to burst open and set into a thick jelly, eaten with milk, spices, honey, currants or raisins – was the perfect meal for millions of farm laborers in years gone by.**

BREAKFAST CEREALS

CORNFLAKES:
ENERGY PER STANDARD PORTION 108KCAL.
MUESLI:
ENERGY PER STANDARD PORTION 184KCAL.
PORRIDGE:
ENERGY PER STANDARD PORTION 133KCAL

❊ *Whole grain cereals are complex carbohydrates providing slow-release energy for several hours.*

❊ *A good source of soluble and insoluble fiber, especially oats, which aid bowel function and cholesterol elimination.*

❊ *A source of B vitamins – some commercial products also have added nutrients and iron.*

❊ *Oats are one of the great mood-enhancing foods, due to their vitamin B and lysine content.*

❊ *Many commercial brands are high in sugar and salt.*

You might think that these early-morning foods are a product of the late twentieth century. But archaeologists have found evidence of oats being

BRAN

used by the ancient Greeks and Romans. As early as the first century AD the Chinese cultivated them; tribes in northern Europe used oats to make porridge, and the practice spread to Ireland and Scotland.

In the early nineteenth century oatmeal was used as a nourishing food for the sick, and in America it could only be bought in pharmacies. As an aid to convalescence and to help recover from depression, oats are an invaluable mood-enhancing food (see also p.53).

In America, the history of breakfast cereals is inextricably linked with the famous health pioneer Dr. John Kellogg, and with his sanatorium at Battle Creek, Michigan. He is best known for inventing cornflakes in 1899, but was also responsible for inventing "granola," which he developed during the 1860s. Together with Shredded Wheat and Weetabix (the only cereal actually invented in England), these variations on natural cereals were developed as "health foods," which, with the addition of milk, provided a highly nutritious start to the day.

Most modern commercial breakfast cereals, however, contain large amounts of added sugar, and sometimes salt. Products aimed at the children's market tend to be by far the worst in nutritional terms, some being 50 percent sugar by weight – whether from added honey, glucose, or sucrose. The largest amounts of

added salt and sugar are found in some high-fiber products promoted as constipation remedies.

The majority of commercial mueslis are also a pale and nutritionally inferior substitute for the real thing. The famous Swiss physician and pioneer of the natural health movement, Dr. Max Bircher-Benner, who established his first sanatorium in Zurich in 1897, discovered muesli when he shared a shepherd's supper in the Swiss mountains – a porridge-like dish common to the country peasants. Made from oats, wheat, or barley with milk, nuts, and fruit, it was soon – and is still to this day – part of the ritual at the Zurich clinic.

● **A traditional homemade recipe consists of 30 percent rolled oats, 30 percent toasted wheat flakes, 10 percent golden raisins, 10 percent hazelnuts, and 20 percent fresh apple or other seasonal fruits. This is lower in calories and fat than commercially available variations, has less than half the sugar, more fiber, less salt, and more of the B vitamins – it is also half the price.**

CORNFLAKES

BRAN

WHEAT BRAN
ENERGY PER STANDARD PORTION 14KCAL

❧ *Wheat and oat bran are super sources of fiber. Two heaped tablespoons provide the daily requirement of 18g.*

❧ *Oat bran contains much more soluble fiber than wheat bran. This helps to reduce cholesterol and is less irritant than insoluble fiber.*

❧ *Best eaten as part of a cooked product, like whole wheat bread, porridge, or muesli.*

❧ *Raw wheat bran in excess interferes with mineral absorption, especially the absorption of calcium, iron, and zinc, causes flatulence, and may cause irritable bowel syndrome.*

BRAN FLAKES

Wheat bran is the outer husk of wheat grains and is a very rich source of dietary fiber. One tablespoon of bran (21g) will give you just over 9g of fiber. There is now no doubt that an adequate intake of fiber is essential for the proper functioning of the large bowel (colon). It is interesting to note that where indigenous people have a diet that is high in fiber, bowel cancer is virtually unknown. Dr. Dennis Burkitt, for many years a British government medical officer in Africa, was one of the earliest observers of this fact. There is also a direct relationship between low fiber consumption, constipation, and the subsequent onset of varicose veins and hemorrhoids caused by excessive straining when trying to pass hard and compacted stools.

Unfortunately, in the rush to raise the overall consumption of bran, most people ignored the fact that uncooked bran contains phytic acid, which interferes with the way in which the body absorbs many minerals, such as calcium, iron, zinc, and magnesium. Most women have low iron levels anyway and, due to constant weight-loss diets, are also likely to have low levels of calcium intake. Taking uncooked bran can therefore increase the risk of anemia, and of osteoporosis in later life.

Unpleasant side effects of excessive bran consumption are flatulence and bloating of the abdomen. A mixture of cereal, vegetable, and fruit fibers, like pectin, reduces the unwanted side effects. Some of the high-bran breakfast cereals also contain significant amounts of salt and sugar and do not represent a healthy answer to preventing or treating constipation. Another unfortunate side effect of excessive raw bran intake is that it can be extremely irritant to the bowels. This may have something to do with the dramatic increase in irritable bowel syndrome since bran became a popular "cure-all" medication.

The soluble form of fiber found in oats, beans, apples, and pears has a double benefit, however. First, it

acts as "smoothage," rather than "roughage," speeding up the digestive process and preventing constipation. Second, it combines with cholesterol during digestion and carries it out of the body as part of the normal bowel function.

An average portion of baked beans on two slices of whole wheat toast, a generous bowl of unsweetened, good-quality muesli or an average serving of green peas, broccoli, and a baked potato will each provide the major proportion of the 18g minimum recommended daily intake of fiber.

● **It is far healthier to eat whole wheat bread than bran (four slices equal a tablespoon of bran), as the phytic acid is destroyed by enzymes in the yeast while the bread cooks.**

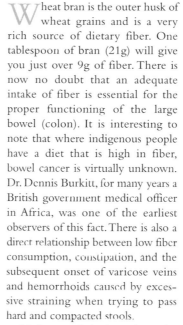

FAST FOOD AID

• *Although it may be irritant to the insides, bran is a wonderful remedy for skin problems. For the treatment of eczema and psoriasis, put four or five large tablespoons of bran onto a handkerchief-sized square of muslin or cheesecloth. Gather up the four corners, twist into a neck, and tie with string. Soak the ball of bran in warm water and use like a sponge to wash the affected areas of skin. The gentle, abrasive effect, combined with the vitamin E and demulcents in the bran, is an aid to healing. You can also hang the bag under the running tap as the bathtub fills, dissolving these beneficial substances into the bathwater.*

Pasta

PENNE

PASTA

WHITE PASTA:
ENERGY PER STANDARD PORTION 239KCAL
WHOLE WHEAT PASTA:
ENERGY PER STANDARD PORTION 226KCAL

❦ *Good for providing energy and especially for athletes.*

❦ *Useful for convalescence.*

❦ *Good for weight loss.*

The history of pasta in Europe starts with Marco Polo, who allegedly found people eating it in China and took pasta back to his native Italy in 1295. This claim is hotly disputed by Italian foodies, who maintain that their national dish was being eaten in Italy long before Marco Polo's time. Whatever the truth, pasta, along with sun-dried fruit and vegetables, cured, smoked, and air-dried fish and meat,

SPAGHETTI

FARFALLE

was among the first true convenience foods. Once made and dried, it can be kept for months and prepared in minutes, simply by boiling it in water.

Though there are many variations of pasta, there are only two basic types – the one made with flour and water and the one made with eggs – and they are very different. Traditional Italian pasta is made from nothing but flour and water, but it is the type of flour, made from durum wheat, that is so important. Known as semolina to the Italians, this flour is high in gluten and is the only flour suitable to produce the best dried spaghetti and all those other wonderful pasta shapes.

Egg pasta is the kind that you can make yourself at home or, increasingly, can buy fresh in your local delicatessen or supermarket. It is made with a much softer wheat flour, with a lower gluten content, and is known to every Italian housewife as *"pasta all' uovo."* In some regions, especially in the far southern areas of Apulia, olive oil and a pinch of salt are sometimes added too.

Although most pasta that is consumed is the traditional dried variety, made from white durum wheat, whole wheat pastas are now far more widely available, and are lighter and more palatable than early versions. For people with celiac disease and others who are allergic to gluten, pasta made from rice flour can also be found in specialty stores. There are now also pastas which are colored and flavored with squid ink, tomatoes, and spinach.

Pasta is an excellent source of complex carbohydrates, which provide sustained, slow-release energy. Although whole wheat pasta is richer in fiber, minerals, and B vitamins, both white and whole wheat pasta are healthy foods. The idea that pasta is fattening is one of the longest-surviving food myths of the twentieth century – it is what you put on the pasta that makes it fattening. A creamy carbonara sauce made with bits of fatty bacon, a pile of Bolognese sauce made from high-fat ground beef, or a lasagne that is more cheese than pasta are indeed fattening. But the classic *aglio e olio* – spaghetti with garlic and olive oil – or a simple mixture of extra-virgin olive oil, garlic, parsley, rosemary, thyme, and basil – *spaghetti alle erbe* – or a dish of pasta with tuna fish and scallions are all wonderful meals: satisfying, delicious, and a weight-watcher's treat.

● **With practice and imagination you can soon become adept at making meals in minutes using the enormous variety of pasta. From stir-fried Chinese noodles to the most exotic pasta with seafood, you can enjoy good nutrition and the added bonus of the mood-enhancing benefits of a high carbohydrate intake.**

TRADITIONAL ITALIAN PASTA

Pasta lunga (long pasta) – all the spaghettis, spaghettinis, angel hair, linguini, fusilli, etc.

Fettucce (ribbons) – tagliatelli, fettuccini, tagliolini, etc.

Tubi (tubes) – all the variations of penne, macaroni, rigatoni.

Pasta shapes – farfalle, conchiglie, orecchiette, lumache, fusilli, plus tomato-, spinach- and various other colored pastas, such as beet and mushroom.

Stuffed pastas – ravioli, cappelletti, tortelloni, canneloni, lasagne, etc.

FUSILLI

SQUID INK SPAGHETTI

Rice

**WHITE LONG
GRAIN RICE**

**BROWN
LONG
GRAIN
RICE**

RICE

BROWN RICE:
ENERGY PER STANDARD
PORTION 212KCAL
WHITE RICE:
ENERGY PER STANDARD PORTION 248KCAL

For centuries rice has been the dietary staple of the East, where it provided a basis for good nutrition. It is low in fat, provides protein, and most of the B vitamins, but not vitamins A, C, or B12. It is a gluten-free cereal, so it is suitable for those with celiac disease. It was traditionally eaten as brown rice, which contains all the nutrients in the germ and outer layers of the grain, but with the arrival of modern milling techniques and the production of white rice, most of the B vitamins (especially thiamin) were lost. With white rice came a disastrous epidemic of beri-beri – a disease of the brain and nervous system caused by deficiency of thiamin – that spread like wildfire around the Eastern world. Parboiling the rice before milling pushes some of the vitamins back into the grain and reduces the thiamin loss to about 40 percent instead of 80 percent.

● **Plain boiled brown rice is a universal folk remedy for diarrhea – as is the water in which it is boiled. Boiled rice mixed with puréed apples is recommended by some European doctors as an aid to reducing blood pressure.**

TYPES OF RICE
The two main types of rice are long-grain and short-grain. Long rice grains are about five times as long as they are wide, while short grains are much more rounded.

American long-grain rice can be used for most dishes and is best cooked by the hot-water method *(see box left)*. Brown rice will take about 30 minutes, while white rice takes 15–20 minutes.

Arborio rice is the Italian variety used to make risotto. Its short grains clump together as they cook and tend to break down more, resulting in a smooth, creamy texture with a distinctive nutty flavor. There is no quick way to make good risotto – you need to stand by the pot, adding liquid gradually and stirring constantly. It's worth the effort.

Basmati is the classic long-grain rice of Indian cooking. It is slightly aromatic with a definite flavor of its own, and the grains separate well when cooked, making them ideal for pilafs and salads. Best cooked by the absorption method *(see box left)*, it takes 15–20 minutes.

Easy-cook rice has been pre-processed to shorten the cooking time and is designed to cook by the absorption method. Follow the cooking instructions on individual manufacturers' labels.

BROWN RICE

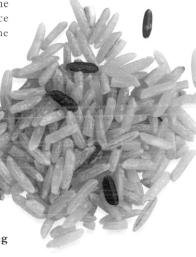

Japanese short-grain rice is the wonderfully shiny, glutinous rice served in every Japanese restaurant at the end of the meal, or used to prepare the vinegar rice that goes so well with sushi.

Pudding rice is another short-grain variety, which becomes very soft during cooking. It is nearly always used in sweet dishes. White rice takes 20 minutes, brown about 40 minutes. The traditional oven-baked rice pudding takes around an hour and a half.

Thai rice is delicately flavored with jasmine and goes well with European as well as Thai dishes. It is another short-grain rice, is best cooked by the absorption method, and takes only 15 minutes. Its delicious flavor combines well with simple chicken or fish dishes.

COOKING RICE

The hot-water method Add rice to a large saucepan of boiling, lightly salted water. Plenty of water, combined with a large pan, allows the rice grains to move about freely and not stick together. Simmer until the rice is cooked. Pour into a strainer and rinse with boiling water.

The absorption method This method uses a specific amount of water, which is completely absorbed by the time the rice is cooked. Put one measure of rice and two and a half measures of cold water in a saucepan with a pinch of salt. Bring to a boil, stir briskly, cover, and let simmer for 15 minutes. Leave to stand for another 15 minutes, fluffing the rice with a fork before serving.

**BASMATI
RICE**

WILD RICE

ENERGY PER STANDARD PORTION 248KCAL

This is not rice at all, but the seeds of an aquatic freshwater grass, which is native to the Great Lakes region of North America and can be found in shallow lakes and rivers of the northeastern US and eastern Canada. For over a thousand years wild rice was harvested by the native Americans, who bent the willowy grass across their canoes, then tapped it gently so that the grain fell into the canoe, leaving the plants unharmed to allow the next lot of seeds to ripen.

Wild rice is an incredible nutritional storehouse, containing more protein than even oats or brown rice. Its B vitamin content exceeds that of most other cereals and it is rich in the nutritionally valuable linolenic acids. Wild rice also contains significant quantities of essential minerals. The long, black grains have a nutty flavor and are more chewy than ordinary rice.

● **It is expensive, but for a treat serve it mixed with brown rice. Since it needs longer cooking, give it 10 minutes in boiling water before you add the brown rice, then cook as normal.**

WILD RICE

FAST FOOD AID

• *A poultice of manioc, wheat flour, and dried ginger is used in Chinese medicine to draw out pus from infected boils, cuts, or grazes.*

**PUDDING
RICE**

Dairy

CREAM

MILK AND CREAM

WHOLE MILK:
ENERGY PER STANDARD PORTION 386KCAL

SEMISKIMMED MILK:
ENERGY PER STANDARD PORTION 269KCAL

SKIMMED MILK:
ENERGY PER STANDARD PORTION 193KCAL

❧ *Good for growth, strong bones, and for convalescence.*

❧ *Best drunk straight from the refrigerator or used in recipes.*

Nutritionally, milk is a valuable source of essential nutrients, especially during pregnancy, for children and adolescents. It is a cheap and easily consumed, rich source of calcium, protein, zinc, and riboflavin (B2).

Unfortunately there are drawbacks to this apparent wonder-food. Naturopaths have long believed that cow's milk may be a trigger of infantile eczema and catarrh, excessive mucus and chestiness in both children and adults. Studies at the British College of Naturopathy and Osteopathy in Hampstead, London have shown that breastfeeding mothers consuming a large amount of cow's milk tend to have babies that are more prone to infections such as eczema and chronic catarrh – and who also get more colic.

FRESH MILK

Adults are not immune to milk-related problems either and there are populations throughout the world, especially in India, Japan, and China, where there is frequently an inability to digest cow's milk. This is caused by the lack of a normal digestive enzyme, lactase, which is essential for the breakdown and digestion of the milk sugar, lactose. After 35 years in practice, I am still surprised at how often the simple expedient of removing all cow's milk from a patient's diet can resolve chronic digestive problems, which may have existed for 20 years.

One of the drawbacks of milk is its high fat content, so it is always better to choose semiskimmed or skimmed varieties, even though these contain fewer vitamins A, D, and E than the full-fat product. For this reason, and for the substantial reduction that skimmed milk shows in calorie content, these fat-reduced milks should not be given to the under-fives.

But it is not even certain that you will get the full range of nutrients from your milk. Pasteurization loses 25 percent of the vitamin C, and the remaining proportion decreases even further by the time you get your milk home. Riboflavin (vitamin B2) is extremely sensitive to ultraviolet light, so if your milk stands for two hours on your doorstep or on a sunny windowsill, you lose half of the riboflavin - and even on a dull day the losses are substantial. To make matters worse, fluorescent lighting also destroys riboflavin, so further losses occur in your local deli or supermarket if the milk is stored in bottles, although this does not seem to happen to cartoned milk. When the riboflavin is broken down, the residual chemicals destroy most of the vitamin C that is left. When all the vitamin C has gone, boiling your milk also puts paid to the folic acid that it contains.

For the elderly, who may not be eating well, the growing young, pregnant women, or active people who rush around all day and burn up nutrients in the gym or on the track, milk has a vital part to play – 2½ cups/600ml provides just over half the calcium and vitamin B2 needed by pregnant or breastfeeding women, and more than that needed by everyone else. It also contains more than a day's dose of vitamin B12. Roughly one-third of everyone's protein requirements can also be met by the same amount of milk, along with 15 percent of your energy needs.

For those whose allergies, such as eczema and asthma, are triggered by cow's milk, goat's milk is often an acceptable alternative. But take care with babies, as goat's milk contains substantially less folic acid, which is reduced even further by boiling the milk and can result in babies becoming anemic.

Milk is only as good as the food fed to the cows or goats, so whenever possible buy organic milk, which is now available in many supermarkets. Humans are the only living creatures who continue to consume milk after they have been weaned (hedgehogs and cats only drink it because we give it to them). But there is no doubt that overall most people benefit from this food.

● **Cream may be delicious, but it is full of calories, most of which come from fat. As an occasional treat it is fine, and it is worth remembering that whipped cream is mostly air and actually contains far less fat than double cream. Use it sparingly and enjoy it with relish.**

CREME FRAICHE

HEALTH WARNING

People suffering from rheumatoid arthritis often find their symptoms aggravated by cow's milk. The same is true for eczema, catarrh, sinus problems, and sometimes asthma. Before depriving anyone, especially children or women, of all dairy products, seek professional advice to make sure that calcium deficiency does not ensue.

GOAT'S MILK

Dairy

YOGURT

LOW-FAT PLAIN YOGURT:
ENERGY PER STANDARD PORTION 84KCAL
ORGANIC YOGURT:
ENERGY PER STANDARD PORTION 84KCAL

❦ *Good for diarrhea (caused by antibiotics), the prevention and treatment of osteoporosis, most general digestive problems, the immune system, thrush, and cystitis.*

❦ *Best eaten as low-fat yogurt (but not for the under-fives), unpasteurized, and regularly.*

Yogurt in some form or other has been made since time immemorial. It is believed that the ancient Bedouin, carrying fresh milk across the desert in goatskin bags, found that the combination of heat, movement, and some bacterial contamination with the right bugs resulted in a delicious food, which kept much better than fresh milk.

Many health problems start in the gut, when the balance between the good bacteria and the bad ones swings in the wrong direction. Fermentation, putrefaction, gas, constipation, and poor absorption are the result. Most commercial yogurts are made from the starting point of pasteurized milk, which is inoculated with cultures of highly beneficial bacteria like *Lactobacillus acidophilus* or *bulgaricus*, *Bifidobacteria* or *Streptococcus thermophilus*. But many yogurt products, especially those with long sell-by dates, are pasteurized after manufacture and contain none of the live and beneficial organisms that give yogurt its unique properties. They comprise a host of chemicals, stabilizers, emulsifiers, artificial flavorings, colorings, preservatives, and large amounts of sugar or artificial sweetener, although even some of the much healthier live yogurts contain a selection of these.

Live, or "bio" yogurts contain the health-giving bacteria that will help to restore the balance in the gut. These cultures act on the digestion in several ways. They synthesize some of the B vitamins, biotin, folic acid and B$_{12}$; increase the uptake of calcium and magnesium; and regulate bowel function. Their presence in the intestines prevents the development of pathogenic bacteria. Even people who cannot digest milk can normally cope with yogurt, so whenever you are prescribed a course of antibiotics, do eat a tub of yogurt each day. Antibiotics kill all bugs – good and bad – but yogurt replaces the bacteria your body needs and so helps to prevent the diarrhea caused by sterilizing the gut. The B-vitamin synthesis encouraged by the yogurt bacteria also helps to prevent the almost inevitable feelings of depression that follow even quite short periods of time on antibiotics.

There is a slowly emerging but growing body of serious scientific evidence that suggests another remarkable protective role for these amazing little bugs. Veterinary scientists have found that these "probiotics" can actually produce enzymes that are absorbed directly through the gut wall, and enhance the activity of the body's immune defense mechanisms.

So, for your health's sake, choose live or bio natural yogurts and, if required, add your own unsweetened, puréed fruit. A comparative newcomer among the ranks of healthy bugs is the *Lactobacillus casei Shirota*, discovered by a Japanese scientist of the same name. He introduced it to the Japanese population as a fermented milk drink, which could be well tolerated despite the almost universal milk intolerance of the Japanese population. Shirota's pioneering work did much to improve the calcium and vitamin D consumption of the Japanese, as well as delivering a huge dose of live active and protective bacteria. There is growing evidence that all of these probiotic bugs may be protective against stomach cancer, which is highly prevalent in Japan.

For many people, dairy products present a digestive problem, since they lack the enzyme lactase, which is essential for the digestion of the milk sugar, lactose. This problem is particularly prevalent in the Chinese, Japanese, and Indian subcontinent populations. But as the fermenting process of yogurt results in a thicker curd, this is held for longer periods in the stomach than ordinary milk, so giving the smallest quantities of lactase more time to get to work on the lactose.

YOGURT WITH FRUIT

NATURAL YOGURT

Yogurt is an excellent source of calcium, with one 5oz/150g tub providing 210mg – well over a quarter of the minimum daily requirement; for weight-conscious people, low-fat varieties contain even more calcium, at 285mg per tub. Yogurt also contains small traces of vitamin D, which is essential for the absorption of calcium, making it an even more important source of this mineral.

The therapeutic properties of yogurt and other cultured milk products are nothing new. Traditional practitioners, herbalists, and naturopaths have praised yogurt's healing powers since the nineteenth century. But in 1908 the great Russian scientist Metchnikoff published a book entitled *The Prolongation of Life*, based on his observations of the enormously long lifespans of Bulgarian peasants, who consumed vast quantities of yogurt made with *Lactobacillus bulgaricus*. Metchnikoff's word was enough encouragement for most of Europe to take up eating fermented milk products on a grand scale.

● **Many women, having suffered years of distress as a result of chronic thrush and cystitis, can testify to the benefits of eating live yogurt on a daily basis. It not only helps to relieve the symptoms of thrush and cystitis, but continuing use acts as a serious preventive.**

FAST FOOD AID

• *For thrush and cystitis, apply small amounts of natural live yogurt to the inflamed areas each night. A couple of teaspoonfuls can be placed inside the vagina if necessary, which is most easily done using a tampon with its inserter.*

• *An effective facial scrub can be made with live yogurt by adding two teaspoons of coarse sea salt to a tub. Stir well, then massage thoroughly into the face. Leave for 15 minutes and wash off with plenty of cold water.*

Cheese

CHEESE

BRIE:
ENERGY PER STANDARD PORTION 128KCAL
CHEDDAR:
ENERGY PER STANDARD PORTION 165KCAL
COTTAGE CHEESE:
ENERGY PER STANDARD PORTION 87KCAL

❧ *Useful for building strong bones, and for both the prevention and treatment of osteoporosis.*

❧ *A good source of protein, especially for vegetarians.*

❧ *Good for preconception, pregnancy, and breastfeeding (but not unpasteurized cheeses during pregnancy).*

❧ *Beneficial for male sexual function.*

❧ *Best eaten fresh, with good whole wheat bread or, since cheese can be high in salt, compensate with virtually salt-free matzos.*

❧ *Combines well with most fresh fruit.*

❧ *Can be eaten cooked either in sauces or as toppings.*

CHEDDAR

The great combination of excellent cheese, wonderful bread and a glass of good red wine takes a great deal of beating as food for the mind, body, and spirit. Unfortunately there are some drawbacks, in that most cheeses have a high content of saturated fat, the type that is known to cause cholesterol deposits in the arteries and heart disease.

To me it's very sad that the ever-increasing amount of fat in the Western processed diet has led to an obsession about dairy foods among the health-conscious. As part of a healthy balanced diet, cheese has enormously important contributions to make, so allow yourself to savor the wonders of good cheese.

Making cheese must be one of the most ancient of all food-preparing techniques. In 3000 BC the Sumerians made 20 different varieties and it is likely that the earliest shepherds and goatherds were producing soft cheeses from their flocks when these animals were first domesticated around 10,000 BC. It was another 3,000 years before man domesticated cattle and started to make cheese from cow's milk.

Both the ancient Greeks and Romans developed sophisticated cheeses, but much of the cheese-maker's art was lost during the Dark Ages and survived only among isolated mountain dwellers, in the abbeys and monasteries. Today, happily, there is a huge resurgence of interest in farm-made regional cheeses and small producers are making wonderful-quality cheeses from cow's, sheep's, and goat's milk, although Britain does not yet have the strict *"Appellation d'Origine Contrôlée"* applied to the 300 or so French cheeses. But the average Briton consumes a total of only 8.1kg/18lb of cheese per year, whereas in Australia the average is 20¼lb/9.2kg, in Canada 33¾lb/15.3kg, in Holland 32½lb/14.8kg and in France – where they have far less heart disease than in Britain – it is 49lb/22.3kg.

I grow increasingly concerned that many people, especially young women, interpret a low-fat diet as being a no-fat diet and exclude most dairy products from their regular food intake, often in the pursuit of thinness. But as a source of calcium (for building strong bones), of essential protein, vitamin D (to help absorb the calcium), a selection of B vitamins (for the central nervous system), vitamin A (as a cancer-protector

and for healthy skin), and a spread of essential minerals, a little good cheese is hard to beat.

There are variations in the nutritional value of cheeses, but it is worth knowing that 3½oz/100g of Cheddar cheese supplies more than a day's dose of calcium, half the required protein, nearly half the zinc, half the vitamin A, one-fifth of the selenium, quarter of the iodine, three-quarters of the vitamin B12, and one-fifth of the folate that a woman needs each day.

In general, the harder the cheese, the higher the fat content – with the obvious exception of cream cheese, which is the fattiest of all. Stilton, Cheddar, blue cheese, and Parmesan are all high in fat, but Camembert, Brie, Edam, and feta contain considerably less. There are now many "low-fat" cheeses made from skimmed milk, which contain around 15g of total fat per 3½oz/100g. Cottage cheese contains only 4g per 3½oz/100g and curd cheese around 11g. Many processed cheeses – they hardly deserve the name anyway – are high in fat, though they are good sources of calcium and protein.

● **Cheese is a very useful source of zinc, which is vital for normal male sexual function; though not present in enormous quantities, the zinc is in an easily absorbed bio-available form – 3½oz/100g of most cheese provides over a quarter of a man's daily zinc needs.**

GOAT'S CHEESE

HEALTH WARNING

With the growing availability of real farm-made cheeses, many are made from unpasteurized milk, which may be contaminated with bacteria, particularly *Salmonella* and *Listeria*. These cheeses are eaten by millions of people without problems, but anyone with a compromised immune system should avoid them, as should pregnant women, as *Listeria* can have serious effects in pregnancy. The chronically ill and elderly may be seriously affected by *Salmonella*, so unpasteurized cheeses should be avoided by them.

Cheeses contain a chemical called tyramine, which can trigger migraine attacks, and most cheeses are best avoided by migraine sufferers unless they have excluded it as a culprit for themselves. Soft goat's and sheep's cheeses, cottage and cream cheese contain very little tyramine and are usually okay.

Some antidepressant drugs can react badly with tyramine, causing a dramatic increase in blood pressure, and fatalities have been known to result. Anyone taking monoamine oxidase inhibitors (MAOIs) should try to avoid cheese, especially very mature hard cheese.

GOAT'S AND SHEEP'S CHEESE

Most goat's cheese is eaten very young and soft and has a characteristic taste. As it matures it becomes slightly firmer, developing a definite tang. Sheep's milk is usually mild but it matures to a much firmer texture. Spanish manchega is an exceptional variety – hard with a full, mild flavor. French roquefort, Italian pecorino, and Greek feta are strong sheep's cheeses. Both sheep's and goat's cheeses are lower in fat and lactose.

Eggs

EGGS

CHICKEN EGGS:
ENERGY PER STANDARD PORTION 90KCAL
DUCK EGGS:
ENERGY PER STANDARD PORTION 122KCAL
QUAIL EGGS:
ENERGY PER STANDARD PORTION 75KCAL

❦ *Good for rheumatoid arthritis and osteoarthritis.*

❦ *Useful for cancer and heart protection.*

❦ *Good for anemia.*

❦ *Beneficial for male sexual function.*

❦ *Best eaten boiled or poached to avoid added fat.*

How sad it is that the obsession with cholesterol, especially in the US, has resulted in the humble egg being branded as the villain in the story of heart disease. The confusion arises because of a lack of understanding of the difference between dietary cholesterol and blood cholesterol. There is no doubt that raised levels of blood cholesterol – the cholesterol that the body manufactures from a high intake of saturated animal fat – increase the risk of coronary heart disease. But the cholesterol in food such as eggs and shellfish *(see p. 111)* does not add to the circulating blood cholesterol and should not be a concern, except in people suffering from extremely high cholesterol levels or those who have the hereditary disease that causes them to manufacture far too much cholesterol.

While British and US experts advise eating no more than three or four eggs per week, the World Health Organization advocates a total of 10 (including those used in cooking). Eggs are an amazing source of protein, although it is not the quantity of protein in a food but its quality that is important. Nutritionists use the term NPU – Net Protein Utilization – to measure the biological availability of different protein sources. For example, lentils have an NPU of 30,

soybeans of 63, fillet steak 67 and cheese 70 but eggs are rated at 94, and just two boiled eggs provide more than a quarter of a day's protein for women and over one-fifth for men. Eggs are also a rich source of zinc, vitamins A, D, E, and B, and especially B_{12}. This vitamin is often lacking in vegetarian diets, but two eggs, especially if they are free-range, provide more than a day's need of this essential nutrient.

CHICKEN EGGS

One of the most important substances in egg yolk is lecithin which is vital as part of many of the body's metabolic processes, including the dispersal of dangerous fat deposits and cholesterol. Lecithin prevents the development of heart disease and the formation of gallstones and also encourages the speedy conversion of body fats into energy.

Whether you choose hen, duck, quail, gull, or goose eggs, they are all nutritionally similar. The one exception is factory-farmed battery hens, and their eggs should be avoided wherever possible. Battery eggs mean unhappy chickens, less vitamin B_{12} and all the extras in the artificial feed on which these poor creatures live. There is also a much higher risk of *Salmonella* infection from intensively reared hens so, unless you are certain that yours are genuinely free range, they should be eaten thoroughly cooked.

● **Because of their high lecithin content eggs are an important brain food, contributing not only to memory and concentration, but also to a balanced mental and emotional status.**

FAST FOOD AIDS

Eggs are an excellent and cheap natural beauty product and can be used in the following ways:
• *For dry hair, whisk one egg together with a cup of beer and apply after shampooing for beautifully conditioned and glossy hair.*

• *For oily skins, whisk the white of one egg together with the juice of half a lemon and apply to the face for five minutes (avoiding the area around the eyes) for a wonderfully astringent face mask.*

QUAIL EGGS

DUCK EGGS

Herbs

The history of herbs and spices is as old as the history of humanity. From the earliest cave dwellers, who scattered fragrant leaves on the fire when they were cooking that day's catch, to the ancient Romans sprinkling wild thyme on their hot-pot and the mandarins of Peking growing garlic in their gardens, knowledge that combined the medicinal value of herbs and spices with their ability to enhance flavor was passed from father to son and mother to daughter.

Some of the great advances of medicine started life in the cooking pots of the native North Americans, the Himalayan tribesmen, and the crofter's cottage. It is not by accident that we eat mint with lamb, sage with pork, nutmeg with rice, chili with beans, or bay leaves with rich stews. They all impart a unique flavor, but they also aid the digestion of the foods with which they are combined.

Since the first century AD, when Dioscorides wrote *De Materia Medica,* the most ancient of Western herbal books, the use of herbs as both medicine and food has been inseparable. In 1597 John Gerard compiled his *British Herball,* which was as much about gardening and cooking as about healing.

Today, the medicinal value of herbs has been recognized once again, as more people prefer to rely on age-old natural remedies and cures rather than risk the side effects of pharmaceutical drugs prescribed by orthodox medicine.

- **Most of the herbs and spices that are in common use today are utilized not just for their flavors, but also because they have specific health benefits in relation to the foods with which they are commonly used.**

BALM

Otherwise known as lemon balm, this herb is equally helpful for calming nervous tension or the anxious indigestion that so often accompanies it. It is useful for children's problems too – in Spain it is considered a nursery cure-all. It is the volatile oils that give lemon balm its wonderful smell. The tonic effect of balm acts as a gentle calmer-down during stressful situations, but it is also very helpful in the treatment of mild to moderate depression. Use the leaves to make a soothing tea and enjoy the delicate aroma of citronella and the other flavonoids in the plant. It is delicious added to salads.

FAST FOOD AIDS

- *A traditional treatment for the painful swellings of gout is a compress soaked in warm lemon-balm tea and applied to the inflamed area.*

- *Also use lemon-balm leaf to soothe insect bites and stings.*

ANGELICA

This can be taken either as an infused tea, which makes an excellent remedy for indigestion, or as a tincture – a small teaspoon three times a day for mild chest infections. Best known in its candied form, as a decoration for cakes and cookies, angelica contains volatile oils, a little vitamin A and B, but is rich in tannins. Herbalists often use the dried root in the treatment of liver disorders, arthritis, and as a gentle, stimulant. American angelica *(Angelica atropurpurea),* sometimes called "bellyache root," is an effective remedy for wind and heartburn. Chinese angelica *(Dang gui)* brings great relief from menstrual discomfort. Its pungent taste makes an interesting addition to cooking and is the traditional way in which the Chinese use angelica to treat anemia.

FAST FOOD AIDS

- *Sprinkle a few leaves into your bath – they are stimulating and ease the pain of aching joints.*

- *A handful of crushed leaves tied into a cheesecloth bag makes an excellent air freshener to hang inside your car. The aroma is slightly stimulating and helps prevent travel sickness.*

MINT

FAST FOOD AID

• *Peppermint oil is widely used in aromatherapy and, diluted five drops to 1fl oz/25ml of grapeseed oil, it makes a good rub for tired and aching muscles. The same mixture massaged into the temples relieves headaches.*

This herb contains the essential oils menthol, menthone, menthyl acetate, and flavonoids. Soothing to the stomach and still listed in many national pharmacopoeias, mint is helpful in irritable bowel syndrome, spasm of the muscles of the intestine, and colon. Peppermint tea made from fresh leaves and taken after meals is popular throughout the Middle East as an aid to good digestion – a custom well worth copying. Mint tea is also used to relieve headaches, especially when caused by stress. Chewing spearmint leaves or drinking the tea stimulates the cortex of the brain and leads to improved concentration and a sense of spiritual well-being. Most commonly used as a sauce to go with lamb dishes, mint is also frequently added to sweet desserts to bring out their delicate flavors.

HEALTH WARNING

Some people may be allergic to contact with the oil so always do a small patch test before applying it to large areas. Do not use peppermint oil on babies.

BAY

The distinctive flavor of bay leaves is an intrinsic part of the classic French bouquet garni, and they are prized as much for their antiseptic properties as for their assistance in digestion, helping to ward off gas and cramps. Tuck a bay leaf or two inside a chicken you have just brought home, but remove it before cooking. Add bay to soups, stews, and casseroles for a wonderfully aromatic seasoning. It contains the volatile oils geraniol, cimeol, and eugenol, it is antiseptic, and is a mild stimulant. When used in recipes its stimulation of the digestive juices improves the absorption of nutrients from the food.

Bay leaves are a most beneficial addition to the diets of people recovering from serious illness, and especially anorexia nervosa, optimizing the patient's nutrition.

Prized by the Romans and sacred to the Greeks, the bay leaf was made into the laurel wreath which was awarded to athletes, scholars, and the gods.

HEALTH WARNING

Essential oil of bay can cause allergic reactions and should only be used in very dilute mixtures. Test a small patch of skin before using. On no account take it internally.

FAST FOOD AID

• *Add a decoction of bay leaves to a hot bath to relieve aches and pains.*

HEALTH WARNING

The alkaloids in borage can be toxic and the fresh leaves can cause contact dermatitis, so be sure to wear gloves when picking it.

FAST FOOD AID

• *For dry, scaly skin, place your head under a towel and over a bowl containing 5pt/2.25 liters of boiling water and a couple of handfuls of borage leaves. Allow the steam to wash over your face for 8–10 minutes, then rinse with cool water.*

BORAGE

Mostly popular in Britain as an addition to the summer drink Pimms, borage flowers are also used as a decorative, but edible, garnish for chilled soups. Borage helps reduce high temperatures, stimulates the kidneys, and aids chronic chest problems. It contains a number of alkaloids as well as tannins and mucilage, but most interestingly large amounts of gamma linoleic acid (GLA). Their presence make borage an excellent remedy for PMS, rheumatoid arthritis, and eczema. Borage is also an aid to a more restful sleep – throw some leaves into a mug, add boiling water, cover for ten minutes, strain, then drink one hour before bedtime.

Herbs

CAMOMILE

Insomnia, nervous indigestion, and the jitters all respond well to this magically calming herb, which makes one of the most pleasant of all herbal teas. Whenever ordinary tea or coffee are contraindicated, this should be one of your first choices. It also has a good antiinflammatory action, which helps with joint problems and period pains. This wonderful herb contains volatile oils, flavonoids, tannins, and cumarins, all of which make it a most effective and easy to use remedy. Its benefits to the digestion have been known since the first century and camomile tea will help with bloating, stomach ache, and even, suitably diluted, with baby colic. As a remedy for sleepless children, high temperatures, and general irritability, it is hard to better and can even reduce the severity of hay fever symptoms.

A strong infusion of camomile can be used as a mouthwash to soothe inflammations of the mouth. As an inhalation, camomile can help relieve those suffering from nasal catarrh – add half a cup of flowers to 5 pt/2*l* boiling water to make a steam treatment. Cover your head with a towel and inhale the steam, taking deep breaths.

FAST FOOD AID

• *Three camomile teabags in a warm bath relieve the terrible itching of eczema. For sore and itchy eyes, pour boiling water over two teabags, leave to cool, squeeze out the surplus water, and place one bag over each closed eye for ten minutes. For cracked and painful nipples when breastfeeding, put four camomile teabags in a scant cup/200ml of boiling water. When cool, soak clean cloths in the tea and apply to the affected nipples. Keep the mixture in the refrigerator and repeat applications after each feed.*

CHIVES

This herb shares many of the wonderful healing properties of garlic and onions, which belong to the same Allium family of plants. When used as a seasoning in cooking, chives should not be added until the last minute or their uniquely delicate flavor is lost. They have an antiseptic action, and both their smell and taste improve the appetite and encourage the flow of digestive juices.

FAST FOOD AID

• *Not an aid for people, but for plants this time. Planting a border of chives around your rosebed protects the roses against black spot.*

BASIL

The natural accompaniment to all tomato dishes and a principal ingredient of pesto sauce, basil contains volatile oils, especially linalol, limonene, and estragole. It is good for flatulence, helps digestion, and its antiseptic properties are said to benefit acne. It is also a mild sedative and makes an excellent evening snack to help those suffering from insomnia: tear up three or four leaves into small pieces and them add to a sandwich of lettuce and tomato for a natural tranquillizing effect.

FAST FOOD AIDS

• *Tear eight basil leaves into small pieces, then add to a scant half cup/100ml of cider vinegar. Leave for three weeks, shaking occasionally. One tablespoon added to your bath water is antiseptic and invigorating.*

• *Also rub a crushed basil leaf on exposed skin – it makes a good insect repellent.*

CORIANDER

Of all the spices to be grown in America, coriander was among the first. Both the seeds and leaves (cilantro) are used, though they have very different flavors. This strongly aromatic plant contains linalol, pinene, terpinine, and flavonoids. It is one of the most popular of all the food plants of India, the fresh leaves being sprinkled over curries. Ayurvedic physicians use it as a diuretic, as a digestive aid, and to enhance male potency.

FAST FOOD AID

• *Tea made from a heaped teaspoon of chopped coriander leaves in a cup of boiling water helps with wind, irritable bowel syndrome, and stress. A teaspoon of crushed and roasted seeds in a glass of warm water makes a good gargle for oral thrush.*

DILL

Widely used in pickles, soups, and fish dishes, dill contains the volatile oils carvone, limonene, and phellandrine, as well as cumarins and xanthones. It is extremely effective in the relief of gripe, flatulence, and stomach pain. Most babies are given dill in the form of gripe water. Its name comes from a Saxon word meaning "to lull."

FENNEL

This herb is used mostly in fish dishes. It contains volatile oils, mainly anethole and fenchone, and some flavonoids. It makes an exceptional aid for flatulence, stimulates the liver, and improves the digestion. Most fennel is grown for its feathery leaves and seeds, although the Florence fennel produces a large white bulb that is delicious either raw in salads or cooked. Fennel is a useful diuretic and an infusion of the seeds is helpful for kidney stones and cystitis. In the past the leaves, roots, and seeds were all eaten to improve strength and fitness and to help in weight control.

HEALTH WARNING

Excessive amounts of fennel seeds can be toxic so do not exceed the recommended dose.

MARJORAM AND OREGANO

People get very confused by these two herbs, but it is simply a question of names. *Origanum vulgare*, known as oregano throughout the Mediterranean and in the US, is the original wild oregano. In Britain the same plant is known as wild marjoram. It was taken to America by the early settlers, where its name was changed in the 1940s. Oregano contains highly active essential oil with a number of components including thymol, carvacrol, and origanene, and it is these constituents that make it such an important medicinal plant. It has a powerful antiseptic action and is very effective in the treatment of all respiratory problems, coughs, bronchitis, and even asthma. A cup of oregano tea is an instant answer to anxiety and nervousness. With a little honey, it is also a perfect calming and relaxing bedtime drink for insomniacs.

FAST FOOD AID

• *Chew a leaf or two to help alleviate toothache.*

Herbs

PARSLEY

FAST FOOD AID

• *Chew a few leaves of fresh parsley to freshen the breath after onions, garlic, or too much alcohol.*

The most widely used of all culinary herbs, parsley is, sadly, often sent back to the kitchen as an unwanted garnish. It contains the essential oils apiole, myristicin, and limonene, as well as cumarins and flavonoids. It is also rich in vitamins A and C, iron, calcium, and potassium. Traditionally used as a diuretic and antiinflammatory, it is also a strong antioxidant. By aiding the elimination of uric acid it is useful in treating rheumatism and gout. Yet another herb valued by the Greeks and Romans. They knew it as a digestive aid and diuretic. Modern herbalists know that the seeds are a more powerfully diuretic than the leaves and can be used just like celery seeds. I recommend parsley, celery, carrot, and apple juice to patients who experience uncomfortable fluid retention in the days before the onset of menstruation. Parsley tea is simply made – put a large handful of chopped leaves into a jug, add 2pt/900ml boiling water, cover, leave for ten minutes, then strain. When cool, keep a pitcher of this tea in the refrigerator and drink a glass every three hours as a gentle, natural diuretic.

HEALTH WARNING

Large doses of parsley seeds can be toxic. Do not use them at all if you have kidney disease or are pregnant.

ROSEMARY

Valued for its powers of "remembrance," rosemary is both a tonic and stimulant of the brain's cortex. It eases general debility, improves memory loss by enhancing the cellular uptake of oxygen, and reduces nervous tension. Used with lamb and chicken dishes throughout the Mediterranean, rosemary contains the volatile oils borneol, camphor, limonene, flavonoids, and rosemaricene. Rosemary is also antiinflammatory, stimulates the gall bladder and increases the flow of bile, so aiding fat digestion. In addition the rosemaricene acts as a mild painkiller – rosemary tea is an excellent natural remedy for headaches. Rosemary also aids good circulation and strengthens weak blood vessels. It is used in many herbal shampoos because of its refreshing, tonic quality and an infusion of rosemary with borax can be used as a rinse to treat dandruff. Rosemary is a true food for the mind and spirit – a perfect tonic for anyone who feels "one degree under" and deserving of its reputation in classical Greece as an effective remedy for depression and despondency.

FAST FOOD AID

• *Hang a bunch of rosemary sprigs under the hot tap of your bathtub to make the water truly invigorating and reviving to both body and spirit.*

SAGE

Known and used since ancient times, sage's botanical name, Salvia, comes from the Latin word *salvere,* literally meaning "to be saved" but colloquially "to be in good health," referring to the healing properties of this remarkable herb. It is used in stuffings with rich meats like pork and venison, in sausages and in any heavy meat dish, as it stimulates the bile and improves the digestion of fats. It contains volatile oils, thujone (a strong antiseptic), bitters, flavonoids, and phenolic acids and is a cleansing antiseptic and antiinflammatory herb. Herbalists use it to help with menstrual problems, to reduce excessive sweating, and for chest infections.

Red sage, a Chinese relative known as *Dan shen,* is listed in the very earliest Chinese herbal writings as stimulating the blood flow. In fact, this variety contains tanshinones, which improve the efficiency of the heart by stimulating coronary circulation. Red sage is also powerfully antiseptic and makes a very effective gargle for sore throats. A teaspoon of the fresh, chopped herb added to a glass of boiling water, covered for ten minutes, then strained can be used as a gargle when cool enough. Sage tea can also be used as an effective mouthwash for gum infections and mouth ulcers. It is the thujone in ordinary sage that is a phytoestrogen and helps in the regulation of menstrual problems. For the same reason consumption of sage on a regular basis helps women through the difficult times of the menopause by controlling hot flushes.

HEALTH WARNING

Sage can interfere with the flow of breast milk so don't overuse this herb when breastfeeding.

FAST FOOD AID

• *Rubbing the skin with sage leaves reduces the discomfort of insect bites and stings.*

THYME

HEALTH WARNING

Essential oil of thyme is toxic – do not take it internally. If you are pregnant do not use the essential oil for massage or in the bath.

FAST FOOD AID

• *For rheumatic aches and pains add five drops of thyme oil to a hot bath.*

This herb is used as a tea and very widely used in cooking. Ancient Greeks put it in baths, the Romans used it to purify their houses and it formed part of the eighteenth-century "nosegay" to protect against the smell of disease. It always forms part of a bouquet garni and is good in stews, casseroles, marinades, and chicken dishes. It contains the essential oils thymol (still widely used as a base for many antiseptics and mouthwashes) and carvacrol, as well as flavonoids. It helps in the breakdown of fats, and thymol and carvol have a specific effect on the smooth muscle of the trachea, which explains the expectorant benefits of thyme. Thyme oil is widely used in pharmaceutical and cosmetic products, as well as for flavoring. Tea made from thyme makes a good gargle for sufferers of sore throats and mouth ulcers. Thyme oil added to a hot bath can also help to ease rheumatic pain.

Spices

Like herbs, spices have a long history of both culinary and medicinal use. With their exotic scents and intense flavors, they offer one of the easiest ways of adding savor and bringing exciting variation to everyday foods. Many of these spices are known to aid the digestion and stimulate the appetite, and they can also be a useful alternative to salt for those on a low-sodium diet.

namaldehyde, which has a mild sedative effect, acts as a painkiller, and helps to lower raised blood pressure. Cinnamon is also a digestive aid and helps to control sickness and diarrhea. Ayurvedic practitioners traditionally use it in the treatment of anorexia and as an expectorant.

FAST FOOD AID

• *A cinnamon stick boiled in water produces an excellent steam inhalation for blocked sinuses and chesty coughs.*

FAST FOOD AID

• *For a warming massage oil, especially for aching muscles after sport, put 1 cup/250ml of grapeseed oil into a bowl and add 1³⁄₄oz/50g of finely chopped chili pepper. Stand the bowl in a saucepan of hot water on a very gentle heat and leave to infuse gently for at least one hour. Strain the oil into a dark glass bottle and keep in the refrigerator. Use sparingly and massage well into the affected muscles.*

CARDAMOM

FAST FOOD AID

• *Chewing a few cardamom seeds cleans the mouth and disguises the odour of even the hottest curry or Spanish garlic soup.*

This herb is helpful for all digestive problems, especially diarrhea, colic, and gas. The pods are used equally in sweet and savory dishes, and in India they form a vital ingredient of many curry dishes. In Ayurvedic medicine, cardamom seeds are regarded as a cardio-tonic and an expectorant.

ANISE

Also called aniseed, its flavor and medicinal value come from the essential oils, anethole and estragol. The seeds are helpful for dry coughs and for breaking up mucus. Tea made from the seeds relieves flatulence, stimulates the appetite, and aids digestion. It was the traditional remedy to improve the flow of milk in nursing mothers.

CARAWAY

In Central Europe caraway seeds are a well-known aid to digestion. They contain the compounds carvone, limonene, and pinene, which make them effective in coping with wind or flatulence. Add them to potentially windy dishes, such as cabbage or beans, or make an infusion of them to soothe indigestion. They are a gentle diuretic, an expectorant, and are often used in children's cough remedies.

FAST FOOD AID

• *A mixture of five drops of essential oil to 1fl oz/25ml of grapeseed oil is useful in the treatment of scabies.*

CINNAMON

This spice is a stimulant, a tonic, and an antiseptic. It warms the whole system and helps combat the fatigue and listlessness that so often accompany a bout of flu or other viral infections. Bruise a stick of cinnamon and add it to a hot, sweet toddy at the start of a cold, or whenever you feel low. Its most important constituent is the volatile oil cin-

CAYENNE

The cayenne chili is one of many members of the Capsicum family. This fiery plant has always been popular with herbalists for use in acute illness, where the body becomes chilled and the pulse slows down. Its most important chemical constituent is capsaicin, which accounts for cayenne's amazing ability to stimulate the circulation and, added to your food, chili – fresh, dried, or powdered – helps those suffering from cold hands and feet and chilblains. Capsicidins from the seeds also have quite a strong antibacterial power. Cayenne acts as a digestive stimulant and helps to protect against stomach bugs and food poisoning.

HEALTH WARNING

People with sensitive skins can react to hot peppers so wear gloves when preparing cayenne.

CLOVES

These are a powerful antiseptic and a warming stimulant to the circulation. Add a bruised clove or two to any herbal tea to give you an extra lift. Its major constituent is the volatile oil eugenole. The Indians, like the Chinese, regarded cloves highly as a breath freshener, and its use in the Indian spice mixture garam masala imparts a distinctive taste to Indian cooking. Ayurvedic practitioners knew about the clove's ability to ease the pain of toothache long before clove oil became a popular remedy in the Western world. Sadly, its value in the West has been mostly culinary.

FAST FOOD AIDS

• *For toothache, either chew a clove or rub a couple of drops of essential oil around the affected tooth and repeat as necessary.*

• *For the treatment of boils, dab two or three drops of essential oil of cloves onto the surface of the boil (see bread poultice on p.112).*

Spices

GINGER

Widely used in all Asian cooking, ginger is a common ingredient in both sweet and savory dishes. It contains zingiberene, gingerols, and very pungent shogaols in the dried form – so dried ginger is much more pungent than the fresh root. It is useful for the relief of coughs and colds, is generally a warming plant, and is extremely valuable in the prevention of travel sickness and early-morning sickness during pregnancy. Fresh ginger grated into hot lemon and with a teaspoon of honey as a bedtime drink can stop a cold in its tracks.

FAST FOOD AID

• *Ginger tea is good for morning sickness, travel sickness, post-operative sickness, and as a warming drink. Peel and grate ½in / 1cm of ginger root into a cup. Add boiling water, cover, and stand for ten minutes. Strain, add a teaspoon of honey, and sip slowly.*

MUSTARD

Mustard seeds contain sinigrin, which is converted to allyl isothiocyanate, which gives mustard its taste, smell and inflammatory qualities. Most modern medicinal use is external, though mustard is both diuretic and emetic (induces vomiting). Mustard flour mixed to a paste with water can be spread on cloth and applied to the lower back for lumbago and sciatica, to the chest for the treatment of bronchitis and pneumonia, and elsewhere for the relief of neuralgia. Used as a condiment, mustard stimulates the gastric juices and so aids the digestion.

FAST FOOD AIDS

• *Add a dessertspoon of mustard powder to a large bowl of hot water to make an invigorating foot bath for the relief of headaches and to bring a quick end to colds and flu.*

HEALTH WARNING

When applied to the skin, mustard may cause blistering – intentional as a counterirritant in Chinese medicine – so test it on a small area of skin before using mustard poultices.

HORSERADISH

This belongs to the same species, Cruciferae, as watercress, and shares many of its tonic and curative powers, including a strong antibiotic action. For centuries it was cultivated primarily as a medicinal herb and its powerful antibacterial and cancer-protective properties come from its siligrin content, which breaks down to form isothiocyanates. The plant is rich in sulfur and its traditional English use as a condiment with roast meats and oily fish acts an aid to their digestion. Horseradish is a wonderful remedy for coughs and sinus problems. A teaspoon of fresh grated root with some honey in a cup of boiling water is a remedy for sore throats, blocked sinuses and flu.

FAST FOOD AIDS

• *A poultice of grated horseradish steeped in hot water can be applied to unbroken chilblains.*

HEALTH WARNING

Contact with the skin can cause blistering. Horseradish also contains goitrogens, which can affect the thyroid gland and interfere with the drug thyroxin. Those with thyroid problems should make sure they use this herb sparingly.

JUNIPER

These tiny berries are what gives gin its unique flavor and they impart a powerful tang when used in cooking. Herbalists use them as a stimulating diuretic for diseases of the urinary tract, particularly cystitis. They can be used for rheumatism or gout, as they promote the excretion of uric acid. Like so many culinary herbs, they are tonic to the digestive system.

HEALTH WARNING

Do not take juniper if you suffer from kidney disease or acute urinary infection or if you are pregnant.

FAST FOOD AID

• *Essential oil of juniper – five drops to 1fl oz / 25ml of grapeseed oil – is helpful when massaged over areas of cellulite, as it speeds up the elimination of waste products stored under the skin. But do not use juniper oil externally if you are pregnant.*

NUTMEG AND MACE

These spices both come from the same plant, an evergreen tree whose botanical name is *Myristica fragrans*. The flavor and smell of nutmeg and mace are much the same, although mace tastes slightly more bitter. The major component of nutmeg in terms of its effects on the body is myristicin, which has a profound effect on the brain and is chemically similar to mescalen (from the famous peyote cactus in Mexico). Nutmeg stimulates the appetite and is a valuable digestive remedy for food poisoning, diarrhea, and nausea. In Indian Ayurvedic medicine it is regarded as extremely important for a glowing skin. It is also added to traditional remedies for insomnia, coughs and nausea.

FAST FOOD AID

• *For severe food poisoning, add a little nutmeg to a glass of peppermint tea and drink every four hours.*

HEALTH WARNING

Nutmeg and mace are highly toxic in large quantities, so use sparingly in food. Quite moderate doses can irritate the cortex of the brain and result in hallucinations, rapid heartbeat, and double vision.

Salt

SALT

Eating too much salt causes high blood pressure, strokes, and heart attacks. Salt also aggravates the fluid retention that occurs around period time and also in heart failure. Too much salt is linked to cancer of the stomach and makes asthma worse. But Professor MacGregor of St. George's Hospital, London, says that there is even worse news – too much salt causes loss of calcium from the body and is a major factor leading to osteoporosis (brittle bone disease). He believes that we should halve our average salt consumption, from ¼oz/10g to ⅛oz/5g a day – the level at which there is no risk of stomach cancer, high blood pressure, or fluid retention, and no loss of calcium from the bones. We actually need a mere 1g daily.

But it is not that easy as most of our salt is added by food manufacturers during processing. Salt is cheap, gives flavor to bland ingredients, soaks up water to make some products heavier, is addictive, and makes you thirsty – and many salty snacks are manufactured by brewers and soft-drink companies. There is far too much salt in bread and you will find it in cornflakes and other breakfast cereals, and lurking in all meat products, so it is hard to avoid. It is the most widely used legal substance that puts your health at risk.

Salt is a chemical substance called sodium chloride and it is the sodium that causes the problems. The kidneys work harder to get rid of it, the heart works harder, pumping more blood through the kidneys, and the blood pressure goes up. Since none of us needs to add salt to our food – there is more than enough there naturally – it makes sense to reduce our salt consumption as much as possible, both as a protective measure and as an essential part of the treatment for all those who suffer from high blood pressure.

I always try to wean my patients off salt, and it isn't as hard as you might think. Start by taking the salt cellar off the table. Use more of the savory and aromatic herbs in your cooking. Then start to reduce the amount of salt that you add to recipes (I never suggest that people should use the "low-salt" salts). Within two months you and your family will be enjoying the real taste of food, and not the flavor of salt. Vegetables cooked without salt taste better steamed rather than boiled, which is a healthier method anyway.

When you go shopping, look at food labels carefully. The nearer the top of the list of ingredients that salt is, the more salt there is in that particular food. And watch out for monosodium glutamate, saccharin, bicarbonate of soda, baking soda, sodium nitrate, sodium nitrite, and many others – all of these substances contain sodium.

Some of the worst offenders are take-outs, especially Indian, Chinese, hot dogs, and pizzas. Go easy, too, on processed foods, chips, salted nuts, savory nibbles, and most bottled sauces. Bacon, ham, sausages, smoked fish, canned and package soups, pickled meat and fish, baked beans, cornflakes, all foods canned in brine, yeast extracts and even bread all contain high levels of salt.

British food manufacturers often show "mg of sodium per 100g [3½oz]" and this looks deceptively small. Multiply by 2.5 and you will get the amount of salt – and remember, 5g a day (just a teaspoonful) should be your total intake.

● **It is never too late to cut down on the salt in your diet. Help your family to better health, and make those changes straight away. Get your children into good habits now and you will protect them for life.**

Vinegars

Since our earliest beginnings we have practiced the ancient art of vinegar-making. In earliest China and Japan, and in the ancient Greek and Roman civilizations, this age-old craft flourished.

ENERGY PER STANDARD PORTION 1KCAL

❦ *Valuable as a method of preserving.*

❦ *A useful flavoring.*

Although much modern vinegar is produced by high-tech industry, the very best-quality vinegars are still made by the Orléans process, which has not changed in centuries and is extremely slow, taking at least three months before the necessary acidity is reached.

All vinegars start with alcoholic liquid, which is acidified using a group of micro-organisms that are called acetobacter, ending up with 4–6 percent acetic acid in the finished product.

The sharp tangy taste of vinegar is an excellent fat-free dressing for salads, adding extra flavor for those on a low-fat diet who must avoid mayonnaise.

● **The word "vinegar" comes from the Latin *Vinum acer* which means "sharp wine." Vinegar is the oldest of all known flavorings and is also an invaluable way of preserving food.**

BALSAMIC VINEGAR

Little known outside its home town of Modena in northern Italy until recent years, balsamic vinegar has however long been popular with great chefs and gourmets and highly prized by Italians. It is made from grape must, which

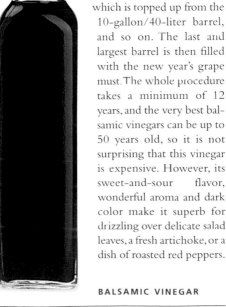

HERB VINEGAR

should ideally come from the Trebbiano grape. As soon as the must begins fermenting it is simmered carefully and reduced in volume by 50 percent, leaving behind a concentrate that is about one-third sugar. The cultures are introduced and then the real process begins, starting with a collection of between five and twelve barrels, each made of different wood – oak, chestnut, cherry, ash, and mulberry are the most popular. The barrels decrease in size from 16 gallons/60 liters to 5 gallons/20 liters, and when half of the 5-gallon/20-liter barrel is drained to use as balsamic vinegar, it is topped up from the 8-gallon/30-liter barrel, which is topped up from the 10-gallon/40-liter barrel, and so on. The last and largest barrel is then filled with the new year's grape must. The whole procedure takes a minimum of 12 years, and the very best balsamic vinegars can be up to 50 years old, so it is not surprising that this vinegar is expensive. However, its sweet-and-sour flavor, wonderful aroma and dark color make it superb for drizzling over delicate salad leaves, a fresh artichoke, or a dish of roasted red peppers.

BALSAMIC VINEGAR

Vinegars

CIDER VINEGAR

This is particularly popular in the US, where the starting alcohol is cider or apple wine. It is not as acidic as malt vinegar but has a distinctive, crisp, acidic flavor that is reminiscent of some of the old-fashioned varieties of apple. It is perfect for light, delicate salad dressings. It is also one of the great traditional home remedies of North America where it is used for the relief of rheumatism and arthritis.

FAST FOOD AIDS

• *Vinegar is a good antiseptic and, with the addition of garlic, a powerful anti-fungal. For athlete's foot, add two crushed cloves of garlic and four tablespoons of cider vinegar to 3½ pt/1.7 liters of hand-hot water. Soak the affected foot for 15 minutes once a day – you will smell like a French fry, but the fungal infection will clear amazingly quickly.*

**MALT
VINEGAR**

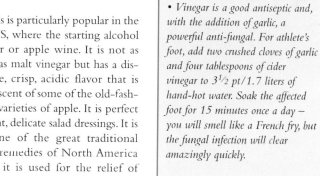

MALT VINEGAR

This is the commonest variety in the UK and is the vinegar you use to pickle your onions, gherkins, or walnuts. Malt vinegar is made by fermenting malted barley with yeast and then adding the acetobacter cultures, and may be given a darker color by the addition of caramel. Distilled malt vinegar is a clear distillation of ordinary malt vinegar, without any colorings, and is most commonly used for pickling and preserving.

RICE VINEGAR

The traditional vinegar of the Far East, this can be made from rice itself, or from rice wine (sake). It is less acidic than other vinegars and is a delicate accompaniment to Chinese and Japanese food.

WINE VINEGAR

The main variety produced in Europe, wine vinegar starts with low-alcohol wine – red, white, or rosé – to which the cultures are added. Traditionally it is a slow process, which takes place in wooden barrels and results in the end product containing a large number of aromatic compounds, which give good wine vinegar its wonderful flavor.

All of the real vinegars, with the exception of balsamic, can be flavored and spiced to suit specific purposes. Chillis, garlic, rosemary, tarragon, bay leaves, even fruits such as raspberries and strawberries, can be added to vinegar and it is fun to experiment with them. As well as the flavors that you add, you also reap the medicinal benefits of the individual herbs.

In his best-selling book *Folk Medicine*, Dr. D.C. Jarvis advocates the traditional American folk remedy for arthritis of two teaspoons of apple cider vinegar and two teaspoons of pure honey in a glass of hot water, to be taken three times a day with meals and at bedtime.

Thrush is another condition that responds to vinegar. Its acidity is the same as that in the vagina and restoring acidity to the proper level makes it more difficult for the *Candida* yeast, which causes thrush, to survive. Douching with a solution of 2½ cups/600ml of warm water and four teaspoons of vinegar can be a great help to those who are suffering from recurring and chronic vaginal thrush.

SYNTHETIC VINEGAR

• *This is not made by fermentation and is not really vinegar. It is known commercially as NBC (nonbrewed condiment) and is usually what is in the bottle on the counter of your local fast-food store. It is artificially colored with caramel, then flavored with sugar, artificial flavorings, and salt. This cheap product of the chemical factory is best avoided, particularly by people with allergies or hyperactive children.*

**RED WINE
VINEGAR**

Fats and oils

Saturated, polyunsaturated, mono-unsaturated, trans; cholesterol, high-density lipoprotein, low-density lipoprotein; omega-3, omega-6 – these are all varieties of fats, but are they beneficial or harmful? Do we really need any of them in our daily diet?

❦ Provide essential fatty acids for healthy skin and development of body cells.

❦ Rich source of fat-soluble vitamins A, D, E, and K.

The whole question of fats is complicated and confusing, but understanding the different types of fats – what they do, how much we need, and how much is healthy – is a vital step to nutritional good health.

Of all the components of our food fat contains the highest number of calories by weight and (with the exception of fat-reduced spreads) all fats – whether lard, butter, margarine, or olive oil – contain nearly the same number of calories in every 3½oz/100g and more than twice as many calories as starchy foods: 3½oz/100g of lard supply 891 calories, but 3½oz/100g of boiled new potatoes only 76 calories. But turn your potatoes into French fries and you'll get 253 calories, or a massive 533 from a packet of chips, because of the added fat.

GRAPESEED OIL

The average consumption of fat in the British diet represents around 40 percent of our total energy, 3½oz/100g a day, of which we get 50 percent from meat, milk, cream, cheese, eggs and oily fish, 30 percent from butter, margarine, and other fats and oils, and 8 percent from cookies, cakes, and pastries.

The first step in reducing your fat consumption is to cut down on

FAT FACTS

Food	Amount containing ¼oz/10g of fat
Butter	⅖oz/12g
Cheddar cheese	1oz/30g
Cheesecake	1oz/30g
Chocolate cookies	1⅙oz/35g
Cream cheese	⅔oz/20g
French fries (frozen)	1¾oz/50g
Fried bacon (streaky)	⅔oz/20g
Fried scampi	1⅚oz/55g
Heavy cream	⅔oz/20g
Lamb chop with fat	1oz/30g
Lard	⅓oz/10g
Light cream	1¾oz/50g
Margarine	⅖oz/12g
Mayonnaise	⅖oz/12g
Meat pasty	1¾oz/50g
Milk chocolate	1⅙oz/35g
Pork pie	1⅙oz/35g
Pork sausage	1oz/30g
Potato chips	1oz/30g
Quiche	1⅙oz/35g
Roast duck with skin	⅞oz/25g
Scotch egg	1¾oz/50g
Sponge cake	1⅓oz/40g
Stilton cheese	⅞oz/25g
Taramasalata	⅔oz/20g
Traditional shortbread	1⅓oz/40g
Vegetable oil	⅓oz/10g

all the visible fats – such as butter, cheese, cream, the fat around your steak or chop, or on the outside of a slice of ham. Much more difficult is to avoid the hidden fats in meat products like sausages, salamis, pâtés, pies, and pasties, in cookies, cakes, Danish pastries, and chocolates. The only way to avoid them is to read all labels very carefully.

Before you set off for the supermarket, look at the chart on the left and see how little you need to eat of some of these high-fat foods to provide just 10g of fat – one-third of your total recommended consumption for a day.

The populations of Britain and the US divide into three camps: the majority who, sadly, ignore all the risks of a high animal-fat diet; a smaller but growing number who take on board the messages of healthy eating and are gradually reducing the total calories from fat in their daily diets; and a small but significant band of "health freaks" who believe that a low-fat diet means a no-fat diet, and so avoid all oily fish, all vegetable oils, and even the super-nourishing avocado.

● **There is now an irrefutable link between both heart disease and breast cancer and a high intake of animal fat in the diet. The British government is aiming to reduce the total**

CHEESE

percentage of calories from fat to 35 percent, and in the US they are recommending a reduction to 30 percent.

But without some fats in our diet we cannot absorb the fat-soluble vitamins A, D, E, and K, and for this reason some fat is vital. But what sort?

Saturated fats are nearly all animal fats: butter, lard, the fat on your meat, and the fat in your cheese, cream, and milk. Some vegetables also produce saturated fat, especially coconut and palm. The body is able to manufacture its own saturated fatty acids so you do not actually need to eat them.

Polyunsaturated fats are found mainly in vegetable oils like soybean, corn, sunflower, and safflower. They also occur in oily fish and although containing virtually as many calories as saturated fats, are extremely important and should form a regular part of your diet.

Mono-unsaturated fats occur mostly in olive oil, rapeseed oil, nuts, and seeds and are important as heart-protectors. The enormous consumption of olive oil in all Mediterranean countries is thought to be one of the factors that results in a much lower level of heart disease in these southern countries than those that occur in northern Europe and North America.

CORN OIL

Fats and oils

LARD

Essential fatty acids are the omega-6 and omega-3 fatty acids, which are vital building blocks of body cells, especially brain and central-nervous-system tissue. They are found in both mono-unsaturated and polyunsaturated fats. Without them normal development of a baby's brain during pregnancy and in early childhood can be adversely affected. Recent studies have expressed concern at the lack of some of these essential fatty acids in the diets of pregnant vegetarian women. Omega-6 fats are found in olive oil and sunflower oil, while the omega-3 fatty acids are abundant in oily fish, soybean and rapeseed oil, and walnuts.

Cholesterol levels in the blood are a key marker of an individual's risk of heart disease. Though other factors are involved – such as smoking, obesity, lack of exercise, and overall diet – cholesterol is of fundamental importance. It is an essential constituent of every cell in the body, but we do not actually need to consume cholesterol, as we manufacture it from other fats.

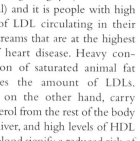

WALNUT OIL

Most people with raised cholesterol levels can reduce them by cutting down on the amount of saturated fat in their diet, whereas lowering the intake of cholesterol itself benefits only a small percentage of those with raised levels. There is no cholesterol in plant foods, but it is found in all animal and animal-based foods, the highest amount being present in organ meats and egg yolk.

There are two ways in which cholesterol circulates in the body. It is attached either to Low-Density Lipoproteins (LDLs) or High-Density Lipoproteins (HDLs). LDLs are the bad guys and HDLs the good guys (remember: L = lethal) and it is people with high levels of LDL circulating in their bloodstreams that are at the highest risk of heart disease. Heavy consumption of saturated animal fat increases the amount of LDLs. HDLs, on the other hand, carry cholesterol from the rest of the body to the liver, and high levels of HDL in the blood signify a reduced risk of heart disease.

High-cholesterol foods that contain little other saturated fat seem to make very little difference to blood cholesterol levels, except in the small number of people suffering from genetic disorders of cholesterol metabolism. Eggs, fish roe (taramasalata), and some shellfish have been unfairly labeled in this way. It is true that the British Heart Foundation and the American Heart Association advise eating no more than three eggs a week, but the World Health Organization is happy to recommend ten eggs a week. Of course, it all depends on what the rest of your diet is like. There are many foods, especially those high in soluble fiber, that encourage the body to eliminate surplus cholesterol (see heart disease, p 184).

Trans fats are not listed on food labels, although you may occasionally find a margarine that declares itself to be free of, or low in, trans fats. After decades of being told that margarines are safer for your heart than butter – an argument with which I have never agreed, since butter is a natural product and margarine the synthetic product of a

DRIPPINGS

factory – American research points the finger directly at these previously ignored culprits.

Liquid oils go through a process called hydrogenation in order to convert them into solid or semi-solid margarines. Commercial cooking oils are also partially hydrogenated, which gives them a longer life in the deep-fat fryer and so makes them commercially attractive. A by-product of this process are the trans fats, and enormous population studies in the US have revealed that these trans fats are as bad as, and possibly worse than, saturated fats as a cause of serious heart disease.

Following information that I received from the Center for Science in the Public Interest, Washington, more than ten years ago, I wrote articles informing the British public that McDonalds used rendered beef tallow for all their frying. Now it seems that matters have got even worse. In common with the majority of fast-food chains, they use partially hydrogenated oils and the trans fats from these, combined with the saturated fats already in the food, make a staggering contribution to our total consumption of heart-risk fats.

US guidelines advise a maximum daily consumption of 20g of saturated fat, and the British Department of Health a maximum 5g of trans fats. With all the hidden trans fats in fast food, you are now likely to find a mixture of saturated and trans fats totalling 12g in some French fries, 9g in fried chicken pieces, around 4g in a packet of popcorn, 6g in chocolate jelly rolls or a modest portion of chocolate fudge cake, up to 10g in some doughnuts, and a massive 15g in some commercial cheesecakes.

BUTTER

FAST FOOD AID

• For dry, brittle, and perm-damaged hair olive oil makes a superb deep-conditioning treatment. Comb the oil into wet or damp hair and then wrap up in a towel. Leave for a couple of hours (or overnight if possible), then shampoo as normal.

Fats and oils

HARD MARGARINE

BUTTER

ENERGY PER STANDARD PORTION 74KCAL

This is delicious and, in modest use, it is certainly better for you than nearly all margarines. The bad news is that it is virtually all fat, and 60 percent of that comprises saturated fat. $3\frac{1}{2}$oz/100g of butter provides 740 calories, but it is a rich source of vitamins A, D, and E. Some brands are much higher in salt than others – it may contain anything from no salt at all to 1300mg per $3\frac{1}{2}$oz/100g. In the UK, butter may be colored but may not contain antioxidants, unless the finished product is exclusively for manufacturing or catering use.

● **Unlike most other dairy products, butter is a poor source of calcium and contains virtually no B vitamins at all. Long before the trans fats scare I advised patients to use modest, even sparing, amounts of butter, rather than margarine.**

BUTTER

HEALTH WARNING

On no account use butter or margarine as an emergency treatment for burns or scalds. Although this was advised in the past, the heat from the wound in fact causes the butter to fry – even up to an hour after scalding. Hold the affected area under cold running water for at least ten minutes.

MARGARINE

ENERGY PER STANDARD PORTION 74KCAL

This is a complex chemical product combining oils, fats, flavoring, and coloring made by a process first invented by the French chemist Mège Mouriès, in Paris in 1869. It is usually a blend of vegetable, animal, or fish oils, which hydrogenation converts from liquid to solid or soft margarine. This is the process that produces the harmful trans fats as a by-product.

Low-fat spreads are much lower in calories and fats and, similar to polyunsaturated margarines, are cholesterol-free. Remember, though, that cholesterol-free does not mean fat-free. By law margarine in Britain has to be fortified with vitamins A and D and is responsible for nearly half the amount of vitamin D in the British diet. The total amount of fat in all but low-fat spreads is about the same in margarines as it is in butter. But while $3\frac{1}{2}$oz/100g of butter provides 54g of saturated fat, hard margarines contain only 36g and polyunsaturated margarines only 16g.

● **Margarines do however provide considerably more vitamin E than butter, but even this fact could not persuade me to eat it.**

FAST FOOD AIDS

In traditional folk medicine, a spoonful of olive oil taken while fasting, first thing in the morning, to which a little lemon juice may be added, has always been recommended for liver problems.

Olive oil can be used as a cuticle softener during a manicure. Mix half a cup of olive oil with half a litre of warm water and soak fingertips for 10–15 minutes. Then gently push back cuticles with a cotton bud.

Use vegetable oil or olive oil as an emollient to soothe very dry skin or psoriasis. They are most effective if you apply them after a bath.

SOFT MARGARINE

HEALTH WARNING

A low-fat diet does not mean a no-fat diet. Those who avoid all fat (a group that comprises mainly intelligent, successful women in the 25–55 age group, who are frequently obsessive exercisers or dieters and much too thin) are as much at risk of serious disease as the overweight, fat-eating segment of the population.

Fats and oils

VEGETABLE OILS

ENERGY PER STANDARD PORTION 99KCAL

Like all fats, oils are enormous providers of calories – 899 per 3¹/₂oz/100g. Most vegetable oils contain little saturated fat and good supplies of vitamin E. Palm and coconut oil, both contain large amounts of saturated fat and coconut oil virtually no vitamin E. It is likely that either of these oils will be a constituent of anything labeled "vegetable oil," so make sure that you buy only named varieties of oil or, if you are buying food canned in oil, avoid any that are labeled just vegetable oil.

Keep vegetable oils in a cool, dark place as heat and sunlight make them deteriorate quickly. If they are not in dark bottles, I advise you to wrap them in cooking foil. The polyunsaturated fats in vegetable oils are extremely important because they contain essential fatty acids that our bodies do not make for themselves. Sunflower is the richest of all in vitamin E, containing 49µg per 3¹/₂oz/100g of oil. When used in baking bread and cakes, oils retain the majority of their nutritional value, but when they are used for frying the percentage of polyunsaturated fats is gradually reduced by up to 20 percent in quite a short period of time.

Sunflower, corn, and safflower oils are ideal for light salad dressings and for cooking, though none has quite the flavor of really good-quality olive oil. Specialty oils like walnut, soybean, and sesame seed have really come to the fore in recent years with the increased interest in Oriental cooking and stir frying. Cooking in a wok at very high temperatures with small amounts of oil and little water means that the food is cooked very quickly and little of the extra oil is absorbed into the ingredients of your dish. Almond oil is good for salad dressings, and rapeseed oil (canola) has very little flavor but is useful for frying, as it has a high smoke point and is high in mono-unsaturated and polyunsaturated fats. Hazelnut oil has a distinctive flavor but a low smoke point – good for sauces, but not for frying food.

● **Peanut (groundnut) oil has a distinctive nutty flavor and a high smoke point, is low in saturated and high in mono-unsaturated fats, and has a reasonable amount of polyunsaturateds. It makes a good all-purpose oil.**

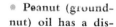

OLIVE OIL

SUNFLOWER OIL

HEALTH WARNING

It is a serious health hazard to overheat or repeatedly use the same oil for frying food as this results in the production of toxic chemicals. Once your frying oil has "smoked," it must never be reused. Extra-virgin olive oil is wasted used for frying, as its delicate flavor is destroyed.

OLIVE OIL

ENERGY PER STANDARD PORTION 99KCAL

For years nutritionists have been telling us that the higher polyunsaturated fats were, the better for our health. This put olive oil – a mono-unsaturated fat – way down the list. Scientific research has now confirmed the peasant wisdom of the Mediterranean area that olive oil is a marvelous food-medicine.

Polyunsaturated fats can combine in the body with oxygen to form peroxides – otherwise known as free radicals. The more unsaturated the fat, the more free radicals may be created. And these unstable compounds are highly destructive: they can seriously damage cell membranes and even damage the structure of DNA. This process of peroxidation – which turns fats rancid – can be kept at bay by substances known as antioxidants. One of the most powerful antioxidants is vitamin E, and olive oil is lavishly supplied with the most active – alpha – form of this vitamin. It actually has antioxidant activity to spare, and generous amounts of the best quality olive oil can be consumed without risk. Nutrition expert Ancel Keys was astonished to learn that Cretan peasants quite often breakfast on a chunk of bread and half a tumbler of olive oil. Because of this high antioxidant factor, olive oil is now considered to have a protective effect against maladies in which free-radical activity is implicated, among them cancer, arthritis, premature senility, and cardiovascular disease.

This antioxidant value would be enough in itself to account for the protective effect on the heart of the Mediterranean diet. But intensive research in Italy has revealed other active chemical components in olive oil that can help counteract a high-fat, high-cholesterol diet. One of these components, cycloarthanol, neutralizes cholesterol during the absorption cycle. Two other recent studies have shown that, on diets rich in olive oil, volunteers showed marked reductions in their blood cholesterol. Blood cholesterol levels, however, are now being seen as much less significant markers for potential heart problems than the quantity in the blood of HDLs or high-density lipoproteins, which scour excess cholesterol out of the bloodstream into the liver. Regular olive-oil eaters also have more beneficial HDLs, possibly contributing to the heart-protective effect of the Mediterranean diet.

Recent research has shown that while all fats promote the secretion by the gall bladder of bile – the digestive fluid that emulsifies fats for digestion – the bile-promoting effect of olive oil is both more intense and longer-lasting. This explains why, on a digestibility rating of 100 set up by the US Food and Drug Administration, olive oil scored full marks, sunflower oil 83, groundnut oil 81, and corn oil only 36. Olive oil is also more efficiently absorbed and promotes intestinal peristalsis – those rhythmic, squeezing movements that carry food through the body. For all these reasons, olive oil is the friend of the liverish, the dyspeptic, and the ulcer victim.

● **If you can possibly afford it, always choose extra-virgin olive oil. In this mechanically produced oil the vital antioxidants are preserved to give the oil the maximum biological value.**

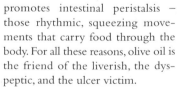

SUNFLOWER OIL

Sugars and sweeteners

WHITE SUGAR

*T*he sugar industry pours millions of dollars and pounds into trying to persuade us that sugar is a pure, natural food product, but nothing could be further from the truth. The sugar you buy in your local store, whether it is white or brown, is not natural or good for you.

BROWN SUGAR:
ENERGY PER 3¹/₂OZ/100G 362KCAL
WHITE SUGAR:
ENERGY PER 3¹/₂OZ/100G 394 KCAL

Sugar will not directly cause a heart attack, diabetes, behavioral disturbances, or acne, but it is often the first link in an inevitably progressive chain that leads to health disasters. Reducing the total sugar consumption by 50 percent in Britain and the US would have an enormous impact on health.

The government, schools, institutions, and, above all, parents must do something about the high sugar content of food that our children eat. The link between nutrition and crime can no longer be ignored, and eating too much sugar can have a disastrous effect on the behavior of some people, particularly teenagers. Research in the US has shown that changing the diet of young offenders in correctional institutions can

MOLASSES

make significant improvements in their behavior. In one study youngsters eating a healthier diet were compared with a group of offenders fed on the usual high-sugar prison fare. Prisoners on the better diet committed 45 percent fewer acts of antisocial behavior. Criminologist Professor Stephen Schoenthaler, who carried out this study, has now persuaded penal institutions throughout America to improve the food served to inmates, and has seen better behavior result from his work.

A regular diet that supplies too much refined sugar can lead to a condition known as hypoglycemia *(see p. 154)*, where there is, in fact, too little sugar present in the blood. This may be caused by diabetes *(see p. 168)* or by a disease of the pancreas, but is often the result of bad eating habits. Sweating, shaking, faintness, dizziness, headaches, and confusion can all develop when your blood-sugar level is too low.

Refined sugar, an essential ingredient of so many jams, cakes, puddings, cookies, canned fruits, and soft drinks, contains absolutely no nutritional value – all you get from it is a large helping of calories and rotten teeth. And there is now a growing suspicion that poor eating habits,

DEMERARA SUGAR

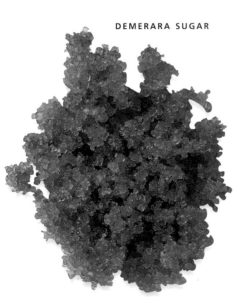

irregular meals, and a high sugar intake may seriously damage your state of mind.

The average consumption of sugar in the UK is around 2lb/1kg per head each week. – or more than 100lb/45kg a year for every man, woman, and child. Since adults tend to consume fewer high-sugar foods, just think how much sugar most children and teenagers are eating. Most of it comes from soft drinks, candies, and chocolate bars, and large quantities of processed food, and the hidden sugar in many manufactured products is alarming. Some breakfast cereals may contain up to 60 percent sugar, masquerading as dextrose, sucrose, corn syrup, molasses, or even honey – but these are all forms of sugar.

Over the years it has become increasingly clear to me that by encouraging patients to eat better food, to time their meals with more care, and to reduce their overall consumption of refined sugars, significant improvements can be made in their mental states.

Depression, fatigue, irritability, poor concentration, PMS, mood swings, poor performance at school, and hyperactivity are just some of the conditions that can be improved – and eating less sugar seems to be the common factor.

Sugar causes other problems too. It represents very poor nutritional value for money and is frequently used as a cheap bulking agent in highly processed convenience foods, so replacing more nourishing produce with empty calories. It is also known to increase the amount of triglyceride fats excreted from the sebaceous glands of the skin, so I am in no doubt that the first step to better skin is a reduction in sugar.

White sugar is bad for you, but brown sugar is good – true or false? Although unrefined sugars are marginally less bad for you, in that they do supply minute quantities of nutrients like potassium, calcium, and magnesium, with a little iron, this is usually absorbed from the processing machinery.

HIDDEN SUGAR

Food	Teaspoons of sugar
One plain graham cracker	0.5
Modest portion of baked beans	1
One chocolate-coated cookie	1
One plain doughnut	1
One scoop of plain ice cream	2
Three teaspoons of jam	2.5
Average slice of sponge cake	3
Average portion of sugar-frosted breakfast cereal	3
3¹/₂oz/100g of jelly	3
Three teaspoons of honey	3
Average fruit yogurt	4.5
11fl oz/330ml can of cola	7
Medium-sized can of fruit in syrup	10
3¹/₂oz/100g bar of chocolate	11
3¹/₂oz/100g pack of hard candies or peppermints	18

● **Honey contains tiny traces of nutrients and has other healing properties, but it is 20 percent water. Maple, corn, and glucose syrups, fructose, and maltose are all sugars under the guise of different names.**

SWEETENERS
Artificial sweeteners crop up everywhere: in regular foods – chips, candies, medicines, sauces, and even savory dishes – as well as in "low-calorie" products. Surprisingly there is little evidence that they help you consume fewer calories. It is true that artificial sweeteners – saccharin, acesulfame-K, and aspartame – contain no calories, but is using them really going to change your eating habits or reduce your taste for sweet things? Your tongue is the

ROUGH SUGAR

only part of your body that is fooled by these chemicals so you'll still crave something sweet, and it makes more health sense to reduce the amount of sugar you use.

There are also bulk sweeteners – mannitol, xylitol, sorbitol – which are used as bulking agents in many processed foods. They do not contain sucrose but do provide about the same number of calories as regular sugar. Their advantage is that they do not cause dental decay,

HEALTH WARNING

When sugar is digested by the body it is converted into glucose and fructose. These enter the bloodstream and end up in the liver. When sugar consumption is excessively high, the fructose does not behave in the same way as glucose but raises the levels of blood lipids – a type of fat that increases the risk of cholesterol deposits in the arteries. Those most at risk from this effect are men, some women on the contraceptive pill, and women past the menopause. Diets that are high in healthy, polyunsaturated fatty acids and low in saturated fats offer protection against this major health risk, but the combination, which is all too common, of a high-fat, high-sugar diet is a serious heart hazard.

so they are often found in candies and chewing gums that carry the "tooth-friendly" label. They can, however, cause diarrhea if taken in excessive amounts.

Artificial sweeteners act just like natural sugars, by stimulating the sweet-sensitive tastebuds on the tongue. Saccharin, for example, is 400 times sweeter than sugar, so tiny amounts can make things taste very sweet indeed. Unfortunately, it also leaves a slightly bitter metallic after-taste, which becomes worse if you use it in cooking.

Manufacturers and the British government state that sweeteners are perfectly safe, but a report in the British Consumers' Association magazine *Which?* explains that the acceptable daily intake (ADI) is calculated by studying experiments on animals to find the maximum amount of sweetener that does not produce harmful effects. This is divided by a safety factor of 100 to establish the maximum quantity that you can eat without danger every day. Critics of sweeteners believe that this is simply guesswork and that it is, in any case, very hard to calculate from the labels on processed foods exactly how much sweetener you are getting in your food.

Few manufacturers reveal the actual amounts of sweetener in their products, and it is not even clear how much of the chemical is in the sweeteners you drop into your coffee or tea. The safe amount of

saccharin for a girl of 6½ weighing 44lb/20kg to consume each day would be 100mg. *Which?* calculates that a couple of glasses of orange drink, a strawberry ice-lolly, a glass of sugar-free lemon drink, a can of sugar-free cola, an individual trifle, a portion of reduced-sugar baked beans, and a packet of shrimp chips, would give her an over-the-limit total of 112mg.

Dr. Michael Jacobson, Director of the Center for Science in the Public Interest (CSPI) in Washington, DC, has serious reservations about the safety of sweeteners. Saccharin may have been used for almost 100 years, but a number of studies during the 1970s linked it with cancer in laboratory animals and the American

SWEETENER TABLETS

government subsequently took it off the list of safe chemicals and finally banned it in 1977. Saccharin was finally exempted from the American food-safety laws and is now regarded as safe by government scientists in the UK, although in the US foods containing saccharin have to carry a warning label about their cancer-causing effect on laboratory animals!

Acesulfame-K Dr. Jacobson has called for a ban on this sweetener in the US, and the CSPI considers it the worst culprit. It claims that ace-sulfame-K is inadequately tested and that tests show that it causes cancer in animals, which means that it may increase the risk for humans. Government experts admitted that the safety data were not ideal but decided that there was enough evidence to prove its safety.

GRANULATED SWEETENER

Aspartame This poses some very specific problems. One of its ingredients is phenylalanine, a natural component of proteins. One in 20,000 babies is born with an illness called phenylketonuria (PKU – remember your baby's pricked heel test) and is not able to break down phenylalanine. Raised levels of this chemical can cause brain damage and retardation. For this reason all products containing aspartame carry the warning, "Contains phenylalanine." Government scientists maintain the product to be safe but some experts believe that a high intake could pose a risk to the babies of pregnant women who carry the trait for PKU. Jacobson says: "Many people (though a minuscule fraction of those who have consumed the additive) have reported dizziness, headaches, epileptic-like seizures, and menstrual problems after ingesting aspartame."

Cyclamate This sweetener is currently banned in America and the UK after tests showed an increase of cancer in laboratory animals fed on it. In Britain, European legislation is likely to come into force soon and so allow cyclamates back onto the market.

● **No healthy person needs extra sugar, let alone chemical sweeteners. If you need to lose weight, then change your eating habits. My advice is: always read food labels carefully to spot hidden sugars; don't use sweeteners if you are pregnant; and don't give them to children.**

Sweet things

CHOCOLATE

MILK CHOCOLATE:
ENERGY PER 3½OZ/100G 520KCAL

❦ *Good for depression – but beware its high sugar content, which may lead to rebound hypoglycemia, exhaustion, and even worse depression.*

❦ *Useful as an emergency food supply.*

❦ *Best eaten in moderation.*

CHOCOLATE

The whole history of chocolate is shrouded in romance and mystery. The name comes from the Mexican *chocolatl* and cacao from *cacauatl,* Mexico being the native home of the cocoa tree. This was so prized by the Mexicans that the seeds were used as currency at the time of the Aztecs.

Both chocolate and cocoa are made from cocoa beans. Cocoa is made by grinding the beans to a paste, adding sugar and starch and removing the fat. For chocolate most of the fat is left in and its quality is determined by the percentage of cocoa solids in the finished product. At least 50 percent cocoa solids is reckoned to be the minimum requirement for "quality chocolate," but for the very best this rises to 70 percent.

The fat, known as cocoa butter, is widely used in industry for the manufacture of cosmetics, and also in the pharmaceutical trade. It is very soothing to the skin and is found in hand and lip balms.

The famous botanist Carolus Linnaeus named the cocoa tree *Theobroma cacao,* "theobroma" meaning "food of the gods." One of the major ingredients of the cocoa bean is a stimulating chemical, theobromine, which is similar to caffeine (also present in the beans), but has a much gentler action. These two ingredients make chocolate a mild diuretic and a gentle stimulant. The theobromine is believed to trigger the release of natural "feel-good" chemicals in the brain, and it is these endorphins that also kindle the feelings of romance, love, and arousal. Theobromine also has a stimulating effect on the heart muscle and the kidneys and was traditionally used by medical herbalists, with the plant *Digitalis,* for fluid retention linked to heart failure.

In spite of its high fat content, chocolate is quite nutritious, dark chocolate especially being a good source of iron and magnesium. Chocolate supplies useful amounts of protein, traces of other minerals, and some of the B vitamins, but it is loaded with calories – over 500 per 3½oz/100g. You would need to walk briskly for two hours, pedal your bicycle for an hour and a half, or swim nonstop for an hour in order to burn off the calories in a 3½oz/100g bar of chocolate.

● **Because chocolate is known to dilate the blood vessels, it can also be useful in the treatment of those suffering from high blood pressure.**

HEALTH WARNING

Migraine sufferers should beware of chocolate. The caffeine that it contains – 20mg per square in dark chocolate, 5mg in milk chocolate – could well be enough to trigger an attack.

LICORICE

LICORICE

ENERGY PER STANDARD PORTION 4KCAL

❦ *Good for coughs, digestive problems (especially ulcers), liver problems, anemia, arthritis, nausea, and vomiting.*

❦ *Best eaten as pastilles or sticks.*

It is the root of the licorice plant that is valuable, containing glycyrrhizic acid, a chemical 50 times sweeter than sugar. Combined with its other phytochemicals, licorice has wide-ranging medicinal benefits and has been used for thousands of years in China for the treatment of liver disease and jaundice, and in Europe as a remedy for stomach ulcers, bronchitis, catarrh, sore throats, rheumatism, and arthritis.

Although most people think of licorice as a commercially produced sweet, it is in fact a powerful anti-inflammatory, which works in the same way as hydrocortisone. The area around Pontefract in Yorkshire, used to make "Pontefract cakes" – small, round, flat disks of licorice confectionery. Powdered licorice root contains a large amount of iron so licorice confectionery supplies over 8mg of this essential mineral per 3½oz/100g.

This herb is an effective laxative. For the treatment of constipation put ¾oz/20g of dried licorice stick in 3 cups/750ml of cold water, bring to a boil, and simmer until reduced by one-third. Strain into a pitcher, cover, and refrigerate. Drink a cupful each morning and evening.

● **Every home should have a handy supply of licorice – licorice sweets will do, but a few sticks of dried root kept in an airtight jar in a cool, dark place can be far more therapeutic.**

HEALTH WARNING

Taking large doses of licorice for long periods can cause high blood pressure. People with high blood pressure should not eat licorice sweets or take it medicinally. Licorice is also best avoided during pregnancy because of its effects on blood pressure.

HONEY

ENERGY PER STANDARD PORTION 49KCAL

In impressive clinical trials, manuka honey from New Zealand has been shown to be an excellent remedy for the treatment of stomach ulcers. A dessertspoon after each meal and at bedtime for a month can eliminate all traces of *Helicobacter pylori* – a major cause of gastric ulcers. During a double-blind study at the University Medical School in Auckland, the honey outperformed the normal medical combination of antibiotics, bismuth salts, and H₂ antagonist acids.

For sore throats and chesty coughs, honey is a sovereign remedy. Mixed with hot water and lemon juice, it is soothing to the throat and an effective expectorant.

FAST FOOD AID

● *Natural honey, unlike the product of sugar-fed bees and that produced by the huge commercial honey industry, has some extraordinary healing powers. Used postoperatively on sterile dressings, it speeds up healing and reduces scarring. Spread on gauze and used on varicose leg ulcers, honey can stimulate the healing process in suppurating ulcers that have been present for months.*

Drinks

COFFEE BEANS

GROUND COFFEE

INSTANT COFFEE

TEA

ENERGY PER STANDARD PORTION – TRACE

☙ *A mild stimulant for those suffering from fatigue and exhaustion*

☙ *A good cancer-protector.*

☙ *Beneficial for the heart.*

☙ *Good for lifting the spirits.*

Tea is almost certainly the most popular of all drinks worldwide. It started life in southeast China, spreading to India, Burma, and Vietnam, then to the rest of the tropics and subtropics. It made its first appearance in Britain in Elizabethan times, when China tea was brought home on ships of the British East India Company. The British imposition of a tea tax and the ensuing Boston Tea Party were the flashpoint for the American Revolution.

Tea is a member of the *Camellia* family, but early attempts to cultivate China tea – *Camellia sinensis* – were a failure in India. It was not until wild plants were found growing in the Assam region that cultivation on this continent was successful.

In the West it is most common to drink black tea, which is the fermented leaf of the Indian tea plant. Green tea, largely drunk in Japan and China, is not fermented, is drunk without milk or sugar, and produces a pale, greenish-yellow-colored liquid. There are some China teas that are partially fermented and their leaf has an appearance halfway between that of green and black tea.

Tea has long been credited with health benefits, but it is only in the last year or so that these have been taken very seriously. Its caffeine content is about half that of coffee, making tea a mild stimulant, which helps to revive the flagging spirits. Black tea supplies important amounts of vitamins E and K, and small amounts of the B vitamins. Tea also contains some very interesting phenolic compounds, and research in Russia and Eastern Europe has shown that these chemicals can strengthen the walls of the tiniest capillary blood vessels.

Tea is also a good source of the important trace elements manganese and fluorine, and contains the astringent substance known as tannin, though green teas have much less of this than black teas. Tannins have an antibacterial effect and may help in the treatment of stomach infections.

But it is the antioxidant and cancer-protective effects of the bioflavonoids in tea, especially quercetin and catechin, that are the most exciting discoveries.

● **There is growing evidence that populations consuming large amounts of green tea have a lower incidence of heart disease and of some forms of cancer. This also now appears to be true, although to a slightly lesser extent, of black tea.**

ASSAM TEA

COMFREY TEA

CAMOMILE TEA

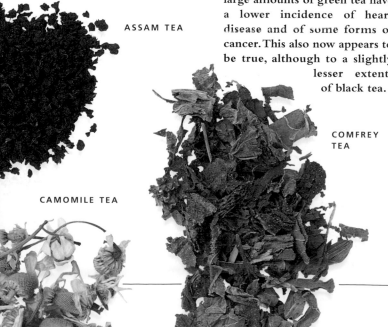

HEALTH WARNING

The tannins in tea can interfere with the body's uptake of essential minerals, especially iron, and those who drink a lot of strong tea are at risk of anemia. The longer the tea is allowed to brew, the more its tannin content increases, though the brewing makes little difference to its caffeine content. Like coffee, tea stimulates the production of stomach acid, and it can be an irritant to those suffering from stomach ulcers.

FAST FOOD AID

• *A couple of used teabags moistened in cooled, boiled water and placed over the closed eyes for ten minutes are extremely soothing and mildly astringent for tired eyes. They are good for irritating, scratchy, or sticky eyes, especially when caused by dust or pollen.*

COFFEE

BLACK COFFEE:
ENERGY PER STANDARD PORTION 4KCAL

☙ *Good for stimulation when tired.*

☙ *Helpful for fluid retention.*

☙ *Beneficial for asthma.*

☙ *Good for headaches and diarrhea.*

☙ *Best drunk filtered and in very small quantities.*

Caffeine is a brain stimulant and can be of value in the treatment of narcotic poisoning (for example in treating snake bites, where large quantities of coffee may keep the subject awake and so prevent coma). Temporary improvements in awareness and performance can be valuable at times of extreme exhaustion, or when it is vital to stay awake beyond one's normal capacity. Caffeine can be useful for some asthmatics, as it is quite similar to theophylline, an effective antiasthma drug. It also increases the effectiveness of some everyday painkillers and is often included in proprietary formulations. And caffeine is used medicinally to restrict blood flow to the brain as part of antimigraine medication. In Indian Ayurvedic medicine the coffee bean has a long history of use, both for the treatment of diarrhea and for headaches.

But while there are positive uses of caffeine, it is important to weigh up the risk/benefit associations, since coffee drinking is implicated in a number of serious health problems.

More than five or six cups a day can lead to caffeinism, or coffee addiction. Coffee affects the blood pressure and avoidance for a few weeks can reduce both systolic and diastolic pressures. Both PMS and cyclic breast lumps are said to improve by avoiding coffee, and there is evidence that consistent and large quantities of coffee can increase a woman's chances of osteoporosis. Three cups of coffee per day may reduce a woman's chances of conception and increase the risk of miscarriage, low-birth-weight babies, and birth defects.

Caffeine can interfere with mineral absorption, and increase the insulin produced by the pancreas, leading to hypoglycemia. It can also seriously affect the digestive system.

● **Smokers actually eliminate caffeine from their bodies twice as quickly as non-smokers. To maintain their heightened sense of awareness they need to drink twice as much coffee.**

Water

Water is one of the most powerful, and easily available, of all medicines. Used by man in the form of hot and cold springs, sulfur springs, as sea water, river and mountain water, it has provided external as well as internal therapy for centuries.

The art of hydrotherapy, using showers, baths of different temperatures, steam, and alternate hot and cold bathing, has been part of the history of healing over many centuries. But most important of all is the water we drink – and few people drink enough.

Mineral waters not only taste good, but have health-giving properties as well. Nearly all tap water, on the other hand, is recycled, and if you live in New York, London, or any other big city, yours could be the seventh pair of kidneys that your glass of water has passed through! And many of the chemicals used in farming – insecticides, pesticides, fungicides, herbicides, growth hormones, and even antibiotics – seep into the ground to eventually contaminate the water.

This does not happen to mineral waters. The bottles that you buy today contain rain water that fell up to 80 years ago. It has been filtered through hundreds of feet of layers of purifying sand, shale, and rock, enriching the water with natural minerals – the most beneficial of which are calcium (for building bones), magnesium, (an important trace element to increase the body's resistance to disease) and the less beneficial sodium. Although these minerals are present only in minute quantities, it is worth bearing them in mind when choosing your favorite water. Anyone with high blood pressure or heart disease should avoid those with a high sodium content. If you are suffering from digestive problems, then water containing more of the minerals would certainly help.

But taste is also a major factor. After recent years of low rainfall, leading to major hygiene problems in the water industry, chemical accidents at purifying plants, and the uncertainty of supply, mineral waters look a lot more appetizing.

In Victorian times, people flocked to Bath, Buxton, Leamington, Cheltenham and Harrogate in the UK, to Evian, Vichy, Baden-Baden, and Sangermini in Europe, and to Hot Springs Calistoga, Saratoga Springs and Poland Spring in the US, to take the waters'. Now 100 years later, we are rediscovering their taste and value.

It is important to know exactly what you are drinking. Faced with rows of supermarket shelves stacked with different bottles, choosing the right one can be confusing.

Kidney problems, cystitis, migraine, headaches, skin disorders, and constipation may all have their roots in a lack of fluid intake. The huge rise in the popularity of mineral waters has helped make people more aware of water, which we so often take for granted.

MINERAL WATER

ENERGY PER STANDARD PORTION 4KCAL

These must come from a single underground source and be free of dangerous bacteria and polluting chemicals. The mineral content of the water must always be the same and although the water can be filtered and exposed to ultraviolet light, no other sterilizing or disinfecting process is allowed. Water can be naturally gassy when it comes out of the ground and this fizziness can be increased by the addition of carbon dioxide, or reduced by mechanical methods. Mineral water must be bottled at, or very close to, its source. The label must always indicate the mineral content and there are strict conditions governing the use of terms such as "low mineral content," "very low mineral content," "rich in mineral salts," "suitable for a low-sodium diet," and claims concerning the content of other minerals.

SPRING AND TABLE WATERS

ENERGY PER STANDARD PORTION 4KCAL

These may come from a spring or out of a tap connected to your local water authority. As long as the contents of the bottle meet the same standards as those required for tap water, bottling companies can virtually do what they like. They need not identify the source of the water. They can mix water from different sources, filter it, disinfect it, and put very little information on the label.

RESTAURANT BOTTLED WATERS

ENERGY PER STANDARD PORTION 4KCAL

Some restaurant chains are making enormous profits by stocking only their own in-house bottled water. This may be nothing more than tap water that has been through a plumbed-in filtration system to remove the taste of chlorine and some of the minerals. Unless you like the taste of a particular bottled water with your meal, you're better off asking for a large jug of ice water and giving it a good stir for two or three minutes to remove some of the excessive chlorine.

CHECKLIST

1. Check that the cap and seal are unbroken and that they show no signs of tampering – in some Third World countries empty bottles are refilled with local (even river) water and resealed for sale.
2. Check the expiry date.
3. Check the mineral contents on the label, especially if you suffer from high blood pressure, kidney or liver disease.
4. Check the sodium content if you are on a low-salt diet.
5. Use only very low sodium or low mineral waters for babies and young children.

HINTS AND TIPS

1. If you're a big bottled-water user, some brands are now available in very large containers, which can save you a lot of money.
2. Few people drink enough water, so encourage the family by putting miniature bottles in lunch boxes, briefcases, and sports bags.
3. Still mineral water may contain tiny, safe amounts of bacteria. If you keep the water beyond its sell-by date, these can multiply – so don't buy six months' worth at a time.
4. Once opened, keep water refrigerated and use within a week.
5. Don't drink straight out of the bottle – bugs from your mouth could contaminate the water and create a health hazard.
6. It is safer to boil all water for babies, including tap water.
7. If your only reason for buying bottled water is the taste of chlorine in tap water, why not buy a filter jug and produce your own? One major manufacturer calculates that the cost of using their filter, including buying the jug and changing the cartridges, works out at just a few cents per 2pt/1 liter – you also get tea without the scum on it.
8. A jug of tap water that has been refrigerated overnight will taste much better by the morning, as all the chlorine evaporates.

CHILTERN HILLS
STILL AND CARBONATED

Source:
From the chalky hills just outside Tring, Hertfordshire, UK

Calcium content (mg/l)	104
Magnesium content (mg/l)	1.4
Sodium content (mg/l)	8
Total mineral content	low
Taste	slightly acidic, bland flavor

Comments
The first English water recognized as a natural mineral water, it comes from an area of outstanding natural beauty adjoining Ashridge National Trust. It takes at least 50 years to filter through the limestone and contains minute amounts of fluoride, which is good for the teeth.

MALVERN
STILL

Source:
From the springs in the hills above Malvern, Hereford & Worcester, UK

Calcium content (mg/l)	83
Magnesium content (mg/l)	15
Sodium content (mg/l)	34
Total mineral content	low
Taste	almost no taste

Comments
Probably the best-known, and certainly the oldest-established, of the English brands. As the springs above Malvern are granite, little of their composition dissolves into the water, so it is low in minerals. Widely used as a mixer with Scotch because of its lack of taste.

HIGHLAND SPRING
STILL

Source:
From the Ochil Hills, Perthshire, Scotland

Calcium content (mg/l)	39
Magnesium content (mg/l)	15
Sodium content (mg/l)	9
Total mineral content	very low
Taste	clean, fresh taste

Comments
This is one of the best-selling of the British waters. It is good to drink on its own, slightly chilled. Low in sodium and nitrates, it is suitable for those with heart and kidney problems. I often recommend this water to patients.

BUXTON
NATURALLY STILL

Source:
Buxton, Derbyshire, UK

Calcium content (mg/l)	55
Magnesium content (mg/l)	19
Sodium content (mg/l)	24
Total mineral content	low
Taste	very light, clean-tasting

Comments
This water comes from an underground reservoir almost 5,000 ft/1,525m deep. It comes out of the ground at a temperature of 82°F/28°C and was drunk by medieval pilgrims and Mary, Queen of Scots. My favorite of all the British waters and still available at St. Ann's Well, the public drinking fountain in Buxton.

SAN PELLEGRINO
CARBONATED

Source:
Italian Alps

Calcium content (mg/l)	203
Magnesium content (mg/l)	56.9
Sodium content (mg/l)	46.5
Total mineral content	medium
Taste	a refreshing, distinctive flavor

Comments
Leonardo da Vinci drank this water still, very warm, and with its metallic aftertaste, just as it came straight from the spring. Modern carbonated water loses most of the mineral flavor, which is replaced by a sparkling crispness.

SPA
STILL

Source:
Spa Reine, Belgium

Calcium content (mg/l)	3.5
Magnesium content (mg/l)	1.3
Sodium content (mg/l)	3
Total mineral content	very low
Taste	just a hint of flavor

Comments
This Belgian variety has been exported for more than 400 years. It has a very low salt content and is one of the best-known mineral waters in the world. Peter the Great, Charles II, and Disraeli were all fans. Perfect for those on a low-salt diet.

Water

VOLVIC
STILL

Source:
Clairvic Spring, France

Calcium content (mg/l)	9.9
Magnesium content (mg/l)	6.1
Sodium content (mg/l)	9.4
Total mineral content	low
Taste	very plain, hardly flavored water

Comments
This mountain water, from the deserted volcanic region of the Auvergne, takes many years to drain through the basalt rocks. It is best drunk chilled and, thanks to its low sodium and calcium and reasonable magnesium contents, is good for making up baby foods and for skin problems. Some say it makes the best coffee.

EVIAN
STILL

Source:
Evian, Lake Geneva, France

Calcium content (mg/l)	78
Magnesium content (mg/l)	24
Sodium content (mg/l)	5
Total mineral content	low
Taste	Pure, very clean taste

Comments
The spa at Evian has been famous since the eighteenth century for the treatment of kidney stones and urinary infections. Evian water takes 15 years to filter down from the alpine snows to the spring in the town and more than 200 laboratory checks are made each day at the bottling plant. The biggest seller of all the still waters in its native France, ideal for the whole family, and the only water that the French government recommends for mixing baby foods.

BADOIT
NATURALLY SPARKLING

Source:
Badoit, Saint-Galmier, France

Calcium content (mg/l)	200
Magnesium content (mg/l)	100
Sodium content (mg/l)	160
Total mineral content	medium
Taste	slightly alkaline and very refreshing

Comments
This wonderful water was the first to be bottled in France, and when Louis Pasteur was working in Italy in the late 1800s he used to order 50 bottles at a time. It emerges from a 1,640-ft/500-m fissure in the granite, slightly sparkling, with its high bicarbonate content making it the best of all the sparkling waters to drink with food. It contains enough fluoride to give local children better teeth than those in any of the surrounding villages.

VICHY
NATURALLY FIZZY

Source:
Vichy, France

Calcium content (mg/l)	100
Magnesium content (mg/l)	9
Sodium content (mg/l)	1,200
Total mineral content	high
Taste	very alkaline, very slightly fizzy

Comments
The most fashionable and elegant of all the spas in the 1800s, Vichy was frequented by Napoleon III and most of the crowned heads of Europe. It is the water for digestive problems, rheumatism, and kidney stones. With the elegant old hotels restored, the original thermal treatment center updated, and aimed at a new health-conscious market, Vichy is once again a fashionable place.

MOUNTAIN VALLEY SPRING
STILL AND CARBONATED

Source:
Hot Springs National Park, Arkansas, USA

Calcium content (mg/l)	68
Magnesium content (mg/l)	8
Sodium content (mg/l)	2.80
Total mineral content	low
Taste	very slightly alkaline

Comments
This is the American equivalent of the great spas of Europe, its waters revered for their healing properties by the native North Americans. Once the railroad reached Hot Springs, the spa blossomed – Theodore Roosevelt was a regular visitor, and the purity of the water was unrivaled. Its most famous current supporter is Bill Clinton – his home town is Hot Springs.

POLAND SPRING
STILL AND CARBONATED

Source: Poland Spring, Maine, USA	
Calcium content (mg/l)	nil
Magnesium content (mg/l)	1.6
Sodium content (mg/l)	3
Total mineral content	very low
Taste	very clean

Comments
This water filters through fine sand and gravel deposited 10,000 years ago by moving glaciers and is exceptionally pure with a mineral content totalling only 46mg/l. Originally promoted by the Ricker family, who owned a local inn around the turn of the nineteenth century, as they believed the water helped their ailments and started to publicize its benefits.

Alcohol

BEER

ENERGY PER ½PT/330ML 70–125KCAL

❦ *Good for anemia, TATT (tired-all-the-time syndrome) but not chronic fatigue syndrome, and fluid retention.*

❦ *Best drunk at cellar temperature if it is real ale and you are British; most other people seem to prefer an ice-cold fizzy drink – perhaps the coldness disguises its lack of flavor.*

Making beer from fermented grains is a process as old as humanity and has been developed by civilizations from Africa to Asia, from Europe to Australia. In the UK every medieval home made its own brew of traditional ale, using whatever cereal happened to be available. During the latter part of the fifteenth century hops were first brought to Britain from Flanders – Belgian monks already being expert brewers – and beer soon ousted ale to become the more popular drink.

Energy is mostly what you get from beer – anything from 70 to 125 calories in each half-pint. All beers contain alcohol but no protein and, with the exception of potassium, beer contains virtually no other minerals. It is, however, an exceptionally good source of vitamin B12, unlike almost all non-meat foods. Two pints of beer will supply a day's need of vitamin B12,

around 400 calories and not much more, apart from 550mg of potassium. Of all alcoholic drinks, beer is about the weakest, but is often consumed in the greatest quantities.

There are great differences between a traditionally brewed real beer and the lagers and keg bitters. Barley is first sprouted and then malted. The resulting "wort" is boiled with hops and then brewer's yeast is added to start the fermentation process. Hops are rich in a number of resins, which not only prevent unwanted bacteria from growing but also impart the unique flavor to beer. Stouts are generally sweeter due to their higher sugar content, while regular lagers contain slightly less alcohol than beer or stout. Due to their higher sugar content, stouts also have the highest calorie content of all beer varieties – 222 per ½ pint/330ml.

In the UK in recent years there has been a huge resurgence of traditional cask beers, which are brewed in the old-fashioned manner without chemical additives, kept in wooden barrels, and lifted from the cellar by manual pumps without the aid of compressed carbon dioxide. In much of Europe and the US, the taste is for lighter and more gaseous beers and lagers, but consumption of these can cause bloating and abdominal discomfort.

● **Sadly, the idea that stout is highly nutritious is a myth created by very clever, though now outlawed, advertising. Nonetheless, in modest quantities beer is an effective diuretic, a good source of vitamin B12 and energy, which helps with anemia, lethargy, and tired-all-the-time syndrome, and contains very little alcohol.**

FAST FOOD AIDS

• *To add a really good luster to dull and lifeless hair, rinse it with beer after shampooing thoroughly. This helps the cuticles on the hair shaft lie flat to give you a glossy mane.*

RED WINE

WINE

RED WINE:
ENERGY PER STANDARD GLASS 85KCAL
WHITE WINE:
ENERGY PER STANDARD GLASS 93KCAL

❦ *Good for cardiovascular protection, improving circulation, mild depression, and anemia.*

❦ *Best drunk in moderation.*

❦ *The above benefits depend on modest consumptions only. Larger quantities have the reverse effect.*

While the nutritional value of wine is limited solely to its calorie and iron content, it contains a large number of chemicals that have both positive and negative effects. There is still some controversy over the benefits of wine drinking, but it does seem clear – much to the delight of wine drinkers – that modest intakes can have a significant benefit in terms of reduced heart and circulatory disease. But it is vital to realize that these benefits only accrue from really low consumption. Most medical experts, especially the hepatologists, agree that consumption should not exceed 14 units per week for women and 21 units per week for men, a unit being one regular measure of spirits, one small glass of wine, or half a pint of normal beer or cider.

Though most wine is made from grapes, all countries have a tradition of making wine from other forms of fresh produce – elderberries, gooseberries, rhubarb, parsnips, apples, or almost any other fruit or vegetable with a reasonable sugar content. Commercial wine production from grapes often includes a number of chemical substances, some of which can cause health problems. Colorings, flavorings, and preservatives may also be added, and there is normally no requirement for wine makers to declare these on the label. Sulfur dioxide, for instance, a common preservative in wines, is a frequent trigger of asthma in susceptible people. And the substances known as congeners are suspected of being the culprits in red wine that trigger migraine. Organic wines are now developing a large following, but the chemicals used during the growing of the grape are, to my mind, far less of a hazard than those used in wine production.

Although the amounts of iron in both red and white wine are comparatively small – around 1mg in an average glass – they are extremely well absorbed. Indeed, alcoholics, who frequently have a low-protein diet, may absorb so much iron from alcohol that it causes serious liver damage.

Contrary to popular belief, alcohol in any form is in reality not a stimulant, but a depressant, although in very small amounts the combined social and chemical effects of sharing a glass or two of wine with a friend could do a great deal to lift the spirits and assuage panic.

● **In general, the cheaper the wine the more chemicals it will contain and the worse your hangover will be. For your health's sake, buy the best quality wine you can afford, and drink less of it.**

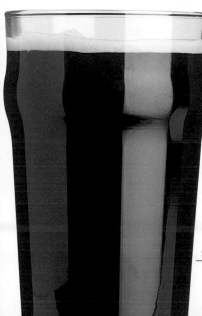

STOUT

WHITE WINE

PART THREE

AILMENTS THAT FOOD CAN HELP TO HEAL

T his section looks at common ailments and conditions that an adjustment in diet, a new eating program, or the boosting of a specific food can help. Covering over 100 conditions from acne to whooping cough, it is arranged alphabetically for easy access. Each entry comprises a précis of the ailment's common symptoms and an indication of the nutritional deficiency or imbalance that either causes or aggravates it. The entries conclude with at-a-glance lists of what to eat more of and what either to avoid or cut down on.

Although the main emphasis is on common ailments, there is also nutritional advice for people suffering from serious chronic diseases, like diabetes, cancer, AIDS, and HIV, and an entry on hyperactivity and diet in children. Useful recipes and dietary regimes, health warnings, hints, and tips support the main text.

ABOVE *Cabbage helps anaemia, respiratory disease, stomach ulcers, cancer, and gastric ulcers.*

ABOVE *Coffee beans supply caffeine, useful in small quantities for diarrhea, asthma, and fluid retention.*

RIGHT *Pumpkin seeds are packed with zinc and are helpful for acne, prostate problems, impotence, and infertility.*

A

ACNE

SYMPTOMS

❖ *Red, pustular and angry zits.*

❖ *Zits usually occur between the ages of 12 and 24.*

ACNE affects 80 percent of young people. Hormone changes are the trigger, but it is certainly aggravated by emotional ups and downs and may be closely related to diet. A high blood-sugar level encourages bacteria and a diet that contains too much fat stimulates the over-production of sebum. This is the skin's natural protective oil, but excessive amounts attract dirt, which blocks the sebaceous duct allowing bacteria to grow in the tiny glands producing the oil.

In general, acne will be helped by eating plenty of whole grains, fresh fruit, and vegetables, together with a reduction in the consumption of dairy products. Exclude refined carbohydrates like sugar, candies, cakes, and sweetened drinks. A high consumption of animal fats is also likely to make the condition worse. Caffeine never seems to do much good for the skin, and alcohol, in more than very modest quantities, can also be a bad thing.

The best healing foods are carrots, which are rich in beta-carotene, as are all the dark-green and orange vegetables and fruit, such as spinach, apricots, and mangoes. Avocados, wheat-germ, extra-virgin olive oil, and other cold-pressed vegetable oils are all good sources of vitamin E, which is the skin's best friend. Eat plenty of oats for their B vitamins and the minerals calcium, potassium, and magnesium. Pumpkin seeds, nuts, and shellfish provide plenty of zinc, which is also vital for a healthy, glowing skin.

Vitamin C protects against infection and acne sufferers should eat lots of citrus fruit and kiwi fruit to make sure they have plenty of this vitamin to spare.

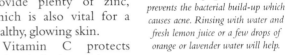

ABOVE *Keeping the skin clean prevents the bacterial build-up which causes acne. Rinsing with water and fresh lemon juice or a few drops of orange or lavender water will help.*

▶ **Eat more** dark-green and orange vegetables and fruit for their beta-carotene; shellfish, poultry, and pumpkin seeds for their zinc; citrus fruit for their vitamin C; avocados and seeds (pumpkin, sunflower, and so on) for their vitamin E, and vegetable oils.

▶ **Eat less** sugar and all sugary foods and drinks, high-fat foods, pastries, cakes, cookies, candies, and chocolate.

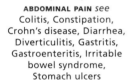

ABDOMINAL PAIN *see* Colitis, Constipation, Crohn's disease, Diarrhea, Diverticulitis, Gastritis, Gastroenteritis, Irritable bowel syndrome, Stomach ulcers

---

AGE-RELATED MACULAR DEGENERATION (AMD)

SPECIAL CAROTENOIDS

A study by Dr. Johanna Seddon at Harvard examined the diets of people with macular degeneration and compared them with similar people without the disease. Her conclusion was that people with a higher consumption of carotenoids have a much lower risk of getting AMD. Two very special carotenoids, lutein and zeaxanthin, seem to be most directly linked with the prevention of AMD. Many foods that are rich in beta-carotene do not contain these two special carotenoids, so in order to gain optimum protection against AMD you need a regular consumption of the recommended foods.

SYMPTOMS

Gradual development of a dark spot at the center of the visual field; loss of color vision; difficulty in judging distances.

AGE-RELATED macular degeneration (AMD) is the most common cause of visual impairment in the West and there is no treatment that helps. Although seldom leading to total blindness, it can progress to the stage where only the vaguest peripheral vision is possible. Pouring a drink into a glass becomes a hit-and-miss affair, judging steps and curbstones is difficult, while threading a needle becomes impossible.

LEFT *Spinach is a delicious way to maintain carotenoid intake. Young spinach leaves make an excellent salad on their own or mixed with other lettuce, served with a few mushroom shavings and a lemon dressing.*

Until recently, taking vitamin supplements did not appear to reduce the incidence of this dreadful disease, presumably because the pills did not contain the special carotenoids required – lutein and zeaxanthin *(see box)*, which are powerful antioxidants and filter out the damaging blue light that causes degeneration of the macula. The macula is the circular yellowish area on the retina responsible for the sharpest, most detailed vision. Up-to-the-minute supplements, containing both lutein and zeaxanthin, are now available and are best taken with a little olive oil or with oily food. Both carotenoids are fat-soluble and the consumption of small amounts of oil stimulates the release of bile and improves their absorption.

There is no evidence as yet that taking supplements has any effect on the existing condition, but here is one example of prevention being better than cure. Eating the right greens can reduce the risk of AMD by almost 60 percent – and if you can't bear to eat them, then at least take the right supplement.

▶ **Eat more** spinach, curly kale, spring greens, and collard greens for their carotenoids – lutein and zeaxanthin.

AIDS

SYMPTOMS

❖ *Gradual or sudden appearance of general malaise, fatigue, muscle and joint pain.*

❖ *Fever, sweating, swollen glands, rash on the back or front of the body.*

❖ *Weight loss, pneumonia, Kaposi's sarcoma, tuberculosis.*

AIDS is a disease that destroys the body's ability to defend itself against infection by reducing the number of specific white blood cells called T-helper cells. Infection with HIV (Human Immunodeficiency Virus) does not necessarily imply the development of AIDS immediately, nor in fact of other symptoms. More than 70 percent of infected people have no symptoms at all for up to five years, although around 30 percent will develop full-blown AIDS within three to five years.

What is it that decides how long the HIV sufferer has before developing AIDS? The answer is a better immune system. The immune system depends on an adequate consumption of essential vitamins and minerals, a sufficient amount of the natural protective plant chemicals, and an adequate supply of antioxidants to mop up the free radicals. In order to function at its optimum level, the immune system also needs to be protected against the antinutrients. High intakes of fats, sugars, alcohol, caffeine; exposure to heavy metals like cadmium, lead, and mercury; smoking, and pollution can all compromise natural immunity.

An adequate consumption of good protein is essential, and a selection of vitamin A, beta-carotene, and the other carotenoid-containing foods should be eaten every day – deficiency in these impairs immune responses, while only a small increase in consumption improves them.

Deficiencies of the vitamin B complex are known to interfere with natural immune responses, so white fish, oily fish, poultry, spinach, peas, kidney beans, garbanzo beans, brown rice, and bananas should all be on the daily menu. Another reason for including large amounts of oily fish in the diet is their high content of vitamin D, which is also essential for the immune system. They are also rich suppliers of the important vitamin E, together with olive oil, nuts, avocados, wheatgerm, and whole grain cereals. Citrus fruit and all fresh produce are needed for their vitamin C and bioflavonoids, large amounts of which appear to increase levels of immunoglobulin, whereas deficiency causes delayed reaction of the immune system.

One of the commonest and least recognized nutrient deficiencies that affects the immune system is zinc, while the essential fatty acids present in fish oils and cold-pressed safflower and linseed oils are also vital.

Repeated treatment with antibiotics can severely compromise the immune system; the typical Western diet of high-fat, high-sugar, and low-fiber content is equally damaging. And few people understand the relationship between stress and lowered immune responses. Positive attitudes, laughter, enjoyment, and satisfaction raise the white cell count and increase immunity; negative attitudes, depression, and dissatisfaction reduce it.

Throughout the world practitioners of natural medicine have been working with traditional herbal remedies for the treatment of AIDS. From the remedies of the native North Americans to the traditional herbs of China, from the Brazilian rainforest to everyday plants like golden seal, echinacea, and licorice, there is evidence of antiviral activity. And in the fight against HIV and AIDS, anything known to be nonharmful is worth trying.

▶ **Eat more** oily fish, poultry, lean meat, legumes and cereals for their high-quality protein; spinach, sweet potatoes, carrots, liver, apricots, dark-green leafy vegetables, and dairy products for their beta-carotene and vitamin A; garbanzo beans, whole grain cereals, seaweed, bananas, oily fish, brewer's yeast, and wheatgerm for their B vitamins; olive oil, safflower oil, nuts, and seeds for their vitamin E; citrus fruit, berries, red, yellow, and green sweet peppers, and cherries for their vitamin C and bioflavonoids; shellfish and pumpkin seeds for their zinc; Brazil nuts for their selenium.

▶ **Eat fewer** animal fats, highly processed carbohydrates, and less sugar; consume less alcohol and caffeine – these can all reduce natural immunity. **Avoid** smoking; all foods that carry a risk of food-poisoning bacteria – undercooked chicken, raw shellfish, unpasteurized cheeses, undercooked burgers, pâtés, reheated food, refrozen food, raw or undercooked eggs, the cold buffet left in the sun to get warm, unsafe drinking water.

DIET FOR BOOSTING THE IMMUNE SYSTEM

Certain foods are known to boost the immune system. Try to build meals around as many as possible of the foods suggested below. Many of them can be eaten as snacks.

ABOVE *Avocados, carrots, sweet peppers, and kiwi fruit are all packed with vitamins.*

ABOVE *For protein, choose oily fish, shellfish such as oysters, and shrimp.*

ABOVE *Pumpkin seeds, sesame seeds, and Brazil nuts are particularly useful.*

BELOW *A positive attitude has a beneficial action on the immune system; keeping up with favorite sports when possible and making sure that what you eat is helping rather than harming you all contribute to a better quality of life.*

NUTRITIONAL SUPPLEMENTS

When seriously ill, AIDS sufferers may have a very poor appetite, so it is essential to institute a long-term regime of nutritional supplements in order that the immune system can function at its optimum level. The daily plan should be:

• 2,000mg vitamin C with bioflavonoids, morning and evening, a half hour before or after meals

• 7,500 IU vitamin A, with morning and evening meals

• 6mg natural beta-carotene, with morning and evening meals

• 1 megadose vitamin B complex, with midday meal

• 50µg selenium (non-yeast formula), with midday meal

• 15mg zinc + 1mg copper, with midday meal

• Chewable mixture of bromelain and papain enzymes before each meal

• Milk-free acidophilus capsules, taken morning and evening with cold water

ALLERGIES

SYMPTOMS

❖ *Blotchy skin, hives, swollen mouth and throat.*

❖ *Streaming eyes, paroxysms of sneezing.*

ALL ALLERGIES are inappropriate responses by the body's immune system to a substance that is not normally harmful. In some people, the system makes mistakes and wrongly identifies an innocent substance as an invader. The white cells overreact, producing large quantities of the chemical histamine and the symptoms of asthma, hay fever, eczema, or other allergies that plague so many people.

As our society has become more affluent, so the number of people suffering from allergies has risen: our fresh air polluted by traffic fumes; our homes centrally heated, double-glazed, and carpeted, to the delight of the house-dust mite; our work places often without a single opening window. The worldwide supremacy of the supermarket has made it possible to eat our favorite foods all year round, and in ever-increasing quantities. But the more we eat the same foods, the more likely it is that allergies will develop.

The instant reactions that produce large quantities of histamine also produce instant symptoms. But it is also possible for allergic responses to be delayed, and this is caused by the T-helper cells reacting to non-protein substances, like nickel and other heavy metals, cosmetics, perfumes, and even food additives, which can take up to 48 hours to develop, making the offenders difficult to identify. Common culprits are citrus fruit, garlic, mangoes, celery, and even carrots. Chemicals added to food for coloring, flavoring, or preserving can also work in the same way.

FOOD ALLERGY OR FOOD INTOLERANCE?

About half the world's population does not produce the enzyme needed to digest milk, so it is hardly surprising that milk intolerance is widespread, but milk allergy – an allergic reaction to casein, which is part of milk protein – is actually quite rare, although more violent in its effects. Coffee, tea, cocoa, chocolate, cheese, beer, sausages, canned foods, red wine, wheat, and even tomatoes are other culprits.

Migraine, asthma, eczema, urticaria (hives), irritable bowel syndrome, colitis, Crohn's disease, hay fever, and rheumatoid arthritis are just some of the illnesses that can involve food allergy or intolerance. They may all respond to dietary changes. The only way to relieve your problem is to follow the lengthy and quite laborious task of an exclusion diet *(see p. 65)*. When dealing with children, any major change in eating habits must be monitored by an expert nutritionist or doctor.

BEWARE THE BERRIES!

Sadly, some of the things we most look forward to eating as the weather warms up are just those that are likely to cause allergic reactions. Strawberries must come near the top of the list. In fact, all of the berries often cause allergies. Other foods that you may consume more of when the summer comes, and which are common allergens, are cola drinks, pineapples, cherries, and plums.

If you get the occasional bout of nettle rash for no obvious reason, or even red itchy patches, which fade within a few hours, suspect a food allergy and think back to what you've eaten during the past day. Severe reactions are most likely from nuts, seeds, fish, shellfish, and eggs. Vaguer, more chronic symptoms are normally caused by milk and milk products, soy-based products, food additives and gluten-containing cereals. People suffering from asthma sometimes experience severe reactions to some of these.

NUTRITION AND ALLERGIES

While there has been little scientific research into the connection between nutrition and allergies, there is evidence that increasing consumption of some nutrients, either from foods or from supplements, can lessen allergic reactions. The B vitamins, particularly niacin and pantothenic acid, are thought to help with catarrh, nasal congestion, and hay fever; B_6 may reduce sensitivity to monosodium glutamate; B_{12} is believed to reduce postnasal drip and sensitivity to the sulphite preservatives; the essential fatty acids and omega-3 fatty acids in evening primrose oil and fish oils, together with magnesium, have been shown to help reduce the allergic reaction in atopic eczema.

COMMON ALLERGENS

Of the many things that cause allergies, food is the most common cause although chemicals such as paint and pollution from industrial effluent and car exhausts are also culprits, as is excess sun. Things that can spell disaster for some individuals are shown below.

NUTS   MILK   DAIRY PRODUCTS   EGGS

SHELLFISH   BERRIES   CANNED PAINT   POLLUTION

HEALTH WARNING

If you have a severe "anaphylactic" (increased susceptibility) allergy, see your physician, who will provide you with an emergency injection kit, should the unthinkable happen and you unwittingly eat a peanut or a few sesame seeds, or get stung by a bee or a wasp.

THINGS THAT STING AND BITE

Most of us put up with the occasional insect nibble without too much inconvenience, but for some they can be a matter of life and death. Wasps are one of the summer terrors: 20 people in the UK die each year from their stings, around half due to allergic shock, the rest by asphyxiation after being stung in the mouth or throat. If you are stung, mix up a paste of vinegar and salt to rub into the sting. Bee stings should be removed with tweezers – they are left in the skin – then bathed with a teaspoon of bicarbonate of soda in half a glass of water. If you have a serious reaction to stings, ask your physician about carrying a syringe of adrenalin for emergencies.

N.B. Rush to the nearest hospital if there is any difficulty with breathing, swelling away from the site of the sting, blue skin or lips, a sudden flush or rash, a very fast pulse, or the person passes out.

ALOPECIA

SYMPTOMS

❖ *Sudden loss of hair in clearly separate circular patches, usually on the head, although they may occur in the pubic hair – Alopecia areata.*

❖ *More rarely, loss of all body hair including eyelashes, eyebrows, pubic and head hair – Alopecia totalis.*

GENERAL loss of hair and poor hair condition can be the earliest sign of underlying illness, but alopecia can happen suddenly and without warning. Small, perfectly round, completely bald patches appear in the scalp or beard. They nearly always regrow within about 18 months but often, as one patch starts to regrow, another patch starts to go bald. This can be a very distressing problem, causing great embarrassment to the sufferer.

Stress is nearly always a major factor and has to be dealt with as the root cause. But, as with all hair problems, good nutrition is essential and good circulation, carrying nutrients to the hair root, is vital. The foods rich in vitamins A, B-complex, folic acid, and zinc are the key nutrients and can be usefully combined with the herbal remedy rutin, and with increased consumption of vitamin E for the circulation.

Washing the hair regularly and vigorous scalp massage can speed recovery. Local steroid creams or even injections are sometimes advised, but in my experience the benefits are not as good as, let alone better than, improved nutrition, and the risks are those attributable to steroid therapy.

▶ **Eat more** liver, carrots, and butter for their vitamin A; olive oil and oily fish for their essential fatty acids; shellfish, pumpkin seeds, and red meat for their zinc; bananas, brewer's yeast, wheatgerm, dark-green leafy vegetables, whole grain cereals, and eggs for their B vitamins and folic acid.

▶ **Eat fewer** refined carbohydrates; drink less caffeine.

LEFT The B vitamins are essential to healthy hair; eggs contain plenty and are easy to incorporate into the diet.

AMENORRHEA *see* Menstrual problems

ANEMIA

SYMPTOMS

❖ *Tiredness; breathlessness; pallor, particularly inside the eyelids, mouth, and lips, and on the fingernails; dizziness, fainting, and buzzing in the ears.*

❖ *Loss of appetite, headache, constipation, irritability, and poor concentration; "restless legs syndrome" (see p. 204).*

CONTINUAL loss of blood and, with it, iron, through heavy or prolonged menstrual periods, piles, gastric ulcers, ulcerative colitis, or even severe and untreated gum disease, like gingivitis, may be the cause of anemia, which often develops very slowly. Increased demand for iron during pregnancy and times of sudden growth in childhood and adolescence may also lead to iron-deficiency anemia. Lack of other essential nutrients, such as vitamin B12, folic acid, and vitamin C, can play an important part in this condition as well, so it is vital to make sure that you have plenty of these nutrients in your diet.

Iron is the first requirement *(see the recommended foods)*, followed by folic acid. A lot of folic acid is lost into the water when you cook green vegetables, so add the cooking water to soups, casseroles, stocks, and gravy, and make sure that you eat plenty of green salads. Vitamin B12 occurs in all foods of animal origin, and especially in organ meats. Vegetarians and vegans need to eat substantial quantities of yeast extract and breakfast cereals, which are fortified with vitamin B12. Vitamin C has an important role, as it helps the body to absorb iron. So make sure that you increase your vitamin C intake when eating meals that are rich in iron – a salad with an omelet, an orange after your egg sandwich, sweet green peppers with your broiled liver.

There are some substances that reduce the amount of iron your body can absorb. Tannin and caffeine are the worst offenders, so do not drink tea, coffee, chocolate, or cola drinks at meals that include iron-rich dishes; bran is another substance that should be kept away from iron sources.

▶ **Eat more** liver, black pudding, kidneys, eggs, bread, legumes, cereals, leafy greens, watercress, dried apricots, dates and other dried fruit, molasses, and red meat for their iron; liver, leafy greens, wheatgerm, peanuts, almonds, tomato purée, yeast extract, and brewer's yeast for their folic acid; citrus and other fruit for their vitamin C.

▶ **Eat less** chocolate, bran, and bran cereals; drink less tea, coffee, and cola.

ABOVE Keeping up iron levels is easily achieved by adding more foods such as liver, navy beans, and parsley to meals. An orange eaten afterward can help your body to absorb the iron more easily.

COUNTRY REMEDIES

Stinging nettles and dandelion leaves are rich in iron, and you can make tea from both of them – a teaspoon of chopped leaves to a cup of boiling water. Nettles also make great soup, while dandelion leaves give an unusual bite to your salad – but do pick them where dogs have not been! Elderberries, parsley, watercress, chives, lovage, and fennel are all prime sources of the essential blood nutrients and should be added to salads and fruit dishes.

ANGINA *see* Heart disease
ANKYLOSING SPONDYLITIS *see* Arthritis

ANXIETY

SYMPTOMS

❖ *Vague feelings of foreboding, fast pulse, and shallow breathing.*

❖ *Headaches, insomnia, irritability, uncontrollable muscle twitches, and trembling.*

❖ *Tightness in throat, dry mouth, and problems with speech.*

ANXIETY STATES represent the perfect example of psychosomatic illness. Though it starts as a state of mind, anxiety is soon expressed as a combination of any or all of the above symptoms. Unfortunately, if anxiety states become common in an individual, the cumulative effect of mood swings, irritability, and loss of appetite soon creates nutritional deficiencies through altered eating habits. These deficiencies, notably of the B-group vitamins, adversely affect the central nervous system, which makes the anxiety worse and so the sufferer begins an ever-downward spiral.

None of us can avoid all the situations that cause anxiety and, although counseling, psychotherapy, and hypnotherapy can help, food plays a major role in controlling it. Great benefit can be found in herbs like rosemary, basil, and hops, which can be used in cooking or made into herbal teas.

▶ **Eat more** green vegetables, nuts, low-fat cheese, bananas, and seaweed for their B vitamins; live yogurt for the bacteria that synthesize B vitamins; blackcurrants, blueberries, bilberries, cherries, and cranberries for their vitamin C and bioflavonoids; complex carbohydrates, honey, and dried fruit for their tryptophan.

▶ **Eat less** refined sugar and fewer carbohydrates; drink less alcohol, coffee, strong tea, and cola drinks.

LEFT *If you lead a high-stress life at work, make sure you balance it with some positive relaxation techniques such as yoga.*

ANOREXIA NERVOSA *see* Eating problems

TRYPTOPHAN

The amino acid tryptophan is essential for the formation of the hormone serotonin – a powerful calming factor – and is found in starchy foods and milk. The traditional benefits of honey for the relief of anxiety are due to its natural sugar content, which plays a key role in increasing the effectiveness of tryptophan.

ARTERIOSCLEROSIS AND ATHEROSCLEROSIS

SYMPTOMS

❖ *Arteriosclerosis: thickening of the walls of the arteries, build-up of deposits of calcium, reducing the elasticity of the arterial walls, especially in great arteries like the aorta and its branches.*

❖ *Atherosclerosis: deposit of fat on the inside of the artery walls, resulting in high blood pressure, angina, heart attacks, strokes, kidney damage, and muscle cramp.*

WHILE arteriosclerosis, which affects the arteries (both large and small), is part of the normal aging process, is virtually universal and is determined largely by genetic inheritance, atherosclerosis is almost entirely a disease of civilization, although there are some inherited fat-metabolism disorders. The combination of normal arteriosclerosis with bad diet, poor lifestyle, excessive smoking, and alcohol presents an all too common, but avoidable, picture of impending disaster. In a healthy individual, fat molecules normally pass through the arterial walls, but once an excessive amount of fat interferes with the smooth passage of blood, yellow fatty streaks develop inside the arteries. These get thicker until large plaques of cholesterol narrow the arteries so that the heart ceases to function properly.

A key factor contributing to the dramatic rise in atherosclerosis has been the gradual switch to convenience foods, not only because they are frequently high in salt, sugar, saturated and trans fats, but because they are equally low in the protective antioxidant nutrients *(see also Heart Disease, p. 184).*

Eat at least five portions a day of fresh fruit and vegetables; omega-3 and omega 6 fatty acids from safflower, sunflower, and fish oils, soybean and walnut oils; a diet rich in whole grain cereals, the Allium vegetables, all the legumes, a variety of fish and seafood, and plenty of vegetable protein; modest quantities of poultry and low-fat dairy products, small amounts of lean meat, butter, and a little alcohol. Excessive amounts of sugar, canned drinks, and boiled, reheated or percolated coffee should be avoided, as should margarine containing trans fats.

▶ **Eat more** fresh fruit and vegetables for their antioxidant protection; oats, beans, and whole grain cereals for their fiber; oily fish, olive oil, sunflower-seed oil, nuts, and seeds for their protective fatty acids; garlic, leeks, and onions for their cholesterol-lowering properties.

▶ **Eat less** salt and sugar; fewer saturated fats (animal fat from meat and dairy products), trans fats (from margarine), and hydrogenated fats; drink less alcohol and coffee.

EARLOBE CREASE

One strange and surprising diagnostic predictor for atherosclerosis is believed to be the appearance of a crease across the bottom corner of the earlobe. Though not a sure sign, the link is strong enough to make it foolish to ignore it – although native North Americans and those of Oriental origin do not show this link between the crease and atherosclerosis.

ABOVE *The diagram shows how the fatty deposit known as atheroma gradually builds up. Blood pressure rises and a blood clot may form, blocking the artery completely.*

ARTHRITIS

SYMPTOMS

❖ *Pain, swelling, stiffness, inflammation, and deformity of any joint or group of joints.*

ARTHRITIS means joint inflammation and there are more than 200 different types, the most common being osteoarthritis, though gout, rheumatoid arthritis, lupus, ankylosing spondylitis, spondylosis, and bunions are also prevalent.

In all forms of arthritis food would appear to play a major role. Eating the right foods *(see below)* has both a protective and a therapeutic effect, while eating the wrong ones can greatly aggravate symptoms and may even be a causative factor. There is also the possibility that some allergic reactions to food and food additives may be to blame.

• OSTEOARTHRITIS is a degenerative disease of the weight-bearing surfaces of the joints, affecting cartilage and bone. Injury, repetitive use in occupations, sports, and hobbies, obesity, and heavy manual work can all be the root cause.

• RHEUMATOID ARTHRITIS affects many joints, often in the extremities. Women are affected three times as often as men and there is frequently a family history of rheumatoid arthritis. Steroids, NSAIDs (non-steroidal antiinflammatory drugs), gold injections (in the form of sodium aurothiomalate, which can have severe side effects), joint replacement and fusions are all part of the orthodox treatment for this disease, which may be linked to deficiencies of the immune system.

• ANKYLOSING SPONDYLITIS is gradually progressive inflammatory arthritis in the joints of the spine, most commonly occurring in men between the ages of 20 and 40. It develops very slowly and is identified by the "bamboo spine" seen on X-rays. In time the spine becomes progressively more rigid and sufferers – of whom there are ten times more men than women – can become badly incapacitated.

• SYSTEMIC LUPUS ERYTHEMATOSUS (SLE) also involves the connective tissue in many areas of the body. Again, it is thought to be due to deficiencies in the immune response mechanism. Young women are most frequently affected (ten times more so than men – and, during childbearing years, 15 times more). A number of factors have been identified as triggering the onset of lupus – sudden and unexpected exposure to strong sunlight, infection, severe emotional stress, and some prescribed medication, particularly penicillin, sulphonamides, anticonvulsants, and, occasionally, oral contraceptives. Typical symptoms are fever accompanied by acute joint pain, moving from joint to joint throughout the body. Often there are skin eruptions on the face and hands, exhaustion, loss of appetite, and anemia, together with the classic and typical "butterfly" rash across the cheeks and nose. Those with lupus usually have to avoid exposure to sunlight, so extra vitamin D from fish oils, oily fish, and egg yolk becomes essential. Kidney problems and high blood pressure are common with this condition, so a very low sodium intake and lots of water are vital.

For those suffering from rheumatoid arthritis, ankylosing spondylitis, and lupus, all red meat, meat products, red wine, port, sherry, madeira, refined carbohydrates, sugar, coffee, strong tea, and all dairy products should be avoided. It is best to cut them all out and then add them back gradually *(for more information see the Exclusion Diet on p. 65; for Gout see p. 180.*

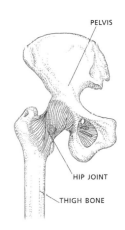

ABOVE *A diet rich in oily fish such as sardine, herring, mackerel, trout, or tuna can help arthritis; celery, brown rice, and strawberries are also useful foods.*

Vegetarians can get the necessary omega-3 fatty acids from soybeans and tofu, and there is growing evidence that a vegetarian diet helps in the relief of all forms of arthritis. The same advice is true for osteoarthritis, except that dairy products and the nightshade family do not seem to have an adverse effect. Some sufferers of all types of arthritis find that their symptoms are reduced if they avoid corn and wheat.

▶ **Eat more** salmon, mackerel, herring, trout, sardines, mussels, and other shellfish for their omega-3 fatty acids; liver, carrots, broccoli, apricots, sweet potatoes, and cantaloup melon for their vitamin A and beta-carotene; kiwi fruit, oranges, brussels sprouts, and cabbage for their vitamin C; avocados, fresh nuts, asparagus, sunflower seeds, and olive oil for their vitamin E; white meat, whole grains and cereals, eggs, and brewer's yeast for their B vitamins.

▶ **Eat less** red meat, game, caffeine, salt, and sodium-based food additives – for rheumatoid arthritis also eat fewer dairy products, less corn, wheat, and also potatoes, tomatoes, sweet peppers, and eggplants (all members of the nightshade family); drink less red wine, fortified wine, such as sherry, port, and madeira, and cut down on large amounts of other alcoholic drinks. Food allergies may be a factor for some sufferers.

(for more information see the Exclusion Diet on p. 65; for Gout see p. 180.

ANTIINFLAMMATORIES

Ginger, turmeric, garlic, and evening primrose oil are great natural anti-inflammatories, so take evening primrose as a supplement and use the others liberally in cooking. Ginger makes a delicious and refreshing tea. But take care with your choice of vegetable oils – otherwise healthy corn, safflower, and sunflower oils can aggravate already inflamed joints, so stick to olive oil.

PELVIS

HIP JOINT

THIGH BONE

ABOVE *A healthy hip joint, an example of a ball and socket joint that allows maximum rotation. It is also subject to a great deal of wear and tear and, along with the knee, is one of the joints that can be surgically replaced. Artificial joints only last for about 15 years.*

LEFT *Arthritis is often erroneously considered to be a natural and inevitable "symptom" of old age. It need not be, and sensible eating can help to prevent or alleviate joint pain and stiffness.*

A

ASTHMA TRIGGERS

There are a number of factors that may bring on an attack:

- emotional stress or anxiety
- sudden vigorous exercise
- chest infections
- sudden changes in breathing patterns, such as laughing or coughing
- irritants – smoke, paint, chemicals, gasoline, diesel emission, gases
- sudden changes in temperature

ABOVE *Emissions from car exhausts are thought to be the trigger for the huge increase in childhood asthma over the last 10 years.*

RIGHT *Much-loved household pets may be the cause of asthma; long-haired varieties may cause the most trouble.*

HEALTH WARNING

Asthma is a serious disease, sometimes fatal. Never underestimate the potential consequences of an asthma attack and, if you're in the slightest doubt, call your doctor.

ASTHMA

SYMPTOMS

❖ *Tight chest, short gasping breaths, wheezing, unproductive cough.*

❖ *Postural changes, anxiety.*

THE INCREASE in asthma over the last 40 years has been dramatic. Although this can be partly attributed to better diagnosis, it is mostly due to the ever-increasing pollution of the air we breathe, a significant rise in the consumption of foods laced with chemicals, and to domestic changes that encourage the number of dust mites in our homes. In the US around 3 percent of the total population suffers from asthma and, although people of all ages get it, most sufferers are children (and twice as many boys as girls).

In childhood, asthma is almost always an allergy and there is usually a family history of allergic conditions. Hay fever and eczema may be present in close relatives and may also develop in the asthmatic child. Some children may show extreme reactions to many of the artificial food colorings, flavorings, preservatives, or other additives, especially monosodium glutamate, tartrazine, sulfur dioxide, nitrites, and salt. Fish, dairy foods, yeast, nuts, wheat, and carbonated drinks may be an important factor for many children.

ABOVE *Dairy products and eggs are often the causes of asthmatic attacks, especially in children.*

Adult-onset asthma is not normally an allergic response to environmental factors, but is triggered by changes in the body – which is why it is called intrinsic asthma. It is sometimes brought on by upper respiratory infections, colds, or a bout of bronchitis. Only 1 in 15 intrinsic asthma sufferers is likely to get hay fever, whereas more than half of allergic, or extrinsic, asthma sufferers will succumb.

There are a number of practical changes that it is vital to implement:

- Turn off the central heating in your bedroom. It creates air currents that waft the microscopic dust-mite droppings into the air. They are then inhaled by the sleeping occupant.
- Don't smoke if you are asthmatic, or allow smoking anywhere in a house where anyone has asthma.
- Avoid furry or hairy pets and cage birds.
- Have smooth, wipeable surfaces in your bedroom: linoleum or wood flooring, window blinds, a mite-proof or antimite impregnated cover on the mattress, duvet, and pillows; damp-dust all surfaces just before bed; vacuum daily with a suction cleaner with a medical filter and include the mattress.

- Encourage children to play any of the wind instruments, as this will help establish good breath control.
- Always take your medication as prescribed by your doctor. Much of it will be for prevention rather than for the relief of symptoms, and it can be harmful to stop some of the cortisone drugs suddenly.
- Wear a mask when you go out or, at the very least, cover your mouth and nose with a silk scarf. This will filter out some of the irritant particles and will also warm up the cold winter air before it reaches the sensitive lining of your lungs.

A diet diary is the next step, so write down every single thing that you put into your mouth. Note when you get an attack and see if there is a pattern that is repeated. Try to reduce the amount of dairy foods in your diet, to avoid sugar and salt, to eat more fresh fruit and vegetables and lots of garlic and onions. Cheap red wine and acidic white wines may make things worse, so avoid them. In any case, large quantities of alcohol are not a good idea.

Some complementary treatments can make a dramatic change to the course of the disease. Osteopathy or chiropractic should be your first choice. Children with asthma are liable to develop curvatures of the spine and pigeon chest, as a result of years of breathing difficulties. Manipulative treatment can improve the movement of the ribs and spine, as well as helping to minimize postural changes. Good breathing exercises are vital to make maximum use of all the available air in the lungs. And remember the healing power of touch and massage.

▶ **Eat more** fruit, vegetables, and salads for their beta-carotene and protective antioxidants; grapes, melons, tomatoes, sweet peppers, and kiwi fruit for their vitamin C; whole grain cereals and dark leafy greens for their B vitamins.

▶ **Eat fewer** dairy products, yeast extracts, nuts, and seeds; less shellfish and salt; drink fewer carbonated drinks. **Avoid** any known allergens, most likely to be food additives – colorings, flavorings, and preservatives – shellfish, the caffeine found in colas, tea, coffee, and chocolate; some children may even be allergic

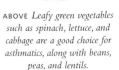

ABOVE *Leafy green vegetables such as spinach, lettuce, and cabbage are a good choice for asthmatics, along with beans, peas, and lentils.*

to naturally occurring substances in fruit and vegetables (*see Hyperactivity, pp. 187–8, for a full diet*). Adults are also often allergic to the chemicals used in beer- and wine-making, so alcohol consumption should be limited and confined to naturally produced wines and beers without chemical additives.

BACK PAIN

SYMPTOMS

❖ *Pain that either comes on gradually, stabs you in the back without warning, or drops you on the floor in screaming agony.*

❖ *When the sciatic nerve is involved, there is pain in the affected leg – sometimes as far down as the toes. Women may think they are having menstrual problems and men sometimes get referred pain in their testicles.*

❖ *Damage to the upper part of the back can produce pain in the front of the chest. Neck problems are a common cause of headaches and of pain in the arms and hands.*

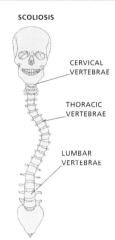

NORMAL SPINE

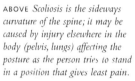

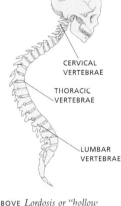

SCOLIOSIS

CERVICAL VERTEBRAE

THORACIC VERTEBRAE

LUMBAR VERTEBRAE

LORDOSIS

CERVICAL VERTEBRAE

THORACIC VERTEBRAE

LUMBAR VERTEBRAE

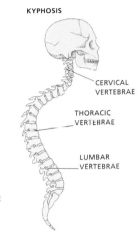

KYPHOSIS

CERVICAL VERTEBRAE

THORACIC VERTEBRAE

LUMBAR VERTEBRAE

EIGHT OUT OF TEN people will have at least one attack of bad back pain in their lives – and once you've had the first attack, it is almost certain that you'll get it again. Because of back pain 67 million working days are lost annually in the UK, there are 2.25 million visits to general practitioners, and 1.5 million people are on invalidity benefit.

Backache has several causes – damaged disks, pressure on the nerves, misalignment or inflammation of any of the 110 joints in the spine, muscle spasm, damaged ligaments, or a combination of these. Injury or some form of arthritic disease is frequently to blame. But postural abnormalities like scoliosis, exaggerated lordosis, or kyphosis, are common causes. Though these are nearly always inherited, they can be due to bad posture at work or play. Improving your posture is the first step to a life without back pain, but dietary adjustments can also help.

▶ **Eat more** oily fish for their omega-3 fatty acids, which help mobility; cabbage for its antiinflammatory properties; turnips to eliminate the uric acid in gout; celery and parsley, which are diuretic; sprouted alfalfa for vitamin B_2; and pineapple, mango, and pawpaw for their pain-relieving enzymes; low-fat dairy products, canned salmon and sardines, nuts, and legumes for their calcium.

▶ **Drink less** coffee – especially instant coffee, which interferes with the brain's production of pain-killing chemicals – and tea, and eat less red meat. If you have gout, *see p. 180*. If you have rheumatoid arthritis, *see p. 151*. Reduce your fat and sugar intake if excess weight is aggravating your back pain. **Avoid** smoking, as nicotine closes down the tiny blood vessels that supply the disks and joints of the back and can delay healing.

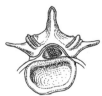

LEFT *Oily fish, nuts, and low-fat dairy products provide calcium for bone strength and fish oils for mobility.*

ABOVE *Scoliosis is the sideways curvature of the spine; it may be caused by injury elsewhere in the body (pelvis, lungs) affecting the posture as the person tries to stand in a position that gives least pain.*

ABOVE *Lordosis or "hollow back" is an exaggerated form of the natural inward taper of the spine; it is usually the result of poor posture or weak abdominal muscles.*

ABOVE *Kyphosis, or "dowager's hump" is the opposite of lordosis. The spine curves outward causing a distinct hump. It is often seen in elderly women.*

HEALING HERBS

There are many herbal medicines that are effective in the relief of back pain, generally those that have an antiinflammatory effect – plants like the humble dandelion, willow, primula, and the more exotic African devil's claw.

For the relief of rheumatism and arthritis, the most effective herbal remedies are a combination of willow and primula, and a liquid extract of devil's claw *(Harpagophytum procumbens)*. Meadowsweet contains the same chemical as aspirin, and an infusion of its flowers makes an excellent tea for the same purpose. Or try ginger tea, made by grating 1in/2.5cm of fresh ginger root into a mug of boiling water, which is then left to stand for ten minutes, strained, and a little honey added. This speeds up the healing process of damaged tissues in the back.

A poultice of hot cabbage leaves applied to the painful area has been a traditional European treatment for arthritis and rheumatism for centuries. Essential oils of lavender, pine, or juniper can be added to a hot bath (ten drops maximum) for their relaxing and circulatory effect, and five drops of any one of these added to ¼ cup/50ml of sunflower-seed oil is useful for massaging into painful joints and muscles.

Oil of evening primrose, combined with fish oil, can help treat arthritically induced backache. Interestingly, neither the Inuits nor the coastal New Zealand Maoris appear to suffer from arthritis. The Inuits' traditional food is whale blubber and that of the Maoris, the New Zealand green-lipped mussel. There are now commercially available mussel extracts and many varieties of fish oil on the market.

One of the most valuable and freely available plants for the treatment of arthritis is the stinging nettle. Make it into soup or make nettle tea *(see box on p. 149)*.

SLIPPED DISK

Disks do not actually slip, they bulge. Officially they are prolapsed intervertebral disks. The five in the lower back (lumbar vertebrae) are the most likely to cause trouble.

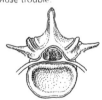

ABOVE *Spinal vertebrae are separated by disks of rubbery, fibrous material filled with a jelly-like substance. These act as shock absorbers for the spine, and help protect the spinal nerves.*

ABOVE *If one of the disks ruptures or "slips," its soft center presses on the nerve nearest it, causing pain in that area.*

BLOOD-SUGAR PROBLEMS

SYMPTOMS

❖ *Irritability, loss of concentration, and fainting may be symptoms of hypoglycemia (low blood sugar).*

FOOD IS converted into sugar and then to energy by the body. It is important to keep your blood-sugar level on a reasonably even keel, to avoid the risks of too much sugar, which may lead to diabetes *(see p. 168),* or the discomfort of too little, causing hypoglycemia.

When you eat sugar, it gets into your bloodstream very quickly. The pancreas pumps out insulin to destroy it and your blood-sugar level tumbles. This triggers a craving for yet more sugar, so you reach for the cookie jar and the cycle repeats itself. Your brain needs a constant supply of sugar to function properly, but not spoonfuls of it. Eat a balanced diet and the body converts food into sugar that is gradually released, avoiding the highs and lows triggered by high-sugar foods and artificially induced hypoglycemia.

Nondiabetics are seldom at risk, but poor eating habits, slimming diets, or simply not stopping for food can cause problems in the form of fluctuating blood-sugar levels. A good mixed diet of whole grain cereals, plenty of fruit, vegetables, and salads, good protein and regular meals is the way to avoid this kind of self-inflicted hypoglycemia.

Breakfast is vital. Good cereals, whole wheat toast with peanut butter, cheese, broiled tomatoes, an egg, or baked beans are great, but always eat a piece of fresh

HEALTH WARNING

If you are constantly tired, passing urine more frequently than usual, thirsty, and your weight changes for no reason, see your physician to make sure you don't have diabetes *(see p. 168).*

fruit. Keep a bag of dried fruit and nuts handy to supply both instant and slow-release energy, and a hoard of other nutrients too. Banish the sugar bowl and don't be fooled by so-called "health bars" or by the inclusion of honey, brown sugar, sucrose, glucose, syrup, or molasses.

Eat regularly, as long gaps between food lead you into the sugar trap. Good snacks are whole wheat bread or crispbread with hummus and cucumber, a cheese and tomato sandwich, a salad sandwich with a variety of green leaves, a baked potato, a small can of tuna fish mixed with kidney beans and salad, a hard-cooked egg or a tomato and a whole wheat roll.

▶ **Eat more** almonds, pine kernels, walnuts, dried apricots and raisins, bananas, dates, beets, carrots, brown rice, millet, oats, whole wheat, wheatgerm, and sunflower seeds. They all provide slow-release energy and some, like dried and fresh fruit, provide a mixture of rapid- and slow-release calories.

▶ **Eat fewer** refined carbohydrates like sugar, white flour, cakes, and cookies; drink less alcohol and high-sugar canned and bottled carbonated drinks.

SUGAR MADNESS

The average sugar consumption in the UK is around 30 teaspoons a day, and in the US it is more than 40, most of which does not come out of the sugar bowl but from soft drinks, candies, and chocolate bars, as well as large quantities of processed foods. Sugar contains 394 empty calories per 3½oz/100g, which no one needs, so read the labels on all packaged food carefully. The hidden sugar in many manufactured products is alarming, and there is little doubt that it may be a major factor in hypoglycemia and consequent behavioral disturbances.

BOILS

SYMPTOMS

❖ *A red, round, raised lump with pus in the middle, very tender to touch, and throbbing pain; sometimes fever and swelling of the nearest lymph glands.*

REGULAR RECURRENT boils are a sign of lowered resistance caused by illness, or of poor-quality nutrition. You are also more at risk of having boils if you are a diabetic, are taking immunosuppressant drugs, or if you have an otherwise compromised immune defense system.

Vitamin C and zinc are the key factors in nourishing the immune system, so the recommended foods must be eaten in abundance, particularly citrus fruit, fruit juices, shellfish, pumpkin seeds, and red meat. Selenium and vitamins A and E are also significant, so eat liver, carrots, and butter. Nutritional supplements will speed healing and help prevent recurrent infections.

Scrupulous hygiene is important in the treatment of boils, and the infected area should be washed at least three times daily with hot clean water, clean cotton wool, and a suitable antiseptic – tea-tree oil is ideal and can also be added to the bath.

▶ **Eat more** kiwi fruit, citrus fruit, blackcurrants, blueberries, and fruit juices for their vitamin C and bioflavonoids; liver, carrots, and butter for their vitamin A; shellfish, pumpkin seeds, and red meat for their zinc; garlic and cabbage for their antibacterial effects.

▶ **Eat less** sugar and refined carbohydrates; drink fewer sweetened carbonated drinks.

ABOVE *Cabbage is excellent for boils as it has antibacterial properties. Cabbage leaves make an excellent poultice for boils; just wash them and lay them over the affected area (see p. 86).*

DRAWING A BOIL

A traditional bread poultice is the quickest way to draw the boil to a head and eliminate the infected pus. Remove the crusts from a good-sized piece of white bread, break it into small pieces, and cover with boiling water. After one minute pour the contents through a wire strainer, squeeze out any surplus water, and scoop the remaining hot bread paste onto a piece of clean cotton. Fold into a pad and apply to the boil as hot as is tolerable. Leave in place until cool. Repeat two or three times a day, or until the boil bursts.

BRONCHITIS

SYMPTOMS

❖ *Acute bronchitis: persistent cough, wheezing, and shortness of breath, together with green or yellow phlegm; if untreated, this may develop into pleurisy or pneumonia.*

❖ *Chronic bronchitis: copious amounts of phlegm and repeated fits of coughing.*

BRONCHITIS is caused when the air-carrying tubes connecting the trachea (the windpipe) to the lungs become inflamed, causing bouts of coughing and lots of sputum. The condition can be acute – a short, sharp, and sudden attack – or chronic. Both conditions occur more often in people who smoke or live in places where the air is heavily polluted with industrial or traffic fumes.

Acute bronchitis is nearly always a secondary infection following on from a cold or flu, when the original virus weakens the immune system and allows secondary infection by bacteria. It is commonest during the winter months, and those who already have an existing lung disease such as asthma, the elderly, very small children and babies and, of course, smokers are much more likely to get bronchitis. As the bacteria attack the lining of the airways, the sensitive mucous membranes swell up and the mucus becomes infected.

Chronic bronchitis, in which each episode lasts for three months or more, and which recurs year after year, can be an extremely debilitating condition.

Reduce your consumption of dairy products – they encourage the production of mucus – and keep your consumption of sugar, cookies, and other sweetened foods to an absolute minimum, as they are all anti-nutrients and deplete the body's stores of essential vitamins and minerals. If you continue to cut down on dairy products for more than four weeks at a time, take a calcium supplement.

High intakes of fats, sugars, alcohol, and caffeine; exposure to heavy metals like cadmium, lead, and mercury; smoking and general atmospheric pollution can all compromise your natural immunity.

Improved nutrition strengthens natural resistance, so get protein from fish, poultry, low-fat dairy products, cereals, and legumes, and vitamin A from lots of carrots, spinach, sweet potatoes, melon, and a small portion of liver each week. Lack of vitamin B also lessens natural immunity. Get all you need from fish, poultry, spinach, peas, kidney beans, garbanzo beans, brown rice, and bananas, together with plenty of vitamins C and D. Zinc is vital for high immunity, and good sources are shell-fish, pumpkin seeds, lean beef, and, best of all, oysters.

▶ **Eat more** garlic, onions, leeks, scallions, and chives, as these all belong to the Allium family of plants, which has been used in traditional medicine for centuries for the treatment of chest complaints. Also eat carrots, sweet potatoes, spinach, and cabbage for their beta-carotene; blackcurrants and lemons for their immune-boosting vitamin C and bioflavonoids; celery and parsley as natural diuretics; olive and safflower oils for their vitamin E; garbanzo beans and whole grain cereals for their B vitamins; oily fish for its protein and vitamin D. Use lots of rosemary, thyme, cloves, and cinnamon in your cooking for their antiseptic and decongestant qualities.

▶ **Eat fewer** dairy products, animal fats, refined carbohydrates, and less sugar; cut down on alcohol and caffeine.

BRUISING

SYMPTOMS

❖ *Discoloration of the skin and underlying tissues by blood leaking from tiny damaged blood vessels, usually as a result of local injury.*

FREQUENT and substantial bruising from minor injuries, or bruises that appear with no obvious cause, may be the result of underlying illness and should be investigated. Poor nutrition, anemia, insufficient vitamin C and bioflavonoids, low consumption of iron or untreated chronic blood loss, serious obesity, lack of clotting factors, or leukemia could be responsible.

Prescribed and over-the-counter drugs from the pharmacy can also increase the risk of bruising – aspirin, anticoagulants, antihistamines, antidepressants, steroids, and anticonvulsants can all be triggers in this respect.

Bruises are normally caused by local injury that does not involve breaking the skin. A simple bruise caused by a fall or walking into a hard object is of little consequence. Severe bruising or hematoma (a large volume of blood trapped under the skin) can be more serious, however. The immediate application of ice-packs and eating fresh pineapple will speed up the dispersal of bruises.

▶ **Eat more** pineapple (fresh, not canned) for the enzyme bromelain.

ABOVE *Fresh pineapple, one of the more delicious ways to clear up unsightly bruising quickly.*

THE WORK COST

Chronic bronchitis is more common in the UK than anywhere else and is the most frequent cause of lost working days – more than 30 million of them occur each year.

SPICY GARLIC SOUP
aids bronchitis

SERVES 4

10 CLOVES GARLIC
1 LARGE ONION
3 TBSP OLIVE OIL
1 TSP ANISEED SEEDS
ABOUT 2 SLICES OF SLIGHTLY STALE WHOLE WHEAT BREAD

Chop the garlic and onion and sweat gently in the olive oil until golden. Add the aniseed and stir for 1 minute. Pour over 4½ cups water. Bring to a boil and simmer for ten minutes. Add the bread and simmer for another ten minutes until it has broken down and thickened the soup.

BULIMIA *see* Eating problems

BOXING AID

The enzyme bromelain, present only in fresh pineapples, helps dissolve the congealed blood cells that cause bruising – boxing trainers have known about this since the 1950s and fresh pineapple has long replaced raw steak as a treatment for black eyes.

CANCER

SYMPTOMS

❖ *Depends on the site and the type of cancer.*

THERE IS nothing new in using diet as a treatment for cancer. Max Gerson, Josef Issels, Henry Bieler, Hans Nieper, Gaylord Hauser, Robert McCarrison, and the great Swiss nutritionist Max Bircher-Benner are some of the pioneers who advocated nutritional therapy more than 50 years ago. In addition they were aware of the dangerous free-radical activity created by diets high in animal proteins, saturated fats, smoked and salt-cured foods, refined carbohydrates, and processed meats. They worried about the dangers of rancid fats, oils, and nuts, about the carcinogenic molds that develop on some foods, the toxic substances formed in overheated reused oils, and the cancer-causing chemicals in many food additives and artificial sweeteners.

Now, as then, the emphasis is on a high proportion of raw food – try to make your diet comprise at least one-third raw products. Include as much as you can manage of sprouted seeds, nuts, legumes and grains. Eat some lactofermented foods, like sauerkraut or yogurt, every day. Eat copious quantities of fresh garlic, which is known for its anticancer properties and has been used for centuries in cancer treatment.

Vegetables and fruit contain an anticancer cocktail that we abandon at our peril, but our consumption of fresh produce is generally desperately low. In the UK 1oz/30g a day of salads and vegetables and 2oz/60g of fresh fruit is the average. Three-quarters of adults don't eat a single piece of citrus fruit, half of them don't eat an apple or a pear, and two-thirds don't touch a green vegetable in a whole week. For maximum cancer protection and treatment, as well as for general health benefits, we should all be aiming at eating a minimum of 1lb/450g of fresh produce each day, excluding potatoes. Maximum protection comes from the widest selection, so don't just eat frozen peas.

Any dietary regime used in the treatment of cancer must, of course, depend on the general state of health of the individual patient. Very extreme diets, which provide insufficient calories for the maintenance of body weight, are not acceptable. *In extremis,* very sick people should eat whatever they like. But recovery through nutrition is possible, and at the end of the day better eating can result in improved quality of life, even if it does not result in greater quantity.

An eating plan for cancer must include adequate fluid, which should be pure water, and plenty of freshly pressed or lactofermented fruit and vegetable juices.

EATING PLAN

Breakfast Carrot juice, muesli with dried apricots, almonds, and low-fat live yogurt; or tomato juice, porridge, papaya, grapes, and dates.

Main meal Beet juice, with a casserole made from mixed millet, buckwheat, lentils, kidney beans, mushrooms, onion, garlic, and sweet red and green peppers; or mixed orange and grapefruit juice, steamed, baked or poached salmon, halibut, turbot, or mackerel with broccoli and carrots.

Light meal Beet juice, raw carrot, celery, radishes, cauliflower, and sweet red pepper with a dip made from crushed garlic, low-fat live yogurt, cucumber, mint, and olive oil, with 100 percent rye bread; or carrot juice, brown rice, and watercress soup, and a bowl of mixed raisins, sultanas, almonds, cashew nuts, and pine kernels.

BELOW *Consult a qualified nutritionist if you find the amount of information too difficult to deal with; you do not want to create unnecessary anxieties. He or she will help you create an eating program to keep up strength and boost immunity.*

LEGUMES

FRESH FRUIT

FRESH VEGETABLES

FRESH FISH

LEFT *Choose fresh food over canned, preprepared, or convenience. Fruit, vegetables, and fish are particularly helpful. Try to eat at least 1lb/450g fresh fruit and vegetables a day, making sure you have a good mixture. Lentils and beans (especially sprouting varieties) are also considered useful for cancer sufferers.*

▶ **Eat more** whole foods – nothing added, nothing taken away; all whole grain cereals and bread and pasta made from them; fresh fruit, vegetables, and salads (organically grown if possible); fresh unsalted nuts and seeds; fresh fruit and vegetable juices; beans, peas, and lentils; extra-virgin olive oil; garlic; deep-sea fish; free-range organic poultry and eggs.

▶ **Eat fewer** animal fats, smoked foods, convenience, packaged, and processed foods; eat less salt and sugar; drink less caffeine and alcohol. **Avoid** red meat, all meat products, dairy products (except low-fat organic live yogurts), artificial colorings, flavorings, sweeteners, and preservatives.

HEALING FRUIT AND VEGETABLES
The following list shows the relationship between specific foods and specific cancers.

Bladder cancer: Carrots in particular, but plenty of all vegetables and fruit, seem to protect against this.

Breast and uterine cancers: There is some evidence (but less than for other cancers) of improvement where fruit and vegetables make up a sizeable part of the diet.

Colon cancer: All the cruciferous vegetables, such as cabbage, kale, brussels sprouts, broccoli, cauliflower, mustard, radish, rutabaga, Chinese cabbage, and carrots are important.

Lung cancer: Eating plenty of carrots and green leafy vegetables specifically reduces the risk of lung cancer.

Pancreatic cancer: Almost every study has shown that eating a variety of vegetables and fruit leads to a lower risk.

Rectal cancer: There are consistent reports of a lower incidence in those eating lots of vegetables and fruit.

Stomach cancer: An increase in fruit consumption and lettuce, onions, tomatoes, celery, and garlic are associated with a reduced risk.

Upper respiratory/digestive cancers: Increased consumption of fruit is linked to a lower risk of cancers of the mouth, pharynx, larynx (also vegetables), and esophagus.

CATARACTS

SYMPTOMS

❖ *Blurred vision, which is worse in bright light, and sometimes double vision; in advanced conditions, milky-white opaque pupils.*

CATARACTS are a major cause of blindness and, although most common in the elderly, there is an alarming increase of cataracts in the young. In some people there is a reduced ability to metabolize the milk sugar galactose and this can lead to cataract formation, as the process demands much more riboflavin (vitamin B₂) and causes a subsequent deficiency in the body. Deficiencies of vitamin C and calcium may also trigger early cataracts, as can high blood-sugar levels, particularly in diabetics. Injury, inflammatory conditions of the eye, such as iritis or uveitis, X-rays, microwaves, infrared rays, and German measles during pregnancy, which affects the unborn child, can all be causes of cataracts, too.

An increase of vitamin E and riboflavin, together with increased vitamin C intake, may reverse the development of cataracts, and you should eat the recommended foods to gain maximum protection against them.

Donald Pitts, Professor of Visual Science at Houston University, Texas, and adviser to NASA, has found that many commonly prescribed drugs increase the sensitivity of the skin and eyes to ultraviolet light. He believes that the increase in the number of young people who are developing cataracts is due to these medicines, which are often prescribed for long periods of time. They include oral contraceptives, tetracyclines, many tranquilizers, some diuretics, sulphonamides, oral diabetic drugs, antifungals, and steroids.

If you are taking any of these drugs for long periods, you must take extra care of your eyes.

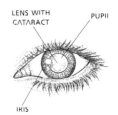

ABOVE *Apricots are an excellent source of vitamin A, which is necessary for visual acuity.*

▶ **Eat more** liver, eggs, apricots, spinach, and broccoli for their vitamin A and beta-carotene; kiwi fruit, citrus fruit, berries, and currants for their vitamin C; olive oil, avocado, nuts, and seeds for their vitamin E; brewer's yeast, whole grain cereals, molasses, peas, and beans for their riboflavin (vitamin B), shellfish, leafy green vegetables, canned sardines, nuts, and beans for their calcium.

▶ **Eat less** sugar, in all forms, and dairy products.

HEALTH WARNING

Don't use sunbeds and make sure that you have high-quality sunglasses that filter out UVA and B rays. These have the added bonus of inhibiting the production of the hormone melatonin, an excess of which has also been linked to cataracts.

LENS WITH CATARACT   PUPIL

IRIS

ABOVE *Cataracts usually occur in people over 65 years of age, or in diabetics. The lens at the front of the eye becomes opaque and vision declines. Cataracts can be surgically removed, leaving the sufferer able to see but unable to focus.*

CATARRH

SYMPTOMS

❖ *Nasal passages blocked by catarrh, swollen mucous membranes, cough, earache.*

WHEN YOU have catarrh, it's a great temptation to turn to the proprietary decongestants. But constant use of decongestants frequently produces a "rebound" effect and eventually, when you try to stop using them, the symptoms return with a vengeance. Instead of using decongestants, change your diet. Attack the problem with a 24-hour diet of fruit, vegetables, and salads (excluding root vegetables, bananas, and beans). In the second 24 hours add some of the starchy foods, and in the third 24 hours include light protein such as eggs, fish, and poultry. Drink at least 3½pt/1.7l of fluid each day – water, unsweetened fruit juices (especially pineapple), and herbal teas.

After the fourth day return to normal eating, but avoid all dairy products and keep your consumption of sugar, cookies, and other sweetened foods to an absolute minimum. If you continue to exclude dairy products for more than four weeks, take a reputable brand of calcium supplement.

There are some natural essential oils that really help to ease catarrh. Use a mixture of two drops each of basil, thyme, and lemon oil in a bowl of hot water, cover your head and the basin with a large towel, and inhale the steam for ten minutes. You can also mix the same ingredients with two tablespoons of grapeseed or sunflower oil, kept in a tightly stoppered bottle in the refrigerator, and massage a few drops into the forehead, temples, and sinuses.

Herbal teas made with ginger and cinnamon will help to keep the mucus free-flowing.

▶ **Eat more** garlic, onions, leeks, scallions, and chives, as these all belong to the Allium family of plants, which has been used in traditional medicine for centuries for the treatment of chest complaints. Also eat carrots, sweet potatoes, spinach, and cabbage for their beta-carotene; blackcurrants and lemons for their immune-boosting vitamin C and bioflavonoids. Use lots of rosemary, thyme, cloves, and cinnamon in your cooking for their antiseptic and decongestant qualities, and make liberal use of ginger and horseradish, which stimulate the flow of mucus.

▶ **Eat fewer** dairy products and refined carbohydrates, and less sugar.

CLEARING THE NASAL PASSAGES

At nighttime use a fragrancer that works with a nightlight candle to heat three drops of lavender oil and three drops of eucalyptus oil in the water container on the top. This helps to keep the nasal passages clear as you sleep.

ABOVE *If you suffer from catarrh and have to cut down on dairy products, step up your nut intake to provide sufficient fat.*

CELLULITE

SYMPTOMS

❖ *Altered appearance of the skin of the buttock, thigh, upper arm, and sometimes the abdomen, to produce the "orange-peel" or "mattress"-like pitting and dimpling of the surface.*

THE BENEFIT OF MASSAGE

Massaging the affected areas briskly – always rubbing toward the heart – has the mechanical benefit of stimulating the circulation and lymph flow, but it does not rub away the cellulite. If you combine the massage with an extract of horse chestnut, the benefit can be even greater.

MOST DOCTORS deny the existence of cellulite, while most alternative practitioners claim that it is caused by a build-up of "toxins." But they are both wrong. Cellulite does exist – ask any woman who has it (and 98 percent of sufferers are women) – and it is nothing to do with toxins.

This is not a disease: it is simply a combination of skin-structure differences between men and women, a change in female hormone levels, age, inactivity, and weight gain, though it must be said that this distressing affliction can affect all women – the skinny as well as the overweight.

Cellulite is truly a feminist issue and it occurs because women have a thinner outer skin than men, a thinner underlying level of the dermis, and a very different arrangement of fat cells in the subcutaneous layer. Although cellulite is a cosmetic problem, it causes a huge amount of unhappiness to those who suffer from it. Throughout the world women spend millions of dollars and pounds on remedies that do not work, being easy prey to every entrepreneur who comes up with a "miracle cure."

Naturally prevention is the best treatment, but since any woman's total number of fat cells is partly determined by what her mother ate during pregnancy, there are many women who are more susceptible to cellulite than others. Regular exercise and maintaining constant body weight dramatically reduces the chance of suffering from cellulite.

Since the problem is more prevalent in overweight women, the first step is to lose weight. Remember, though, that rapid weight loss can make cellulite worse, so sensible eating and more exercise are the two essentials. A diet high in complex carbohydrates ensures an adequate intake of both soluble and insoluble fiber, which in turn helps remove cholesterol from the body and keep fat out of the diet. Beta-carotene and vitamin A are essential nutrients for skin health, and it is also very important to avoid substances that interfere with the efficient circulation of blood to the skin, such as alcohol and salt, is very important.

▶ **Eat more** complex carbohydrates – whole wheat bread, pasta, brown rice, whole grain cereals (especially oats), beans, potatoes, apples, and pears for their fiber; carrots, spinach, sweet red and yellow peppers, and broccoli for their beta-carotene; small quantities of liver for its vitamin A.

▶ **Eat fewer** refined carbohydrates – sugars, cakes, cookies, desserts, candies, chocolates, etc.; drink less alcohol; eat less salt and fewer foods that are high in saturated fat.

CHILBLAINS

SYMPTOMS

❖ *Sore, itchy, inflamed, and sometimes swollen patches of skin.*

❖ *Commonly found on the backs of fingers, tops of toes, ears, and thighs.*

CELIAC DISEASE *see* Gluten intolerance

CHICKEN POX *see* Childhood diseases

HEALING AIDS

Unbroken chilblains can be treated by rubbing them with a slice of lemon dipped in coarse sea salt. Broken or unbroken chilblains will be soothed by the application of aloe vera gel.

CHILBLAINS are caused by reduced circulation in the tiniest capillaries, which supply the skin of the extremities. Restriction of the blood supply, usually aggravated by cold weather, and often made worse by the pressure of ill-fitting shoes, causes damage to the skin. At worst, skin can be broken and bleeding, creating the additional risk of infection. It is obvious that keeping the extremities warm – best done by several layers of loosely fitting clothing, and thermal socks and gloves – and wearing the right-sized shoes are the first essentials of good treatment.

Nicotine is a powerful vasoconstrictor, closely followed by all caffeine-containing foods and drinks, and these should either be avoided or kept to a minimum.

Small amounts of alcohol – one or, at most, two units – can act as vasodilators and improve the peripheral circulation, but any more has the opposite effect and can make your chilblains worse.

It is important to maintain the efficiency of overall circulation, so keep saturated fat consumption to a healthy level to avoid clogging up the arteries. A high intake of vitamin C from citrus fruit, bioflavonoids from cherries, blueberries, bilberries, and blackcurrants, and vitamin E from avocados, nuts, and seeds will contribute to improved efficiency of the circulation, and adding generous amounts of garlic to your cooking further improves the blood flow and helps relieve the discomfort of chilblains.

▶ **Eat more** nuts, seeds, avocados, and olive oil for their vitamin E; citrus fruit for their vitamin C; blackcurrants, blueberries, bilberries, and cherries for their bioflavonoids; buckwheat for its rutin.

▶ **Drink less** alcohol; consume less caffeine. **Avoid** smoking.

CHILDHOOD DISEASES

MOST CHILDREN are likely to experience one or other of the common childhood diseases. Whatever the illness, here are some general guidelines.

A child with fever loses fluid much faster than an adult, so it is essential to encourage drinking, even if swallowing is painful or the child doesn't want to drink. This becomes even more important if the child is vomiting or has diarrhea, as fluid loss can then become critical quite quickly. This can lead to severe dehydration, a disturbance of the body's electrolyte balance, and kidney damage. In this situation use proprietary rehydration mixtures or make your own, by adding one teaspoon of salt and eight teaspoons of sugar to 4½ cups/1l of water, making sure that the water is thoroughly boiled. Let cool and administer a few spoonfuls every 15 minutes.

Most ill children don't want to eat much; providing they have plenty of fluids, this is not a problem for a day or so. Actually it can be a benefit, as fasting increases the number of white blood cells, which form the key part of the body's immune system. If they do want to eat, then it's worth taking a little extra time and trouble to present food in an appealing way, suitable to the age of the child. If the illness includes an upset stomach, remember the BRAT diet – bananas, rice, apples, and dry toast *(see Diarrhea, p. 169)*. And if the child is taking antibiotics, make sure to include a small tub of live yogurt every day – adding fresh fruit to plain yogurt.

Children often get high temperatures very quickly, sometimes for no apparent reason, although these should always be taken seriously and the child seen by a doctor. Tepid sponging (do not use cold water) can help lower the temperature very quickly; sponge the child all over and leave to dry naturally, as it is the evaporation of the water on the body surface that lowers the temperature.

▶ **Drink more** fluids – water, diluted unsweetened fruit juices, vegetable juices, and herbal teas (especially weak camomile with a little honey), to counteract the fluid loss caused by fever; eat more light, simple foods rich in vitamins A, C, and E to boost the immune system – citrus fruit, grapes, melons, kiwi fruit, nectarines; thin fingers of whole wheat toast, or corn chips with dips like hummus, guacamole, tahini, or satay sauce (peanuts) for their beneficial calories, vitamins B and E and minerals; eggs for their protein and iron; small quantities of nourishing clear soups, like chicken or beef; porridge made with water and honey for its calories; yeast extracts as drinks for their B vitamins; bananas with very low-fat yogurt and honey for their easily digested calories, potassium, and protective lactobacilli.

▶ **Eat less** sugar, salt, and meat; consume less caffeine; eat fewer fats and fried foods.

CHICKEN POX

SYMPTOMS

❖ *Fever, headache, occasionally vomiting.*

❖ *Within 24 hours: a rash of small spots, spreading from the mouth and throat to the trunk, arms, and legs; spots become blisters filled with clear fluid, which burst, forming crusts.*

CHICKEN POX is a highly infectious illness caused by the same virus responsible for shingles – *Herpes zoster*. The symptoms develop between 10 and 21 days after exposure to the virus and it is contagious from one day before the rash appears until all the scabs have dried and fallen off. To soothe the irritation and prevent scratching, sponge the affected areas with an infusion of elderflowers or weak elderflower tea.

Adult chicken pox can be extremely serious, with acute pneumonia as a common complication. In adults chicken pox should be treated with antiviral drugs from the earliest possible stage.

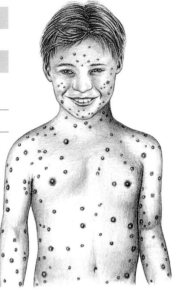

ABOVE *The chicken pox rash is recognizable by its small, raised spots which appear over several days. They can develop into blisters which become inflamed, especially when scratched or picked.*

GERMAN MEASLES

SYMPTOMS

❖ *Slight cold, sore throat, possibly conjunctivitis.*

❖ *A rash may appear one to two days later, starting on the face, spreading down the trunk, glands at the back of the neck may be swollen and tender.*

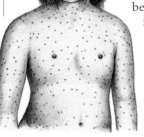

ABOVE *The German measles rash usually starts on the face, then down over the chest. The small spots are pale pink, and may not itch. Sometimes only a few appear.*

GERMAN MEASLES is a mild viral infection, which is extremely infectious from the first appearance of the symptoms until a week after the appearance of the rash. The incubation period is between 14 and 25 days from initial exposure. Because German measles can have catastrophic effects on the fetus, children who have it or who have been recently exposed to it must be kept well away from any woman who might be, or knows she is, pregnant. This may be difficult, for no rash may appear or the pale pink spots may resemble a mild form of measles.

FEVER REMEDY

Weak camomile (or lime-blossom) tea sweetened with a little honey is a very effective traditional European remedy for children with fever. Children under six should be given two teaspoons of either, four or five times daily; from six to ten, use a quarter of a teacup; from ten upward, a whole cupful.

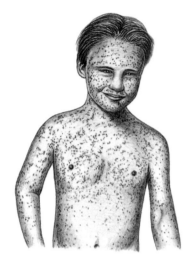

ABOVE *The measles rash of brownish red spots spreads down from the face. The spots are blotchy and may run together. Small, red, white-centred spots which appear inside the mouth on the cheek linings are a sure sign of measles.*

MEASLES AIDS

Pineapple juice should be taken liberally, diluting it 50:50 with hot water, especially if there is earache. Onions and garlic should be added to all food and particularly eaten as onion soup, to help with the cough. This should be made in the traditional way and then liquidized to make it easier for the child to swallow.

ABOVE *Mumps are instantly recognizable by the lump that develops when the infected parotid gland in the neck swells up.*

CHILDHOOD DISEASES CONTINUED

MEASLES

SYMPTOMS

❖ *Cold-like cough, then increasing fever, sore eyes, and discomfort caused by bright light; a day or two later small white spots like grains of salt appear on the insides of the cheeks, level with the back teeth – a fairly certain sign of measles.*

❖ *Rash appears on the face around the third or fourth day – red, slightly raised, and may form blotches; the child is now miserable, with a cough and a fever of 102°F/38.5°C or more.*

❖ *The rash spreads to the lower limbs, then fades to a brownish stain, which lasts another few days; rash is seldom itchy.*

A VIRAL INFECTION attacking the respiratory system, measles can also affect adults and is highly infectious, being spread by coughs and sneezes. The incubation period is 7–14 days from exposure, and the patient is infectious from four days before the rash appears until five days afterward. Middle-ear infection is a common result of severe measles and the cough may develop into bronchitis, croup, or even pneumonia. Measles is a serious illness and your doctor must be consulted.

MUMPS

SYMPTOMS

❖ *Pain around the ear or when eating; slight fever and malaise.*

❖ *The next day one of the parotid glands (the salivary glands over the angles of the jaw on both sides) becomes swollen; the other is usually, but not always, affected within five days.*

❖ *Fever may increase considerably; swelling and temperature gradually subside, returning to normal within ten days.*

MUMPS is a viral infection spread by droplets of saliva, normally affecting children aged five to 14. It can affect adults, and in males this can be serious. If both testicles are affected, there is a risk of sterility if the infection has been severe. The incubation period is 14–21 days and the disease is infectious from several days before the initial feeling of being unwell until all the swelling has subsided – usually ten days.

Due to pain in the jaw, eating is often a problem in small children with mumps. Give plenty of fluids and puréed or very soft foods. Cold compresses applied to the swollen glands are extremely soothing, and pineapple and noncitrus juices should be given for their high vitamin C content.

SCARLET FEVER

SYMPTOMS

❖ *Sore throat accompanied by a scarlet rash, fever, inflamed tonsils with pus-filled spots, and a bright red raw tongue.*

SCARLET FEVER is caused by bacterial infection, which is spread by droplets and occurs mainly in children. The incubation period is between one and seven days, and the illness is infectious from several days before the symptoms until 24 hours after the start of antibiotic treatment. Severe infection may produce a rash a bit like sunburn, which spreads all over the body, and a flushed face with a white patch around the lips.

Complications include middle-ear infection, sinusitis, and swollen, painful glands in the neck. Scarlet fever should be treated with antibiotics to prevent the risk of secondary infection. Cold compresses around the throat and neck are very comforting and 500mg of soluble vitamin C should be given three times daily (once daily to the under-sixes).

ABOVE *The "strawberry tongue" is a classic symptom of scarlet fever; the tongue becomes bright red and raw, and there may be a rash like sunburn on the skin.*

WHOOPING COUGH

SYMPTOMS

❖ *Cough, runny nose, conjunctivitis, sore, pink eyes.*

❖ *Paroxysms of uncontrollable coughing followed by a characteristic "whoop," difficulty in breathing, vomiting.*

WHOOPING COUGH is an acute, highly infectious bacterial illness, which affects the respiratory system and is spread by droplet infection through coughs and sneezes. This is a serious illness and complete recovery can take up to three months. The incubation period is 5–21 days, but normally 10. It is infectious from the onset of the first symptoms until six weeks after the start of coughing. During the worst two weeks of uncontrollable coughing, all sorts of complications may occur: ruptured blood vessels, pneumonia, hernias, and even brain damage through lack of oxygen. During this period the child may keep very little food down, so fluids become of major importance. Avoid dairy products as far as possible at this time.

CHOLESTEROL PROBLEMS

CHOLESTEROL is essential to the body, but problems can arise if you have too much in your blood. If your level is higher than it should be – simple tests are now widely available – your doctor will advise following a healthier diet and lifestyle: stop smoking; take more exercise; eat less saturated fat and more fiber. We now know that taking garlic can help lower the amount of "bad" LDL- (low-density lipoprotein) cholesterol and raise the level of "good" HDL- (high-density lipoprotein) cholesterol. It also makes blood less likely to clot, improves circulation, and helps lower moderately raised blood pressure.

The soluble fiber in oats, apples, and pears, also present in other fruit and vegetables, has a part to play too. Eating an abundance of these foods keeps cholesterol levels down and helps lower them if they are raised. Men more commonly have high levels of blood cholesterol, since women benefit from the protection of the hormone estrogen. Unfortunately this female protection ceases after the menopause, one of the reasons why post-menopausal women are as much at risk of heart disease as men.

The major risk from raised cholesterol levels is heart disease and it is important to keep the levels of cholesterol in your blood within safe limits. To this end, a low-fat diet, plenty of fiber, regular exercise, a modest consumption of alcohol, and good stress management are key factors. But low-fat does not mean no-fat – the body needs essential fatty acids. However, cutting down on saturated animal fats and being aware of which foods have the highest cholesterol levels is a good starting point, especially if you have high-risk cholesterol levels or genetic conditions that predispose you to heart disease.

MEASURING CHOLESTEROL

Levels of cholesterol are given as milligrams per deciliter, and are written as "mg/dl":

300 mmol/l or more	High risk
250-300 mg/dl	Moderate risk
200-250 mg/dl	Average risk
200 mg/dl or less	Low risk

ABOVE *Your choice; low-cholesterol food includes oats, whole wheat bread, fruit, and vegetables; high-cholesterol food includes bacon, salami, butter, cheese, cakes, and cookies.*

HIGH-CHOLESTEROL FOODS

in mg per 3½oz/100g:

Egg yolk	1500
Fish roe	895
Kidney	610
Fried eggs	435
Fried liver	330
Caviar	285
Ghee	280
Boiled shrimp	280
Soft margarine	275
Unsalted butter	230
Liver pâté	169
Bacon	158
Sausage and egg roll	145
Quiche	140

CHRONIC FATIGUE SYNDROME/ME

SYMPTOMS

❖ *Loss of energy and stamina, muscle pain, flu-like symptoms, depression, mood swings, lack of concentration, digestive problems.*

CHRONIC FATIGUE syndrome, myalgic encephalomyelitis (ME), post-viral fatigue syndrome, or what is sometimes derogatively known as "Yuppie flu" causes loss of energy and stamina and muscle pain, and the condition can be totally disabling. The depression that follows is secondary to the illness, though some people with ME-like symptoms may have psychological problems as the root of their symptoms. Depressive illness, and even eating disorders like anorexia, may be buried under the guise of chronic fatigue syndrome. For these reasons early diagnosis is vital.

There is currently widespread ignorance and mismanagement of this illness and patients often encounter a lack of support. The sooner they are taken seriously and offered the right treatment, the less likely it is that the illness will become chronic.

Some extreme therapies have been advocated for chronic fatigue syndrome – restrictive "anti-Candida" diets, enormous doses of supplements, food exclusion diets, and even total removal of amalgam fillings to prevent mercury toxicity. In reality good nutrition, a sensible lifestyle that conserves energy, and allowing the body time to heal itself are the answer. The antioxidant vitamins A, C, and E, vitamin B_{12}, the trace elements selenium and magnesium, and essential fatty acids top the list of requirements. They are all abundant in the recommended foods. And it's essential to avoid the energy-robbers that are antinutrients.

So include easily digested and nutritious foods daily, such as those given below – and take 50 percent of your diet in the form of fresh fruit, salads, and vegetables. Avoid refined carbohydrates, excessive fats, alcohol (which destroys vitamins C and B), caffeine (which interferes with your uptake of iron), nicotine (which interferes with vitamin B absorption and reduces oxygen in the blood), and high-energy drinks.

▶ **Eat more** almonds, apricots, bananas, broccoli, spinach, brown rice, seeds, whole wheat bread, potatoes, pasta, eggs, oily fish, poultry, fruit, and salads. Together these will provide you with good protein, powerful antioxidants, and the essential vitamins and minerals that you need, plus enough good calories to provide that vital energy.

▶ **Eat less** sugar, white flour, cakes, cookies, candies, and puddings, and drink less tea, coffee, chocolate, and cola drinks, which rob you of energy and interfere with the body's absorption of nutrients.

BELOW *The cause of chronic fatigue syndrome is still unknown, but it affects people of both sexes. The chief symptom is loss of energy and stamina, accompanied by depression.*

CIRCULATION PROBLEMS

SYMPTOMS

❖ *Depend on the individual complaint.*

CIRCULATORY problems include coronary heart disease, angina, high blood pressure, strokes, visual disturbances, senile memory loss, Raynaud's disease, intermittent claudication, chilblains, and complications arising from diabetes; whatever the specific problem or symptoms, the nutritional advice remains the same.

Herbs and spices have a part to play in nearly all circulatory problems. Horseradish, ginger, cinnamon, cayenne, paprika, and chilis are all circulatory stimulants and should feature prominently in your eating plan. But, no matter how well you are eating, a healthy circulation requires regular exercise in order to stimulate the entire cardiovascular system. You don't have to become a fitness freak, a marathon runner, or an aerobics addict: a half hour's brisk walk three or four times a week, ten minutes of vigorous housework or gardening two or three times a day, playing your favorite sport, going for a swim, or bicycling are all fine. Exercise becomes even more vital for the elderly, incapacitated, and disabled. Arm and hand movements, foot and ankle rotation, knee exercise, hip, thigh, and even abdominal muscles can be exercised while sitting in a chair or lying in bed. No matter how little you think you can do, the more you do, the more you will be able to do and the easier it will get.

▶ **Eat more** garlic, onions, oats, apples, and pears for their cholesterol-lowering benefits; cabbage, carrots, broccoli, and sweet peppers for their beta-carotene; blackcurrants, cherries, and citrus fruit for their vitamin C and bioflavonoids; buckwheat for its rutin; oily fish for its omega-3 fatty acids; nuts, seeds, avocados, and extra-virgin olive oil for its vitamin E.

▶ **Eat fewer** saturated fats in all meat and meat products – burgers, sausages, salamis, pâtés, meat pies – and bakery goods, such as jelly rolls, Danish pastries and ice creams; artificially hardened and hydrogenated fats; consume less caffeine, sugar, and salt; cut down on excess alcohol. **Avoid** smoking.

COLDS

SYMPTOMS

❖ *Sore throat, runny, sore or blocked nose, postnasal drip,. headache, general aches and pains.*

COLDS ARE caused by viruses, which are caught from somebody else with a cold. They do not come from getting wet feet, being out in the cold weather, leaving home with wet hair, or not wearing a vest. They are spread by droplet infection and are much more common in people who spend time on public transport or in overcrowded, underventilated, and overheated buildings. Americans spend one billion dollars a year on cold remedies, but none of these – or the same medicines bought in the UK – treats the illness: they only relieve the symptoms.

Simple natural remedies are best, as they have no side effects and won't interfere with the body's own immune responses. Inhaling steam containing eucalyptus oil as a decongestant, rubbing a mixture of pine, eucalyptus, and neroli oils on the chest or using them in a vaporizer will all help to keep the nasal passages clear. But nutritious food and plenty of fluids are the quickest cold cure.

The British Common Cold Research Unit has suggested that zinc has the ability to shorten the duration of colds, so make sure you eat foods that are rich in zinc and in selenium, which is known to improve natural immunity.

Double Nobel Prizewinner Linus Pauling advocated large doses of vitamin C, which is important in the healing process and in the optimum performance of the body's natural immune system. Onions and garlic have been traditional cold cures around the world. The antibacterial effect of garlic has been well proven in many scientific studies, so add plenty of both to your salads, soups, and even sandwiches.

The UK Consumers' Association suggests that commercial cold and flu medicines could be a waste of money. Their advice, and mine, is as follows: keep it simple, with hot lemon drinks with honey, simple inhalations, lots of rest, and lots of water to drink.

▶ **Eat more** citrus fruit and pure juices for their vitamin C and bioflavonoids; spinach, garbanzo beans, kidney beans, pumpkin seeds, and pilchards for their zinc; shellfish, whole grain cereals and Brazil nuts for their selenium; onions and garlic for their antibacterial effect. Drink plenty of water to prevent dehydration.

▶ **Eat fewer** dairy products and cut down on caffeine.

COLD SORES *see* Herpes simplex

COLITIS

SYMPTOMS

❖ *Pain and diarrhea, frequently accompanied by blood, mucus, or both.*

COLITIS is inflammation of the part of the large intestine called the colon. This condition occurs all over the world, but seems to be more prevalent in countries where the largest quantities of refined foods are eaten. Sometimes thought to be caused by infection, especially the organism *Campylobactor*, colitis is commonly triggered by the use of antibiotics, which kill off the good bacteria that live in the intestine and protect it from invading organisms.

Large amounts of refined carbohydrates in the diet are a common cause of colitis and other bowel disorders, as they produce stools with very little bulk. To propel these through the bowel requires more intense muscle contractions, resulting in inflammation.

The consumption of large amounts of unrefined bran, which is insoluble, can cause flatulence, distension, and inflammation. Similarly, excessive amounts of alcohol are also an irritant to the stomach and the rest of the digestive tract. As long ago as the 1960s it was

known that allergic reactions to cow's milk were sometimes implicated in colitis.

Colitis may cause nutritional deficiencies, which in turn interfere with the healing process in the damaged gut. Absorption of the fat-soluble vitamins A and D can be reduced, so it is important to eat foods that are rich in these. Anemia is common in people with severe colitis, so it is vital to have high intakes of iron so that the body can manufacture more hemoglobin. For maximum absorption eat iron-rich foods together with a good source of vitamin C.

▶ **Eat more** porridge, apples, and cooked, green leafy vegetables for their soluble fiber; oily fish, canned salmon, sardines, and tuna for their vitamin D; carrots, spinach, sweet potatoes, cantaloup melon, pumpkin, and liver once a week for their beta-carotene and vitamin A respectively; dried brewer's yeast, wheatgerm, eggs, poultry, and natural yogurt for their pantothenic acid (vitamin B_5); parsley, lentils, dates, and watercress for extra iron.

▶ **Eat fewer** manufactured high-bran foods, dairy products, and refined carbohydrates (especially sugars), cut down on red meat and alcohol. **Avoid** adding uncooked bran to anything you make yourself.

CONSTIPATION

SYMPTOMS

❖ *Infrequent passing of stool, resulting in excessive straining on the lavatory; the quality of what is passed, as well as the frequency, is also important.*

IN GENERAL terms, the longer that digested food residue remains in the bowel, the more water is absorbed from it, the harder it gets, and the more difficult it is to pass.

White bread, refined breakfast cereals, and a low intake of fruit, salads, and vegetables are a major factor in the reduction of the bulk of fecal material. Add to this, the fact that most people do not drink nearly enough fluids and a situation arises where an already dry mass takes longer and longer to pass through the system. The abuse of bran in the treatment of other conditions has also caused serious problems.

Constipation can also be caused by bad and irregular toilet habits and, surprisingly, by laxative abuse. Occasional bouts of constipation are common, especially when normal routines are disrupted. In this situation, or to break the cycle of chronic constipation, there is no problem with the short-term use of laxatives. The most natural and safest of these are concentrated extracts of plants like tamarind, figs, and senna,

which are normally produced as compact fruit cubes. But avoid linseed, which interferes with the body's uptake of fat-soluble vitamins A, D, and E and can lead to deficiencies.

Start improving the diet by increasing your total fluid consumption and aim to drink a minimum of $3\frac{1}{2}$–5pt/1.7–2.25l daily. If you have always been a white-bread eater, take half your bread as whole wheat (brown, granary, or any other label simply is not good enough), and eat porridge or muesli every morning. Add two teaspoons of bran to a tub of live yogurt, or to your cereal, each day for a week; three teaspoons in the second week; and a heaped tablespoon in the third week – by which time you should be eating solely whole wheat bread.

Be prepared for some discomfort in the form of wind, bloating, and a bit of pain for the first few weeks, particularly after you add $3\frac{1}{2}$oz/100g of dried fruit to your daily diet in the second week, and lots of extra fruit, vegetables, and salads.

▶ **Eat more** porridge, apples, pears, beans, and cooked, green leafy vegetables for their soluble fiber; whole wheat bread, brown rice, and other whole grain cereals for their insoluble fiber. Drink at least $3\frac{1}{2}$pt/1.7l of water each day.

▶ **Eat fewer** refined, processed carbohydrates.

TRIGGER FOODS

With colitis is always worth trying an exclusion diet (see p. 65) to establish whether any specific foods trigger episodes of colitis, as many sufferers are either allergic or sensitive to certain foods that may be the culprits.

OAT AND APPLE CRUMBLE

provides essential soluble fiber

SERVES 4

1LB APPLES

2 TSP SOFT BROWN SUGAR

1¼ CUPS OATFLAKES AND GROUND ALMONDS

1 TBSP RUNNY HONEY

2 TBSP FLAKED ALMONDS

¼ CUP BUTTER

Peel, core, and finely slice the fruit. Put into a lightly greased pie dish. Add the sugar and 2 tbsp water. Mix the oatflakes and ground almonds together and spread over the fruit. Drizzle the honey on top, then scatter the flaked almonds over. Dot with diced butter. Bake in the oven at 400°F for 20 minutes.

FIBER FACTS

The average daily consumption of fiber in the UK is around 12g, but COMA (the Committee on Medical Aspects of Food Policy) advises consuming ⅔oz/18g. But to avoid the unwanted side effects of a sudden increase of dietary fiber, bran (which is undoubtedly an excellent remedy for constipation) should be added very gradually (see *Irritable Bowel Syndrome* on p.194).

COUGH

SYMPTOMS

❖ *Coughs may be short, dry and painful, or loose and productive.*

❖ *May occur singly or in paroxysms of violent coughing.*

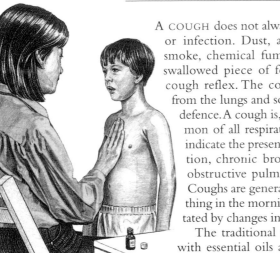

ABOVE *Thyme is a powerful antibacterial agent; in syrup it can soothe coughs, and in oil as a chest rub it can help most minor chest complaints.*

A COUGH does not always indicate chest disease or infection. Dust, atmospheric pollutants, smoke, chemical fumes, or even a wrongly swallowed piece of food can all trigger the cough reflex. The cough expels the irritant from the lungs and so acts as their first line of defence. A cough is, however, the most common of all respiratory symptoms and may indicate the presence of asthma, chest infection, chronic bronchitis, or any chronic obstructive pulmonary disease (COPD). Coughs are generally worse at night or first thing in the morning, and may even be irritated by changes in temperature or weather.

The traditional treatments of inhalation with essential oils and drinking hot water, honey, and lemon do a great deal to soothe the discomfort. Reducing salt intake also reduces the likelihood of fluid retention, which can add to chesty congestion. Naturopaths believe that reducing consumption of dairy products lessens the amount of mucus produced by the body.

Lung tissue requires an abundance of beta-carotene and vitamin A, while all infections benefit from an increase in vitamin C, and herbalists throughout the Western world have traditionally relied on the antibacterial properties of garlic, onions, and leeks in the treatment of all chest infections.

❱ **Eat more** raw fruit and vegetables for their vitamin C and beta-carotene; garlic, onions, leeks, chives, and thyme for their antibacterial effect; lemons and honey for their soothing properties.

❱ **Eat fewer** dairy products and reduce your salt intake.

❱ **Avoid** smoking.

SOOTHING THYME

Thyme is a powerfully antibacterial herb and should be used liberally in cooking and in salads. Five drops of essential oil of thyme in 5tsp/25ml of carrier oil makes a soothing chest rub.

CRAMP

SYMPTOMS

❖ *Sudden and acutely painful contraction of the muscles, commonly occurring in the calves, but possible in any of the large muscle groups – the neck, back, abdomen, and even the face.*

SOMETIMES CRAMP occurs during or immediately after vigorous exercise, when it is caused by a gradual build-up of lactic acid, which is a by-product of muscle activity. Another common cause is repetitive movement, such as writer's cramp, finger cramp in musicians and keyboard operators, or even keeping a group of muscles fixed in an awkward position for long periods.

There is a widely held belief that excessive sweating is a cause of cramp, due to the loss of salt. But there is no scientific evidence that cramp will either be prevented or cured by salt tablets. When I was involved in the organization of professional tennis tournaments, I advised the world's top players to give up salt tablets and start eating bananas. Not only do bananas prevent cramp, they are also a terrific source of easily digested carbohydrate energy.

The most distressing and commonest form of cramp is the kind that strikes in the middle of the night, usually in the calves, and leaves you feeling as if you've been kicked by a donkey. In older people it may be related to narrowing of the superficial blood vessels in the legs. For this reason simple dietary intervention often leads to improvement.

For night cramps eat a few nuts or seeds, some extra-virgin olive oil, or an avocado each day for the extra vitamin E, which helps improve the circulation. Similarly, the bioflavonoid rutin, which occurs in buckwheat, can be a great help. So either cook the grain or use buckwheat flour in other recipes two or three times a week – combined with the circulatory stimulation of chilis, it comes as a neat package in Mexican tortillas.

Quinine is one of the great traditional remedies for night cramps and is still used by doctors today. Get a small daily dose from a glass of tonic water, taken at bedtime. And if you like your tonic with gin, a very small measure of alcohol each day can help improve the circulation.

Cramp should not be confused with severe pain in the calves after walking only a short distance – a condition called intermittent claudication (*see Circulation Problemsn, p. 162*), or with restless legs (*see p. 204*).

❱ **Eat more** bananas for their potassium; avocados, nuts, seeds, and extra-virgin olive oil for their vitamin E; buckwheat for its rutin. Drink tonic water for its quinine.

❱ **Take less** caffeine, nicotine, and avoid large quantities of alcohol – but a small tot during the evening can help.

FAST FOOD AID

Try these two examples of fast food aid. They are traditional remedies that really work.

Mix together 1tsp/5ml each of cloves, lemon juice, and honey. Add 1tbsp/15ml of ginger wine and ⅔ cup/150ml of boiling water. Stand the mixture in the refrigerator for 24 hours, then take 3tbsp/45ml before bedtime each night.

A mustard footbath is great for cramp. Put 1tbsp/15ml of bath mustard powder (traditional English mustard powder but less refined and cheaper than the condiment) in a large bowl. Add enough hot water to cover the feet and soak them for five minutes, three times a week, splashing the back of the calves with the mixture.

CROHN'S DISEASE

SYMPTOMS

❖ *Severe abdominal pain, often after eating, frequently in the lower right part of the abdomen.*

❖ *Diarrhea, nausea, intermittent fever, appetite and weight loss, general malaise.*

NUTRITIONAL deficiencies are one of the major problems of Crohn's disease and occur partly because this inflammatory bowel disease reduces the quantity of nutrients absorbed through the bowel wall, but also because patients with Crohn's disease have poor appetites. This is either due to the general malaise of the condition, or because they stop eating to avoid the pain that follows.

There is a great deal of controversy about the best way to deal with this disease: oral steroids and sulphasalazine are the normal drugs prescribed, and surgery is sometimes required to remove the affected segment of bowel. The exact cause is not known but the inci-dence of Crohn's disease is rising. It most commonly starts between the ages of 15 and 35 and women seem to be slightly more affected than men. Together with ulcerative colitis, these inflammatory bowel diseases do seem to have a partly genetic link.

Some alternative practitioners claim success in the control of Crohn's disease symptoms through the use of allergy diets. Since many sufferers already have severe nutritional deficiencies, it is vital only to exclude foods that you know cause adverse reactions, and to follow exclusion diets for limited periods only. The most likely allergens are wheat, corn, dairy products, and all foods containing carrageen – a seaweed extract widely used in food processing and known to be a bowel-irritant.

Deficiencies – particularly those that are compromised by normal drug regimens – must be made up with vitamin and mineral supplements: calcium, vitamin C, potassium, zinc, vitamins B6 and D, folic acid, and iron. It is essential to maintain adequate caloric inputs, as sufferers can lose weight extremely quickly.

▶ **Eat more** foods that are high in soluble fiber – oats, apples, pears, buckwheat, rice, and beans (in small quantities only); chicken and fish for their protein; all other fruit and vegetables that are well tolerated.

▶ **Eat fewer** dairy products, refined carbohydrates, and convenience foods; less wheat; consume less caffeine and alcohol.

MEASLES AND CROHN'S DISEASE

Professor Pounder and his team at the Royal Free Hospital in London have established a link between the measles virus and Crohn's disease, particularly when babies are exposed to infection in the early weeks of life. For this reason the professor advises against very early measles vaccination

---

BARLEY WATER

Pour 5 cups/1.2l of boiling water onto ½ cup/110g of barley and the grated rind of two unwaxed, well-washed lemons, add 3tbsp/30g of brown sugar, stir thoroughly and add the juice of the two lemons. This is soothing and healing to the whole urinary tract, like camomile tea.

CYSTITIS

SYMPTOMS

❖ *Stinging, burning sensations, and increased frequency of passing urine, pain just above the pubic bone, backache, cloudy urine, sometimes traces of blood, painful intercourse.*

CYSTITIS HAS the horrible habit of acting like an unwelcome guest who won't take a hint. It is an infection of the bladder or urethra, the tube through which urine passes. It is far more common in women and young girls than it is in men, and attacks often follow sex – honeymoon cystitis is not uncommon – or may be due to an allergy to food or bath products.

Make sure your partner is treated as well – if you've got it, he's got it too, and it frequently produces no obvious symptoms in men.

Avoid too much washing, use a soft, smooth cloth and warm water only, and shower rather than bath.

It is vital to keep your fluid intake really high – at least 3½pt/1.7l a day, most of which should be water. This dilutes the urine, making it less acidic, so that it is less uncomfortable passing water. Avoid strong tea, coffee, and citrus juice. Drink plenty of cranberry juice and homemade barley water *(see boxes).*

Eat a handful of parsley every day; chew it, chop it and add 2½ cups/600ml of boiling water, then drink it like tea. Add dandelion leaves to your salads. Both of these plants are diuretics.

Each night for a week add three drops of tea-tree oil to a dessertspoon of sunflower-seed oil, then dip the end of a tampon into the mixture until it's all absorbed. Insert into the vagina and leave overnight.

▶ **Eat more** parsley, celery, and dandelion leaves for their diuretic action; cranberry juice for its antibacterial protection; camomile tea to soothe the irritation.

▶ **Drink less** alcohol, coffee, tea, and cola drinks; eat less sugar and chocolate.

CRANBERRY JUICE

Three glasses a day of cranberry juice diluted 50:50 with water is the greatest natural remedy for cystitis. It forms a barrier on the lining of the urinary tract and bladder, which prevents bacteria from getting established and multiplying. If you are prone to cystitis, this should be a regular form of prevention as well as treatment.

CRANBERRY JUICE

DANDRUFF *see* Hair and scalp problems

THE RULES OF GOOD MOUTH-KEEPING

• Clean your teeth after each meal or snack.

• Always brush down on the top teeth and up on the bottom ones, never from side to side. Brush for 3 minutes.

• Buy a good-quality, medium-bristle brush and change it at least every 3 months.

• Use dental floss after each meal.

• Protect your gums by eating plenty of the recommended foods.

• Sugar-free gum is a good alternative to brushing your teeth, when you are away from home.

• Candies, sugary foods, most carbonated drinks, and sweetened juices are deadly to your teeth and gums.

• Three times each week treat your mouth to a cleansing and antiseptic wash, using sage tea, made from one teaspoon of dried (or two of fresh, chopped) sage in a mug of boiling water. Let stand for ten minutes, strain and use as a mouthwash.

• Give pure juices, diluted one-third juice with two-thirds water, to babies and children instead of sweet drinks.

DENTAL PROBLEMS

SYMPTOMS

❖ *Swollen, bleeding gums, sensitivity to hot and cold.*

❖ *Toothache, bad breath.*

HAVE YOU stopped smiling because you are ashamed of your teeth? Taking care of your own teeth and gums is just as important as regular visits to the dentist – and good mouth-keeping starts here.

• **GINGIVITIS,** or gum infection, quickly becomes serious if untreated. Gums bleed at the slightest pressure when you are eating or brushing your teeth. If left untreated, dental plaque and hard deposits of tartar collect around the gum margin and pockets of infected pus develop at the base of the teeth. Bad breath and abscesses will follow. The teeth become loose and finally start to fall out. Poor oral hygiene, lack of roughage, and insufficient vitamin C are all part of the problem. In the UK 80 percent of patients have gingivitis in at least one site and in some areas this rises to almost 100 percent.

• **TOOTHACHE** may be caused by an abscess, or more commonly by tooth decay, and although good oral hygiene and healthy eating minimize the chances of this occurring, it is still always a possibility. If you do get raging toothache, rubbing some clove oil around the affected tooth with a cotton bud provides some instant relief until you can get to the dentist.

ABOVE *Cloves are a traditional cure for toothache; rub oil of cloves onto the affected gum, or chew a whole clove.*

▶ **Eat more** fruit, salads, and fresh vegetables for their vitamin C; crisp foods like apples, raw carrots, and celery, which massage the gums when you chew; olive oil, sunflower-seed oil, and sprouted seeds for their vitamin E; carrots, dark-green leafy vegetables, and liver for their vitamin A.

▶ **Eat fewer** high-sugar foods; drink fewer sweetened drinks, undiluted fruit juices, highly acidic canned drinks – especially colas – and carbonated water.

DEPRESSION

SYMPTOMS

❖ *Increased or decreased appetite.*

❖ *Sleep disturbance, fatigue, and lethargy.*

❖ *Loss of libido; loss of interest in normal activities, feelings of guilt, loss of self-esteem, thoughts of suicide.*

AROUND 25 percent of the population can expect to suffer some degree of depressive illness during their life, and women are slightly more susceptible than men. Depression is a multifactorial illness and may be a combination of external problems (lifestyle, behavior, relationships) and internal factors (biochemical, physiological, hormonal, and nutritional).

Of all the potential triggers, attention to nutrition is the easiest and most basic first step on the road to recovery. Keeping blood-sugar levels on an even keel is a primary requirement in order to avoid hypoglycemia. As well as eating the vitamin B-rich foods in the list below, an adequate supply of good calories, healthy proteins, and all the essential minerals is of the utmost importance.

The most difficult problem is persuading the depressed patient to eat or dissuading them from endless binges on high-fat, high-sugar foods of poor nutritional quality. Frequent small meals that

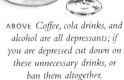

ABOVE *Coffee, cola drinks, and alcohol are all depressants; if you are depressed cut down on these unnecessary drinks, or ban them altogether.*

are appealing, attractive, and nourishing should be the order of the day. Homemade soups, freshly squeezed fruit and vegetable juices, and lots of good whole grain cereals make up the ideal basic menu.

Zinc deficiency can be a major factor in the whole depression story. Many people who go to their doctor complaining of fatigue are automatically assumed to be suffering from depression and prescribed antidepressant drugs. Unfortunately many of these drugs interfere with the body's uptake of zinc, and low levels of zinc in the body not only lead to fatigue (which can in turn be exacerbated by antidepressants), but can also be a factor in the cause of depression itself. It is therefore important to get adequate amounts of zinc in your diet, either from shellfish, pumpkin seeds, mushrooms, soybeans, and organ meats, or by taking zinc supplements.

▶ **Eat more** whole grains, eggs, brewer's yeast, molasses, nuts, legumes, green leafy vegetables, dairy products, wheatgerm, oily fish, and liver for a wide selection of all the B vitamins; shellfish, pumpkin seeds, mushrooms, soybeans, and organ meats for their zinc.

▶ **Drink less** coffee, strong tea, cola drinks and alcohol; eat fewer refined sugars and carbohydrates; food additives or other specific foods if an allergy is suspected.

DERMATITIS

SYMPTOMS

❖ *Red, itching, scaly patches on the skin, initially at the site of contact with an irritant substance, but sometimes spreading to other parts of the body.*

❖ *Scaly patches may crack, weep, bleed, and become infected.*

CONTACT DERMATITIS or contact eczema is the commonest skin allergy. Nickel may be the cause and affects ten percent of women. It is found in costume jewelry, rolled gold, gold plate, watch straps, rings, the clips on bras and suspenders, zippers, coins, keys, scissors, knitting needles, studs in jeans, and even razor blades.

Work can be a major contributory factor to contact dermatitis, which is common among mechanics, engineering workers, hairdressers, nurses, cooks, cleaners, and even beauticians, due to long-term and frequent contact with chemicals, metals, detergents, bleaches, and other irritants. And if you had eczema as a child, take extra precautions, as you are ten times more likely to suffer from contact dermatitis at work.

Perfumes combine plant or synthetic fragrances, which can be irritants. The synthetic musk in aftershave is a powerful allergen, which is aggravated by sunlight; it is also found in soaps, shampoos, shaving creams, deodorants, and perfumed talcs. And cosmetics are all potentially allergenic and may contain preservatives, colorings, and perfumes. Nail varnish does not usually cause problems on the fingers, but may do so after touching the face and neck. This reaction is caused by toluene and formaldehyde, so use hypoallergenic cosmetics if you are susceptible to dermatitis. And continuous use of hair dyes can affect the forehead, neck, face, and shoulders.

Plants, especially primulas, chrysanthemums, poison ivy, rue, and euphorbias, can after the briefest of contacts produce sudden swelling and blistering, which may be severely exacerbated by sunlight. These effects may spread to the face and eyes. But wearing rubber gloves may do more harm than good. Casein – extracted from cow's milk – is added to some gloves during manufacture and it is this, rather than the rubber, that may cause dermatitis. Try cotton-lined PVC or other hypoallergenic gloves instead.

Prescribed medication can also cause contact dermatitis, making the original condition worse. Antibiotic ointments, local anesthetic creams, and some eye drops are common culprits. Stop using them immediately and contact your doctor if this happens.

Avoid the allergens and the condition will get better. And improve your skin by eating foods rich in essential nutrients. Obsessive dieting and ridiculous eating habits will only exacerbate the condition. A low-fat diet doesn't mean eating no fat, as many women believe. Polyunsaturated fatty acids (vegetable oils), omega-3 fatty acids (from oily fish) and vitamin E (from olive oil, nuts, seeds, and avocados) are essential for a healthy skin. Vitamin A is also vital, together with beta-carotene and vitamin B-complex. Add a daily dose of antioxidants, like selenium, with vitamins A, C, and E, 1g of evening primrose oil and fish oil. Keep your skin well hydrated, so drink at least 3½pt/1.7l of liquid each day, most of which should be water.

Avoid bubble baths and soap, which are very drying, and substitute nonsoap bars, bath oils, or a couple of camomile teabags. After bathing use liberal amounts of unperfumed moisturizer and wrap yourself in a large bathsheet or robe to avoid rubbing the skin. Wear cotton next to the skin, avoid biological detergents, rinse all washing thoroughly, and watch out for elastic wearing through on underwear.

For sore patches, boil some watercress in just enough water to cover it, mix with oats, wrap in gauze, and apply to the affected areas. And 4oz/110g of sage leaves, simmered for ten minutes in 2pt/900ml of water, strained and cooled makes a healing compress. Calendula and echinacea ointments are also soothing and healing.

Two cups of stinging-nettle tea taken daily relieves skin conditions – add a teaspoon of chopped leaves to a cup of boiling water, let stand for five minutes, then strain and drink. Wear gloves when picking and preparing, to avoid nettle rash!

For dermatitis and eczema (see p. 171) fresh chickweed used as an infusion or ointment will soothe and heal, as does aloe vera gel by reducing itchiness and promoting healing. And an infusion of astringent blackberry leaves will dry the skin. An infusion of elder leaves can ease the condition too: put 1oz/25g of crushed fresh leaves in 2½ cups/600ml of cold water and bring to a boil, then leave to stand for a half hour.

Finally, if there were ever a good reason for drinking carrot juice, this is it. Bursting with beta-carotene, one large glass per day (fresh if possible, but bottled will do) works wonders for the skin, is a powerfully protective antioxidant, and helps you see in the dark.

▶ **Eat more** melons, peaches, winter squashes, carrots, broccoli, beets, spinach, and parsley for their beta-carotene; sunflower and safflower oil for their polyunsaturates; oily fish for their omega-3 fatty acids; prunes, raisins, walnuts, and soybeans for their vitamin B₆; papaya, sweet peppers, potatoes, and citrus fruit for their vitamin C; liver, eggs, and dairy products (as long as you're not allergic to them) for their vitamin A.

▶ **Eat fewer** sugars, all artificial additives, and less of anything to which you know you are allergic; drink less alcohol.

THE BENEFITS OF LANOLIN

Research shows that 75 percent of women think they have sensitive skin – far more than actually do, but new formulations make the lives of real sufferers much easier. "Lanolin-free claims" are, however, a sales gimmick rather than a necessity and very few people have a genuine allergy to lanolin (only 6 people in every million), which is the most soothing and softening of all substances.

WARM BROCCOLI SALAD
benefits dermatitis

SERVES 4–6
2LB BROCCOLI
3 TBSP WALNUT OIL
1 TBSP WHITE WINE VINEGAR
DASH OF MUSTARD POWDER
2OZ WALNUTS

Cut the broccoli into florets and steam until just cooked (about 5 minutes). Make a salad dressing with three parts walnut oil, one part vinegar, and a dash of mustard powder. Crush the walnuts, sprinkle over the broccoli, and drizzle with the dressing.

D

TABBOULEH

is good for diabetics

SERVES 2–3

³/₄ CUP BULGAR WHEAT

SALT

2 TBSP OLIVE OIL

2 TBSP LEMON JUICE

1 GARLIC CLOVE

1–2 TBSP CHOPPED MINT

3 TBSP CHOPPED PARSLEY

4 TOMATOES

2IN CUCUMBER

¹/₂ AVOCADO

LETTUCE LEAVES TO SERVE

Cover the bulgar wheat
and a dash of salt with
²/₃ cup boiling water and
leave for 15 minutes to
absorb. Add the oil, lemon
juice, peeled and crushed
garlic, and the herbs. Chop
the tomatoes, cucumber,
and avocado and stir in just
before serving on a bed
of lettuce leaves.

BELOW *Diabetes is very hard for
children when they graduate to
teendom: peer pressure and group
activities such as junk food feasts
may encourage them to lose the
nutritional plot. Encourage them
to live as normal a life as possible
while understanding that they
must monitor their intake more
precisely than their friends.*

DIABETES

SYMPTOMS

❖ *Increasing frequency of urination, excessive thirst,
increased appetite.*

❖ *Unexplained bouts of extreme tiredness, decreased resistance
to infection, poor wound-healing, infected spots and boils,
fungal infections.*

Diabetes is classified as follows:

IDDM – **insulin-dependent diabetes mellitus** –
which normally starts in childhood and is caused by
the inability of the pancreas to produce insulin.

NIDDM – **non-insulin-dependent diabetes mellitus**,
or adult-onset diabetes – which is subdivided into
obese NIDDM and non-obese NIDDM.

INSULIN IS essential for the control of the level of sugar
circulating in the blood. If the pancreas is not functioning properly, it produces too little or no insulin,
resulting in IDDM. Where there is sufficient insulin
being produced, but that insulin has become ineffec-
tive, then NIDDM develops. In either case, the level of
sugar in the blood rises too high (hyperglycemia),
causing a wide range of severe symptoms, which can
result in coma and death. Diabetics are also prone to
very low blood-sugar levels (hypoglycemia), which can
also cause coma. Someone suffering from a hyper-
glycemic coma needs insulin, from a hypoglycemic
coma glucose – both are emergency situations.

Diabetes is without doubt a disease of Western civilization and, as a result of the circulatory, kidney, and
nervous-system complications that it causes, it currently represents the seventh leading fatal disease in the
US. This disease currently affects around 4 percent of
the total American population and 2 percent of the
British population.

There are certainly genetic factors that predispose
to diabetes, but the Western diet – high in sugars,
refined carbohydrates and fats, and low in high-fiber
complex carbohydrates, fruit, and vegetables – is the
trigger; 90 percent of diabetics are NIDDM and 90
percent of them are obese. So, in spite of the fact that
many experts claim that diabetes is not caused by
eating too much sugar or by eating a bad diet, too
much sugar and bad diets are the major cause of
obesity. And sugar manufacturers tell us that the
only harmful effect of their product is tooth
decay! Where emerging countries are forsaking
their traditional eating patterns and switching to the
"more desirable" burger, cola, and convenience foods,
the incidence of diabetes is also rising.

Until the mid-1970s diabetics were advised to
follow a high-protein, high-fat, and low-carbohydrate

diet – the exact opposite of that advised by alternative
practitioners – until it was realized that more of them
died of heart attacks than of diabetes. Today's advice is
far healthier and in fact mirrors the general healthy
eating advice for everyone: a diet of complex carbohydrates, high fiber, low fat, and low sugar. This regime is
often enough to control NIDDM without the need for
insulin or other medication.

Using the glycemic index (GI) can be a great help
in compiling diets that suit individual diabetics. The GI
is a way of calculating the rate at which carbohydrate
foods are digested and converted into sugar by the
body. The lower the GI, the longer it takes for food to
be converted into sugar. By mixing low-GI foods into
a meal, it is possible to produce an improvement in
blood-sugar and fat controls in the diabetic patient.

HIGH-FIBER HELPERS

High-fiber foods are helpful for diabetics as they take longer
to be broken down into sugars.

*A high-fiber diet need not be
dull or cut you out of social
activities; whole wheat bread,
fruit, and vegetables, lean meat,*

*pasta, and lentils are all good
foods for diabetics, and should
be easy to build into the
family's usual eating pattern.*

Taking 100 as the standard, based on white bread, then
sugared breakfast cereals, puffed rice, cornflakes, puffed
wheat, cookies, instant mashed potato, baked potato,
glucose, honey, and corn chips all have a higher GI.
Lower, and therefore better, foods for the diabetic are
whole wheat, rye, and pumpernickel, pasta, rice, sweetcorn, buckwheat, bulgar, whole wheat kernels, whole
rye, kernels, pearl barley, shredded wheat, oatmeal, garbanzo beans, soybeans, all dried beans, and low-fat
dairy foods. By combining these with modest amounts
of protein you can create meals that are tasty, satisfying,
and more likely to control NIDDM, and to make the
management of IDDM much simpler.

▶ **Eat more** high-fiber foods, especially whole grain and rye
breads, pasta, rice, sweetcorn, buckwheat, bulgar, barley,
porridge, new potatoes, sweet potatoes, beans, and lentils –
all these have a low glycemic index *(see above)*.

▶ **Eat less** animal protein, sugar, and dried fruit; fewer fats,
bakery goods, and high-salt snacks; drink fewer canned drinks
and less alcohol.

DIARRHEA

SYMPTOMS

❖ *Frequent, very liquid bowel movements*

DIARRHEA is not an illness, but the symptom of an underlying problem. It may be caused by an overindulgence in laxative foods, like figs, prunes, rhubarb, dried fruit, or beer, but is much more commonly the result of a food-borne infection.

Traveler's diarrhea affects at least 40 percent of all international travelers. Where hygiene is doubtful, avoid fruit that you cannot peel, salads, tap water, and ice cubes. Be wary of cold buffets, and avoid any undercooked meat or poultry, raw fish and shellfish, unless it's boiled for at least ten minutes.

Food poisoning *(see p. 177)* is the most common cause of diarrhea and an attack may last any length of time from six hours to three days. Like colds and flu, gastroenteritis *(see p. 179)* may be contracted via droplet infection.

Chronic diarrhea may be a sign of serious underlying illness – Crohn's disease *(see p. 165)*, colitis *(see p. 163)*, diverticulitis *(see below)*, irritable bowel syndrome *(see p. 194)*, thyroid problems *(see p. 208)*, or even cancer of the bowel. Any persistent change in normal bowel habits should be discussed with your doctor. Acute diarrhea can be life-threatening to very

small children and the elderly, as a result of dehydration, so seek medical advice as soon as possible.

The first essential is to replace lost fluids and salts, and although you can buy ready-made sachets of rehydration powders, you can make your own by adding one teaspoon of salt and eight teaspoons of sugar to 2pt/1l of water – but make sure that the water is boiled thoroughly. This quantity of the mixture should be consumed every two hours, if necessary taken as a tablespoon every ten minutes or so.

As soon as you feel like eating – but preferably not in the first 24 hours – follow the BRAT diet (that is, bananas, boiled rice, apples, and dry toast). It is best to eat small amounts at regular intervals. After 48 hours you can introduce potatoes, cooked vegetables (especially carrots), and an egg, and then restore the diet to normal, leaving dairy products as the last type of food to be added.

Garlic is an excellent remedy for diarrhea and it is also protective against stomach infections, so eat plenty when you travel, or take a regular garlic tablet.

▶ **Drink more** water to replace lost fluid. Eat bananas for their energy and potassium, boiled white rice and dry toast for their low-fiber carbohydrate; apples for their pectin.

▶ **Avoid** all other food, especially dairy products, for the first 48 hours.

HERBAL TEAS

Extra fluids can be given in the form of herbal teas, and the following will have a soothing effect on the digestive tract:. Use the same recommendations given for gastroenteritis *(see p. 179)*

DIVERTICULITIS

SYMPTOMS

❖ *Acute episodes: stomach pain, rigidity, flatulence, nausea, vomiting, and a rise in temperature.*

DIVERTICULITIS is a disease of the large bowel (colon). Although it is extremely common over the age of 80, this condition was unknown before the beginning of the twentieth century.

The modern Western diet, which is very low in fiber, causes constipation and excessive straining in order to pass stool, which causes the colon lining to bulge outward where there are areas of weakened muscle fiber. The bulges are called diverticulae. If these little sacs become inflamed, infected, or rupture, they produce the condition known as diverticulitis.

As a result of research published by Dr. Denis Burkitt and Surgeon Commander T.L. Cleave, it is now recognized that diverticulitis is the result of low fiber intakes and, if it is treated with the proper diet, drug therapy and surgery become redundant. It is important to add a quantity of insoluble fiber, like

bran, to the diet, but this is best added to muesli, natural cereals, porridge, or yogurt, rather than taken as commercial high-bran breakfast products. Soluble fiber is a must for the long-term prevention of constipation and the recurrence of diverticulitis.

Diverticulitis is almost always reversible by following the principles of everyday healthy eating, as advocated by naturopaths for the last 100 years. It is interesting to note that vegetarians hardly ever suffer from diverticular disease, as their diet is rich in both forms of fiber and normally contains far less junk food.

A cup of peppermint tea after each meal helps eliminate the problems of wind, and camomile tea at bedtime is a gentle and calming solution for this condition.

▶ **Eat more** porridge, apples, pears, beans, and cooked, green leafy vegetables for their soluble fiber; whole wheat bread, brown rice, and not more than one dessertspoon of bran daily for their insoluble fiber. Drink at least 3½pt/1.7l of water a day.

▶ **Eat fewer** refined, processed carbohydrates.

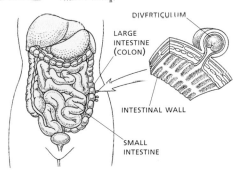

BELOW Diverticulitis affects the wall of the large intestine. The small bulges, or diverticulae, in the gut wall become inflamed and cause the pain often known as "left-handed appendicitis." The condition can be reversed by sensible eating.

DIVERTICULUM

LARGE INTESTINE (COLON)

INTESTINAL WALL

SMALL INTESTINE

DYSMENORRHEA see
Menstrual problems

E

EATING PROBLEMS (ANOREXIA NERVOSA, BULIMIA NERVOSA)

SYMPTOMS

❖ *Obsessive attitude to food, dramatic loss of weight.*

❖ *Cessation of periods in females, laxative abuse, rapid weight fluctuations, periods of bingeing and starving.*

ANOREXIA simply means loss of appetite, which in itself can be caused by a variety of problems – dental, oral, throat, digestive, liver, and gall bladder disorders are a few examples. But mere loss of appetite is a very different situation from the severe eating disorders of anorexia nervosa and bulimia nervosa.

• **ANOREXIA NERVOSA** is a serious disease, in which rejection of eating results in long-term damage to the body. Girls particularly run the risk of infertility and, in extreme cases, anorexia nervosa may be fatal. Although they are obviously emaciated, sufferers become obsessed with the idea that they are fat, often as the result of peer pressure from friends, over-concern with weight from parents, and in children often great fear at the prospect of growing up. Difficult mother/daughter relationships are also common among anorexics and there may well be a history of emotional trauma or disturbance before the onset of the illness. Divorce or the death of a parent or sibling are common triggers.

All forms of treatment are rejected by the anorexic, and no amount of common sense or persuasion will change their own perception of how they look. A major factor in the terrifying spread of anorexia nervosa (ten percent of sufferers are now boys) is the malignant influence of the media. Body images created by the advertising industry, waif-like and emaciated teenage fashion models, the multimillion-dollar slimming industry that pushes diet books, pills, and potions – all of these are putting pressure on young people to be thin.

• **BULIMIA NERVOSA** is a condition that involves alternate starving and bingeing. Sufferers can eat huge quantities of food – enough for six people in one sitting – then purge themselves with laxatives or deliberately make themselves vomit before returning to their starvation diet. Bulimics are not that easy to spot and are usually older than anorexics, around the mid-twenties being common. They are mostly independent, living away from home, either working or studying, and their normal "diet" is just about socially acceptable. They are seldom emaciated and, although sometimes very slim, may also be quite overweight. Bulimia is triggered by the same factors as anorexia – low self-esteem, pressure from ambitious parents, and lack of parental affection and attention – and there is frequently an underlying thread of stress, anxiety, and depression.

Eating disorders require very specialized care under the guidance of an expert psychiatrist, psychologist, or psychotherapist. In fact, patients are often admitted for prolonged in-patient treatment in order to start the healing process. Once under way, this process can be helped along by the gradual introduction of healthy food and the use of vitamin and mineral supplements. The most important of these is zinc, which should be taken in combination with a good all-round multivitamin and mineral formula.

The healthiest calories come from complex carbohydrates, such as whole wheat bread, oats, potatoes, pasta, rice, and beans. But these are very bulky and there is a limit to how much you can eat at one time. Do make sure that they comprise at least half your food. Get extra calories from bananas, nuts (as long as they are unsalted and not covered in chocolate), and dried fruit. Now is the time for you to become a grazer – aim to eat something at least every two hours, starting with a really good breakfast and finishing with a bedtime snack. Raisins, sultanas, dates, and dried apricots are excellent sources of energy, vitamins, and minerals, and also supply useful quantities of fiber. As snacks and nibbles throughout the day, these dried fruits supply a significant number of calories in comparatively small amounts of food.

Once the anorexic patient begins to realize how ill they look, healthy weight gain becomes the prime objective. As well as the need for exercise and plenty of healthy calories, here is a recipe that I have used successfully for years in my own practice. Make it up first thing in the morning, have a glass before breakfast, then keep the rest in the refrigerator, and make sure it has all gone by bedtime. You will need 2½ cups/600ml of whole milk, one certified salmonella-free raw egg, one banana, a dessertspoon each of molasses, honey, tahini, wheatgerm, and brewer's yeast powder, and, finally, four dried apricots. Whisk all the ingredients together in a liquidizer or with a hand-blender.

▶ **Eat more** of anything that provides calories and nutrients, but try to include high-zinc foods like shellfish, pumpkin seeds, liver, cheese, beef, and sardines, as zinc stimulates the appetite.

▶ **Eat fewer** high-fat, high-sugar foods as recovery proceeds, and switch to healthy eating; it is important to avoid the use of bran and bran-based cereals as they interfere with zinc and iron absorption (anorexics are frequently obsessed with improving bowel function and may use bran as an alternative to laxatives).

SEEDS AND NUTS

Among the best sources of healthy calories are seeds, and spreads made from seeds and nuts. Sunflower and sesame seeds are especially good and tahini – a spread made from crushed sesame seeds – together with peanut butter provides a large number of calories and very little bulk.

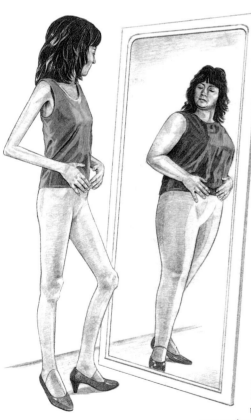

ABOVE *Many anorexia sufferers have a distorted view of their body image: looking into a mirror they see themselves as fat, but in reality they are severely underweight.*

ECZEMA

SYMPTOMS

❖ *Inflammation of the skin – commonly the folds behind the joints of the knees and elbows and around the eyes and mouth; accompanied by redness, flaking, and tiny blisters.*

❖ *Dry, itching, and thickened skin.*

❖ *Family history of eczema, hay fever, or asthma.*

THERE ARE several different types of eczema, the most common being atopic (allergic) eczema, or infantile eczema. This tends to run in families and sufferers often experience other allergies too. Another type is contact eczema, when skin contact with certain substances causes an allergic reaction (see Dermatitis, p. 167). Seborrheic eczema affects areas of the skin that are rich in oil-producing glands.

Eczema may be triggered by stress, but the major cause is an allergy to something. The latest research shows that contact allergy to the droppings of the house-dust mite is a major trigger of eczema, especially in children (see Asthma, p. 152). No matter what treatment you are using for eczema, the first three fundamental steps must always be moisturize, moisturize, moisturize. Do this from the inside by drinking at least 5pt/2.25l of water daily; do this from the outside by applying nonperfumed, hypoallergenic moisturizers as frequently as possible throughout the day.

Because food allergies are frequently an aggravating cause of eczema, an exclusion diet (see p. 65) – in which foods commonly associated with allergies are excluded – is often a good idea. Eggs, cow's milk, and artificial additives (and sometimes red meat) are the main products to avoid. A diet that excludes common allergens and is high in green, leafy vegetables, root vegetables, fruit (but not citrus fruit or acidic berries), oily fish, and good-quality cold-pressed vegetable oils will help. For the adult, avoiding excess alcohol and caffeine can also be beneficial.

Eczema may be helped by taking vitamin B complex, vitamin A, and polyunsaturated fatty acids. At least 3g of evening primrose oil daily should be taken for four to six weeks, 2g for the following eight weeks, and a maintenance level of 1g a day for the next three months. Zinc is another vital factor; pumpkin seeds are a good source, so eat 2 tsp/10g a day.

▶ **Drink more** water; eat more green leafy vegetables, root vegetables, and fruit for their beta-carotene, vitamin C, and bioflavonoids; oily fish for their omega-3 fatty acids; olive, safflower, and flax-seed oils, and avocados for their vitamin E and essential fatty acids; pumpkin seeds for their zinc – shellfish too, if they do not cause allergic skin reactions.

▶ **Eat less** meat, animal fat, cow's milk and dairy products, shellfish, wheat, citrus fruit, acidic berries, and eggs. **Avoid** sugar, artificial additives, and alcohol.

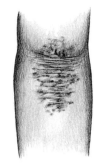

ABOVE *Eczema often occurs in places where the skin folds or creases: inner elbows, knees, groin, and armpit. It is sore and itchy.*

SOOTHING OATS

Porridge oats are a traditional remedy – put 1½ cups/100g onto a large square of cheesecloth, and tie into a bag. Hang under the hot-water faucet on the bathtub so that the water runs over it. The vitamin E and demulcents in the oats are both soothing and healing.

EMPHYSEMA

SYMPTOMS

❖ *Lung stiffness, shortage of breath, and poor peripheral circulation, leading to excessive strain on the heart.*

EMPHYSEMA is a gradually progressive and incurable disease of the lungs. The tiniest air sacs (alveoli) become unnaturally distended with air, which stretches their walls, damages the surfaces, reduces the elastic properties of the lungs, and interferes with the exchange of oxygen and carbon dioxide. The heart needs to pump much harder to push blood through the lungs and, on even the slightest exertion, has to drastically increase its work rate to deliver enough oxygen. Such stresses can lead to heart failure.

Emphysema is almost exclusively the result of cigarette smoking – even chewing tobacco raises the blood level of nicotine, which constricts the blood vessels and can cause further damage to heart and lungs. Even in the later stages, giving up smoking makes a significant difference to the rate of lung deterioration, the degree of disability, and the imminence of death.

Emphysema is treated with the same type of medication as asthma, namely bronchodilators and steroids. It is essential that antibiotics are introduced at the earliest sign of a flare-up, to prevent secondary bacterial infection and further damage to the lung tissue.

In terms of food, vitamin A and beta-carotene are essential for good lung health, and vitamin E is needed for its antioxidants. Eat cabbage for its cancer-protective effect and celery, which is a natural diuretic.

▶ **Eat more** garlic, onions, and leeks for their traditional respiratory benefits; all citrus fruit, blackcurrants, and kiwi fruit for their vitamin C; sweet potatoes, carrots, and spinach for their beta-carotene; whole grain cereals, olive, safflower, and sunflower oils, nuts, and seeds for their antioxidant vitamin E. Use lots of rosemary, thyme, cloves, and cinnamon in your cooking, which help your breathing.

▶ **Eat fewer** dairy products and animal fats; cut down on sugar, alcohol, caffeine, and all refined carbohydrates to minimize the production of excessive mucus and constriction of the blood vessels that supply the lungs. **Avoid** smoking and smoke- and fume-polluted atmospheres.

EDEMA *see* Fluid retention

LEEKS WITH LEMON DRESSING
benefits respiratory system

SERVES 2
6 THIN LEEKS
1 LEMON
4 TBSP OLIVE OIL
SALT
2 TBSP CHOPPED PARSLEY

Trim the ends off the leeks, then rinse in cold water. Cook in boiling water until tender, drain, then place in a dish. Grate the lemon and add the zest to the leeks, then squeeze over the lemon juice and add the olive oil and salt. Let marinate for a while. Sprinkle with parsley just before serving.

F

FAINTING

SYMPTOMS

❖ *A feeling of faintness, or actual fainting, most commonly caused by a lack of blood flowing to the brain, leading to a temporary loss of consciousness.*

FAINTING, or syncope, to give it its medical name, can be caused by excessive pain, heat, cold, fear, the sight of blood, or any unpleasant stimulus. A slowing of the heart rate, accompanied by dilating of the major blood vessels in outer parts of the body, can cause a sudden drop in blood pressure and, as the brain is the highest point of the body, it is the first organ to be affected. Fainting is actually the body's self-defense mechanism, as once you are flat on the ground, the head is at the same level as the heart and blood flows rapidly back into the brain tissues.

Postural hypotension is a sudden fall of blood pressure caused by a rapid change in posture – from lying to standing. This is the most common reason for older people fainting, as their compensatory mechanisms do not adjust as quickly as those of the young. Standing for too long in one position, a lack of oxygen in the blood due to anemia, lung diseases such as bronchitis or emphysema, or a fall in blood-sugar levels can all be triggers that lead to fainting.

It is important to keep your blood-sugar level on an even keel, so get into the habit of eating little and often – four to six small meals a day – and avoiding large quantities of refined sugars.

Complex carbohydrates, dried fruits, oats, and beans provide slower energy-release and help to iron out the peaks and troughs of resting blood-sugar level *(see also Blood-sugar problems on p. 154).*

❯ Eat more buckwheat for its rutin; liver and dark-green leafy vegetables for their iron, to prevent anemia; yeast extracts for their B vitamins; dried fruit and fresh nuts for instant energy.

❯ Avoid excessive caffeine or alcohol, and large amounts of high sugar foods like candies, cakes, and cookies.

Anyone unconscious should be put into the recovery position shown here so that their airways are clear, and there is no pressure on the chest or heart. The priority is to clear the airway, then to pull the casualty over onto his or her side.

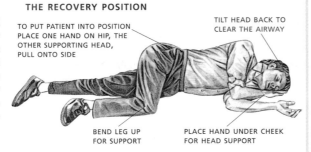

THE RECOVERY POSITION

TO PUT PATIENT INTO POSITION PLACE ONE HAND ON HIP, THE OTHER SUPPORTING HEAD, PULL ONTO SIDE

TILT HEAD BACK TO CLEAR THE AIRWAY

BEND LEG UP FOR SUPPORT

PLACE HAND UNDER CHEEK FOR HEAD SUPPORT

FATIGUE

SYMPTOMS

❖ *Tiredness, depression, loss of concentration.*

❖ *Irritability, stress, anxiety, snoring.*

GENERAL FATIGUE may be caused by many ailments – anemia, insomnia, thyroid disorders, ME, snoring and sleep apnea, glandular fever; by painful diseases such as arthritis, osteoarthritis; by any illness, serious or minor, that interrupts sleep; by nutritional deficiencies, particularly of the B vitamins, iron, and zinc; and by excessive thinness or obesity.

Being underweight can seriously interfere with your sleep, as can constant dieting, which also affects your nutritional status. Obesity, on the other hand, causes fatigue because it increases the risk of snoring and sleep apnea, and the body has to use far more energy just to move the body's bulk from A to B.

Anyone suffering from fatigue without an obvious cause should seek medical advice to rule out underlying disease. By far the most common reasons for fatigue are poor quality of sleep and borderline anemia *(see p. 149)*. Few women of childbearing age manage to maintain adequate levels of iron in the blood or body stores of this vital mineral and, while not displaying obvious signs of anemia, these low levels can be sufficient to cause fatigue and exhaustion.

Good nutrition is the key to combating fatigue: the diet should be rich in all the recommended foods in order to maintain hemoglobin, good blood-sugar levels, and your intake of zinc, a key factor in the production of enzymes that regulate the body's metabolism.

My patients are always horrified when I recommend exercise as the first step in a fatigue recovery programme. Regular exercise stimulates the release of the feel-good hormones, increases the oxygen-carrying capacity of the blood and the energy stores in muscles.

❯ Eat more complex carbohydrates, dried fruit, and root vegetables for their energy; liver, dates, raisins, and dark-green leafy vegetables for their iron; bananas, fish, meat, wheatgerm, and brewer's yeast for their B vitamins.

❯ Eat fewer high-sugar foods; consume less caffeine and alcohol. **Avoid** large meals late at night.

FEVER

SYMPTOMS

❖ *Raised temperature, sweating, chills.*

❖ *Headache, general malaise.*

THE "NORMAL" body temperature is usually considered to be 98.4°F/37°C, but it can range between 96 and 99°F/35.6 and 37.2°C. Infectious diseases cause a rise in body temperature, but exercise, overexcitement, hot baths, adverse reactions to food or prescribed drugs, severe anemia, circulatory, respiratory and heart diseases, and some acute forms of arthritis can also cause the temperature to go up.

The fever can develop gradually or suddenly, and in some situations the temperature remains normal during the day but rockets at night-time. As the temperature climbs, so too do the pulse and respiration rate. Often the tongue becomes coated, dry, and cracked, and the appetite disappears. Nausea, vomiting, or constipation can all be side effects, and the amount of urine passed decreases and becomes more and more concentrated as the body loses a great deal of fluid through sweating. It is essential that your fluid input is at least 2.25l/4pt per 24 hours to protect the kidneys and prevent urinary infection or the formation of stones. Sponging the body with tepid (not cold) water and letting it dry naturally may lower the temperature.

Above 103°F/39.4°C convulsions, fits, delirium, and even coma can occur. Convulsions caused by fever are common in children up to the age of three or four. For more information on how to treat fever in children *see Childhood diseases pp. 159–60.*

The old wives' tale "feed a cold and starve a fever" is, like most of them, correct. Fasting increases the white cell count, which raises the body's natural immune response. Anyone with a high fever should be encouraged to consume only the recommended foods until the temperature returns to normal and the normal appetite is restored.

The traditional European remedy for fever in either adults or children is to drink weak lime-blossom or camomile tea that has been sweetened with honey to taste. This is often effective in lessening a fever.

▶ **Drink more** fluids, particularly water, camomile tea, or tea made from equal quantities of elderflower and peppermint or elderflower and lime-blossom, or a combination of lavender, sage, and rosemary, which is powerfully antiseptic, plus unsweetened fruit juices to replace fluid loss; tomato juice without salt, to replace potassium lost through sweat; eat more cooling fruit, like water melon, mango, pawpaw, and grapes; meat, chicken, or vegetable broth for their minerals and B vitamins.

▶ **Eat less** of everything else.

EXOTIC FRUIT SALAD WITH MANGO PUREE
soothes a fever

SERVES 4
1 RIPE MANGO
8OZ STRAWBERRIES
2 KIWI FRUIT
8OZ GRAPES
1 PAWPAW OR PIECE OF MELON
MINT LEAVES TO DECORATE

Skin the mango, then cut it in half, and chop the flesh into chunks. Liquidize until it is a purée, adding a little water if necessary. Spoon onto 4 plates. Slice the remaining fruit and arrange on the purée, decorating the fruit salad with a few mint leaves.

HEALTH WARNING

Extremely high temperatures, especially when accompanied by delirium, need urgent medical attention.

FIBROCYSTIC BREAST DISEASE (FBD)

SYMPTOMS

❖ *Swollen, painful, and tender breasts, usually occurring just premenstrually; normally affects both breasts.*

❖ *Often a number of cysts of different sizes; sometimes swelling only, with no other symptoms.*

THIS IS THE most common of all breast problems, affecting around one-third of all menstruating women, usually between the ages of 30 and 50. It can vary in severity, from mild discomfort to extreme pain, and is thought to be a slight risk factor for breast cancer. It frequently presents as a part of generalized premenstrual syndrome.

As well as following the general dietary advice for PMS *(see p. 203)*, women who suffer from fibrocystic breast disease need to take additional nutritional steps. Caffeine and its chemical relatives, theophilline and theobromine (found in tea and chocolate) – the whole group of chemicals is known as methylxanthines – must be avoided. Don't forget that many prescribed

and over-the-counter medicines contain quite large amounts of caffeine. Nuts, seeds, extra-virgin olive oil, and avocado should be eaten for their vitamin E content, as this nutrient can help to regulate hormone levels. Beta-carotene also plays a part in reducing the occurrence of these cysts, so the diet should include carrots, broccoli, apricots, squashes, spinach, tomatoes, sweet red and yellow peppers, and whichever dark-green leafy vegetables you like best.

There are great benefits to be had from avoiding meat, and following a vegetarian (plus fish and occasional poultry) regime could make a substantial difference. Where possible choose free-range organic poultry, as this will not contain traces of hormones. A diet that is high in fiber and a regular consumption of live yogurt will ensure good bowel function and healthy gut flora. There is evidence that women suffering from constipation are at much greater risk of fibrocystic breast disease than those who have regular daily bowel movement.

▶ **Eat more/less** *See Premenstrual syndrome on p. 203.*

FIBROIDS

SYMPTOMS

❖ *Sometimes none at all, or irregular and more frequent periods, heavier blood loss.*

❖ *Discomfort or pressure on the bladder and/or rectum, uncomfortable or painful intercourse, anemia.*

A FIBROID is an abnormal growth of cells, which usually occurs in the muscle wall of the uterus. In spite of its name, this comprises not fibrous tissue but muscle cells, which are nearly always nonmalignant.

Fibroids are likely to affect around one-fifth of all women over the age of 35. If you get through the menopause and have never had a fibroid, you are unlikely to develop one thereafter. In fact, if the size of your fibroid or fibroids could be contained until you reach the menopause, they nearly always start to diminish and the need for surgical removal subsequently disappears. Happily, with modern surgical techniques it is often possible to remove fibroids internally without the need for a hysterectomy.

There is no doubt that exposure to hormones does stimulate the growth of fibroids. For this reason eat only organic free-range animal products, as growth hormones are often added, albeit illegally, during intensive farming. The ideal diet is a vegetarian diet, which is high in fiber and in all the essential antioxidant nutrients that are protective of every cell in the body. Short periods of fasting (two to three days) have also been known to reduce the size of these tumors. I advise my patients to do a three-day fast once a month, just before the onset of their next period (*see Safe Fasting on p. 58*).

▶ **Eat more** fruit, vegetables, salads, legumes, whole grain cereals, nuts, and seeds – a vegetarian diet helps control the growth of fibroids.

▶ **Eat less** meat and poultry; fewer dairy products and animal fats; consume less caffeine. **Avoid** the contraceptive pill, and intensively farmed meat or poultry, which is likely to contain traces of hormones – these could accelerate the growth of fibroids.

FIBROSITIS

SYMPTOMS

❖ *Painful inflammation of the muscle fibers – usually the large muscles of the neck and shoulders, especially around the shoulder blades, and the large muscles on either side of the spine – either long-standing and chronic, or sudden and acute.*

AS WELL AS occurring in the neck and shoulders, fibrositis can crop up in other major muscles – the traditional ailment, weaver's bottom, is fibrositis in the buttock muscle, originally caused by sliding from side to side while working at the loom. The modern-day equivalent is seen in organists, people using home-knitting machines, and those whose jobs or hobbies entail long periods of sitting on hard benches.

Conventional medicine has a strong tendency to dismiss fibrositis as being largely psychogenic or originating in the mind, and some texts ascribe it more commonly to women than to men. There is frequently an accompanying problem of disturbed sleep patterns – not surprising in view of the physical discomfort that fibrositis produces. Rheumatologists describe fibrositis as "very difficult to treat," but good massage, osteopathic treatment, and some simple dietary changes frequently work wonders. Practitioners who specialize in "hands-on" treatment are easily able to identify the trigger points of fibrositis and work on them to relieve this painful condition.

It helps to follow a diet that avoids foods likely to inflame the muscle fibers. These are foods that release irritating by-products, especially a group of chemicals called purines, which increase the level of uric acid circulating in the bloodstream. The major sources of this group of chemicals are the foods listed below as being those to avoid. But it is equally important that people with fibrositis eat large amounts of the oily fish – salmon and tuna – that do not contain large amounts of purines, but do supply the omega-3 fatty acids.

Eat plenty of cabbage, which is rich in antiinflammatory chemicals, and all citrus fruit, but especially lemons, which have a high content of bioflavonoids. Celery and dandelion leaves (the latter known in France as *pissenlit* and in the north of England as "wet the bed") are both natural diuretics, which help the body get rid of waste fluids and the inflammatory chemicals that they contain.

▶ **Eat more** salmon and tuna for their antiinflammatory omega-3 fatty acids; more cabbage, also for its antiinflammatory properties; lemons for their bioflavonoids; celery and dandelion for their diuretic effect.

▶ **Drink less** tea, coffee, and cola drinks and cut down on chicken. **Avoid** organ meats, yeast and meat extracts, beef, pork, chocolate, cocoa, sardines, anchovies, whitebait, sprats, herrings, mackerel, mussels, scallops, all fish roe, partridge, guinea fowl, and fortified wines like sherry and port.

TUNA AND BEAN SALAD

is good for fibrositis

CANS OF ASSORTED BEANS (BORLOTTI, RED KIDNEY, FLAGEOLET, GARBANZO, BUTTER BEANS, ETC.)

SCALLIONS OR ORDINARY ONIONS

CELERY

SWEET GREEN AND RED PEPPERS

CUCUMBER

TUNA PRESERVED IN OLIVE OIL

HARD-COOKED EGGS AND COLD, COOKED NEW POTATOES (OPTIONAL)

Rinse all the beans thoroughly. Dice the salad ingredients. Drain the tuna. Combine everything in a large bowl and pour over a good salad dressing made with extra-virgin olive oil.

FLATULENCE

SYMPTOMS

❖ *A sensation of uncomfortable fullness, which is relieved by bringing wind up or passing it down through the colon and out of the anus.*

FLATULENCE, or excessive wind in the digestive system, is perfectly normal. It is an inevitable by-product of the activity of the natural intestinal bacteria on starches and proteins in the food we eat. This wind contains methane, carbon dioxide, and hydrogen, together with air that may be swallowed – more so at times of stress and anxiety – during normal eating. Excessive amounts of wind may be a symptom of several digestive disorders: stomach ulcers *(see p. 207)*, irritable bowel syndrome *(see p. 194)*, diverticulitis *(see p. 169)*, Crohn's disease *(see p. 165)*, hiatus hernia *(see p. 186)*, and also chronic constipation *(see p. 163)*.

Though there is little scientific evidence to justify the Hay Diet *(food combining, see p. 64)*, many people find that this innocuous eating plan produces surprising results and does away with excessive flatulence.

Add at least one tub of natural live yogurt to your daily intake of food to maintain the levels of beneficial bacteria in the gut, and for the synthesis of B vitamins in the large intestine. The latest research from the Institute of Food Science at Reading University, England, now suggests that these natural yogurt bacteria can also protect individuals against severe infections such as *E.coli* 0157: H7, VTEC.

The use of bran and other high-fiber foods in the treatment of constipation and diverticulitis often causes a dramatic increase in wind, which may last for two to three weeks. As the digestive system adapts to the higher fiber intake, this side effect gradually subsides.

▶ **Eat more** live natural yogurt for its beneficial bacteria; drink peppermint tea; thyme, rosemary, sage, caraway, fennel, and dill are all aids to good digestion and help to reduce the amount of gas produced in the gut. Summer savory, known as the "bean herb" in northern Europe, should be added to all bean dishes during cooking, as it makes the beans more digestible. Beans should always be cooked in unsalted water as the salt toughens the skin, leading to poorer digestion and more wind.

▶ **Eat fewer** high-sugar and refined carbohydrate foods, beans, peas, and other "windy" foods, like brussels sprouts, cabbage, and artichokes. **Avoid** all fizzy drinks.

MINT – A VITAL DIGESTIVE

Following each meal with a cup of mint tea is the most natural of all digestives. Mint is one of the most important aromatic medicinal crops grown in the US, and is used largely to manufacture peppermint extract, a safe natural agent, which relaxes the muscles of the colon and relieves the discomfort of excessive wind.

FLUID RETENTION (EDEMA)

SYMPTOMS

❖ *Swelling of the body tissues, usually at the extremities of hands and feet, caused by fluid; pressure causes "pitting," failure of the indentation to spring back to normal when pressure is released.*

❖ *Severe underlying problems may cause generalized edema.*

FLUID RETENTION, or edema, can be caused by heart disease reducing the efficiency of the circulation; by mechanical problems, such as varicose veins or tight-fitting, elastic-topped socks or stockings; by local injury, like severe bruising or scalding; by reduced kidney function or fluid retention. It should always be taken seriously, as it may be a sign of serious underlying heart, liver, or kidney disease, so refer to your medical practitioner straightaway. Prolonged use of steroid drugs, vitamin B deficiency, and severe malnutrition can also cause this uncomfortable problem. The hormone fluctuations that occur in women when they are premenstrual and during pregnancy is another common trigger.

Whatever the cause, the first step is to eliminate salt from the diet, as the sodium part of sodium chloride (common salt) interferes with fluid excretion and causes fluid retention. Swelling of the feet, ankles, and legs can be relieved by regular exercise, raising the legs whenever you sit, drinking large amounts of water, which stimulates kidney function and increases fluid elimination, and eating plenty of the diuretic foods – parsley, celery, and dandelion leaves being the best. If there are dandelions growing in your garden, don't kill them off or let the dogs near them, but use the pale green inner leaves torn up in your salad – they make a delicious addition.

Foods rich in potassium should also be high on your list, as this mineral is another vital piece in the jigsaw of kidney function. Avocados are a rich source of potassium; potatoes, dried fruit, unsalted nuts, and bananas also contain a significant amount. Avoid standing, sitting on hard-edged seats, crossing your legs, and constipation, all of which aggravate the problem.

▶ **Drink more** water; eat more parsley, celery, and dandelion leaves for their diuretic effect; avocados, dried fruit, molasses, potatoes, bananas, and nuts for their potassium.

▶ **Eat less** salt and fewer high-salt foods – preserved meats, smoked fish, savory snacks, instant soups, and bouillon cubes.

DANDELION LEAF SALAD
relieves fluid retention

SERVES 4

A GOOD HANDFUL OF DANDELION LEAVES

1 LETTUCE

2 TBSP OLIVE OIL

JUICE OF ½ LEMON

SALT

Wash the dandelion leaves and lettuce, then tear them into a bowl. Make the dressing with the oil, lemon juice, and salt. Combine together and serve with garlic croûtons, if liked.

FOOD POISONING

SYMPTOMS

❖ *High temperature, stomach pain, headache, nausea, diarrhea (sometimes bloody), flu-like symptoms.*

FOR MOST healthy adults a minor bout of food poisoning is an unpleasant inconvenience, but for the very young, the elderly, pregnant women, and anyone whose immune system is weakened by illness, an attack of *Salmonella* could be fatal.

To protect yourself and your family from the risks of food poisoning, follow the Guide to Good Kitchen Hygiene opposite.

All foods are home to some bacteria, but it is only when foods are not stored or handled properly that problems can arise. Some, such as poultry, burgers, unpasteurized milk products, rice, shellfish, raw or undercooked eggs, present particular hazards *(see Identifying Bacteria, below)*. Correct cooking and storage can overcome these problems.

❭ **Drink copious amounts** of fluid, especially water. Follow the BRAT diet *(see opposite)* for 48 hours, then add live yogurt, but no other dairy products for three days.

❭ **Avoid** all dairy products, alcohol, citrus juices, and high-fiber foods.

IDENTIFYING BACTERIA

Different bacteria cause different problems, so it is important to know what they are:

BACILLUS CEREUS This is found in cooked rice that is not reheated to a high enough temperature or is kept warm. Ideally, keep rice extremely hot, or cool it quickly and put it in the refrigerator. This particular bacteria results in vomiting within an hour of eating contaminated rice, though it may also cause diarrhea later on.

COOKED AND RAW MEAT

CAMPYLOBACTER This is nearly always caused by blood from raw chicken dropping onto already cooked foods stored below it. A high temperature, stomach pain, nausea, and bloody diarrhea begin within two to six days and can continue for up to ten days.

CLOSTRIDIUM PERFRINGENS This bacteria grows on gravy, stuffing, stews, or ground meat left lying in a warm room, or keeping warm in the oven. Within 6–12 hours it causes headache, diarrhea, and stomach cramp, but the symptoms pass after 24 hours.

E. COLI 0157, VTEC (Verocytotoxin-producing *E. coli*) This strain causes violent food poisoning, often from undercooked beefburgers and is strongly linked to careless slaughtering, dirty kitchens, and fast-food take-outs. VTEC is a recent strain, which can also be found in contaminated milk, untreated water, and cheese. Vomiting and severe diarrhea (often bloody) result and, in the very young and very old, there is a risk of kidney failure and death. Problems start within 12–72 hours and may last for ten days and require hospitalization *(for further details see pp. 104–5)*. Never eat burgers that still have the slightest trace of pink in the center.

UNPASTEURIZED CHEESE

LISTERIA This sometimes occurs in soft, unpasteurized cheese and pâtés, and causes flu-like symptoms from four hours to several days after infection. It can be very serious in babies, invalids, and the elderly. The British government advises pregnant women to avoid pâté and soft cheese, as listeria can damage the fetus.

UNCOOKED EGGS AND MAYONNAISE

SALMONELLA This is found in undercooked chicken and turkey, lightly cooked or raw eggs, and all raw egg products, and even cooked food and salads left in the warmth for too long. Salmonella causes stomach pain, vomiting, diarrhea, and

a high temperature within 8–36 hours of infection and is a very common source of food poisoning. Symptoms can last for up to three weeks, but you may be left as a carrier for three months or more. It can be fatal to babies, small children, and the elderly.

UNDEFROSTED CHICKEN

STAPHYLOCOCCUS AUREUS Many healthy people carry this bug in their nose or intestines and it is easily transmitted to food by careless hygiene. It is commonly found in ham, poultry, and cream- or custard-filled cakes and pastries. This is a fast-acting bacteria, which can cause stomach pain, nausea, vomiting, and diarrhea within a few minutes or up to six hours after infection, but has usually gone within 12 hours to two days.

FOOD POISONING

FOOD POISONING BEGINS AT HOME

Food poisoning is the most common cause in adults of episodes of nausea and vomiting, usually accompanied by diarrhea. But mention food poisoning and most people immediately think of Delhi-belly, "gyppy tummy," "Turkey trots," or "Montezuma's revenge" – all related to foreign travel, strange food, and contaminated water. However, the worrying truth is that the number of reported cases of food poisoning in people who have not traveled abroad has rocketed in recent years – from 20,000 in Britain in 1985 to 90,000 in 1996. Bearing in mind that only an estimated ten percent of people bother to report everyday occurrences, this number represents just the tip of an alarming iceberg. And, contrary to public opinion, food poisoning is more frequently caused in the home than by eating out in restaurants or fast-food take-outs.

Throughout the food chain there are places where infection can occur. Intensive food production and the use of antibiotics in animal feed has produced many resistant strains of bacteria; the huge expansion of food processing means more handling and a greater risk of contamination; the mushrooming fast-food take-out business is frequently dirty and unhygienic; and many home cooks know little about the fundamental rules of kitchen hygiene.

BEWARE THE BUFFET!

Cases of food poisoning increase as the weather gets warmer, because bacteria multiply much more quickly at high temperatures. One of the most hazardous sources is the buffet, where flies and bugs proliferate. Cold food like mayonnaise, cream, mousses, and dips gets gradually warmer, and the hot vol-au-vents, cocktail sausages, chilis, and rice get cooler. Be very careful what you choose, and if you arrive late, you're probably safest with a cheese sandwich and fresh fruit salad.

Shellfish are a particular hazard as they are often grown in water polluted by sewage. Cockles, mussels, and oysters can be contaminated by small, round-structured viruses (SRSVs). These cause violent vomiting, which spreads the viruses into the air, so that you don't even have to eat a poisoned mussel yourself – you can get the virus from someone else who has. Never eat raw or undercooked shellfish.

ACTION TO TAKE

If you do get a bout of food poisoning, you should go to the doctor, though most people do not. Try to keep a sample of the food that caused it in a sealed container in the refrigerator so that your local Environmental Health Officer can have it analyzed and can check on the original source. If you work in the food industry, you must see your doctor and tell your employer, to make sure that you are not a carrier of the infection. Babies, small children, and the elderly must get medical attention for any severe episodes of diarrhea and vomiting, and the same is true for healthy adults, if the illness continues for more than a day or two.

It is vital to replace lost fluids, and although you can buy rehydration preparations from the pharmacist, you can make your own by adding one teaspoon of salt and eight teaspoons of sugar to 2pt/1l of boiled water. Try to drink ⅔ cup/150ml every 15 minutes. When you do feel like eating – but preferably not in the first 24 hours – stick to the BRAT diet (that is, bananas, rice, apples, and dry toast). As vomiting is reduced, start by eating plain, toasted whole wheat bread and vegetable broth. By the next day, boiled rice, bananas, and grated apple can be introduced and by the evening, steamed carrots and other root vegetables. Get back to normal eating over the next two or three days.

GUIDE TO GOOD KITCHEN HYGIENE

• If your refrigerator does not have a built-in temperature gauge, buy a thermometer and make sure that it is always between 32° and 41°F/0° and 5°C. Get another for your freezer and keep it below 0°F/-18°C.

• Don't take chilled or frozen food with you on a shopping spree. Use a proper cold-bag and get the food into your own refrigerator or freezer as soon as possible.

• Don't use the same knives and chopping boards for raw and cooked foods. And it is safest to keep separate ones for raw fish and raw meat.

• Keep cooked foods at the top of the refrigerator and raw meat, poultry, and fish at the bottom.

• Always wash your hands before and between handling different foods.

• Never allow household pets onto kitchen counters or to eat off plates or bowls that you use yourself.

• Unless frozen packaged foods say they can be cooked from frozen, make sure they are thawed out first. Frozen poultry should be left to defrost very slowly in the refrigerator – never try to defrost it in hot water.

• Never refreeze previously frozen food.

• Make sure you remove all the stuffing from cooked chicken or turkey before storing it in the refrigerator. It's actually better to cook the stuffing separately if you anticipate having leftovers.

• Cold food should be kept below 41°F/5°C and hot food above 145°F/63°C.

• All poultry and burgers must be cooked right through, until there are no pink areas and the juices run clear.

• Cooked food should be covered and cooled as quickly as possible before refrigerating.

• Be very careful with microwaves. If the instructions on a package are not clear, or you do not know the wattage of your microwave, check with the manufacturer.

FRACTURES

SYMPTOMS

❖ *Pain in the affected joint.*

MOST FRACTURES occur as a result of injury, and they are most common in elderly people but are frequently "pathological" fractures – they occur from a very minor impact, which you would not expect to inflict severe damage, but which does so due to a pathological weakening of the bone structure. This most commonly occurs in women after the menopause, when they start to develop osteoporosis, but may also be the result of underlying conditions like cancer, or long-term treatment with drugs such as steroids or diuretics. In any of these situations, spontaneous or stress fractures may occur without warning in the legs, vertebrae, ribs, or arms. Those with osteoporosis must act immediately to reduce the risk of fractures, while anyone who has just sustained a fracture can shorten their healing period by paying careful attention to the way in which they eat.

In order for calcium to be deposited in the bones, your body needs calcium, magnesium, boron, and vitamin D working together. So the first priority is a dramatic increase in your consumption of the recommended foods.

There is some controversy in the medical profession about the value of calcium and vitamin D supplements, and of hormone replacement therapy (HRT), in the elderly. But most orthopedic surgeons I have spoken to are convinced that it's never too late for either therapy. There are also other drugs that increase the strength of bones without the need for HRT, with its associated side effects (*see Osteoporosis on p. 201*).

Plenty of fresh air and exercise, which must be weight-bearing exercise, will make a considerable difference to the course of osteoporosis and thereby reduce the risk of pathological fractures.

High salt intakes increase the body's loss of magnesium and calcium, thus hastening the onset of osteoporosis and interfering with the normal healing process of a fracture. So make sure you ask for a low-salt diet if you are in hospital, and when you get home, read the labels on everything and try to keep your total salt consumption to no more than 4g per day.

▶ **Eat more** low-fat dairy products, whole grains, nuts, and legumes, for their calcium; oily fish for its vitamin D; almonds, Brazil nuts, brewer's yeast, whole wheat flour, dried peas, and shellfish for their magnesium; alfalfa, lettuce, peas, dates, prunes, and hazelnuts for their boron.

▶ **Eat less** uncooked bran and cut down on foods rich in oxalic acid, like rhubarb and spinach, which form insoluble salts with calcium; and on junk foods rich in phosphorus, such as cola drinks and burgers.

COMFREY

Another important aid to rapid healing is the herb comfrey (*Symphytum officinale*), traditionally known as "knitbone," which has been used in the treatment of fractures for centuries. There has been some concern over the liver toxicity of comfrey in recent years, but this applies to preparations of the root, while the leaves are considered safe. Two cups of comfrey tea a day, after sustaining a fracture, should be taken for three to four weeks. Put one teaspoon of chopped leaves in a cup of boiling water. Leave to stand, covered, for five minutes, strain, then add a little honey, and drink.

BELOW *A simple fracture of the radius, one of the two bones in the forearm. Sometimes fractures are difficult to diagnose if the skin is not damaged.*

INABILITY TO MOVE WITHOUT PAIN

SWELLING AROUND INJURY

POSSIBLE BRUISING OR DEFORMATION

GALLSTONES

SYMPTOMS

❖ *Mild discomfort in the upper abdomen to frequent bouts of violent, projectile vomiting, and very severe pain.*

AN OLD medical school mnemonic tells us that the five "f"s – female, fair, fat, flatulent, and forty – are the key to gallstones, which are indeed twice as likely to occur in women as in men. The risk rises even more for women who are on the contraceptive pill or who are pregnant. In spite of their common incidence, only about one-third of gallstones actually cause problems, when a stone in the gallbladder obstructs the opening of the bile duct. Most stones are made of crystallized cholesterol and calcium salts.

Obesity, constant yo-yo dieting, irregular meal times, and a high sugar consumption (particularly from candies and fizzy drinks) are all linked to the formation of gallstones. If the gallbladder becomes inflamed and

LEFT *Overweight women over forty are more likely to suffer from gallstones.*

there is severe pain and vomiting, then surgery to remove the stones, the gallbladder, or both may be necessary. However, because they eat far less animal fat, vegetarians are only half as likely to get gallstones as meat eaters. One common factor in nearly all patients with gallstones is insufficient consumption of water. Aim to drink at least 3½pt/1.7l every day.

If the symptoms settle down after the initial episode, it is feasible to reduce the size and number of the stones through dietary manipulation. A considerable increase in soluble fiber is the first step. Increasing your intake of vitamins C and E and essential fatty acids should be next on the list, by eating plenty of citrus fruit, nuts, seeds, olive oil, and safflower seed oil.

▶ **Eat more** high-fiber foods, especially soluble fiber from porridge, apples, pears, bananas, and dates to reduce cholesterol levels; globe artichokes, which are a known stimulant to gallbladder function. Drink plenty of water.

▶ **Eat fewer** refined carbohydrates and, most importantly, drastically reduce your sugar intake.

PLANT AIDS

Plants can be a great help. The globe artichoke contains the chemical cynarnine, which stimulates the gallbladder and increases the production of bile. Herbal extracts of dandelion root and the milk thistle (*Silybum marianum*) also have beneficial effects on the gallbladder.

GASTRITIS

SYMPTOMS

❖ *Heartburn, vomiting, and flatulence, often accompanied by a burning sensation at the top of the stomach, which may travel up to the chest.*

GASTRITIS is either acute or chronic. Acute gastritis is usually caused by a sudden inflammation of the stomach lining, normally associated with drugs like aspirin, with nonsteroidal antiinflammatory drugs, or even with alcohol abuse – albeit a one-off binge, rather than regular heavy drinking. Acute ulcers can also arise at times of very excessive stress, following severe burns, injury, psychological trauma, liver or kidney disease. An acute attack of gastritis after a night on the town and too much alcohol needs little specific treatment, apart from a very bland diet made up of the recommended foods listed below.

Chronic gastritis, which is much more common in the elderly, is now thought to be linked to presence of the bacterium *Campylobacter* in the gut. Another bacterium, *Helicobacter pylori*, is also strongly linked with gastritis and ulcers and can be well treated by the use of a special type of honey *(see box)*.

In a very small number of people (less than 5 percent of the population) there is considerable damage to the lining of the stomach, which seems to be linked to cigarette smoking, rather than to alcohol, and may subsequently cause gastric ulcers. Thyroid disorders, diabetes, and pernicious anemia also affect the integrity of the stomach lining.

Happily, the days of treating any form of gastric ulceration or gastritis with diets of boiled fish, rice, and bread soaked in milk are long gone. Certainly it is a good idea to avoid highly irritant foods, like large quantities of alcohol, coffee, strong tea, and very hot spices. But relief can be found in the regular consumption of small meals, with the emphasis on positive foods, and by never allowing long periods to elapse without eating.

▶ **Drink more** water to replace lost fluid. Eat bananas for their energy and potassium; boiled white rice and dry toast for their low-fiber carbohydrate; apples for their pectin; manuka honey for its antibacterial residues *(see box)*.

▶ **Avoid** all other foods, especially dairy products, for the first 48 hours; cut down on very hot spicy foods, like chilis and curries, alcohol, coffee, and strong tea.

MANUKA HONEY

Manuka honey is produced in New Zealand by bees that feed on the flowers of the manuka tree. A dessertspoon with each meal and another at bedtime has been reported in the New Zealand medical press as producing dramatic benefits within a month, because the antibacterial residues in the honey kill off the *Helicobacter*.

GASTROENTERITIS

SYMPTOMS

❖ *Gastric discomfort, vomiting, diarrhea, and mild fever.*

THE COMMONEST culprit in gastroenteritis is food itself, and while this condition is often associated with diarrhea and "traveler's tummy," it occurs most frequently in the home as a result of poor hygiene, lack of thought, or just plain carelessness. The *Salmonella* bacterium is most likely to be found in badly handled stews, casseroles, ground meat, poultry, cooked rice, meats, milk and cream, eggs, seafood, coconut, chocolate, dried foods, and spices.

Food poisoning *(see pp. 176–7)* is the most common cause of gastroenteritis and an attack may last anything from six hours to three days.

Bottle-fed babies are far more likely to contract gastroenteritis than those who are breastfed, due to the obvious extra areas of potential contamination – the bottle, the teat, the formula itself, and the milk or water with which it is made up.

Some people suffer from a form of allergic gastroenteritis, and so food allergies or food intolerances should never be ignored as the possible cause. A history of chronic and repeated attacks of gastric discomfort, in which there are no signs of either acute food poisoning or excessive consumption of nicotine, coffee, or alcohol, are always suspect. Young women with chronic gastroenteritis may be abusing laxatives in order to keep their weight down.

Relieve the discomfort of gastroenteritis with the BRAT diet – that is, bananas, boiled rice, apples, and dry toast *(see p. 177)*. It is best to eat small amounts at regular intervals.

Severe diarrhea and vomiting can be life-threatening in the very young and the elderly. Fluid and mineral replacement are essential *(see p. 177 for a rehydration formula)*, and medical advice should be sought if the symptoms do not abate within 24 hours.

▶ **Drink more** water to replace lost fluid. Eat bananas for their energy and potassium; boiled white rice and dry toast for their low-fiber carbohydrate; apples for their pectin.

▶ **Avoid** all other foods, especially dairy products, for the first 48 hours.

HERBAL TEAS

The following will have a soothing effect on the digestive tract: raspberry-leaf tea – two cups a day sipped very slowly (except in early pregnancy); ginger tea – up to three cups a day; cinnamon tea made with a teaspoon of powdered spice simmered for 20 minutes with a little honey.

GENITAL HERPES *see* Herpes simplex

GERMAN MEASLES *see* Childhood diseases

GINGIVITIS *see* Dental problems

G

BELOW *A gluten-free diet need not be unappetizing; rice, potatoes, fruit, vegetables, cheese, and meat are all tolerated.*

GLUTEN INTOLERANCE (CELIAC DISEASE)

SYMPTOMS

❖ *Failure to thrive in infants and children, weight loss in adults.*

❖ *Distension and pain in the abdomen, flatulence, foul-smelling loose stool, mouth ulcers.*

❖ *Anemia, signs of multiple vitamin deficiency in chronic sufferers.*

GLUTEN INTOLERANCE, known as celiac disease, is an abnormality of the lining of the small intestine, which is triggered by gluten, a substance present in wheat, rye, barley, oats, and triticale – a cross between wheat and rye.

This disease can occur at any age and, in addition to the general symptoms outlined above, the overall picture is one of malnutrition, as even a balanced diet that includes gluten results in very poor absorption of nutrients. Numbness, tingling and pins and needles in the hands and feet, bleeding, cramp, muscle weakness, rickets, and menstrual disorder are virtually all reversible by eliminating gluten. Definite diagnosis can only be reached by observing the symptom pattern, taking a biopsy that confirms structural changes, starting a strict dietary regime, seeing the symptoms abate, and, finally, repeating the biopsy one to two years later and finding a normal lining.

Though there is certainly some hereditary factor in celiac disease, it is believed that early feeding of cow's milk and cereals to infants may also play a part.

Vitamin and mineral deficiency is common in celiac patients, who may have had a mild undiagnosed form of the disease for years. So vitamin supplementation is vital in the early stages of treatment, the fat-soluble vitamins A, D, E, and K, the B vitamins, iron, and especially zinc all being important.

Constipation can be a major problem for celiacs, so make sure you avoid it by drinking at least 5pt/2.25*l* of fluid daily and by eating regular amounts of dried fruit, brown rice, peas, beans, millet, buckwheat, fibrous vegetables, and plenty of apples and pears.

Today most countries have a celiac self-help organization, which publishes details of guaranteed 100 percent gluten-free products. But if in doubt, don't eat it.

▶ **Eat more** fish, poultry, and meat for their protein; calf liver, chicken liver, and dark-green leafy vegetables for their iron and folic acid; millet, maize, brown rice, dried beans, potatoes, and grits for their fiber, starch, and calories; shellfish and pumpkin seeds for their zinc; all fresh fruit, vegetables, and salads for a spread of nutrients.

▶ **Eat fewer** dairy products in the first few weeks of treatment. **Avoid** wheat, rye, barley, oats, and triticale, in any form. Great care must be taken to avoid manufactured products containing extracts of any of these.

GOUT

SYMPTOMS

❖ *Acute pain in the affected joints, which are red, hot, swollen, and excruciatingly painful; sometimes fever; shiny red skin over the affected joints.*

GOUT is a serious and increasing condition, more common in men (16 in every 1,000) than in women (3 in every 1,000 and rarely occurring before the menopause). The big toe is commonly affected, but gout can also occur in other joints. Acute attacks require medical treatment.

Caused by deposits of uric acid in the joints, gout often has a family history. Uric acid is a waste product and is removed from the blood as it passes through the kidneys. The group of organic compounds known as purines are part of this process, and although it is unlikely that particular foods cause gout, those foods rich in purines do aggravate the disease.

Your weight should be kept down and the following purine-rich foods should be avoided altogether:

organ meats; yeast, yeast and meat extracts; oily fish; mussels, scallops, roe, taramasalata, and even caviar! Also avoid partridge and guinea fowl. Other meats contain fewer purines, but chicken, turkey, and lots of white fish are better for you than beef roast or steak.

Caffeine is another purine and can aggravate this condition, as can diets that are very low in carbohydrates. Drink lots of water to reduce the risk of kidney stones – 5pt/2.25*l* a day is the minimum, and more in hot weather.

▶ **Eat more** of the cabbage family of plants, onions, leeks, cherries, and apples for their antiinflammatory action, and celery and parsley as diuretics, every day; drink lots of water.

▶ **Drink less** coffee and tea; eat less chocolate and salt. **Avoid** alcohol; game, liver, kidney, heart, sweetbreads, yeast and meat extracts, oily fish, roe, mussels, and scallops.

GLANDULAR FEVER *see* Mononucleosis

GOITER *see* Thyroid problems

RIGHT *Sufferers from gout should avoid red meat of all kinds, including organ meats.*

HAIR AND SCALP PROBLEMS

SYMPTOMS

❖ *Deterioration in hair or scalp condition.*

❖ *Loss of hair, either in patches or all over.*

❖ *Flakes of dandruff.*

HAIR IS ONE of the earliest barometers of health and your hairdresser will often notice a deterioration in the condition of your hair or scalp before other symptoms appear. Many factors can affect the health of your crowning glory and most of them can be improved by paying more careful attention to the way you eat.

▶ **Eat more** fruit, vegetables, and salads for their beta-carotene and vitamin C; whole wheat bread, brown rice, and oats for their B vitamins; oily fish for their omega-3 fatty acids and vitamin D; shellfish and pumpkin seeds for their zinc; liver, dates, dried apricots, raisins, and prunes for their iron; low-fat dairy products for their calcium; Brazil nuts for their selenium; olive and safflower oil, for their polyunsaturates; avocados, sunflower-seed oil, and peanut butter (natural, unsalted) for their vitamin E; eggs for their cysteine and methionine.

▶ **Eat fewer** refined carbohydrates, saturated fats, and full-fat dairy products, and less bran; drink less alcohol.

DAMAGED HAIR

Many of the things you and your hairdresser do to your hair can cause damage. Bleaching, dyeing, perming, straightening, heated rollers, and blow-drying can all dry out the hair and make it break and split, while many of the chemicals can irritate the scalp and may cause contact dermatitis.

> #### OLIVE OIL MASSAGE
> For dry hair and a flaky scalp, warm a cup of olive oil in a bowl of hot water, massage into the hair, wrap in a towel for one hour, shampoo, then rinse with a cup of cider vinegar to 2½ cups/600ml of hot water.

DANDRUFF

Excessive loss of skin from the scalp is known as dandruff and is caused by too little or too much natural oil being secreted by the sebaceous glands. Dry, white flakes appear when there is too little sebum, and oily yellow flakes when there is too much. Wash the hair with camomile shampoo, and add a cup of the cider vinegar mixture described below to the final rinse. A weekly application of a tub of live yogurt, massaged well into the hair after washing, left for ten minutes, then rinsed with hot water to which you have added two tablespoons of cider vinegar and two teabags of stinging-nettle tea is beneficial.

GREASY HAIR AND SCALP

This is caused by overactivity of the sebaceous glands, which can be stimulated by a high intake of sugar and saturated fats. Try to wash your hair every day in a mild, non-detergent shampoo like rosemary or nettle. All the stories about too much washing making hair greasier are simply old wives' tales. Dirty hair is dull and lifeless hair, and you would not dream of leaving your face dirty for a whole week – would you?

> #### NEUTRAL SHAMPOO
> Using a neutral shampoo is really important on greasy hair, as this helps maintain the protective acid layer of the scalp.

HAIR LOSS

Male-pattern baldness is hereditary and none of the proprietary preparations have any real long-term benefit. Some pharmaceutical creams derived from blood-pressure medication do stimulate a coarse growth, more like pubic hair, but only if you continue to use the expensive treatment, and an unwanted side effect may be a clinically significant drop in blood pressure. *(See also Alopecia on p. 149.)*

All women lose some hair as they get older, and after the menopause it tends to become fine and thin. Women also frequently suffer hair loss two or three months after childbirth, although the hair soon regrows.

> #### ANEMIA
> For both men and women anemia can trigger hair loss. Though this is more common in women, especially those with heavy periods, an increase in iron-rich foods could make a significant improvement.

GENERAL HAIR CARE

Many herbs combine cleansing and conditioning qualities, but different hair types will respond to herbs in different ways. Some herbs, however, such as rosemary, thyme, and marjoram, are suitable for all hair types. Camomile shampoo and a rinse of camomile tea are especially good for fair hair. And a cup of beet juice in four cups of hot water with a teaspoon of salt, massaged through the hair, then rinsed out makes a great conditioner for dark hair.

> #### DIET AIDS
> No matter what else you do, a diet comprising all the recommended foods is essential to ensure adequate vitamins, minerals, and all the other nutrients necessary for a healthy scalp and a luxuriant head of hair.

FOOD FOR HAIR

You can find many effective hair remedies in the kitchen cupboard. Some are shown below.

Beer shampoo is available commercially, but a glass of flat beer in the final rinse can be just as effective.

Egg shampoos are good for dry hair.

Lemon juice in the final rinse helps greasy hair to look good. Neat lemon juice left on the hair to dry in the sun produces natural highlights.

Olive oil makes an excellent treatment for dry scalp. Warm some oil, massage it in, wrap the head in a towel, and leave for an hour before shampooing.

Rosemary conditions greasy hair; make an infusion of rosemary leaves, let cool then use as a rinse.

Almond oil is very mild and safe to use on sensitive skin or babies over 3 months; use it on the scalp as indicated for olive oil.

etc.

HALITOSIS (BAD BREATH)

SYMPTOMS

❖ *Bad-smelling breath.*

HALITOSIS is usually a trivial complaint, but it can be embarrassing, and unpleasant for others. The most likely causes of bad breath are problems in the mouth (an obviously bad tooth, a build-up of tartar, inflamed and infected gums, rotting food stuck in unbrushed crevices, or a crop of suppurating ulcers), the nose and sinuses, the lungs, or the stomach and the digestive tract. Chronic sinus problems, catarrh, oral thrush, tonsillitis, and chest infections such as chronic bronchitis, or a lung abscess can also make your breath smell.

It is important to seek professional dental or medical advice if the cause is not obviously simple and easily remedied. Food odors can be avoided by chewing a few dill seeds or a couple of coffee beans. Regular brushing with a good toothbrush, changed at least every three months, and plenty of fiber-rich foods like raw vegetables, apples, and pears help massage the gums and keep them healthy. Avoid plaque by cutting out sugary snacks and drinks, and brush your teeth as soon as possible after eating.

Sinus problems and catarrh can be helped by reducing your intake of dairy products and by eating decongesting herbs and spices such as ginger, cinnamon, mustard, and horseradish. Steam inhalations over a bowl of hot water containing five drops of eucalyptus oil will also help. Chronic chest infections need medical attention, but help yourself by eating plenty of carrots, broccoli, spinach, and citrus fruit for their beta-carotene and vitamin C, which protect lung tissue.

Constipation, ulcers, and indigestion can all provoke bad halitosis. Deal with the cause, by increasing your soluble fiber and fluid consumption. Many digestive problems, including constipation, respond well to the Hay Diet *(food combining, see p. 64).*

❯ **Eat more** carrots, broccoli, spinach, and citrus fruits for their beta-carotene and vitamin C; fibrous raw vegetables, apples, and pears to protect the gums; ginger, horseradish, mustard and cinnamon for the sinuses; whole grain cereals and lots of water to avoid constipation.

❯ **Eat less** sugar, candies, cakes, and cookies and drink fewer fizzy drinks, to protect the teeth and reduce tartar; and cut down on dairy products to reduce mucus. **Avoid** alcohol and all tobacco products.

ABOVE A gargle and mouthwash made up of 30 drops of tincture of myrrh in a glass of warm water also helps to keep breath sweet. Do not overuse patented antiseptic mouthwashes, as they kill good bacteria too.

BELOW Hay fever is characterized by bouts of sneezing and red streaming eyes.

HAY FEVER

SYMPTOMS

❖ *Violent bouts of sneezing, itchy and watery eyes, catarrh, blocked sinuses. Disturbed sleep and all-round misery.*

IF YOU ARE among the 40 percent of the population who show a susceptibility to allergy or the unfortunate 20 percent of people who suffer from hay fever or asthma, don't lose heart! There is a great deal of self-help that can ease your misery.

When your white cells overreact, they produce large quantities of the chemical histamine and the symptoms of hay fever, which is an allergy to pollens (specifically those from grasses, trees, and flowering plants). The symptoms start when the plants are in flower, and some people may suffer from spring right through to the fall.

The same symptoms can also be triggered by mold, feathers, dust, the house-dust mite, and animal dander. If you react to these nonpollen allergens, you have "perennial rhinitis" *(see Asthma on p. 152 for practical tips on prevention).*

There are natural alternative treatments for hay fever. An instant way to stop an attack of the sneezes is to sniff cold water up your nose and spit it out through your mouth. This simple trick washes all the pollen

grains out of the nasal passages, and you will be symptom-free until you go out again.

Keep a bottle of distilled water in the refrigerator, and use it in an eyebath to irrigate the eyes (using clean water for each eye). A used, cold, damp teabag placed over each eye for two minutes also helps stops the irritation. And if you go out when the pollen count is high, use a filter mask (available from pharmacies).

Reducing the amount of dairy products in the diet controls the production of mucus and makes life more comfortable, but do replace the calcium with a daily supplement including vitamin D, and don't deprive children of milk without professional advice.

❯ **Eat more** locally produced honey for its homeopathic pollen protection; lemons, oranges, blackcurrants, and blueberries for their vitamin C and bioflavonoids; extra-virgin olive oil, safflower oil, and avocados for their antiinflammatory fatty acids and vitamin E; garlic, leeks, onions, chives, and scallions for their antimucus and antibacterial properties; thyme, rosemary, cinnamon, cloves, ginger, horseradish, and chili for their antiseptic and expectorant effect.

❯ **Eat fewer** dairy products and refined carbohydrates; less animal protein. **Avoid** known allergenic foods and food additives.

PRACTICAL STEPS

There are obvious steps to take that often get ignored:

• Don't go out early in the morning or late in the evening, when pollen counts are high.

• Keep windows closed, especially in the bedroom.

• Don't bring flowers into the house.

• Make someone else mow the lawn.

• Wear glasses or sunglasses when you do go out – they keep the pollen out of your eyes.

• Even if it's hot, keep car windows closed – sweating is better than sneezing.

HEADACHES AND MIGRAINES

SYMPTOMS

❖ *Throbbing pain in the head, tension in the temples or behind the eyes, nausea, stiff neck.*

HALF OF ALL women get headaches, but only one-third of men, while twice as many women as men endure the form of torture known as migraine. All forms of headache are related to changes in the blood supply to the brain. For this reason foods that help this, and foods that are likely triggers of your pain, are a vital part of the headache diet.

Keep a food diary and carefully note when you get your headaches; then you should be able to make the right deductions from this simple piece of detective work. Sometimes it's easier to exclude all the possible triggers and then add them back one at a time.

Tension headaches are the most common of all. The tension can be mental, physical or both, and the pain is caused by pressure on the nerves at the base of the skull, in the scalp and face, and on the blood vessels.

Warm baths, with a few drops of lavender oil added, massage, gentle stretching exercises, aromatherapy, and some of the calming herbs, like valerian, will all help. Camomile, lime-blossom, or elderflower tea is relaxing, safe and effective.

A headache is often the first sign of hunger, and starts as your blood sugar level falls. Eat something as soon as possible or, better still, have a good breakfast and the pain will go within a few minutes.

A stuffy or constantly dripping nose and bunged-up sinuses frequently result in severe discomfort and headache. Reducing the amount of dairy products you consume also reduces the amount of mucus you produce, and eating at least two cloves of fresh garlic a day helps to clear the nasal passages.

Gasoline fumes, varnish, paint, and even nice smells like perfume are sometimes responsible for headaches. Where you work, or sleep, can also have an effect. Apart from postural considerations, air-conditioning, poor lighting, central heating, noise, soft beds, and too many pillows are the main culprits. Too much or too little sleep is another consideration.

The "ice cream" headache is started by eating, or drinking, very cold substances. The pain is sharp, but will not usually last longer than a minute or two. But the combination of sex and a headache is no joke. The muscles at the back of the neck sometimes get very tense as a result of sexual arousal and the peaceful after-glow may be marred by a headache. Some gentle massage is usually all that is needed.

▶ **Eat more** oily fish – salmon, mackerel, pilchards, and sardines – and take a fish-oil supplement, all of which have a gentle antiinflammatory action. Use ginger in cooking, take it in tea or as tablets to relieve nausea and stimulate the circulation. Green olives, seeds, liver, lobster, and, best of all, oysters are useful for their high copper content, a deficiency of which appears to be linked with recurrent headaches. Extra virgin olive oil, avocados, pine kernels, sunflower seeds, sesame seeds, and wheatgerm are rich in vitamin E, which is essential for the vascular system.

▶ **Eat less** chocolate, citrus fruit, red wine, cheese, yeast products, and herrings, which contain amines. **Avoid** nitrates and nitrites used as preservatives in meat products such as hot dogs, salami, ham, bacon, salt beef, pastrami, and pâtés; caffeine – in coffee, tea, and cola drinks; monosodium glutamate in packet soup, many meat products, and lots of other preprepared foods. Baked beans, butter beans, fava beans and mangouts (snow peas, sugarsnap) are unlikely causes of headaches but more common than you might think, together with nuts and even peanut butter.

FOODS TO AVOID

CHEESE

CHOCOLATE

CITRUS FRUIT

RED WINE

MIGRAINE

Sadly, there is no mistaking an attack of migraine. It often starts with an "aura," so that there is a sense of an impending attack. You may get a blind spot in your vision, experience flashing lights or zigzag patterns, or a dislike of bright light. The warning signs last for anything between a few minutes and an hour.

The pain and an upset stomach come next: nausea, an aversion to food and food smells, vomiting, severe pain (usually on one side of the head, behind the eye), sometimes sensations of numbness in the side of the face, and alternate feelings of cold and sweat – during an attack most people go to bed in a dark room. Migraines last for anything from 6 to 72 hours and disrupt life completely. The strain soon tells on family

relationships, and the social impact of migraine can be every bit as serious as the medical condition.

Feverfew (*Tanacetum parthenium*) is one of the great aids for migraine and is best used as a preventive. Put a couple of leaves in a sandwich and eat one of these each day, but don't nibble on plain leaves as the parthenolide – the constituent of the plant that relieves the pain of migraine – may cause mouth ulcers. A hot compress on the nape of the neck and a cold one on the forehead will also help to break the cycle of an attack and lying down on your back with a rolled-up towel in the nape of your neck to stretch the joints and muscles is often a great comfort.

BELOW *Relaxing your muscles can dispel the tension that often causes headache. Try this simple exercise. Lie flat on your back, knees raised and slightly bent, arms at your sides, your mouth open to relax your jaw. Starting with your toes, focus on each part of your body and consciously relax the muscles. Feel the tension drain away. Get up slowly.*

HOW TO LEAD A HEART-FRIENDLY LIFE

- Don't smoke.
- Keep your weight/height ratio within the recommended limits (see p. 200).
- Drastically reduce your intake of animal fats.
- Eat more whole grain cereals and complex carbohydrates, whole wheat bread, pasta, brown rice, potatoes.
- Eat more fish and poultry without the skin.
- Eat at least five portions a day of fresh fruit, vegetables, and salads.
- Cut down on sugars and salt.
- Keep alcohol consumption down to one, or at most two, drinks a day.
- Use herbal teas as a substitute for some of your cups of coffee, use skimmed milk, and never use non-dairy creamers or whiteners.
- Take regular exercise – a half hour's brisk walk three times a week will do.
- Make time for some relaxation: yoga, meditation, self-hypnosis, and relaxation exercises are all useful.
- Use your time wisely, plan your day, avoid over-commitment and the stress that comes in its wake.

ABOVE *Foods that promote low blood pressure and healthy circulation support the heart at its pumping station. Leeks, onions, garlic, oily fish, and red wine in moderation can help.*

HEART DISEASE

SYMPTOMS

❖ *Depends on the individual complaint.*

HEART DISEASE in all its varied forms is the single largest cause of premature death in the Western world. It encompasses coronary artery disease, diseases of the heart muscle and heart valves, angina, heart attack, and atherosclerosis.

A major heart problem in later years is angina, which now affects two million Britons each year. It is caused by damage to the coronary arteries. If these become narrowed by deposits of cholesterol, even modest exertion can mean that the heart muscles do not receive enough blood for them to function adequately. Pain in the chest and one or both arms comes on severely and suddenly, and all you can do is to stand absolutely still until it passes. But it is never too late to make the changes to your lifestyle outlined below.

Heart disease is triggered by a number of risk factors: a family history of the illness, smoking, obesity, a diet high in saturated animal fat and low in fiber and fresh produce, high blood pressure, high cholesterol levels, inactivity, alcohol abuse, stress. The real risk comes with a combination of two or more of these factors, but the biggest risk of all still seems to be smoking. Deal with that first, then turn your mind to reducing the other risk factors.

Despite worldwide publicity, the response to healthy eating and lifestyle messages has been varied. It is true that death from heart disease is declining, but much more slowly in Britain (which is right at the top of the heart-disease league) than in the US. In the UK someone dies prematurely and preventably every three minutes from coronary heart disease. That's the equivalent of a full jumbo jet crashing at London's Heathrow Airport every day of the week.

Epidemiologists studying the patterns of heart disease in different countries have produced the fascinating theory of "The French Paradox." Why is it that the French – like nearly all Mediterranean nationalities – smoke more, drink more, and have quite a high intake of animal fat, yet show a much lower incidence of heart disease than people in Britain, northern Europe, and the US? The answer appears to be the Mediterranean diet *(see p. 63)*. If we were all to adopt this diet, I believe

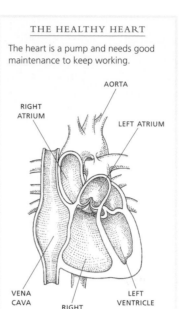

THE HEALTHY HEART

The heart is a pump and needs good maintenance to keep working.

AORTA

RIGHT ATRIUM

LEFT ATRIUM

VENA CAVA

RIGHT VENTRICLE

LEFT VENTRICLE

the drop in heart-disease-related deaths would be phenomenal.

A healthy heart starts in the womb. Professor Michael Crawford at the Institute of Brain Chemistry in London has now shown that bad maternal nutrition can lay the foundations for later heart disease in the growing fetus.

Keeping animal fats to sensible levels, and eating all the high-fiber foods that help to eliminate cholesterol, combined with regular exercise, will protect against atherosclerosis. Controlling obesity is the next key step and starting your children out in life with a healthy attitude to food is guaranteed to work. If you get half your calories from complex carbohydrates and eat five portions of fruit and vegetables a day, there is going to be little room left for the antinutrient foods.

Garlic has long been used as a remedy that lowers cholesterol, lowers blood pressure, and makes blood less likely to clot. Modern science has now confirmed all these properties and more besides.

Far from prohibiting alcohol, we now know that small quantities benefit the heart and circulation by opening the tiniest blood vessels, the capillaries. This helps reduce blood pressure and improve blood flow. Research has now shown that any form of alcohol (not just red wine) taken in modest amounts performs the same function. But don't get carried away – three or more units a day can spell disaster.

▶ **Eat more** fruit, vegetables, and salads for their nutrients and protective antioxidants; complex carbohydrates and dried beans for their energy and fiber, which lowers cholesterol; oily fish for their protective omega-3 fatty acids; other fish for their fat-free protein; garlic, onions, leeks, chives, and scallions for their cardio-protective benefits; Brazil nuts for their heart-protective selenium; extra-virgin olive oil, safflower oil, walnuts, almonds, avocados, sunflower seeds, pine kernels, and sesame seeds for their essential vitamin E; drink not more than two glasses of red wine a day for improved circulation; Chinese green tea for its antioxidant protection.

▶ **Eat less** saturated animal fat, meat, and fewer meat products – bacon, ham, corned beef, salt beef, sausages, salami, pâté, hot dogs, burgers, meat pies; salt and preserved meats containing sodium nitrates and nitrites; smoked foods, salted nuts, and other nibbles; refined carbohydrates, cakes, cookies, and white bread; high-sugar, high-fat bakery goods, Danish pastries, doughnuts, chocolate bars, and ice creams.

HEARTBURN

SYMPTOMS

❖ *Burning pain behind the breastbone, severe discomfort behind the V at the front of the ribcage.*

❖ *Belching, reflux of stomach contents into the back of the throat and mouth, sore throat, difficulty in swallowing.*

HEARTBURN is not a disease but a symptom, commonly caused by hiatus hernia *(see p. 186)*. It is very common in the later stages of pregnancy when the baby is pressing up against the underside of the diaphragm and squeezing the stomach. It can be aggravated by stress, bad and irregular eating habits, and being severely overweight.

If you suffer from heartburn, you must first deal with these problems. Stop smoking, as this is a common trigger of over-acidity, and keep your alcohol intake to not more than two units a day. Many commonly prescribed and over-the-counter drugs can also be the cause of heartburn, including aspirin, non-steroidal antiinflammatories, and corticosteroids.

Eat little and often – don't go for more than three hours without food – and make sure to include lots of the digestion-friendly herbs, like mint (mint tea), basil, thyme, rosemary, dill, fennel, and caraway. If you're very pregnant, try raising the head end of your bed by 3 inches/7.5cm and if you have to bend, use your knees, don't fold over at the waist.

▶ **Eat more** live yogurt for its beneficial gut bacteria; boiled white rice, fish, bananas, potatoes, and dairy products, all of which are easy to digest; sauerkraut, cooked onions, garlic, and vegetable juices for their healing properties

▶ **Eat less** very spicy food; fewer high-fat foods – sausages, pâtés, meat pies, salamis; acidic pickles, chutneys, relishes, and raw onions. **Avoid** alcohol and coffee (even decaffeinated).

ABOVE *Heartburn commonly affects pregnant women as the growing baby pushes the stomach upward. Try to avoid taking drugs for this temporary condition*

HEPATITIS

SYMPTOMS

❖ *Fever, headache, exhaustion, appetite loss, nausea, vomiting, dark urine, pale feces, yellowing of the skin and whites of the eyes.*

HEPATITIS is inflammation of the liver, sometimes caused by medicines, disorders of the immune system, or alcohol. Most commonly, however, with hepatitis A, B, or C, it is a viral infection that is the trigger. There are vaccines available which prevent hepatitis A and B, but not, so far, for C.

● HEPATITIS A is transmitted via infected food or water and increases with the growing amount of travel to developing countries – a major outbreak in America recently affected many hundreds of school children, who ate contaminated frozen strawberries from Mexico. It is also known as infectious, epidemic, or short-incubation hepatitis and the incubation period is about one month. It can cause prolonged periods of illness and liver damage, though sufferers of hepatitis A rarely die of it.

● HEPATITIS B is acquired through infected blood or other body fluids, frequently during sex. It is a hundred times more infectious than HIV and kills between one and two million people worldwide each year. It is second only to smoking as a cause of cancer. There is an effective vaccine, widely used in Europe and the US, but not routinely in the UK. It is also called serum or long-incubation hepatitis and the incubation period is from two to six months.

● HEPATITIS C is a blood-borne virus, most common today among injecting drug-users (infecting 60–80 percent of them), for which there is no vaccine. Hepatitis B and C can be present without you knowing and can be passed on unintentionally. Unprotected casual sex, needle-sharing, or even using someone else's razor or toothbrush can all be roots of infection.

Where hygiene and sanitation are questionable, avoid untreated water, undercooked food, raw meat or fish, raw vegetables, milk, and all shellfish.

Hepatitis needs a careful diet, low in fats and animal proteins to reduce the workload on the liver, and low in sugars, which increase liver enzyme activity and raise the blood level of triglyceride fats. Foods rich in vitamin B_{12} and folic acid and high intakes of vitamin C will also aid recovery.

Globe artichokes, black pepper, and the milk thistle should all be eaten to stimulate improved liver function. The young stalks of thistles can be peeled, soaked, and cooked like asparagus, and young leaves (with the prickles cut off) can be used in salads or cooked just like spinach.

▶ **Eat more** globe artichokes, which are protective and curative; oily fish, yeast extracts, rabbit (very low fat), brussels sprouts, red cabbage, and garbanzo beans for their vitamin B_{12} and folic acid; oats for their fiber; beets, carrot and lemon juice, and dandelion leaves to improve elimination; kelp, brewer's yeast, almonds, and bananas for their potassium.

▶ **Eat less** red meat and sugar; drink less caffeine, sweetened carbonated drinks, and tea. **Avoid** alcohol, animal fats, and sugar.

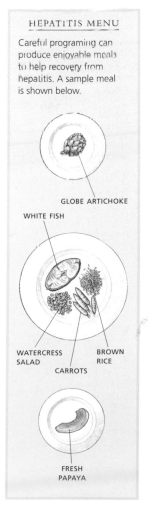

HEPATITIS MENU

Careful programing can produce enjoyable meals to help recovery from hepatitis. A sample meal is shown below.

GLOBE ARTICHOKE

WHITE FISH

WATERCRESS SALAD

CARROTS

BROWN RICE

FRESH PAPAYA

HERPES SIMPLEX (COLD SORES AND GENITAL HERPES)

SYMPTOMS

❖ *Cold sores: a burning, prickling sensation around the margin of the lips, followed by a crop of tiny blisters, which coalesce and crust over to form a cold sore.*

❖ *Genital herpes: small, painful, tender, highly infectious blisters on the genital region, sometimes on the thighs and buttocks; the first attack is always worst and accompanied by fever and swollen glands.*

• **COLD SORES** are highly infectious and most children have picked up the virus by the time they are five. It lies dormant in nerve tissue in the lips for ever, until triggered into activity. Any illness that lowers the natural resistance, or the trauma of high temperature, a cold, a sore throat, very cold weather, or exposure to intense sunlight are common causes.

If you are prone to cold sores, boost your immune system with all the recommended foods, and use total sunblock on your lips in appropriate circumstances.

• **GENITAL HERPES** are caused by a slightly different strain of the *Herpes simplex* virus, but around ten percent of all cases are caused by oral sex with a partner who has cold sores. They are very common in young people and the first attack can be extremely painful and debilitating. The blisters may rupture, forming open sores

that cause great discomfort. Normally, however, the blisters crust over within ten days and then disappear. The lucky sufferers have one mild attack and appear not to suffer again, but many people with genital herpes have frequent recurrent attacks for many years. Genital herpes during pregnancy can have serious consequences for the baby, which is likely to be infected during birth. There does seem to be a slightly increased risk of cervical cancer in women who have genital herpes, so regular screening is essential.

In both forms of herpes, lowered resistance is the main trigger. Stress, anxiety, lack of sleep, poor general health, depression, menstruation, and even sexual intercourse can trigger an outbreak. Supplements of vitamin B-complex, extra vitamin B_{12}, and the essential amino acid L-lysine are worth taking to shorten an attack and build up resistance.

▶ **Eat more** citrus fruit (especially the pith), apricots, cherries, tomatoes, and papaya for their vitamin C and bioflavonoids; liver, oily fish, eggs, and chicken for their vitamin B_{12}; safflower oil, olive oil, unsalted peanut butter, and avocados for their vitamin E; live yogurt for its synthesis of the B vitamins; green tea for its powerful antioxidant effect.

▶ **Eat less** sugar and salt, and fewer high-salt foods; drink less alcohol.

HIGH BLOOD PRESSURE
see Hypertension

HIV (human immunodeficieny virus) *see* AIDS

HIVES *see* Allergies

HIATUS HERNIA

SYMPTOMS

❖ *Chronic heartburn, indigestion, wind and, at its worst, painful burning in the back of the throat, which can lead to esophagitis (inflammation of the esophagus).*

HIATUS HERNIA is a very common problem for both men and women, but it usually affects the over-fifties. Constipation, obesity, pregnancy, and repeated strain on the muscles from heavy lifting can all increase the chances of developing this unpleasant condition. The opening in the diaphragm through which the esophagus (food tube) passes becomes too loose. This allows the acid contents of the stomach to leak upward into the esophagus, causing most disruption at nighttime when lying down.

The first practical step to minimize this disruptive discomfort is to raise the head of your bed by about 3in/7.5cm, using proper bed blocks or a brick under each leg. Do not prop yourself up on six pillows – this never works and you simply end up with a stiff neck, as well as heartburn.

Avoid anything that aggravates the symptoms. Don't eat large meals, but opt for four or five smaller meals each day. Avoid very acidic foods, cut down on alcohol and fizzy drinks, particularly those containing caffeine, and try not to mix starch and protein at the same meal, by following the Hay Diet *(food combining, see p. 64)*. Do not eat or drink anything in the three hours before you go to bed for the night.

A large paunch puts extra pressure on the diaphragm – even more so when you sit or bend – and obesity is certain to aggravate the symptoms of hiatus hernia.

▶ **Eat more** rosemary, basil, thyme, parsley, and sage, aromatic herbs that aid digestion; high-fiber foods such as porridge, whole wheat bread, apples, pears, dried apricots, and vegetables to prevent constipation.

▶ **Eat fewer** dried beans, peas, and brussels sprouts, and drink fewer fizzy drinks to avoid flatulence; cut down on coffee and especially instant coffee (even decaffeinated), which are acidic. **Avoid** pickles, vinegar, acidic foods like rhubarb, gooseberries, and unripe fruit, and anything fried. Stop or cut down on smoking.

HYPERACTIVITY AND ATTENTION DEFICIT HYPERACTIVE DISORDER

SYMPTOMS

❖ *Constant overactivity, being on the move, fidgeting.*

❖ *Poor coordination, emotional instability, short attention span, lack of concentration, failure to listen.*

❖ *Tendency to violent, destructive, self-damaging outbursts.*

IN RECENT YEARS there has been much controversy surrounding the question of hyperactive children. This term does not apply to those who are simply naughty, badly behaved, or even difficult. It applies to children who are impossible: disruptive, destructive both of themselves and property, violent and extremely aggressive, with short attention spans and great difficulty in concentrating, learning difficulties, an inability to sit still and to sleep.

For years such children were treated as behaviorally disturbed until, in the late 1960s, Dr. Ben Feingold, an allergist working in America, stumbled across a possible chemical cause for hyperactivity. While working on a project connected to flea-bite allergies in children, he devised a special diet that excluded a group of chemicals called salicylates – related to the aspirin family and similar to the substances produced by fleas. A number of children who were extremely allergic to flea bites were put on this diet and Feingold was astounded when many of the parents told him that not only were the children reacting less severely to the flea bites, but their behavior had improved as well.

He then began a large-scale study of hyperactive children who had been institutionalized. A considerable percentage responded dramatically to the diet, their behavior changing within days, although, when given a doughnut filled with artificially colored and flavored jam, their behavior deteriorated within hours. Feingold established that many of the chemicals used as artificial food additives were salicylates, which, together with the natural salicylates occurring in some foods, were the root of the problem for some children.

All children with ADHD (Attention Deficit Hyperactive Disorder, as it is now more generally known) may be sensitive to some of these chemicals. Among the worst offenders is the yellow coloring tartrazine, which is widespread in convenience foods and especially in many of the drinks, candies, and cookies aimed directly at children. Over the last 20 years I have seen dozens of children (and their parents) restored to sanity and sleep by the simple expedient of avoiding food additives. It is worth noting that some of these can also be the trigger for asthmatic attacks, eczema, urticaria, and irritations.

ABOVE *Most children go through the tantrum stage, but a hyperactive child seems to be in a permanent state of stress and overexcitement, unresponsive to normal calming methods.*

▶ **Eat more/less** *See the advice below and on p. 188.*

THE ADHD DIET

I have used this diet for over 20 years. It doesn't work for every child with ADHD, but for many it is like pressing a switch and going from darkness to light. Persevere, for you will not achieve any degree of success unless you follow the diet properly, as follows.

1. Keep a diet diary and write down everything your child eats. It is important to keep this diary going even after any improvements have occurred. It is worth keeping a column for general behavior and school progress. If the diet is working but there is a sudden deterioration in behavior, suspect that one or other of the baddies has crept in, either by accident or by cheating.

2. Any fruit or vegetable that is not on the prohibited list in Group I is allowed, unless you suspect that it causes problems in your particular case.

3. Read all labels and reject anything that is not 100 percent free of artificial additives.

4. Nearly all the permitted foods are available at the supermarket.

5. All children enjoy the occasional sweet treat, but you will have to make cakes, cookies, pies, pastries, puddings, and even simple candies at home – there are plenty of recipe books Make your own ice cream too, as fruit, nuts, or chocolate may contain additives.

6. The best way to ensure success is to get the whole family following the diet – would you like to watch while everyone else is eating all the goodies that you're not allowed? The restriction on fresh fruit and two vegetables can be relaxed after four to six weeks. Only give one new food in any 48-hour period, so that you can spot those that might still present a problem.

7. If you are going to succeed, this must be a 100 percent effort – anything less will not work. If your child has a mouthful of tartrazine on Sunday and another on Wednesday, it could cause hyperactivity for a week.

8. Usually a good response will be obvious within 7–21 days, and in some children behavioral improvements may be noticed within two or three days; in others it might take seven weeks. If your child is one of those sensitive or allergic to these chemicals, then you will reap the benefit for all your efforts, so do persevere.

9. Severely hyperactive children are frequently prescribed behavior-modifying drugs and you should never make changes without consulting your doctor.

10. Until recently many children's medicines contained flavorings and colorings that might cause the problems. Most medicines are now available without these addditives.

BROILED FISH WITH WHITE CHEESE

is suitable for hyperactive children

1 STEAK FRESH COD OR OTHER WHITE FISH PER PERSON

SALT AND PEPPER

OLIVE OIL

1 TBSP NATURAL (WHITE) CHEESE, SUCH AS MOZZARELLA OR GOAT CHEESE, PER PERSON

Pat the fish dry and season. Heat the broiler to maximum. Pour a little oil into the broiler pan. Put the fish in, then turn it immediately. Press on the sliced cheese. Broil for up to 5 minutes, depending on the thickness of the fish, until cooked right through.

FOODS TO AVOID

GROUP 1

This is the list of fruit and vegetables that contain natural salicylates. They must be omitted in any and all forms – fresh, frozen, canned, dried, as juice, or as an ingredient of prepared foods.

FRUIT

Almonds, apples, apricots, berries (blackberries, gooseberries, raspberries, strawberries), cherries, currants, grapes and raisins or any product made from grapes (e.g. wine, wine vinegar, jellies), nectarines, oranges (NB: grapefruit, lemons and limes are permitted), peaches, plums, and prunes

VEGETABLES

Cucumbers (pickles); tomatoes and all tomato products

Try adding these foods *one at a time* for about three or four days. If there is no unfavorable reaction, another item can be added. Follow this procedure until all the items in group 1 have been tested and those to which there is no adverse reaction are restored to the diet.

GROUP 2

All foods that contain artificial coloring and artificial flavoring are prohibited (it is not practical to list them all here, and the following list is meant simply as a guide for shopping and food preparation). It should be emphasized that this diet is not concerned with food preservatives, except for Butylated Hydroxy Toluene (BHT), to which the occasional child may show an adverse reaction. *The safest approach is to read all labels carefully.* And there are some permitted food items that must be prepared at home in order to avoid synthetics.

Cereals with artificial coloring and flavoring

All instant-breakfast preparations

All manufactured cakes, pastries, sweet rolls, doughnuts, etc.

Pie crusts

Frozen baked goods

Many packaged baking mixes (usually dyed, unless 100 percent whole wheat)

Luncheon meat, bologna, salami, frankfurters, sausages, meat loaf, ham, bacon, pork (when colored or flavored, usually indicated on the package)

Poultry: all barbecued types, all "self-basting" turkeys and/or with prepared stuffing

Frozen fish fillets or fish sticks that are dyed or flavored

Manufactured ice cream (unless the label specifies no artificial coloring or flavoring); the same applies to sherbet, ices homemade from pure gelatin, junkets, puddings

All powdered puddings

All dessert mixes

Flavored yogurt

All manufactured candies, hard or soft

Cider

Wine

Beer

Diet juices

Soft drinks

All instant breakfast drinks

All quick-mix powdered drinks

Tea and coffee, hot or cold

Prepared chocolate milk

Any margarine containing artificial additives

Colored butter

Preprepared mustard

Cider or wine vinegar

Ketchup

Homemade mayonnaise

Colored cheese

All toothpastes and toothpowder

All mouthwashes, cough drops, throat lozenges

Antacid tablets

Perfumes

PERMITTED FOOD

Any cereal without artificial coloring or flavoring, dry or cooked

Manufactured cakes without artificial colorings or flavorings

Homemade bakery items

All commercial breads, except egg bread and whole wheat

All other meat not listed to avoid

All other poultry not listed to avoid

All fresh fish

Homemade ice cream without artificial flavorings or colorings

Gelatin, with permitted natural fruit or fruit juices

Tapioca

Homemade custards and puddings

Plain yogurt, fresh fruit may be added

Homemade candies without almonds

Grapefruit juice

Pineapple juice

Pear nectar

Guava nectar

Homemade lemonade or limeade from fresh lemons or limes

Milk

Butter frosting, not colored or flavored

Jams or jellies made from permitted fruit, not colored or flavored

Honey

All cooking oils and fats

Mustard prepared at home

Distilled wine vinegar

All natural (white) cheese

Salt and soda mixture for cleaning teeth

MILK SHAKES

ICE CREAM

CARBONATED DRINKS

RIGHT *A few of the guilty foods: sadly, these dominate some children's diets.*

HAMBURGERS

CANDIES

HYPERTENSION (HIGH BLOOD PRESSURE)

SYMPTOMS

❖ *None, until stroke, kidney failure, or heart disease occurs.*

HIGH BLOOD pressure is one of the most important factors in the cause of heart disease, the condition that kills prematurely more people in the Western world than any other illness. You can reduce your chances of getting it, and even reduce your blood pressure, by making simple dietary and lifestyle changes.

Blood pressure is a direct measurement of the amount of work actually being done by the heart. The higher the pressure, the more work your heart has to do in order to pump blood around the body. Throughout daily life your blood pressure varies considerably, depending on what is needed, but your brain must get a regular supply of 750cc each minute, regardless of what the rest of your body is doing. If your arteries are narrowed, due to hardening, silting up with cholesterol, or constriction by nicotine, caffeine, or excess alcohol, then the heart has to pump harder to push the blood around the system, and up goes your blood pressure.

Blood pressure is written as a fraction, with the larger number (representing systolic pressure, when the heart contracts) on top and the smaller number (diastolic pressure, when the heart relaxes) on the bottom. The normal reading for a healthy adult is around 120/80, and any readings that exceed 140/90 are an indication that it is time to take some action. The lower figure is the more important, as this shows the minimum pressure that the artery walls have to withstand, all the time. If it is constantly too high, then they will suffer progressive damage, which can in turn produce heart disease and even strokes.

It is at this point that self-help is the first, and most important, step. Treating high blood pressure with drugs is not a cure for the condition, merely a way of controlling the symptom. Many of my patients have been able to reduce the amount of medicine they need, or even cut it out completely. But never change your drug regime without your doctor's advice.

There are three steps on the road to reduced blood pressure: first, changes to your diet; second, taking some form of exercise; and third, changing some of the social habits that have a seriously adverse effect on blood pressure.

Your intake of all animal fats must be reduced, so eat less butter, modest amounts of low-fat cheese, use skimmed milk, don't eat more than six eggs a week, and don't use cream at all. You must avoid all foods containing "hidden" fats: sausages, salami, pâté, meat pies, processed meats, most take-out meals, cakes, and cookies made with fat, and all fried foods.

You need to increase your intake of foods that have a positive effect on the circulation and cholesterol level, so oats, beans, apples, garlic, oily fish, and whole grain cereals should all be eaten in abundance. Red meats are best cut out of the diet altogether, but poultry, cooked without the skin, is okay. I have found that the best results come by avoiding all animal protein except oily fish.

Any form of aerobic exercise will help in the reduction of high blood pressure. Walking, swimming, cycling, or just avoiding using elevators will gradually increase the efficiency of the heart and circulation and help to reduce blood pressure. Exercise also has a positive effect on your feelings of "well-being," reduces tension, and encourages relaxation.

Social factors, such as smoking, too much alcohol, tea, and coffee, will all add to the problems. Caffeine and nicotine are both chemicals that make the tiny blood vessels at the ends of the system close up, increasing the pressure. One or at most two glasses of wine, small measures of spirits, or a can of regular beer may be good for the heart, but several are not.

Relaxation is most important, and relaxation exercises, meditation, yoga, or self-hypnosis can all have a positive result if you persevere. Massage is a wonderful aid to overcoming stress, so buy one of the many books on massage and have a go.

The ever-increasing amount of salt in the average diet is certainly a major factor in the epidemic of high blood pressure throughout northern Europe, Britain, and the US. But few people realize how widespread very large amounts of salt are in many everyday foods *(see Salt on p. 130)*. If you have a problem with your blood pressure, do cut down on your salt intake.

▶ **Eat more** fruit, vegetables, and salads for their nutrients and protective antioxidants; complex carbohydrates and dried beans for their energy and fiber, which lowers cholesterol; oily fish for their protective omega-3 fatty acids; other fish for their fat-free protein; garlic, onions, leeks, chives, and scallions for their cardio-protective benefits; Brazil nuts for their heart-protective selenium; extra-virgin olive oil, safflower oil, walnuts, almonds, avocados, sunflower seeds, pine kernels, and sesame seeds for their essential vitamin E; drink not more than two glasses of red wine a day for heart protection and improved circulation; drink Chinese green tea for its antioxidant protection.

▶ **Eat less** saturated animal fat and meat, and fewer meat products – bacon, ham, corned beef, salt beef, sausages, salami, pâté, hot dogs, burgers, meat pies; salt and preserved meats containing sodium nitrates and nitrites; fewer smoked foods, salted nuts, and other nibbles; refined carbohydrates, cakes, cookies, and white bread; high-sugar, high-fat bakery goods, Danish pastries, doughnuts, chocolate bars, and ice creams.

ABOVE *Stress and tension are one of the major causes of high blood pressure. More men suffer than women. Bad diet exacerbates problems, but you should try to root out the cause of tension in the first place as well as adjusting your food intake.*

SUPPLEMENTS

I always think that it is a good idea to add some simple supplements to the diet. Garlic tablets, fish oils, 250 units of vitamin E, and two cups of lime-blossom tea should be taken daily.

HYPERTHYROIDISM *see* Thyroid problems

HYPOGLYCEMIA *see* Blood-sugar problems

HYPOTHYROIDISM *see* Thyroid problems

I

IMPOTENCE

SYMPTOMS

❖ *The inability of a man to have or maintain an erection.*

FOR MANY YEARS the orthodox view has been that most impotence is psychosomatic in origin, except that caused by specific diseases or by medication – diabetes, thyroid disorder, infections, drugs for high blood pressure, or alcohol abuse. Although stress, anxiety, fear of failure, and emotional disturbances can adversely effect male potency, anything that reduces the circulatory efficiency and, specifically, blood flow to the penis reduces the efficiency of the erectile mechanism.

Around half of men over the age of 50 with erection problems are known to suffer from cholesterol deposits in their arteries, including the one that directly supplies the penis. Stress control is important *(see p. 189)*, but dietary improvement is fundamental to improved performance. Most ancient folklore about aphrodisiacs was on the right track, advising the consumption of foods rich in the zinc essential for sperm formation and sexual function.

Avoiding high-fat foods and increasing consumption of cholesterol-lowering ones will make a great difference. Vitamin E is necessary for the good health of artery and vein walls. Small amounts of alcohol help to stimulate blood flow, but too much is disastrous – as Shakespeare tells us in *Macbeth:* "It provokes the desire, but it takes away the performance."

Nicotine is a major culprit, causing narrowing of the blood vessels and thus reducing the flow of blood to the penis. A leading French heart surgeon once told me that advising his bypass patients to quit smoking seldom had much effect, but telling men that abandoning cigarettes would give them bigger erections nearly always worked. *(See also Infertility on p. 192.)*

▶ **Eat more** shellfish (especially oysters), liver, cheese, lean beef, whole grain cereals, nuts, and pumpkin seeds for their zinc; olive oil, avocados, sunflower and sesame seeds for their vitamin E; citrus fruit and blackcurrants for their bioflavonoids; garlic, oats, and beans for their cholesterol-lowering effect.

▶ **Eat fewer** animal fats; drink less caffeine and alcohol. **Avoid** nicotine.

ABOVE *Oysters have become a byword for seduction, and there is a reason why; oysters are one of the most pleasurable ways of eating zinc, the mineral that supports the reproductive system.*

THE BENEFITS OF MASSAGE

Exercise, especially of the abdominal muscles, improves digestion and massaging the stomach can bring instant relief. Start in the bottom right-hand corner, work your way up to the ribs, across to the left and down to the bottom left-hand corner.

RIGHT *A glass of soothing peppermint tea can soothe digestive upsets or refresh a jaded appetite.*

MINT TEA

Mint tea is the traditional herbal remedy for indigestion and it really does work. Use a teabag or two teaspoons of fresh chopped leaves to a cup of boiling water after every meal.

INDIGESTION

SYMPTOMS

❖ *Heartburn and severe discomfort around the breastbone.*

MILLIONS OF people spend tens of millions of pounds each year on remedies for indigestion, but this is the ultimate example of prevention being cheaper, more effective, and much safer than the cure. Indigestion is usually caused by the acid contents of the stomach getting back into the esophagus (the tube connecting the mouth and the stomach), which is resistant only to alkali. Excessive amounts of wind also cause indigestion and pain by distending the stomach, putting pressure on the diaphragm. Obesity, pregnancy, and overindulgence are often to blame.

Chronic indigestion is unpleasant and socially embarrassing. But the solution is simple: identify and eliminate the behavior patterns that cause the problem. Rushed meals, insufficient chewing, swallowing air, long gaps without food, smoking, alcohol, excessive coffee, fizzy drinks, pickles, vinegar, even simple things like cucumbers and peppers, can all play their part. Stress can be a major factor too, so take time to unwind before you eat. Indigestion may also be a symptom of other digestive problems.

Constant self-medication with antacids is unhealthy, as those containing calcium can lead to kidney stones, while the aluminum-based ones may be linked to

Alzheimer's disease and can reduce vitamin D absorption so severely that it may lead to bone disease. Sodium bicarbonate, a popular form of self-medication, can have a severe effect on folate (folic acid). Deficiencies of this part of the B complex are known to cause birth defects in children, so any woman planning to become pregnant should avoid sodium bicarbonate antacids for at least three months beforehand.

Even the more modern antacids are not without problems, as some of them interfere with vitamin B_{12}. Anyone taking them for more than a week or so should make sure that they also take a B_{12} supplement. Regular sufferers of indigestion need to consult their doctor to exclude underlying disease.

Unexplained chronic indigestion often responds extremely well to a month or so on the Hay Diet *(food combining, see p. 64).*

▶ **Eat more** fiber-rich foods, like oats, brown rice, whole wheat bread, baked potatoes with their skins on, fruit, and vegetables.

▶ **Drink less** alcohol, coffee, and fizzy drinks; eat fewer refined, processed carbohydrate foods. **Avoid** acidic pickles, raw onions, bran, raw sweet green peppers, very hot chilis, and unripe bananas.

INFECTION

SYMPTOMS

❖ *Depends on the individual complaint.*

BACTERIA, viruses, and parasites lie in wait at every turn, hoping to come across a human being whose natural immunity is low enough for them to take up residence. In order to fight infection you must feed your immune system and protect it against the anti-nutrients. High intakes of fats, sugars, alcohol, and caffeine; exposure to heavy metals like cadmium, lead, and mercury; smoking and general atmospheric pollution can all compromise natural immunity.

Due to modern intensive methods of farming and horticulture, much food may be nutrient-deficient and contaminated with residues. Even a sensible diet may not supply the optimal nutrient needs of the immune system, so it is important to eat regular amounts of high-nutrient foods. An adequate consumption of good protein is essential, while a selection of vitamin A and beta-carotene-rich foods should be eaten every day. Carrots, spinach, sweet potatoes, melon, and a small portion of liver each week is sufficient.

Deficiencies of the vitamin B complex are known to interfere with natural immune responses, so white and oily fish, poultry, spinach, peas, kidney beans, garbanzo beans, brown rice, and bananas should all be on the daily menu. Citrus fruit and all fresh produce are needed for their vitamin C. Another reason for including large amounts of oily fish in the diet is their high content of vitamin D and the important vitamin E.

One of the commonest and least recognized nutrient deficiencies that affects the immune system is zinc, while the essential fatty acids present in fish oils and cold-pressed safflower and linseed oils are another vital component in the integrity of the body's defences.

If disaster strikes and you do succumb to infection, you will probably be prescribed antibiotics. Though these amazing drugs can be life-saving, they cannot tell the difference between good bugs and bad bugs, so they kill them all, including the beneficial probiotic bacteria that are responsible for some digestive processes, the synthesis of B vitamins, and, it is now believed, the health of your immune system. These beneficial bacteria also keep up a constant fight against the fungus-causing organism, *Candida albicans (see p. 207),* and when they are destroyed, Candida gets the upper hand and you end up with thrush.

So it is essential that whenever you take antibiotics, you also consume a daily tub of natural live (not pasteurized) yogurt, as the bacteria it contains are these very probiotics. The "sterilized" gut resulting from antibiotic treatment not only causes diarrhea, flatulence, and often nausea, but also results in lowered levels of B vitamins in the system, which is why a B-complex supplement should always be taken as well as the live yogurt. The onset of irritable bowel syndrome *(see p. 194)* frequently dates from a prescribed course of antibiotic treatment.

It is not just viruses and bacteria that can invade the human body; parasites too are an ever-present hazard. The ones most likely to cause you problems are parasitic worms. The three major roundworm infestations are caused by eating infective eggs, which find their way onto vegetable and salad crops through the use of human feces as fertilizer. Roundworm *(Ascaris lumbricoides),* whipworm *(Trichuris trichiura),* and threadworm *(Enterobius vermicularis)* are thought to affect around 1,000 million people in the world and up to one-third of all inhabitants of tropical Africa. Heavy infections can cause serious illness and nutritional imbalance, including vitamin A deficiency and night blindness, vitamin C deficiency, and the protein-deficiency disease kwashiorkor.

- **TAPEWORMS** *(Cestoda)* are flat and range in size from a few millimeters to several meters or yards. There are four common varieties that affect humans.
- **THE BEEF TAPEWORM** *(Taenia saginata)* can grow to 11 yards/10 meters in length and is widespread throughout the Middle East, Africa, and South America. To avoid it, all beef should be thoroughly cooked, and rare steak and burgers present a considerable risk.
- **THE PORK TAPEWORM** *(Taenia solium)* is rather more serious, as its eggs can be regurgitated back into the stomach and the larvae are able to migrate to the brain or eye, causing epilepsy and blindness. This parasite is most common in eastern Europe, Southeast Asia, and Africa, where eating undercooked pork or pork products like sausages should be avoided.
- **THE DWARF TAPEWORM** *(Hymenolepis nana)* is no more than 1½inches/4cm long and commonly occurs in Latin America, India, the Mediterranean, Egypt, and Sudan. It gets into the human host from food contaminated with infected mouse droppings and, like the beef tapeworm, confines itself to the intestine, where it seldom causes symptoms.
- **THE FISH TAPEWORM** *(Diphyllobothrium latum)* may also grow up to 11 yards/10 meters long. It is acquired by eating pickled, undercooked, or raw fish and is common in China, Japan (beware the sushi), Southeast Asia, Scandinavia, the Baltics, and the lake regions of Switzerland. Expert Japanese chefs are past masters at detecting infected fish, so there should be little risk in quality Japanese hotels and restaurants, but it may be wise to avoid street vendors. Fish tapeworm seldom cause symptoms but there is usually a vitamin B12 deficiency.

ABOVE *Plain live yogurt restores friendly bacteria to the digestive system.*

SPINACH SNACK

fights infection

SERVES 2

3 CLOVES GARLIC

5 TBSP OLIVE OIL

SMALL HANDFUL OF PINE NUTS

1LB READY-WASHED BABY SPINACH LEAVES

2 SLICES GOOD WHOLE WHEAT BREAD

JUICE OF 1 LEMON

Slice the garlic and sweat very gently in the oil for 10 minutes. Add the pine nuts and cook for another 5 minutes. Wilt the spinach in boiling water, drain and arrange on the slices of bread. Pour the oil mixture over. Drizzle with lemon juice and serve at once.

I

INFECTION CONTINUED

• **THE ROUNDWORM** *(Anisakis simplex)* is a surprising source of infestation which commonly occurs in herrings. Where herrings are eaten virtually raw – as they are in Holland and in Scandinavia – there is considerable risk of acquiring this parasite. Fortunately the Anisakis worms cannot survive freezing, and storage at -4°F/-20°C for three days will render them harmless.

All worm infections need appropriate medical treatment and, though tourists will not be at risk if they take sensible precautions, any vague symptoms appearing after foreign travel should be checked by a doctor. There are many traditional and herbal remedies for parasites, but one that uses fresh pumpkin seeds *(see p. 83)* is safe and effective.

▶ **Eat more** oily fish for its omega-3 fatty acids; poultry and lean meat for their protein; spinach, sweet potatoes, and carrots for their beta-carotene; garbanzo beans and whole grain cereals for their B vitamins and folic acid; olive oil, safflower oil, nuts, seeds, and avocados for their vitamin E; citrus fruit, cherries, and berries for their vitamin C and bioflavonoids; low-fat dairy products for their calcium and vitamin D.

▶ **Eat less** sugar; fewer animal fats, highly processed carbohydrates, processed, prepackaged and ready-made foods; consume less caffeine and alcohol.

NATURAL RESISTANCE

Have you ever stopped to wonder why, when there is an epidemic of flu, there are always those who don't succumb? The answer is that some individuals have a natural resistance to infection, raised to peak levels by an efficient, well-nourished immune system – and that's all down to diet.

LEFT *The body's defense system relies on vitamin C to fight its battles with infection of all kinds. Delicious fruits such as oranges, grapes, kiwis, guavas, mangoes, papayas and pineapple are all rich sources.*

RIGHT *Natural herbal antiseptics such as thyme, sage, oregano, and especially garlic all help to keep the blood clear of infection. They are best eaten fresh or raw, but incorporate them in your cooking as a preventative as well as a cure.*

FERTILITY ENHANCERS

Down the ages folk medicine has enshrined many foods as fertility enhancers: sesame seeds, oysters (Casanova ate 70 a day), and milk, all of which we now know to be rich sources of zinc; honey, as recommended in the *Kama Sutra*; and even sarsaparilla and licorice, as prescribed in North American folklore.

INFLAMMATORY BOWEL DISEASE
see Colitis; Crohn's disease; Diverticulitis; Irritable bowel syndrome

INFERTILITY

SYMPTOMS

❖ *Inability of a couple to conceive due to male or female problems, or both.*

THERE ARE MANY reasons that prevent couples from conceiving, but the commonest cause is sub-optimal nutrition, resulting from bad eating habits or ill-advised weight-loss diets – around 50 percent of women with fertility problems are found to have been following slimming regimes. Large quantities of food are not necessary, but adequate essential nutrients are.

Women who are much too thin – dieters, obsessive exercisers, gymnasts, ballet dancers, élite athletes – stop ovulating and menstruating, which is a common cause of infertility. Female fertility requires high intakes of zinc, magnesium, iron, essential fatty acids, and vitamins A, C, and E, all supplied by the foods in the above list.

Long-term use of the contraceptive pill may lower fertility and prevent conception for some months. Eat the foods recommended below, with the specific addition of foods rich in manganese (oats, wheatgerm, chestnuts, rye bread, and peas) and vitamin B6 (bananas and oily fish).

Essential for male fertility are vitamins A, B, C, and E, zinc and selenium. Large quantities of vitamin C are also necessary for healthy testicles, and the common problem of the clumping (sticking together) of sperm may be overcome by taking 1g of vitamin C daily. Male patients taking part in research at Texas University Medical School were given 500mg of vitamin C daily for a month. As a result their percentage of sperm clumping fell from an average of 37 percent to about 11 percent.

▶ **Eat more** pumpkin and sesame seeds for vitamin E and zinc; avocado and extra virgin olive oil for their vitamin E; citrus fruit for their vitamin C; carrots, dark-green vegetables, and beet tops for their beta-carotene; organic free-range meat, organ meats, and poultry for their iron and protein; brown rice, wheatgerm, legumes, bananas, oily fish, oats, and fresh nuts for their B vitamins; soybeans, almonds, and shellfish for their magnesium.

▶ **Drink less** alcohol, tea, and coffee; eat fewer intensively reared animal foods (which may contain growth hormones); fewer large amounts of refined carbohydrates, processed foods (which are likely to be deficient in selenium), and food containing unnecessary additives.

INFLUENZA

SYMPTOMS

❖ *Headache, loss of appetite, muscle pains, general malaise.*

❖ *Fever up to 102°F/39°C, with chills and shivering, rapid pulse, dry cough.*

AN EFFECTIVE immune system enables the body to fight off invading viruses and bacteria and good nutrition is the key. As an extra insurance policy, take a simple multivitamin, together with 1g of vitamin C and a zinc and selenium supplement each day during the winter months. If you do catch an influenza virus, follow the quick nutrition plan to get you back on your feet in record time.

▶ **Eat more** citrus fruit for their vitamin C; seeds and nuts for their vitamin E and minerals, particularly pumpkin seeds for zinc and Brazil nuts for selenium; salads, vegetables, and all other fruit; whole grain cereals for their protein – all for protection and to provide a good balance of nutrients for the immune system. Drink more juices, water, and herbal teas; eat more cinnamon, ginger, grapes, melon, mango, and pineapple – all for treatment of influenza, to improve elimination, reduce fever, and ease the symptoms.

▶ **Eat fewer** refined, denatured processed foods, sugars, and fats, for prevention of influenza; eat fewer starches and dairy products for the first 48 hours, for treatment.

QUICK NUTRITION PLAN

DAY ONE

On rising: A glass of water.

Breakfast: Juice of half a grapefruit in half a glass of hot water, topped up with apple juice, a dessertspoon of honey and a sprinkle of cinnamon; a bunch of grapes and an apple.

Mid-morning: A glass of hot water and honey, with a sprinkle of cinnamon; a few grapes.

Lunch: A large glass of water; a large bowl of dried fruit that you soaked overnight. Squeeze a little lemon juice into it and add a teaspoon of sesame seeds and a dessertspoon of pumpkin seeds.

Mid-afternoon: Hot blackcurrant and pineapple juice with a little honey

and half a teaspoon of dried ginger.

Evening: A mixed salad of raw vegetables with a dressing of extra-virgin olive oil, lemon juice, two crushed cloves of fresh garlic, chopped onions and parsley; fresh fruit and a large glass of water.

Bedtime: A large glass of hot water, with a teaspoonful of honey, ginger, and a slice of lemon.

DAY TWO:
same as Day One until evening

Evening: A mixed salad with the dressing as above, plus a medium baked potato with low-fat live yogurt, chives, and garlic.

Bedtime: Hot water as before.

DAY THREE

On rising: A large glass of water.

Breakfast: Soak a bowl of oatflakes in pineapple juice overnight. In the morning, stir in a teaspoonful of fresh lemon juice, a tub of low-fat live yogurt and a banana; a cup of camomile tea.

Mid-morning: Vegetable juice.

Then back to the "flu-fighter" better eating plan, as described in the list of recommended foods. Don't go back to work too soon – flu is serious and can leave you weak, depressed, and vulnerable to other infections. Carry on with the vitamins listed above, but add an extra dose of a B-complex.

INSOMNIA

SYMPTOMS

❖ *Inability to get to sleep; waking regularly during the night.*

❖ *Waking early and not getting to sleep again.*

IN GENERAL, anxious people sleep less well than happy people, who have better appetites and a better ability to absorb food than those suffering from anxiety. As always, there are exceptions that prove the rule, and occasionally the response to anxiety, stress, and unhappiness is "comfort eating" and subsequent weight gain, although this is far less common.

Bad eating habits can also interfere with sleep. If you are already suffering from insomnia, don't go on a weight-loss diet. If you are underweight, putting on a few pounds will help improve your sleep. Serious obesity, on the other hand, can also interfere with your sleep, as it adversely affects breathing, increases the likelihood of disruptive snoring, and may lead to sleep apnea – serious interruption of breathing during sleep, which puts extreme pressure on the heart and creates chronic fatigue, believed to be the cause of many early-

morning traffic accidents. Never go to bed hungry; and never go to bed on an over-full stomach. Too little food and you'll have a restless night; too much and you'll suffer indigestion and heartburn.

As starchy foods encourage the release of a natural chemical called tryptophan, which is also present in milk, a bedtime sandwich often helps. The best filling is a mixture of basil and lettuce, both of which are soporifics but do not overload the digestive system.

Coffee, tea, chocolate, and cola drinks all contain caffeine, which keeps you awake. High-protein foods such as meat, fish, and cheese suppress the body's production of tryptophan and should not be eaten last thing at night, unless you need to stay awake.

▶ **Eat more** whole wheat bread, oats, and bananas, and drink more milk for their starch content; sesame seeds, honey, basil, rosemary, sage, fennel, camomile tea, and lime-blossom tea are all traditional aids to sleep.

▶ **Drink less** coffee, tea, chocolate, alcohol, and fewer cola and carbonated drinks; eat fewer late-night greasy or very spicy take-outs, and late-night protein meals.

FOODS TO AVOID

Insomniacs should avoid late-night cups of coffee or cheese sandwiches.

CHEESE

COFFEE

HONEY AND HERBS

Honey has long been a favorite folk remedy for insomnia. Take it mixed with a little warm milk, in a cup of camomile tea, or in hot water with lemon. Many of the herbal teas can help you in your search for better sleep – balm, fennel, lime, and valerian being among the best.

IRRITABLE BOWEL SYNDROME (IBS)

SYMPTOMS

❖ *Severe abdominal pain, bloating of the abdomen, diarrhea, or alternating diarrhea and constipation.*

IRRITABLE BOWEL SYNDROME (IBS) is a prime example of what is known as iatrogenic disease – an illness caused by the treatment given for another illness. It affects twice as many women as men and seems to be on the increase.

In many cases the illness dates from a severe bout of food poisoning, or from repeated or very lengthy courses of antibiotics. Quite a large proportion of patients are believed to have some food intolerances – according to Elizabeth Workman, Dr. Virginia Alun Jones, and Dr. John Hunter at England's Addenbrookes Hospital, Cambridge, who were among the earliest orthodox physicians to use an exclusion diet *(see p. 65)* with considerable success. Milk products (due to their lactose content), wheat and other cereals (because of gluten), and meat are some of the commonest foods to cause problems.

However, as the craze for using large amounts of bran as a treatment for constipation has grown, the number of people suffering from IBS has risen dramatically. Bran also features as a component of some totally unscientific but popular slimming diets, which should be avoided like the plague.

Having first ruled out any underlying illness by proper investigation, the sufferer should strongly resist any suggestion that they are in need of tranquilizers, antidepressants, psychiatric help, or surgery.

The most successful solution is through diet. You should obtain a reasonable fiber content from ordinary foods, not from bran or bran tablets. A large proportion of your fiber should be of the soluble form, occurring mainly as pectin in apples, pears, dates, and other fruit and vegetables; glucans, in oats, barley, and rye; and inulin, in globe and Jerusalem artichokes, and, to a lesser extent, other root vegetables. Peas, bean, and leafy vegetables contain insoluble fibers and should be eaten in balance with the soluble sources.

Meals should be taken regularly, and eating little and often can be a great help in relieving the discomfort of IBS. Keeping the stool soft by drinking at least 3½pt/1.7*l* of water a day, and including a tub of live natural yogurt to maintain the gut flora, is essential.

◗ **Eat more** oats, apples, pears, dates, Jerusalem artichokes, and globe artichokes for their soluble fiber; live natural yogurt for its beneficial bacteria. Drink at least 3½pt/1.70 of water a day.

◗ **Avoid all** high-fiber cereals and commercial breakfast cereals with added bran, and never add wheatbran to your food. Avoid sorbitol – a widely used sugar substitute – which is a common cause of diarrhea.

MINTY REMEDIES

Spasmodic contractions of the colon are abated by drinking mint tea, a traditional herbal remedy, after each meal. Scientists have also obtained beneficial results using capsules of peppermint oil.

JAUNDICE

SYMPTOMS

❖ *Yellow coloring of the skin and whites of eyes.*

❖ *Dark urine, very pale stool, itching, symptoms of whatever is the underlying cause.*

THE LIVER IS probably the most important single organ in the body and anything that affects it can have dramatic repercussions on health. Overindulgence, too much saturated fat, the occasional alcoholic binge or gastronomic feast can all upset its complex functions.

Jaundice occurs when too much bile pigment ends up in the blood. When jaundice is caused by obstruction of the bile duct, usually by gallstones, the stool is very pale and the urine very dark. Jaundice without pale stool has another cause: hepatitis, parasites, alcoholism, toxic substances, medication (commonly a paracetamol overdose), and tumors can all affect the liver and produce symptoms of jaundice.

Pernicious anemia also causes jaundice, as so many red blood cells are destroyed that the liver cannot cope

with them and their pigment remains in circulation. And a rare cause of jaundice is the fava bean, another name for which is the broad bean, and this type of jaundice is known as favism. It occurs due to a genetic deficiency of the enzyme needed to break down the chemicals in the bean.

But the dietary requirements remain the same. Avoid all fat, alcohol, sugar and refined carbohydrates. Eat large amounts of whole grain cereals as their fiber improves fat elimination and bowel function. Raw fresh fruit and vegetables together with vegetable juices (particularly cabbage, celery, and celeriac) all help to stimulate liver function.

◗ **Eat more** dark-green leafy vegetables for their iron and folic acid, especially watercress; whole grain cereals, including oats, for their fiber; globe artichokes and dandelion leaves for liver cell protection and bile stimulation; as far as possible, organic produce.

◗ **Eat fewer** animal fats, dairy products, refined sugars and carbohydrates; consume less caffeine. **Avoid** alcohol.

PLANT PROTECTION

The globe artichoke and dandelion leaves have long histories as folk recipes for liver and gallbladder disease. They not only help protect and regenerate the liver, but produce both an increase in bile production and a contraction of the gallbladder, which improves bile flow.

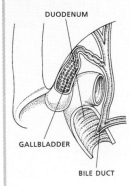

DUODENUM

GALLBLADDER

BILE DUCT

JOINT PAINS

SYMPTOMS

❖ *Pain, with or without swelling, stiffness and inflammation in any joint or joints.*

ANY OF THE body's many joints can become painful as a result of disease, injury, overuse, or underuse. The pain can be caused by a muscle, ligament, tendon, bone, or cartilage, any of which can be damaged or inflamed *(for specific details see entries on Mobility on p. 18; Arthritis on p. 151).*

Whatever the cause, local and systemic treatments are usually necessary, and massage, physiotherapy, acupuncture, osteopathy, hot and cold packs, and anti-inflammatory drugs all have value. But whatever treatment you are receiving, eating plenty of the right foods, and avoiding the wrong foods, will speed recovery.

The omega-3 fatty acids in fish oils stimulate the production of prostaglandins – antiinflammatory hor-mones – and insufficient of the antioxidants selenium and of vitamins A, C, and E increases the risk of joint problems. So eat regularly from the recommended food list for an abundance of joint-protective nutrients. Phytochemicals in cabbage and its relatives are benefi-cial to joints, and you can even use a cabbage-leaf poultice to relieve pain, inflammation, and swelling *(see Boils p. 154 and p. 86).*

▶ **Eat more** salmon, mackerel, herring, trout, sardines, mussels, and other shellfish for their omega-3 fatty acids; liver, carrots, broccoli, apricots, sweet potatoes, and cantaloup melon for their beta-carotene; red and yellow sweet peppers, kiwi fruit, oranges, brussels sprouts, and cabbage for their vitamin C; avocados, fresh nuts, asparagus, sunflower seeds, and olive oil for their vitamin E; white meat, whole grains and cereals, eggs, and brewer's yeast for their selenium.

▶ **Eat less** red meat, game, salt, and sodium-based food additives; drink less alcohol, especially red wine, and caffeine.

ROAST PEPPERS

combat joint pains

A MIXTURE OF RED, YELLOW AND GREEN SWEET PEPPERS (ONE PEPPER PER PERSON)

FRESH THYME

CHILI OIL

Put the whole peppers in the oven at 350°F for 20–30 minutes, until starting to brown. Remove, cover with a dish towel and leave to cool slightly – the skins will then lift off easily. Quarter the peppers, remove the seeds and membranes, then cut the quarters in half. Arrange on plates, sprinkle with chopped thyme, and drizzle with oil. Serve warm.

KIDNEY PROBLEMS

SYMPTOMS

❖ *Increased or reduced volumes of urine, which may be dark, cloudy, and strong-smelling.*

❖ *Kidney failure, severe edema, severe pain in the kidney region, blood in the urine, fever, nausea, headache – all dependent on the underlying cause.*

SOME SERIOUS illnesses like hypertension *(see p. 189),* Lupus erythematosus *(see p. 151),* and TB *(see p. 209)* can have a serious effect on the kidneys. Urinary infec-tion can spread to the kidneys and kidney stones can damage their structure. Sudden kidney failure may be caused by a stone that blocks the flow of urine or by tumors, spinal injury, violent trauma, or sudden severe hemorrhage.

In addition, as we get older, the kidneys tend to become less efficient at getting rid of waste products. Worryingly, this is associated with many drugs and elderly people are more likely to be taking long-term medication. Any appearance of the symptoms listed above should be treated as urgent and medical advice should be sought straight away.

Diet is very important, and in severe kidney disease this needs to be calculated exactly for each individual and often results in a regime of strictly weighed and measured portions. In general, people with kidney problems must reduce their salt intake, restrict their protein consumption, avoid foods containing oxalic acid, and be sparing with foods rich in potassium and phosphorus. The recommended foods cover the basic guidelines for those with kidney problems.

Dandelion leaves, parsley, radish, and finely chopped baby leeks should be eaten daily, and tea made from chopped parsley and the cooking water left over from leeks should be drunk on a regular basis.

Avoid excessive sweating, so keep out of the hot sun, avoid saunas, and don't perform stren-uous tasks in hot weather.

▶ **Eat more** parsley, celery, and dandelion leaves for their diuretic effect; whole wheat bread, boiled vegetables, and rice-based cereals for their fiber; drink magnesium-containing mineral waters, barley water, and diluted cranberry juice for their healing benefits; diluted cider vinegar, honey, and water.

KIDNEYS

The kidneys filter out waste products from the blood, which are passed through the ureters and collect in the bladder to be excreted.

KIDNEY

URETER

BLADDER

▶ **Eat less** animal protein, salt, and fewer salty, preserved and smoked foods; avocados, dried fruit, bananas, molasses, soy flour, wheat bran, raw salad vegetables, French fries, nuts, eggs, and dairy products, all of which are high in potassium. **Avoid** spinach, beets, rhubarb, and chocolate, which contain oxalic acid; coffee, tea, and cocoa, which are very rich in potassium.

LUPUS ERYTHEMATOSUS
see Arthritis

RIGHT *A gargle made with honey (a natural antiseptic) can soothe the inflammation of laryngitis. Mix one teaspoon of honey into a glass of hot water, stir, and leave to cool. You can gargle with this as often as you like.*

KIDNEY STONES

SYMPTOMS

❖ *Normally none, until a stone causes a blockage.*

❖ *Then very severe pain, nausea, vomiting, alternating fever and chill.*

KIDNEY STONES are common and they are frequently quite painful. They begin as tiny deposits in the middle of the kidney, where the urine collects, and slowly build into solid stones. They are made of body chemicals such as calcium phosphate, calcium oxalate, or, more rarely, uric acid – and are thought to be caused by an excess of calcium in the urine. A reduced intake of fluid or excessive sweating can lead to more concentrated urine, which makes it more likely that calcium salts will form stones. Kidney infections can also cause stones, and women are more prone to these infections than men.

There are three sizes of kidney stone: very small ones, which are symptomless and can pass unfelt from the kidney; medium-sized stones, and very large stones, which are often the result of an infection. These can fill the area of the kidney where the urine collects and may take on peculiar shapes as a result. Kidney stones may cause no symptoms at all to be felt until they have done so much damage to the kidney tissue that, in a few rare cases, the kidney will have to be removed. But if larger stones become stuck in the ureter, they can block the flow of urine and cause waves of excruciating pain.

Though there are some underlying diseases that cause kidney stones, the other causes are nearly always preventable by avoiding the low-fiber, high-fat, animal-protein, salt-laden, and refined-carbohydrate diet of our times. And the risk of stones is increased still further by vitamin D-fortified foods. Interestingly, vegetarians have a much lower incidence of this complaint, due to their overall healthier eating habits and the omission of animal protein. Two other factors that increase your risk of stones are magnesium deficiency and the long-term use of antacids, so eat plenty of the magnesium-rich foods and avoid aluminum and calcium carbonate indigestion remedies.

The surest way to avoid kidney stones is to drink at least 3½pt/1.7l of fluid every day – Evian water or any other very low-mineral content water is ideal. And prevent fluid loss by making sure that you don't sweat excessively. Avoid constipation by including lots of foods that are rich in fiber.

❧ **Drink more** water, and cider vinegar with honey; eat more parsley, celery, and dandelion leaves, all of which are diuretics; radishes, leeks; cashews, almonds, Brazil nuts, peas, and brown rice for their magnesium; complex carbohydrates and green vegetables for their fiber.

❧ **Eat fewer** dairy foods, especially if fortified with vitamin D; eat less meat, fish, poultry, yeast extracts, nuts (other than those listed above), bran, avocados, bananas, lima and soybeans; sugars and white flour; drink less tea. **Avoid** spinach, beets, rhubarb, and chocolate, which contain oxalic acid.

LARYNGITIS

SYMPTOMS

❖ *Pain when speaking, hoarseness.*

❖ *Excessive production of thick mucus, and extreme discomfort when coughing.*

A CONDITION often confused with a sore throat is laryngitis, which is inflammation of the larynx. That's the part of your windpipe where your voice box is located. Infections, or overuse of the voice, are the most usual causes of laryngitis, and it may follow a cold or a bout of flu. Anyone who uses their voice a lot – actors, singers, teachers, clergymen, or even harassed mums with small children – may get bouts of laryngitis.

If you have been getting frequent bouts of hoarseness or voice loss, or the episode that you are currently suffering has been going on for two weeks without improvement, see your doctor straightaway. These symptoms may be early warning signs of a growth in your voice box – this is more likely to be the case if you smoke and and are over 40.

For self-help treatments and more general information, *see Sore Throat on p. 206.*

❧ **Drink more** water, citrus juices, pineapple juice; eat more citrus fruit, mangoes, pawpaws, avocados, pine kernels, sesame seeds, and natural yogurt.

❧ **Eat less** salt, sugar, pickled, salted and smoked foods, and dairy products; drink less strong coffee and cola drinks.

MENIERE'S SYNDROME

SYMPTOMS

❖ *Severe dizziness, hearing loss, noises in the ear.*

❖ *Sometimes accompanied by sweating, visual disturbance, loss of balance, vomiting.*

DURING 30 years of practicing complementary therapies I have seen many desperate sufferers of Ménière's syndrome in my consulting room. Osteopathic or chiropractic treatment, acupuncture, relaxation techniques, massage, and even self-hypnosis may all help. But nutritional changes must be the first step.

Anything that reduces the likelihood of mucus congestion, minimizes fluid retention, and maximizes blood flow may help. To this end, cut down on dairy products and, if it helps, replace calcium and vitamin D with a simple supplement. Drastically cut down on your salt intake and watch out for other sodium compounds on food labels: monosodium glutamate, sodium bicarbonate, and so on.

Coffee, tea, and alcohol can be a problem as they cause the tiniest blood vessels at the very end of the system to contract and thus restrict the blood supply to the inner ear. Small amounts of alcohol can actually improve the peripheral circulation, but any more has the opposite effect.

Vitamin C is important for the structure of blood vessels, while vitamin E helps to maintain their elasticity, so eat the relevant foods on a daily basis.

▶ **Eat more** citrus fruit, peppers, kiwi fruit, tomatoes, and most fruit and vegetables for their vitamin C; olive oil, sunflower-seed oil, avocados, whole grain cereals, fresh seeds and nuts for their vitamin E; oily fish such as sardines, herrings, mackerel, pilchards, and salmon for their omega-3 fatty acids and antiinflammatory action; ginger, garlic, leeks, onions, scallions, and chives for their anticongestive action and to improve the circulation; oats, whole grain cereals, apples, and pears for their soluble fiber.

▶ **Eat less** salt; fewer dairy and sodium products; drink less coffee, tea, and alcohol.

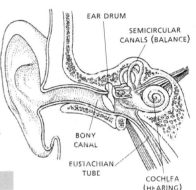

ABOVE *Ménière's syndrome affects both balance and hearing; the inner mechanisms of the ear govern both.*

GINKGO BILOBA

One ancient herbal remedy that I have used with considerable success is an extract of the leaves of the *Ginkgo biloba* tree. This dilates the tiniest capillaries and has long been used in Europe to improve blood flow to the brain. It has no side effects and can be of great benefit to sufferers of Ménière's syndrome.

MENSTRUAL PROBLEMS

SYMPTOMS

❖ *Dysmenorrhea: painful periods.*

❖ *Amenorrhea: missed periods.*

❖ *Menorrhagia: heavy periods.*

ABOVE *Raspberry-leaf tea has a beneficial effect on the uterus, and can help menstrual cramps.*

PAINFUL PERIODS (**DYSMENORRHEA**) affect 50 percent of menstruating women to some extent and are worse between the ages of 18 and 24, but usually stop after childbirth. Niacin may relieve the symptoms, but is more effective in conjunction with vitamin C and the bioflavonoid rutin. Extra iron also helps to reduce or even stop the symptoms. The omega-3 fatty acids in oily fish are a great help as they aid the body's manufacture of prostaglandins, and help to relax the womb muscles. Vitamins E and B₆, and magnesium may also help.

Lack of periods (**AMENORRHEA**) can be caused by underlying disease of the thyroid or by diabetes. Sudden weight loss or gain, obsessive and excessive exercise, or emotional upheavals may also interrupt the cycle. Even changing your type of contraceptive pill can interfere with the normal pattern. Amenorrhea is common in those suffering from anorexia nervosa *(see p. 170)* and in élite women athletes, who induce an artificial menopause, which can have disastrous effects on their bone structure *(see Osteoporosis on p. 201).*

For PMS see p. 203; Menopause see p. 40.

Heavy periods (**MENORRHAGIA**) can be common at the beginning and end of the childbearing years. In between, heavy periods may be caused by fibroids, hormonal imbalance, infection, endometriosis, or thyroid disease. They are a common cause of anemia and chronic iron deficiency. Eating more iron rich foods and taking supplements usually improves the problem. Increasing your consumption of vitamins A and C and bioflavonoids will also help.

▶ **Eat more** olive, safflower and sunflower oils, avocados, brown rice, salmon, and peas for their vitamin E; dried brewer's yeast, yeast extracts, wheatgerm, oatflakes, bananas, nuts, liver, chicken, oily fish, and dried fruit for their vitamin B₆ and niacin; oily fish for their omega-3 fatty acids; liver, shellfish, sardines, whole wheat bread, chicken, and peas for their zinc; soybeans, cashew nuts, almonds, Brazil nuts, peanuts, dried fruit, and shellfish for their magnesium and selenium; liver and kidney meat for their organic and more easily absorbed haem iron; parsley, dried fruit, whole wheat bread, and dark-green leafy vegetables for their inorganic iron; skimmed milk, low-fat cheese, canned sardines, pulses, root vegetables, oatmeal, whole wheat flour, and fish for their calcium.

▶ **Eat less** salt, sugar, other refined carbohydrates, large amounts of dairy products, uncooked bran, animal fats, and margarines containing trans fats and hydrogenated fats; cut down on excessive caffeine and alcohol.

HEALTH WARNING

Any continuing period abnormality, irregularity, more frequent or heavy blood loss, unusual levels of pain or discomfort must be investigated by your doctor. Nutritional medicine may often be the best remedy, but examination and diagnosis are the first requirement.

ME *see* Chronic fatigue syndrome

MEASLES *see* Childhood diseases

MONONUCLEOSIS

SYMPTOMS

❖ *Tiredness, muscle pain, headache, fever, swollen glands and sore throat; usually occurs in children and young adults.*

MIGRAINE *see* Headaches and migraines

MONONUCLEOSIS, or glandular fever, is an acute viral infection common in children and young adults. It spreads rapidly through schools and colleges, hence its popular name, the "kissing disease." It causes debilitating fatigue and mental exhaustion, but is seldom serious. The Epstein-Barr virus or the cytomegalo virus, both members of the herpes family, is usually responsible. Although complete recovery from mononucleosis is normal, the period of illness varies from weeks to many months, with repeated attacks of high fever, night sweats, and weakness.

Fasting raises the white cell count, so start with a 24-hour fast of fresh fruit and vegetable juices, herbal tea made from peppermint and elderflowers (half a tea-spoon of each in a cup of boiling water) – and lots of water to drink. Spend the next 24 hours on fresh fruit, salads, steamed vegetables, water, juices, and herbal tea; then eat one-third raw food, one-third carbohydrates, one-sixth fish, poultry, eggs, and dairy produce, and one-sixth nuts, seeds, and beans.

Drink at least 3½pt/1.7l of liquid daily, and take 1.5g vitamin C and a high-potency vitamin B-complex tablet each day.

❭ **Eat more** citrus fruit, especially lemons, and cherries for their vitamin C and bioflavonoids; yeast extracts and whole grain cereals for their B vitamins; dried fruit for high energy and easy digestion; nuts and seeds for their vitamin E and minerals.

❭ **Take fewer** artificial stimulants, such as caffeine and alcohol; eat fewer empty calories found in refined-sugar foods; low-nutrient convenience meals and take-outs; and less red meat.

MOTION SICKNESS AND NAUSEA

SYMPTOMS

❖ *Nausea, vomiting.*

❖ *Pallor, vertigo, fainting.*

TRAVEL SICKNESS can be caused by any form of motion, in cars, buses. planes, boats, swings, round-abouts, or roller-coasters. When frequent changes of direction upset messages from the balance system in the ear to the brain, it receives messages that don't match what the eyes are seeing. Some people just cannot cope with the situation, and the result is travel sickness, which can cause nausea, vomiting, dizziness, or even fainting.

Your children are much more likely to be affected than you are and most of them – though not all – will grow out of the problem in time. There are lots of adults who suffer as passengers, however, even though they can drive themselves with no symptoms at all.

Setting off at five in the morning on a cup of sweet tea, and stuffing yourself and the kids with candies, chips, chocolate, cans of cola, cookies, and sticky buns, is a recipe for the most certain disaster. Instead, start with a good starchy breakfast – cereals, toast, fruit juice – but avoid the great British fry-up. Take some food with you, such as nuts, raisins, mixed dried fruit; sensi-ble sandwiches of honey, peanut butter, or cheese, and apples, grapes, or bananas, all of which are easy to eat.

A little psychology goes a long way when dealing with car-sick children. Lots of reassurance, keeping them busy with tapes, puzzles, games, and quizzes, and not talking about the problem too much will all help. Give them weak camomile tea and honey to drink. Eating small cubes of crystallized ginger half-hourly is a great cure for motion sickness.

In adults, nausea and vomiting can be caused by irritation of the stomach wall as a result of excessive alcohol or rich food, or by infectious diseases that cause fever. Any of the common childhood diseases can be implicated. Antibiotics are an extremely common cause of nausea, sometimes vomiting and often diar-rhea, although these problems can be mitigated by eating a tub of live, low-fat natural yogurt every day. However, by far the most common cause of nausea is food poisoning *(see pp. 176–7)*, when it is usually accompanied by diarrhea.

Maintaining fluid intake is always the prime essen-tial. Babies and young children dehydrate extremely quickly and need constant fluids *(see Childhood diseases on pp. 159–60)*. As vomiting is reduced, start to follow the BRAT diet *(see p. 177)*. Get back to normal eating over the next two or three days.

❭ **Drink more** fluids, peppermint, ginger, camomile, and melissa tea, and clear vegetable broth; eat more bananas, rice, apples, and dry toast.

❭ **Eat less** of everything – especially dairy products, fatty foods, salt, and all salty foods. **Avoid** alcohol, meat and meat products, and caffeine.

MOUTH ULCERS

SYMPTOMS

❖ *Extremely painful, circular red ulcers with white centers, occurring anywhere inside the mouth.*

PROPERLY called apthous ulcers, mouth ulcers are normally shallow, round white spots, usually with a bright-red inflamed border. They occur anywhere inside the mouth – inside the lips, on the gums, the tongue, or the roof of the mouth – growing as open sores where there is a small injury to the mucous membrane lining the mouth cavity. There may be odd single spots or whole clusters, and their color gradually changes as they grow, often ending up as quite large yellow craters.

Mouth ulcers are extremely painful and appear to be much more common in women than in men. Stress is a factor, so they tend to coincide with the menstrual cycle, though they can be caused by physical injury from a damaged tooth or by an infection, possibly accompanied by a high temperature.

Nutritional deficiencies or food sensitivities are the likely cause, but diets deficient in folic acid, B₁₂, and iron may also be responsible. Eating the beneficial recommended foods will reduce the severity of episodes and their frequency. Zinc deficiency, which is a growing concern in these days of convenience food and intensive farming, is another common factor, so eat more shellfish, wheatgerm, seeds, and eggs.

Allergies or sensitivities may also cause mouth ulcers, the most likely culprits being gluten, dairy products, tomatoes, vinegar, lemon, pineapple, and mustard. It is also worth avoiding boiled candies, alcohol, salty foods, and pickles. For serious recurrent problems try an exclusion diet (see p. 65).

▶ **Eat more** wheatgerm, fresh nuts, liver, chicken, green leafy vegetables, legumes, parsley, and dates for their folic acid, iron, and vitamin B₁₂; shellfish, canned sardines, whole meal bread, eggs, and pumpkin seeds for their zinc.

▶ **Eat less** salt, vinegar, chips, processed nuts, and pickles; drink less alcohol.

MULTIPLE SCLEROSIS (MS)

SYMPTOMS

❖ *General weakness, gradual loss of muscle strength, pins and needles.*

❖ *Visual disturbances, vertigo, gastric problems, incontinence, sexual difficulties.*

WE STILL know little about the origins or causes of multiple sclerosis. It is a "demyelinating" disease, in which the myelin sheath that surrounds and protects the nerves is gradually destroyed. MS affects women rather more than men (60:40) and mostly begins in young adult life, affecting about one in every 10,000 people. There may be periods of remission, sometimes lasting for several years, although people suffering from MS may also be more susceptible to other illnesses.

A number of nutritional therapies have been promoted for the treatment of this debilitating illness, most of them extreme, nutritionally risky, and with little or no scientific basis. Food allergy is currently a popular theory and many MS sufferers have gone onto gluten-free, milk-free, and long-term "Stone Age" or low-allergen diets. There is little evidence, however, that these have been beneficial and it is more than likely that the nutritional deprivation of such regimes only adds to the health burdens already present. Raw food diets, macrobiotic regimes, and other extreme nutritional therapies are best avoided.

The only serious evidence in support of dietary change has shown decreased frequency, severity, and duration of relapses associated with diets that are high in essential fatty acids, polyunsaturated acids, and fish oils, and very low in saturated animal fats. The effect seems to be somewhat enhanced if this type of eating can be introduced early on in the development of the disease.

Avoid all hydrogenated fats and oils, like margarine and vegetable cooking fats. Make sure that you eat no more than ¼oz/10g of saturated fat a day. Get most of your protein from fish – eating this at least four times a week – and from vegetable sources, and try to avoid other animal proteins.

In addition, make a tablespoon of cod-liver oil, a tablespoon of flaxseed oil, and 3g of evening primrose oil part of your daily regime. Also take 200IU of vitamin E morning and evening.

▶ **Eat more** polyunsaturated oils – sunflower, safflower, grapeseed, nut, and fish oils – plus oily fish for their powerful antiinflammatory benefits; legumes and cereals for their vegetable protein; an abundance of fresh fruit, salads, and vegetables for the full spectrum of nutrients; plenty of whole grain cereals and complex carbohydrates for their energy, B vitamins, and fiber; Brazil nuts for their selenium.

▶ **Eat less** saturated animal fat, animal protein, and sugar; drink less alcohol.

MUMPS see Childhood diseases

NAUSEA see Motion sickness and nausea

PASTA WITH TUNA FISH

provides essential fish protein

SERVES 2

4½OZ WHOLE WHEAT PASTA
1 CAN TUNA OR SALMON
1 BUNCH SCALLIONS
2 TBSP CHOPPED PARSLEY
1 TBSP CHOPPED BASIL

Bring some lightly salted water to a boil and put the pasta in to cook. Meanwhile slice the scallions, put a little oil in a pan, and cook the scallions until soft and transparent. Add the drained, flaked tuna or salmon. When the pasta is slightly al dente, strain, and toss back in the pan. Add the scallions, tuna or salmon, and herbs, warm through, and serve at once.

OBESITY

OF ALL THE nutritional disorders that affect the total population, obesity is the most common in our affluent society. It is a major disease of Western civilization and, as well as being irrefutably and closely linked to premature death, it is an almost certain guarantee that you will suffer from a range of other health problems.

Apart from plain bad eating, one of the key factors is an individual's basic metabolic rate (BMR). This is the efficiency with which your resting body can burn up the fuel that you consume as food. The percentage of brown fat in the body – which is able to store huge amounts of energy without causing obesity – is also thought to be significant.

While there are some glandular disorders that cause weight gain, they are comparatively rare and usually treatable. Thyroid disorders are probably the most common cause. Steroid drugs, oral contraceptives, HRT (hormone replacement therapy), and the insulin used by diabetics may also cause weight gain. But the vast majority of overweight people are so because they consume more calories than they burn.

Of all the multitude of weight-reducing treatments, the only one that really works is permanently changing the way you eat. Slimming pills, injections, liposuction, low-calorie crash diets, and "miracle cures" are usually expensive, frequently hazardous to your health, and never work in the long term.

Check your own waist/hip ratio. Measure your waist around the belly button, then measure round the largest part of your hips. Then divide the waist measurement by the hip measurement. For women, the answer should be 0.75 or less, and for men 1.0 or less. As the figure goes up, so your risk of heart disease increases accordingly.

All the ideal height and weight charts are based on averages. I believe the margin of error is greater than is generally accepted, because weight is not the only measure of health and fitness. Spiritual and emotional health are difficult to measure, but they play an enormous part in your total well-being. I am certain that being ten percent overweight and happy is far better than striving to become ten percent underweight and being miserable. In fact, life expectancy statistics confirm this.

▶ **Eat more** good carbohydrates, like whole wheat bread, brown rice, potatoes, root vegetables, beans, and pasta for their high-energy, slow-release calories and their zero fat content; fresh fruit, vegetables, and salads, to provide vitamins, minerals, and fiber; fish, and poultry without skin for their protein.

▶ **Eat fewer** visible fats (if you can see it, don't eat it) – and drink less alcohol (only one unit a day). **Avoid** sugar, full-fat dairy products, all high-fat, high-sugar cookies, desserts, candies, and chocolates, and all processed meat products.

BODY MASS INDEX (BMI)

Body mass index is a universally standard way of calculating the relationship between height and weight. To work out your own BMI, divide your weight in kilograms by your height in meters squared. This calculation is known at Quetelet's Index:

$$BMI = \frac{\text{Weight in kilograms}}{(\text{Height in meters})^2}$$

The resulting number is an excellent guide to obesity – anything between 20 and 25 is within the ideal weight range; 25–30 is overweight; 30–40 is moderately obese; and over 40 is grossly obese. These figures are based on the American Metropolitan Life Insurance calculations.

BELOW *Safe weight-loss meals: porridge and whole wheat bread for breakfast; soup and salad for lunch; grilled lamb chops, peas, and carrots, followed by honey, lemon, and cinnamon yogurt.*

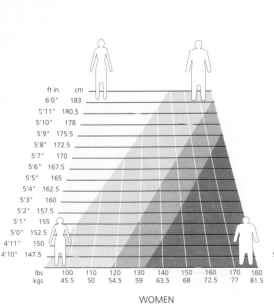

As an approximate guide, here is a chart of relative height and weight measurements. If you are 10–15 percent above the indicated weight, you might consider doing something about it; 20–30 percent above and you should definitely take some action.

DOES YOUR WEIGHT FIT YOUR HEIGHT?

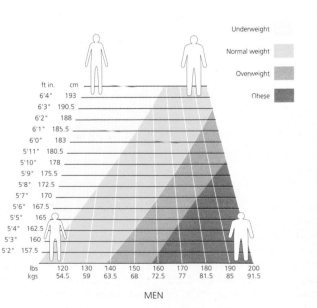

Underweight

Normal weight

Overweight

Obese

ft in.	cm
6'0"	183
5'11"	180.5
5'10"	178
5'9"	175.5
5'8"	172.5
5'7"	170
5'6"	167.5
5'5"	165
5'4"	162.5
5'3"	160
5'2"	157.5
5'1"	155
5'0"	152.5
4'11"	150
4'10"	147.5

lbs	100	110	120	130	140	150	160	170	180
kgs	45.5	50	54.5	59	63.5	68	72.5	77	81.5

WOMEN

ft in.	cm
6'4"	193
6'3"	190.5
6'2"	188
6'1"	185.5
6'0"	183
5'11"	180.5
5'10"	178
5'9"	175.5
5'8"	172.5
5'7"	170
5'6"	167.5
5'5"	165
5'4"	162.5
5'3"	160
5'2"	157.5

lbs	120	130	140	150	160	170	180	190	200
kgs	54.5	59	63.5	68	72.5	77	81.5	85	91.5

MEN

OSTEOPOROSIS

SYMPTOMS

❖ *Usually none until well advanced, then severe backache, height loss, fractures after minor injuries, spontaneous fractures, especially of the vertebrae.*

OSTEOPOROSIS is a condition in which the bones become less dense. It often goes undetected until the bones become so weak that even a minor injury can cause a fracture. Just a cough or sneeze can damage a vertebra, while levering yourself out of an armchair can fracture a wrist and the mildest of stumbles can break a hip. Though it's normal for bones to lose some of their mass from the age of 40 onward, in osteoporosis this bone loss is greatly exaggerated, and this most commonly occurs after the menopause. But there are other reasons for bone loss – thyroid problems, diabetes, poor absorption of nutrients, alcoholism, chemotherapy, long-term steroids, and long-term immobilization due to injury or other diseases.

The best protection against osteoporosis in later life is a diet that builds strong bones throughout the teens, twenties, thirties, and forties, with regular weight-bearing exercise – one hour's walk three times a week is enough – and a reasonably sensible lifestyle. But just looking at changes in lifestyle and diet in Britain and the US over the last few decades tells us why osteoporosis is becoming such a major problem in the Western world. Salt, sugar, and phosphorus are three key nutrition ingredients that increase the excretion of calcium. The average American gets through at least one can of phosphoric acid-filled drink each day, together with ⅔ cup/150g of sugar, masses of refined carbohydrates, and far too much animal protein.

The great British diet is no better, containing more than twice the recommended salt intake, 45–50 percent of calories from fat, huge amounts of sugar, too much meat, and far too little of all fruit and vegetables. Add the ill effects of alcohol and tobacco and you have a recipe for disaster throughout the Western world, which is made even worse by ever-decreasing amounts of physical activity.

A regular intake of vitamin D, sunshine, together with plenty of calcium from low-fat dairy products and supplements, is essential. Supplements containing calcium, boron, magnesium, and B vitamins also help with menopausal symptoms.

Constant dieting, over-exercising, being underweight, or anorexic are common triggers of early bone loss. And women who have had hysterectomies, ovaries removed, a late onset of menstruation, or a close family history of osteoporosis should take special care. Hormone replacement therapy (HRT) is being heavily recommended, but despite its benefits it is not without risk. Any woman deciding to use HRT should be in possession of all the facts, enabling her to make an informed and sensible decision in respect of her own personal circumstances.

▶ **Eat more** low-fat dairy products, nuts, and beans for their calcium; oily fish for their vitamin D – canned sardines and salmon for their calcium, too; citrus fruit and all the dark berries for their bioflavonoids; all other fruit and vegetables for their boron, vitamin K; soybeans, cashew nuts, and almonds for their magnesium.

▶ **Eat less** meat, salt, sugar, and saturated animal fats, and drink less alcohol, coffee, and tea, all of which increase calcium excretion **Avoid** smoking.

ABOVE *Osteoporosis is the result of calcium deficiency; if you have always enjoyed a calcium-rich diet, your chances of bone loss are minimized. Even so, keep up your intake whatever your age. Nuts and low-fat dairy products are excellent sources.*

MEN SUFFER TOO!

Although osteoporosis mainly affects women, men can suffer too and the information given here is just as applicable to them.

OSTEOARTHRITIS *see* Arthritis

PARASITIC INFECTION *see* Infection

PHLEBITIS (THROMBOPHLEBITIS)

SYMPTOMS

❖ *Hardening of portions of a superficial varicose vein.*

❖ *Tenderness to touch, pain, and inflammation at the affected site.*

SUPERFICIAL thrombophlebitis is a consequence of varicose veins. Inflammation and a tiny clot develop after local trauma or infection – possibly from insect bites. The risk of this problem is much greater if you smoke or take the contraceptive pill. If you do both, you are at serious risk. Ideally give up both, but certainly stop smoking – the next clot could be a much more dangerous and life-threatening deep-vein thrombosis. Avoid sitting on hard-edged chairs, don't cross

your legs, when sitting and get back to sensible exercise as soon as the inflammation subsides *(see also Varicose veins on p. 209)*

▶ **Eat more** porridge, apples, pears, beans, and cooked, green leafy vegetables for their soluble fiber; whole wheat bread and brown rice for their insoluble fiber; liver, shellfish, some red meat, canned sardines, and eggs for their zinc; carrots, apricots, and broccoli for their beta-carotene; citrus fruit, blackcurrants, and blueberries for their bioflavonoids and vitamin C; safflower and olive oil, and avocados for their vitamin E; garlic, ginger, cayenne, and pineapple for their ability to break down blood clots.

▶ **Eat fewer** refined, processed carbohydrates; less salt; cut down on excessive coffee and alcohol.

CLOT-BUSTING

Make sure that your diet contains clot-busting items – at the very least, eat two to three cloves of garlic and drink four glasses of pineapple juice every day until all the symptoms have gone. For long-term prevention, follow the nutritional advice.

PILES (HEMORRHOIDS)

SYMPTOMS

❖ *Bright red blood on toilet paper or stool; pain, severe itching, or mucus; small lumps in the anus; sensations of not emptying the rectum after bowel movement.*

PILES, OR HEMORRHOIDS, are varicose veins in the soft lining of the anus. They are either external, lying close to the opening, or internal, when they occur higher up the anal canal. They are frequently caused by constipation and straining. Pregnancy and childbirth commonly cause piles, which can be familial. They are more frequent when your work involves prolonged standing and you take little exercise.

Soluble fiber in oats is the great preventer of hemorrhoids, acting as "smoothage" rather than roughage, and encouraging the easy passage of stool. Soluble fiber from fruit and vegetables, and insoluble fiber from whole grains and brown rice, combined with a minimum of 3½pt/1.7l of fluid each day, relieve the discomfort of piles or prevent them.

Where constant blood loss is a feature, there is the risk of iron-deficiency anemia *(see p. 149)*.

▶ **Eat more** porridge, apples, pears, beans, and green leafy vegetables for soluble fiber; whole wheat bread, pasta, and brown rice for insoluble fiber; drink at least 3½pt/1.7l of water daily.

▶ **Eat fewer** refined, processed carbohydrates.

(see p. 149)

WATER TREATMENT

Contrast bathing, with alternate hot and cold water, is the traditional naturopathic treatment, and nothing relieves the desperate irritation and pain of an inflamed hemorrhoid as effectively as an ice cube.

BREAD REMEDY

A traditional Eastern European folk remedy for pleurisy sounds bizarre but is well documented heat some cubes of dry whole wheat bread in the oven until toasted, grind them into a powder, and mix with hot water, a tiny dash of salt, and a knob of butter, until you have a porridge-like consistency, which should be eaten while warm. Repeat daily until the condition has improved.

MUSTARD POULTICE

One of the best traditional remedies is a mustard poultice. Mix a tablespoon of dry English mustard powder with six tablespoons of white all-purpose flour. Add water slowly, stirring until you have a smooth paste. Spread some thinly onto a cotton dish towel, cover with a second dish towel, and wrap round the chest for a maximum of 15 minutes. Check that the skin is not too inflamed or blistered.

PLEURISY

SYMPTOMS

❖ *Sudden onset of severe pain in the chest, aggravated by coughing and even breathing.*

❖ *High temperature, breathlessness.*

PLEURISY is a lung disease caused by inflammation of the thin envelope of tissue that surrounds the lungs and inside of the chest – the pleura. It is usually a consequence of other chest infections or diseases, though it can be caused by the trauma of a broken rib. The pain can vary from vague discomfort to the most excruciating, knife-like pain, which is greatly aggravated by coughing, laughing, or moving. Pleurisy is a serious illness and requires medical attention and rest. Good

nutrition can help as well. The traditional remedies for all chest infections will help. Drink plenty of hot water with honey and lemon to soothe the discomfort and at least two glasses per day of pineapple juice – it contains the enzyme bromelain, which helps in the healing of scar tissue.

▶ **Eat more** sprouted beans and seeds for their high nutrient value; onions, leeks, and garlic for their specific antibacterial properties; fresh vegetable soups and juices for easy digestion and immune-boosting vitamins and minerals; puréed potatoes, root vegetables, and rice for their calories; unsweetened fresh fruit juices for their vitamin C.

▶ **Eat fewer** dairy products to reduce your mucus; sugars; less salt to prevent fluid retention.

PNEUMONIA

SYMPTOMS

❖ *High temperature, chills. Shortness of breath, chest pain, productive cough – there may be streaks of blood – exhaustion.*

PNEUMONIA may be caused by viruses, bacteria, or Legionnaire's disease and is frequently found in those suffering from AIDS. It is unlikely that viral or bacterial pneumonia can be caught by others but, when caused by the *Mycoplasma* bacterium, it is contagious. Pneumonia usually affects the elderly or people who have low natural immunity, particularly alcoholics, drug users, and people with an otherwise compromised immune system. When it occurs in otherwise healthy people, it is normally the result of other factors, such as smoking or inhalation of irritant or toxic fumes.

Medical treatment is essential but you can help yourself by taking care of what you eat and drink. Plenty of bed-rest, lots of liquids - vegetable soups and juices, herbal teas, and masses of water – and herbal remedies, like echinacea and licorice, boost the immune system.

▶ **Eat more** green leafy vegetables, carrots, sweet potatoes, yams, winter squashes, apricots, and broccoli for all the carotenes; citrus juices, tomatoes, tomato juice, grapes, kiwi fruit, and sweet peppers for vitamin C; shellfish and pumpkin seeds for zinc; bananas and fresh fish for vitamin B_6; thyme, sage, rosemary, and parsley for their antiseptic and diuretic benefits.

▶ **Eat less** sugar and animal fat, both of which seriously deplete the immune system; fewer dairy products to reduce mucus formation; less salt to avoid fluid retention.

PREMENSTRUAL SYNDROME (PMS)

SYMPTOMS

❖ *Bloating, mood swings, irrational behavior, food cravings, weight gain, loss of coordination, proneness to accidents.*

PMS IS ONE of the most common forms of extreme stress, producing physical, emotional, and behavioral changes in millions of women in the few days before the onset of a period. Up to 70 percent of women may suffer, and even those who have mild symptoms will be less efficient at everything they do for one week in every month. Complementary medicine has long held that nutrition is the key. A good diet with extra zinc and vitamin B_6 can work wonders.

In 1987 I undertook an enormous research project to test this theory, in which 670 women took part, keeping a daily record of their diet and symptoms for four months. The women were divided into four groups, some of whom were asked to change their diet, some to take a supplement, others a placebo, and the final group to take a real pill and to change their diets. These are the dietary changes that they made. They are not hard to follow, and if you suffer from PMS, you should give them a try:

- Cut down on your tea and coffee consumption. Try not to have more than two or three cups altogether each day. Instead you should drink herbal teas, unsweetened fruit juices, or savory drinks such as Vegemite. Avoid cola drinks.
- Increase your consumption of whole grain products – whole wheat bread, whole wheat pasta, and brown rice. Use oats, barley, nuts, seeds, lentils, and beans.
- Eat a salad each day, and plenty of vegetables.

- Eat more fish (especially sardines, mackerel, tuna, and salmon); more poultry and less red meat.
- Use less salt and avoid salty foods.
- Cut down on sugar, especially the "hidden" sugar in cakes, cookies, candies, and carbonated drinks.
- Keep alcohol consumption to a minimum.
- Watch out for "hidden" fats in meat products, and cut down on all dairy products.

You may have cravings for all the wrong things just before your period. Try to resist the temptation, for you will feel better if you can.

At the end of the four-month trial women who followed this diet and took a pill (MagnesiumOK, supplied by Wassen International) showed improvements ranging from 47 to 94 percent across the whole range of symptoms.

Bearing in mind that a good, well-balanced diet is a more natural source of nutrients, it would appear that a good compromise is to make as much improvement in eating patterns as you can, and to supplement this with a suitable vitamin and mineral pill.

▶ **Eat more** salmon, cod, herring, liver, bananas, and chili con carne for their vitamin B_6; whole wheat bread, whole wheat pasta, brown rice, oats, barley, nuts, seeds, lentils, beans, shellfish, and pumpkin seeds for their B vitamins and zinc; garbanzo beans, cashew nuts, kidney beans, mackerel, pilchards, whole grain cereals, and most vegetables for their magnesium.

▶ **Eat less** sugar, candies, chocolates, cookies, and cakes; drink less coffee and alcohol.

POST-VIRAL FATIGUE SYNDROME see Chronic fatigue syndrome

ABOVE *Cashew nuts are useful for PMS, but make sure that you do not buy the salted varieties, which can encourage water retention.*

THE TEN MOST COMMON SYMPTOMS OF PMS:

- feeling swollen and bloated
- loss of efficiency
- irritability
- weight gain
- difficulty in concentrating
- tiredness
- mood swings
- tension
- restlessness
- depression

PROSTATE PROBLEMS

SYMPTOMS

❖ *Most commonly enlargement of the prostate gland, causing frequency of urination, especially at night, a weak stream, difficulty in starting the flow, a constant dribble, and sometimes complete obstruction of urine.*

BENIGN PROSTATIC HYPERTROPHY (BPH) – enlargement of the prostate gland – affects around half of all men over the age of 50 and is the most common prostate problem; 1 in 12 men in the UK develops prostate cancer, which kills 8,500 British men a year.

Take care of your prostate by eating plenty of the zinc-rich foods in the following list. Selenium deficiency increases your risk of prostate cancer and is common in the UK, though much rarer in the US. Get

all you need from a handful of Brazil nuts each day. Traditional herbal remedies can also help with BPH, the most effective of which is an extract of saw palmetto, originally discovered by the Native North Americans. Other nutritional benefits can be obtained from sesame seeds, soybeans, almonds, and carob.

Prostate problems must be investigated at the earliest opportunity – most prostate complaints will be BPH or simple infections, but prostate cancer is as common as breast cancer.

▶ **Eat more** oysters and other shellfish, liver, lean beef (if it is organic), cheese, sardines, and pumpkin seeds for their zinc; Brazil nuts for their selenium.

▶ **Drink less** coffee, tea, cola drink, and alcohol; eat less chocolate.

PSORIASIS

SYMPTOMS

❖ *Red, scaly patches, often on the knees, elbows, scalp, or nails, but can be anywhere.*

❖ *Itchiness, weeping; sometimes associated arthritis.*

PSORIASIS, though not caused by diet, can often be improved or exacerbated by food choices. It is the skin cells of sufferers that actually cause the problem, as they multiply about 1,000 times faster than in those without psoriasis – and it is this process that produces the unique silvery, scaly surface of psoriatic lesions.

The same allergic problems can apply as in eczema, and it is equally vital to ensure adequate consumption of the essential skin nutrients. Oily fish – provided there is no obvious allergy to them – must make a major contri-

bution to the regular diet, and many studies have shown that fish-oil supplements can help. Vitamin D is also essential, so aim for at least one portion of fish per day (a minimum of 5oz/150g), although canned oily fish are fine.

All psoriasis sufferers will benefit from an increased consumption of zinc, either from supplements or from eating shellfish (if there is no allergy) and pumpkin seeds. The traditional old-fashioned American cordial made from sarsaparilla is also helpful. Plenty of fresh air and gentle sunshine always improve psoriasis.

▶ **Eat more** oily fish for their omega-3 fatty acids and vitamin D; all orange, red, and dark green vegetables and fruit for their beta-carotene.

▶ **Eat fewer** dairy products, animal fats, sugars, and refined carbohydrates; less meat; consume less caffeine and alcohol. **Avoid** all organ meats.

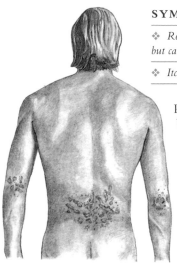

ABOVE *Psoriasis can occur all over the body, but the scalp, back, and arms may suffer in particular. It is not contagious.*

RAYNAUD'S SYNDROME AND DISEASE

SYMPTOMS

❖ *Pale fingertips turning blue and then red, pain, tingling and numbness; long-term damage may include fungal infections of the nail or ulcers on the fingertips.*

RAYNAUD'S SYNDROME affects the circulation in the hands and fingers, and sometimes the toes. The tiny arteries become sensitive to low temperatures and contract in spasms. As the condition gets worse, this may become permanent, giving fingers a "dead" look.

Raynaud's syndrome is caused by factors affecting the circulation as a secondary complication, whereas Raynaud's disease is a specific disorder of the circulatory system. The symptoms and the outcome are much the same, however. Emotional disturbances, the use of

vibrating tools, drugs like beta-blockers, nicotine, and caffeine all cause vaso-constriction.

Avoid vibrating tools. Give up smoking – you will never improve until you do. Cut down on tea, coffee, and chocolate. Drink herbal teas, decaffeinated drinks, and no more than one unit of alcohol a day.

▶ **Eat more** garlic, ginger, and cayenne to stimulate the circulation; olive oil, nuts, seeds, and avocados for their vitamin E; blackberries, blueberries, and blackcurrants for their bioflavonoids.

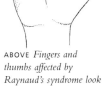

ABOVE *Fingers and thumbs affected by Raynaud's syndrome look bruised and swollen.*

▶ **Drink less** coffee, tea, and alcohol. **Avoid** nicotine.

SPICY REMEDIES

Drink a cup of ginger tea, three times daily, before meals. Alternatively, pour a cup of boiling water onto a level teaspoon of cayenne pepper. Leave for ten minutes, then add a tablespoon of this infusion to half a cup of warm water. Supplements of vitamin E (400 IU), fish oils, and rutin all help.

CIRCULATION STIMULANTS

Simple improvements to the circulation, brought about by hot-and-cold contrast bathing before bedtime, regular walking, and gentle massage, will all help. But the cure is usually achieved by improved nutrition.

RESTLESS LEGS

SYMPTOMS

❖ *Pins and needles, burning sensations, pain and frequent involuntary jerking movements.*

RESTLESS LEGS are common but are frequently misdiagnosed. The symptoms start within a few minutes of sitting down or going to bed. The only relief is to stand up and walk about, but on returning to rest they start again. Iron deficiency is the commonest cause and the symptoms may be the first signs of anemia, due to

gradual and chronic blood loss, or poor diet. Very rarely these spasms can be the result of epilepsy, spinal cord injury, or neurological disease, so symptoms should be checked by your doctor.

▶ **Eat more** wheatgerm, fresh nuts, liver, chicken, green leafy vegetables, pulses, parsley, and dates for their folic acid, iron, and vitamin B_{12}; safflower oil, olive oil, unsalted peanut butter, and avocados for their vitamin E; bananas for their potassium.

▶ **Eat less** salt; drink less caffeine and alcohol. **Avoid** smoking.

RHEUMATISM

SYMPTOMS

❖ *Pain in any joint, muscle, muscle group, tendon, ligament, or capsule, with no underlying joint disease or injury.*

RHEUMATISM is a blanket description covering a range of soft-tissue conditions that cause problems in and around the joints. Medically speaking, it is not serious, but frozen shoulder, fibrositis, tennis elbow, golfer's elbow, carpal tunnel syndrome, repetitive strain injury, Plantar fasciitis, Achilles tendonitis, trigger finger, and sacroiliac strain all interfere with your enjoyment of life. They are often well treated by massage and manipulative therapies.

Caffeine, from coffee, tea, chocolate, and cola drinks, is best kept to a minimum. Also cut down on salt and on foods containing large amounts of salt to minimize fluid retention. Red meat, game, and red wines can also trigger inflammation and make the pain worse. But the omega-3 fatty acids in fish oils stimulate the body's production of antiinflammatory hormones – so eat lots of them.

▶ **Eat more** oily fish and all other foods that provide the antioxidant nutrients, such as vitamins A, C, and E, zinc, and selenium (see Arthritis on p. 151)

▶ **Eat less** red meat, and all other foods that increase uric acid and are likely to cause tissue inflammation (see Arthritis on p. 151)

(see Arthritis on p. 151)

VITAMIN THERAPY

Too little selenium, vitamins A, C, and E, and zinc increases the likelihood of rheumatism, so top up with liver (not for pregnant women), carrots, broccoli, apricots, sweet potatoes, and cantaloup melon, red and yellow sweet peppers, kiwi fruit, oranges, brussels sprouts, cabbage, avocados, Brazil nuts, asparagus, sunflower seeds, and olive oil.

LEFT *Steak and French fries, a favorite with many people, should be avoided if rheumatism strikes.*

SCURVY

SYMPTOMS

❖ *Lethargy, weakness, aches and pains, weight loss.*

❖ *Followed by inflamed, swollen, bleeding gums, loosening of the teeth, failure of wound-healing, hemorrhages for no reason.*

TODAY in the Western world it is rare to see severe scurvy, although chronic vitamin C deficiency can be the result of poor absorption, due to digestive disease or any of the inflammatory bowel diseases.

Eating disorders are probably the most common reason for scurvy and those involved in the extreme "allergy" diets also put themselves at great risk, by excluding many vitamin C-rich foods from their daily

diet. Vitamin C is very sensitive to heat, so poor storage of fresh produce in warm conditions or direct sunlight, overcooking, and keeping cooked fruit or vegetables warm in canteens can destroy it.

Thyroid problems, pregnancy, and breastfeeding all place increased demands for vitamin C on the body, as do severe burns, surgery, and extremes of temperature. It can take from 3 to 12 months after the start of severe vitamin C deficiency before symptoms occur.

▶ **Eat more** citrus fruit, kiwi fruit, peppers, berries, potatoes, and all other fresh fruit and vegetables for their vitamin C.

▶ **Eat fewer** high-fat and sugar foods and overcooked, institutional vegetables. **Avoid** smoking.

SCARLET FEVER see Childhood diseases

ABOVE *Scurvy is an avoidable deficiency disease; make sure you get plenty of vitamin C in the form of citrus fruit or freshly squeezed juices.*

SEASONAL AFFECTIVE DISORDER (SAD)

SYMPTOMS

❖ *Winter episodes of depression, exhaustion, weight gain.*

❖ *Irritability, mood swings, lethargy.*

WHEN THE RETINA at the back of the eye is stimulated by light, the pineal gland is affected so that the amount of the hormone melatonin circulating in the body is reduced. During the winter we don't get much sunlight, so more melatonin is released and we get depressed. Some people are much more severely affected by this than others: their metabolism slows down, there are enormous cravings for sweet and fatty foods, their weight goes up, and depression ensues. It becomes a dark, vicious circle.

Seasonal affective disorder (SAD) responds very well to treatment with high-intensity light. So get as much daylight as you can, but if all else fails you can now buy relatively inexpensively a light box that produces a bright enough light to improve the condition. As well as light, good nutrition is essential. Avoid the energy-robbers, don't go for more than three hours without food.

▶ **Eat more** almonds, apricots, bananas, broccoli, spinach, brown rice, sesame and sunflower seeds, whole wheat bread, potatoes, pasta, porridge, eggs, fish, poultry, lean meat, and low-fat dairy products for mind, body, and spirit fuel.

▶ **Eat fewer** refined carbohydrates – sugar, white flour, cakes, cookies, candies; consume less alcohol and caffeine.

HERBAL STIMULANTS

Parsley, thyme, rosemary, mint, sage, horseradish, ginger, and cinnamon are all good stimulants, so use them in cooking and to make your own herbal teas: put two teaspoons of fresh chopped herb (or one of dried) into a cupful of boiling water. Cover, leave to stand for five minutes, strain, then add a little honey and sip.

S

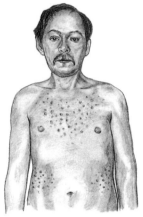

ABOVE *Shingles mainly affects people in mid- or late life; the rash, mostly on the trunk of the body, can be extremely painful.*

RIGHT *Steam inhalation can help clear blocked passages. A few drops of essential oil such as French basil or peppermint in the water will speed the process.*

HERBAL HELP

Include plenty of ginger, thyme, rosemary, horseradish, cloves, and cinnamon in recipes and as teas.

SKIN PROBLEMS *see* Dermatitis; Eczema; Psoriasis

SLE (systemic lupus erythematosus) *see* Arthritis

HUMIDIFIERS AND GARGLES

If your throat is part of a rotten cold, stay in the warm and keep the air moist by using a humidifier or a bowl of water on top of the radiator. Gargles are an essential part of the treatment. Add two tablespoons of honey and the juice of a large lemon to 1¼ cups/300ml of hot water. Gargle thoroughly, then swallow the mixture – it is too good to waste.

SHINGLES

SYMPTOMS

❖ *Slight chill or fever, malaise, irritating burning sensations in the skin at the site of an eruption, where blisters appear up to five days later; streaks of red skin covered in the blisters follow the nerve pathways to the affected region.*

SHINGLES OR HERPES zoster is caused by the varicella-zoster virus. After chicken pox some of the virus survives dormant; then, in middle life, it may reassert itself. Once the rash is present as clusters of small, raised red spots that turn into blisters, shingles is an extremely infectious condition. When the virus affects the eyes, there can be serious consequences, as secondary infection is common. But the major concern is postherpetic syndrome: a condition of excruciating pain, which can last for months or even years.

Improved nutrition after the earliest symptoms reduces the risk of long-term side effects and will help even once they have occurred.

▶ **Eat more** lemons, citrus fruit (especially the pith), apricots, cherries, tomatoes, and papaya for their vitamin C and bioflavonoids; liver, oily fish, eggs, and chicken for their vitamin B_{12}; safflower oil, olive oil, unsalted peanut butter, and avocados for their vitamin E; live yogurt for the synthesis of B vitamins; green tea for its powerful antioxidant effect.

▶ **Eat less** sugar, salt, and high-salt foods; drink less alcohol.

SINUSITIS

SYMPTOMS

❖ *Blocked nose, headache, loss of the sense of smell, pain behind or between the eyes, tenderness over the forehead and cheekbones, pain in the teeth, raised temperature, and malaise.*

SINUSITIS is inflammation of the mucous membranes lining the sinuses – the air spaces in the skull around the eyes. Acute sinusitis is caused by colds or other infections of the nose, throat, and upper respiratory tract. Chronic sinusitis may be caused by nasal polyps (small growths), injury, irritating fumes and smells, allergies, or adverse food reactions. Smoking and secondary smoking are key factors.

Severe infection causes swelling of the face and a thick discharge of purulent, foul-smelling mucus. In children, middle-ear infection is a common sequel. Chronic sinusitis leads to "post-nasal drip," resulting in repeated episodes of unpleasant chest infections.

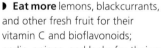

The traditional naturopathic approach has always been nutritional. For the first two or three days of an attack follow a cleansing regime of fresh fruit juices, fresh fruit (plenty of lemons), salads, and vegetables. Take a minimum of 3½pt/1.7l of liquid daily.

▶ **Eat more** lemons, blackcurrants, and other fresh fruit for their vitamin C and bioflavonoids; garlic, onions, and leeks for their antibacterial effect; carrots, spinach, and apricots for their beta-carotene; celery, dandelion leaves, and parsley as diuretics; ginger, rosemary, thyme, horseradish, cloves, and cinnamon for decongestion.

▶ **Eat fewer** dairy products, refined carbohydrates, and less sugar; drink fewer sweetened drinks.

SORE THROAT

SYMPTOMS

❖ *Pain and discomfort in the soft tissues at the back of the throat. Inflammation, swelling, rash.*

ANYTHING that irritates the sensitive mucous membranes that line the back of the mouth and throat can cause a sore throat. The first step is to drink large amounts of liquid. Water, diluted pineapple juice, or cool camomile tea are the best. A cold, damp compress, wrapped around the neck, is very soothing.

I always ask patients with throat problems to change their eating habits for a day or so. For the first 24 hours eat only fresh fruit and drink nothing but fresh fruit juice or water. (This is not suitable for children under two.) Follow this with a few days of eating mainly fruit, vegetables, salads, and light protein. Avoid dairy products and use only small amounts of starch, and no sugar or salt, until the symptoms have gone.

Persistent sore throats should not be ignored, and any sudden changes in the voice, which don't get better after a few days, should be investigated by your medical practitioner. *See also Tonsillitis on p. 208 and Laryngitis on p. 196.*

▶ **Eat more/less** *See Laryngitis on p. 196.*

STOMACH ULCERS

SYMPTOMS

❖ *Pain and discomfort in the upper abdominal region, often within an hour after eating or during the night.*

❖ *Heartburn, sensations of gnawing, cramp, burning.*

GASTRIC AND DUODENAL ulcers are caused when the lining of the stomach does not produce sufficient protective matter and the stomach acids erode areas of the stomach surface. There are many possible causes, including stress and anxiety, alcohol abuse, smoking, excessive coffee drinking, poor eating habits, drugs such as aspirin, nonsteroidal antiinflammatories, corticosteroids, and hyperacidity. But stomach ulcers need proper medical care as well as self-help. Complications like perforation or hemorrhage can be catastrophic medical emergencies, so never try to "go it alone."

In traditional natural medicine it has long been thought that a diet that contains sufficient fiber – both soluble and insoluble – provides good overall protection from ulcers. It is possible that food allergies are part of the overall picture, so I always try my patients on an exclusion diet (*see p. 65*).

Raw cabbage juice and raw potato juice are well-known treatments for gastric ulcers, and a regime of alternating between 2½ cups/600ml of each per day for ten days can heal the ulcers. Plants that encourage the formation of protective mucus in the stomach are also valuable, slippery elm and licorice being the best.

A SOOTHING DIET

Breakfast: Porridge made with water, sultanas and a pinch of cinnamon; a slice of whole wheat toast with Manuka honey (no butter).

Mid-morning: Banana with a tub of low-fat live yogurt.

Lunch: A large jacket potato with coleslaw made from red and white cabbage, carrots, and apple, with olive oil, cider vinegar, garlic, and chopped sage leaves.

Mid-afternoon: A small fresh fruit salad of kiwi fruit, mango, melon, grapes, and dates, sprinkled with sunflower and pumpkin seeds.

Evening meal: Vegetable soup including shredded dark green or Chinese cabbage, florets of broccoli and spinach, chard, or beet tops; chicken or fish risotto with avocado, tomato, and basil salad.

Late-night snack: A lettuce sandwich (without butter or mayonnaise).

Throughout the day drink plenty of water, herbal teas (especially camomile and peppermint) and 2½ cups/600ml of cabbage or potato juice – these can be made more palatable by adding apple, carrot, celery, or beet juice, or all of these.

For thousands of years the Maoris have used honey from the indigenous Manuka tree as a cure for stomach problems (*see p. 179*).

❯ **Eat more** cabbage, sauerkraut, cabbage juice, and potato juice for specific gastric healing; boiled potatoes, white rice, and pasta for their non-irritant carbohydrates; bananas, dry toast, and porridge for their bulk and fiber; Manuka honey for its specific antibacterial benefits.

❯ **Drink less** alcohol and coffee (including decaffeinated); eat less pepper and hot chilis.

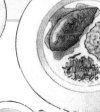

ABOVE *Soothing food for ulcer-sufferers: porridge, homemade vegetable soup, jacket potato, and coleslaw.*

THRUSH

SYMPTOMS

❖ *Thick white discharge, swollen, itching, tender vaginal lips, pain and burning when passing urine.*

THRUSH is the general term for infections caused by the yeast organism *Candida albicans*. Candidiasis – infections with Candida – most commonly affects the mouth, the vagina, the anus, and areas of damaged skin.

Oral thrush can be a problem after antibiotic therapy and is a risk for people using steroid inhalers – but it is preventable by rinsing the mouth out with water after each use of the inhaler and by replacing toothbrushes each month. Boosting immunity is the real preventive, so eat plenty of the recommended foods (*see p. 192*).

For many years complementary practitioners have advised women suffering from thrush to insert a little live yogurt in the vagina to encourage the growth of protective natural bacteria.

Some alternative practitioners believe that thrush sufferers should exclude all foods that may contain any form of yeast. There is little scientific evidence that an extremely trying diet that excludes bread, mushrooms, grapes, wine, yeast extracts, and a host of other foods is any more beneficial than the above advice.

❯ **Eat more** garlic for its antibacterial effect; natural live yogurt for its protective bacteria; complex carbohydrates for their B vitamins; bananas, nuts, and wheatgerm for their vitamin B_6; fresh fruit for its vitamin C; nuts, seeds, olive oil, and avocados for their vitamin E; oily fish for their essential fatty acids; green leafy vegetables, legumes, and oats for their folic acid; liver, red meat, parsley, dates, and dried apricots for their iron; shellfish, cheese, sardines, pumpkin seeds, whole wheat bread, and eggs for their zinc.

❯ **Drink less** tea, coffee, and alcohol, which all interfere with nutrient absorption; eat fewer processed foods, which are low in nutrients and may contain additives that increase local irritation. **Avoid** sugar, chocolate, candies, cakes, and cookies.

COLD COMFORT

The Department of Microbiology at the University of Western Ontario in Canada has treated a patient using a rather more sophisticated technique. After many episodes of thrush, she was given a pessary containing freeze-dried yogurt bacteria, *Lactobacillus*. She was better within two days, and in the following six months she used two more pessaries and remained free of thrush. But don't wait for your physician to prescribe this remedy. If you've got thrush, try the yogurt treatment.

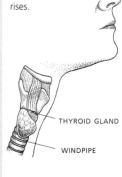

THYROID GLAND

WINDPIPE

ABOVE *People with low iodine levels can increase them by eating iodine-rich foods such as fish; haddock is a good example.*

THYROID PROBLEMS

In principle thyroid problems are the result of the thyroid gland becoming overactive – hyperthyroidism – or underactive – hypothyroidism.

HYPERTHYROIDISM

SYMPTOMS

❖ *Sweating, tremors, overactive, hot, fast irregular heartbeat.*

❖ *Weight loss, bulging eyes, hair loss, anxiety, sleeplessness, goiter.*

HYPERTHYROIDISM usually affects adults between the ages of 20 and 50, and primarily women. It can be the result of abnormalities of the thyroid gland, such as tumors, of disorders or tumors of the pituitary gland, or of conditions affecting the ovaries. There is certainly some familial link and stress does seem to play a part.

Treatment is usually with medication, surgery, or radioactive iodine, which destroys some of the thyroid cells. Increased protein in the diet is really important to counteract the severe drop in weight and muscle loss. The large amounts of extra carbohydrates needed also necessitate extra B vitamins, which are required for carbohydrate metabolism.

▶ **Eat more** meat, fish, poultry, eggs (non-animal protein sources, if you are a vegetarian) for protein to help replace the muscle lost through increased metabolism; whole grain cereals, bananas, wheatgerm, and yeast extracts for their B vitamins; complex carbohydrates for the extra calories.

▶ **Drink less** coffee, tea, chocolate, and fewer cola drinks, and consume less guarana and ginseng – all stimulants.

HYPOTHYROIDISM

SYMPTOMS

❖ *Low body temperature, weight gain, depression, dry skin, sensitivity to cold, constipation, coarse hair and skin, menstrual problems, chronic exhaustion, swelling caused by fluid retention.*

A MOST common cause of hypothyroidism is goiter, enlargement of the thyroid gland caused by a deficiency of iodine in the diet, or by failure of the body to absorb sufficient iodine. But excessive consumption of iodine can also trigger goiter, as it blocks the use of iodine by the thyroid gland. Hypothyroidism has unpleasant side effects – it can interfere with cholesterol metabolism and cause raised fat levels in the blood; it can lead to high blood pressure and greater risk of heart disease; and it can result in spontaneous abortion and stillbirth, congenital abnormalities, retarded mental and physical development.

Selenium is another essential ingredient for thyroid function. Get it from a handful of Brazil nuts each day.

▶ **Eat more** shellfish for their iodine and zinc; liver, carrots, spinach, apricots, and asparagus for their vitamin A and beta-carotene; olive oil, avocado, and sunflower seeds for their vitamin E; wholegrain cereals, bananas, oily fish, and meat and yeast extracts for their B vitamins.

▶ **Eat less** kale, cabbage, sprouts, broccoli, kohlrabi, turnips, rutabagas, rapeseed, mustard, cassava, lima beans, linseed, bamboo shoots, sweet potatoes, pine kernels, peanuts, soybeans, and millet which interfere with iodine uptake.

TOOTHACHE *see* Dental problems

TONSILLITIS

SYMPTOMS

❖ *Tonsils become swollen, inflamed, covered in white or yellow spots. Swollen glands, fever, severe pain, and headache.*

TONSILLITIS is commonest in children when they are first exposed to the myriad bacterial and viral infections carried by other children at school. Children who experience regular episodes of tonsillitis should be seen by a qualified naturopath, as changes in diet may be an important factor in prevention.

Swallowing may be excruciatingly painful and homemade pure fruit ices or frozen yogurt are soothing as well as nutritious. Children should be given lots of fluids, especially pineapple juice, diluted 50:50 with water. Adults should follow a cleansing regime of pure unsweetened fruit or vegetable juices, herbal teas, and lots of water for 24 hours; raw fruit, salads, and vegetables for 24 hours; cooked vegetables, rice, pasta, and cereals for 24 hours; then back to a normal diet.

Cold compresses wrapped around the neck are very soothing, and a gargle with red sage tea will reduce the inflammation.

▶ **Drink more** citrus juices with honey and hot water, other unsweetened juices, and copious amounts of ice water; eat more puréed homemade vegetable soups, including dark-green leafy vegetables, carrots and other root vegetables, onions, and garlic.

▶ **Eat fewer** dry rough foods; pickles, vinegars, and salt; and possibly dairy products.

TUBERCULOSIS (TB)

SYMPTOMS

❖ *In the early stages, mild flu-like symptoms only. Then low-grade chronic fever and fatigue, night sweats, weight loss.*

❖ *Later productive cough with thick, sometimes bloody sputum, breathing difficulties, and chest pain.*

TRADITIONALLY tuberculosis is a disease of poor, overcrowded, badly housed, and very poorly nourished sections of the community. From the late 1950s to the early 1970s it was almost exclusively found in Britain in the recently arrived Asian immigrant population, but was seldom acquired there.

Tragically, due to economic circumstances, high unemployment, and the rising number of homeless people who live on the street, the number of patients with tuberculosis is beginning to rise once again, although with modern antibiotics, this form of tuberculosis is normally curable.

To growing consternation, however, antibiotic-resistant strains of TB have appeared in recent years in the UK and US, where it is one of the common infections affecting people who are HIV positive or have full-blown AIDS. It is vital that people in at-risk groups should try to maintain their natural immunity at peak performance level, though economic circumstances usually militate against this.

It is even more important that patients with TB eat a diet that is overflowing with the protective nutrients essential to the proper functioning of the body's natural defenses.

A combination of all the recommended foods listed below must form the bulk of the regular diet of those suffering from TB, and protective foods like garlic, onions, and all the herbs and spices should be used liberally. Avoiding dairy products helps to control the amount of mucus produced and, since excess sugar compromises the effectiveness of the immune system, this too should be kept to an absolute minimum.

▶ **Eat more** oily fish for their omega-3 fatty acids; poultry and lean meat for their protein; spinach, sweet potatoes, and carrots for their beta-carotene; garbanzo beans and whole grain cereals for their B vitamins and folic acid; olive oil, safflower oil, nuts, seeds, and avocados for their vitamin E; citrus fruit, cherries, and berries for their vitamin C and bioflavonoids; low-fat yogurt for its calcium and vitamin D; garlic, onions, and leeks for specific anti chest-infection activity; thyme, sage, rosemary, and ginger for their respiratory benefits and antibacterial effects.

▶ **Eat fewer** animal fats, all other dairy products, highly processed carbohydrates, processed, prepackaged, and ready prepared foods; less sugar, candies, and puddings; consume less caffeine and alcohol.

VACCINATION CHECK

Tuberculosis is highly infectious, so carers must pay special attention to their nutritional status as well. If you are in an at-risk group, working with people who are at risk, caring for infected patients or planning to travel to areas where TB is endemic, don't be complacent – check your vaccination status.

URTICARIA *see* **Allergies**

VARICOSE VEINS

SYMPTOMS

❖ *Distended, distorted, and sometimes visible veins in the thighs and calves, swollen ankles, pain, eczema, and ulcers.*

VARICOSE VEINS are distended veins, commonly occurring in the legs. If the one-way valves inside the leg veins stop working efficiently, blood leaks back through them, collects in the lower veins and stretches them so much that the vein walls lose their elasticity and are unable to contract back into their normal shape. A weakness of these valves is often hereditary (particularly from mothers to daughters).

Jobs that involve prolonged periods of standing, obesity, pregnancy, and constipation, combined with a sedentary lifestyle, are all part of the pattern that leads to this problem. If varicose veins become severe, then local skin discoloration and varicose eczema are likely to develop. The slightest injury can then result in a varicose ulcer. These can take months or years of repeated treatment, and sometimes surgery, before they heal.

Avoid constipation by drinking at least 3½pt/1.7l of water a day and including a wide selection of the recommended foods in your diet. This will also improve circulation, strengthen the vein walls, and promote healing if you have a varicose ulcer.

Zinc, beta-carotene, bioflavonoids, and vitamins C and E are all essential for the good health of vein walls and for the control of varicose eczema and ulcers.

Take regular exercise – walking is fine. Avoid sitting (especially on hard-edged seats) or standing for long periods without a break, don't ever cross your legs, and do put your feet up whenever you get the chance.

▶ **Eat more** porridge, apples, pears, beans, and cooked, green leafy vegetables for their soluble fiber; whole wheat bread and brown rice for their insoluble fiber; liver, shellfish, some red meat, canned sardines, and eggs for their zinc; carrots, apricots, and broccoli for their beta-carotene; citrus fruit, blackcurrants, and blueberries for their bioflavonoids and vitamin C; safflower and olive oil, and avocados for their vitamin E.

▶ **Eat fewer** refined, processed carbohydrates and less salt; cut down on excessive coffee and alcohol.

HONEY DRESSING

Using a dressing of sterile gauze smeared with honey has proved successful in the treatment of these ulcers.

WHOOPING COUGH *see* **Childhood Diseases**

PART FOUR

USEFUL
INFORMATION

ABOVE *Take all vitamin and mineral supplements with pure water and stick to the RDAs listed in this section.*

T his last section is designed to be a useful appendix to the main volume. It contains information that is relevant to each of the previous sections. It is presented in an easily accessible format with charts and boxes to bring out important data. There is a guide to the vitamin maze and the magic minerals that can boost your health; advice on the recommended daily intake of vitamins and minerals; food additives (the good and the bad) are listed and explained; the effect of medicinal drugs on nutritional uptake is explored. The section concludes with a helpful reading list and some useful addresses.

ABOVE *During pregnancy be even more careful about any supplements that you take. Consult your doctor if you have any doubts.*

ABBREVIATIONS DECODED

Here is a list of abbreviations and acronyms used in the text, with their full names or titles spelled out:

ADHD	Attention Deficit Hyperactive Disorder
ADI	Acceptable Daily Intake
AIDS	Acquired Immune Deficiency Syndrome
AMD	Age-related Macular Degeneration
BMI	Body Mass Index
BMR	Basic Metabolic Rate
BPH	Benign Prostatic Hypertrophy
BRAT diet	Bananas, Rice, Apples, and (dry) Toast diet
BSE	Bovine Spongiform Encephalopathy
CJD	Creutzfeldt-Jakob Disease
COAD	Chronic Obstructive Airways Disease
EU	European Union
FBD	Fibrocystic Breast Disease
FDA	Food and Drug Administration
GI	Glycemic Index
GLA	Gamma Linoleic Acid
HDL	High-Density Lipoprotein
HIV	Human Immunodeficiency Virus
HRT	Hormone Replacement Therapy
IBS	Irritable Bowel Syndrome
IDDM	Insulin-Dependent Diabetes Mellitus
IU	International Units
LDL	Low-Density Lipoprotein
mcg/µg	Microgram
ME	Myalgic Encephalomyelitis
NIDDM	Non-Insulin-Dependent Diabetes Mellitus
NPU	Net Protein Utilization
NSAID	Non-Steroidal Anti-Inflammatory Drugs
PKU	Phenylketonuria
PMS	Premenstrual Syndrome
RDA	Recommended Daily Allowance
SAD	Seasonal Affective Disorder
SLE	Systematic Lupus Erythematosus
SRSV	Small Round-Structured Virus
TATT	Tired All The Time syndrome
TB	Tuberculosis
WHO	World Health Organization

Understanding Vitamins

I *always ask my patients to bring any supplements that they are taking when they come to see me. Lots of them turn up with plastic bags full of them! This really upsets me, as they are certainly spending too much money on them and some of the vitamins and minerals can be dangerous if taken in high doses.*

Although the American recommended daily allowances (RDAs) for vitamins and minerals are generally higher than those in Britain, I am concerned about both of them. Governments make no allowance for the huge variations in the actual nutrient content of today's foods. Intensive growing methods, transporting, storing, handling, and freshness can all reduce the level of vitamins in food. And that is before you buy them, take them home, and cook them. The theoretical vitamin content of what ends up on your plate is often a great deal higher than the reality of what you actually put into your mouth.

There is also an enormous difference between the amount of vitamins and minerals you need in order to avoid deficiency diseases and those that will keep you in peak condition and protect your body against serious illness. On the right are details of what some of the vitamins do, and how much you theoretically need to eat to achieve the RDAs.

THE VITAMIN MAZE

Still confused? I'm not surprised. The burning question most people want to ask is: "Do I need to take extra vitamins?" The theoretical answer is no – not if you are eating a well-balanced diet and getting a wide variety of foods.

In fact, few people manage to do this, and even fewer persuade their partners or children to do so. The pressures of time, working couples, fewer school meals, and the relentless march of the fast-food industry all make it more difficult. So you dash to the pharmacy or health-food store to pick up a pot of pills, and by the time you have read the umpteenth label you're more muddled than ever. Do you choose a multivitamin, six individual bottles, mega-dose or slow-release vitamins, vegetarian capsules, tablets made without gluten, yeast, coloring or sugar, a brand containing 70 different ingredients, one with only five; or, like so many shoppers, do you leave confused and empty-handed?

VITAL VITAMINS

VITAMIN A

Essential for growth, skin, night- and color-vision.

Get all you need for a day from: ⅙oz/5g of liver, 1½oz/40g of old carrots, 2½oz/70g of spinach, butter or margarine, 4½oz/120g of broccoli with 2oz/60g of Cheddar cheese in a sauce.

VITAMIN C

Prevents scurvy, aids wound-healing and iron absorption, and is a vital and protective antioxidant.

The daily dose is found in: one dessertspoon of blackcurrants, one lemon, half a green bell pepper, an orange, half a large grapefruit, a kiwi fruit, 3oz/90g of raw red cabbage.

VITAMIN D

Essential for bone formation, as it is part of the calcium absorption system.

Lack of this vitamin causes rickets in children and bone disorders in adults. The action of ultraviolet light on the skin produces vitamin D. Those at special risk of a deficiency are the elderly and other groups who get little fresh air and daylight exposure. The Asian community is also often at risk, due to traditional clothing, diet, and lifestyle. The 10 micrograms (1 microgram or μg = one-thousandth of a milligram) that are essential will be obtained from one teaspoon of cod liver oil, 1½ oz/45g of herring or kipper, 2oz/55g of mackerel, 2¾oz/80g of canned salmon or tuna, 4¾oz/135g of canned sardines. Eggs and margarine are also fair sources.

VITAMIN B₁, THIAMIN

The main function of thiamin occurs during the conversion of carbohydrates into energy.

If you live on a high starch diet (as some vegetarians do) or you have an excessive consumption of alcohol, your need for B₁ increases. Your daily dose can be obtained from: 2oz/60g of cod roe, 2½oz/70g of wheatgerm, 3½oz/100g of Brazil or peanuts. Oatmeal, bacon, pork, offal, and bread are all good sources too.

VITAMIN B₂, RIBOFLAVIN

Vital for growth, and for the skin and mucous membranes.

6 eggs, 3⅓ cups/800ml milk, 2½oz/65g of liver or kidney, 9oz/250g of Cheddar cheese will each supply the 1.3g you need. Beef, mackerel, almonds, cereals, and poultry are also good sources.

VITAMIN B₆, PYRIDOXINE

Essential for growth. Many women have found it helpful in treating the symptoms of PMS, and it may overcome some of the side effects of the contraceptive pill.

Fish, meat, liver, and cheese are good sources. A large banana and half an avocado will provide the daily dose. A portion of cod, salmon, or a broiled herring will also give you nearly all you need.

FOLIC ACID

Vital during growth and development. Studies now show that some birth defects are related to a low intake of folic acid.

The best sources are dark-green vegetables, liver, kidney, nuts, whole wheat bread, and whole grain cereals. An average portion of lamb's liver supplies 250μg, spinach 140μg, kidney beans, frozen peas, garbanzo beans, and raw red cabbage all around 75μg of the essential daily 200μg.

Even worse, you may waste a lot of your hard-earned cash on supplements you don't actually need, and which may do you more harm than good. Single vitamins and minerals certainly have their place, but as a general rule they are best taken on the advice of your practitioner – certainly in the case of the high-dose ones. If you mix and match yourself, you may find that the products overlap and you get more of some nutrients than you bargained for.

READING THE LABEL
Natural health insurance, in the form of an inexpensive, well-formulated multivitamin and mineral pill, can be a good idea. It will make up for the occasional missed meal, the extra demands of a stressful life, the vitamin losses during storage, transport, and cooking of food, and will buoy you up after an illness.

So what do you look for on the label, and how do you know which supplement to buy? When do you and the family need to take extra nutrients? Are there times when they should be avoided, or when you should increase your intake?

Do read the labels carefully. Avoid pills with artificial colors, flavorings, and preservatives. Watch out for added sugar or sweeteners. Many children, especially those with asthma, eczema, or other allergy problems, and hyperactive children, react badly to many of the food chemicals in some vitamin pills.

On the other hand, some manufacturers are cashing in on the "allergy" syndrome and making expensive products that are gluten-, yeast-, egg-, milk-, and everything-else-free. Unless you know that you are allergic to certain foods – and comparatively few people are – there is no need to go to these lengths.

Most of us are unlikely to need anything more than a good general multivitamin and mineral supplement. Choose those with substantial levels of the main nutrients, rather than huge lists of nutrients you have never heard of. Adult formulations are not normally suitable for children from the ages of two to ten, who should be given the relevant products. Children under two should take vitamin supplements only on professional advice.

SUPPLEMENTS AND MEGADOSES
Single supplements do have a place in the treatment and prevention of certain conditions – extra vitamin C as protection against colds and infections during the winter; B6, zinc, and evening primrose oil for PMS and other menstrual problems; beta-carotene and evening primrose oil for skin conditions; folic acid, calcium, fish-oil (not fish-liver oil), and multivitamins before and during pregnancy; calcium and multivitamins when breastfeeding; calcium and vitamin D for the prevention of osteoporosis (start around your mid-forties); calcium, vitamin D, and multivitamins for the over-sixties; extra B-complex vitamins at times of stress; vitamins E and C and multivitamins before surgery; multivitamins and extra vitamin C and iron when you are dieting.

High doses of single vitamins should not be taken without medical advice, as some of them can be toxic. And there is little evidence that slow-release vitamins are that much better for you, although they can be a lot more expensive.

Some vitamins interfere with medication, so if you are taking prescribed medicines, do check with your practitioner before starting to dose yourself. There are some forms of cancer that develop more quickly if you take extra vitamins, and others that benefit from them, so you must ask your consultant before taking anything other than what he or she has prescribed.

There are some nutritional essentials that it is crazy to get from pills. Fiber is one of these. You would get more fiber, and lots of other nutrients, from a bowl of porridge.

Don't be fooled into thinking that it will not matter what you eat, as long as you take a vitamin pill. This simply is not true. Vitamin supplements are just that – a supplement to healthy eating. If your budget is stretched to the limit, add the money to your shopping instead of spending it on pills.

One of the best comments on vitamins came from Charlton Heston. He told me, over a healthy breakfast, that he takes a multivitamin each day. When I asked him about the American obsession with huge, mega-dose pills, he replied: "Michael, Americans have the most expensive urine in the world."

US FOOD AND DRUG ADMINISTRATION RDAs FOR VITAMINS

A	5,000IU
C	60mg
D	400IU
E	30IU
Thiamin	1.5mg
Riboflavin	1.7mg
Niacin	20mg
B6	2.0mg
B12	6.0µg
Folate	0.4mg
Biotin	0.3mg
Pantothenic acid	10mg

Understanding Minerals

There are certain minerals that your body needs – some in tiny amounts, others in intermediate amounts, and a few in minute traces. They are all essential, and missing out on any – even the trace minerals – can make the difference between health and sickness. For example, a breastfeeding mother needs 1,250mg of calcium each day, but only 15mg of iron and 75µg of selenium.

These magic minerals are nearly always ignored when investigating health problems. Except for the obvious mineral, iron, and perhaps calcium, most practitioners could not tell you what they are, let alone what they do. But the plain fact is that they are often a key factor in the cause of illness, and a simple supplement of the missing substances can produce dramatic improvements.

Because of modern intensive farming methods, soil that has been artificially fertilized and has had the same crop grown on it for years may have its natural stores of trace elements depleted. The crops and the animals fed on them may then contain fewer minerals than we need. The same is true for cereals, fruit, and vegetables.

Two of the trace minerals are of special interest to me, as they are the ones that can be used with dramatic effect, and which are often lacking in our diets.

ZINC

Vital for growth, healthy sex organs, reproduction, insulin production, and for natural resistance.

Lack of zinc can lead to weight loss, skin diseases, ulcers and acne, lower sex-drive, loss of taste and smell, and brittle nails. Too much zinc reduces the amount of copper in the body. The best places to find zinc are in lamb, liver, steak, garlic, ginger root, Brazil nuts, pumpkin seeds, oysters, eggs, sardines, oats, crab, almonds, and chicken.

Zinc deficiency can be a factor in so many conditions that it is a mineral for which I am always on the lookout. You are more likely to have too little zinc if you are a strict vegetarian, are constantly on slimming diets, or if you are into some extreme food fad like macrobiotics.

Premenstrual tension and post-natal depression are two conditions that almost always respond well to small doses of extra zinc (around 15mg per day). People with anorexia nervosa have very low levels of zinc, and deficiency may also be linked to hyperactivity in children. Don't eat vast amounts of bran, as this can inhibit zinc absorption.

SELENIUM

Part of the self-defense system and also important for cholesterol control and for protection against some forms of cancer.

Deficiency may lead to low resistance, heart disease, skin problems, and a significantly increased risk of cancer. You will find most selenium in whole wheat bread made from Canadian and North American flour, in Brazil nuts, butter, oily fish, liver, and kidney.

Back in the 1970s doctors in China studied 9,000 young men living in areas that had very little selenium in the soil. Some were given a supplement containing tiny amounts of selenium, others a placebo, or fake pill. The reduction in the rate of a heart disease that is common in China (Keshan disease) was dramatic.

We now know that selenium works together with vitamin E as an antioxidant, which attacks the free radicals that do so much damage to the body's cells. For this reason it seems to be a key factor in protecting you against high blood pressure, strokes, and heart attacks.

But perhaps the most exciting function of selenium is its apparent ability to protect the body from cancer. American studies have shown that where the soil is richest in this seemingly insignificant substance, the number of people who get cancer is 20 percent lower than in areas of the country which have soil that is low in selenium. A study that was completed in 1996 and published in the *Journal of the American Medical Association* showed a 50 percent lower cancer mortality

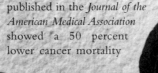

rate in patients who were given a selenium supplement.

In Britain the average daily intake of selenium has almost halved in the last 22 years, to 34µg per day – very low compared with American intakes, and half the recommended minimum amount. Considering that low selenium levels are also linked to a significant risk of spontaneous abortion in women and infertility in men, it must be time to do something about these declining intakes.

Most frightening of all, current research shows that normally harmless viruses can become dangerously virulent when living in a body that is deficient in selenium. This has been suggested as the possible explanation for new flu strains in China, and for the first appearance of AIDS in Zaire. Both these countries have very selenium-deficient soil and, consequently, deficient populations.

You need to take only 100mg of selenium a day to make sure that your body never goes short of this vital element – or else munch your way through half a dozen Brazil nuts.

US FOOD AND DRUG ADMINISTRATION RDAs FOR MINERALS	
Calcium	1g
Iron	18mg
Zinc	15mg
Copper	2.0mg
Sodium	2,400mg
Potassium	3,500mg
Magnesium	400mg
Phosphorus	1g
Iodine	150µg

GERMANIUM The most recently "discovered" trace element. Research in Japan has found that it is essential for life.

It is known to protect plants from infection, and to improve their growth rates and strengthen them in general. It seems that its effect comes from the mineral's ability to act as a scavenger of free radicals.

This is an abundant mineral in nature, and the average diet will give you around 1mg a day. But doses of 50–250mg daily for long periods (4–18 months) can be seriously harmful, and may even cause death. Research is still in its infancy, but don't believe all the extravagant claims made for the germanium pills now on the market. Some of these pills have been withdrawn from sale, and *I never advise anyone to use this mineral as a supplement.*

IRON This combines with oxygen to make hemoglobin, the red coloring of the blood. This transports the oxygen from the air you breathe to every cell of the body. Without enough iron you will suffer from anemia, fatigue, depression, and palpitations and will look pale. Too much iron, on the other hand, can lower your natural resistance and also cause insomnia, tiredness, and depression. Kelp (seaweed), molasses, pig's liver, beef, pilchards, kidney beans, Brazil nuts, dates, raisins, lentils, peanuts, chicken, soy beans, and peas are excellent sources of iron.

A good portion of liver, chili con carne, or any of the game meats or beef, with green vegetables, peas, or dried beans will provide your daily need. Black pudding, oily fish like pilchards, herrings, and sardines, garbanzo beans, shellfish and kidney beans are also good sources. Spinach is not the best source, as

it contains oxalic acid, which makes it more difficult to absorb the iron.

The tannin found in tea also interferes with iron absorption and is a factor in anemia, especially in elderly people, whose diet may be poor and who drink lots of strong tea. Bran and high-wheat-fiber cereals can cause problems too, but vitamin C taken at the same time as cereals improves the uptake of iron.

COPPER Works with iron to make red blood corpuscles, which are important for bone formation, the breakdown of cholesterol and the skin pigment melanin. A deficiency of copper can lead to anemia, hair problems, raised cholesterol levels, and dry skin. Get your daily dose from oysters, nuts, beef, liver, lamb, butter, barley, and olive oil.

CALCIUM A vital mineral for the formation and continuing strength of bones. This is of maximum importance during pregnancy, breastfeeding, childhood, and the teenage years. And in later life women are at risk of osteoporosis, which is caused by a combination of too little calcium in the diet and poor absorption.

The time to do something positive about protecting bones is during childhood. A diet that contains lots of calcium-rich foods is the first step. Your body needs sunlight to make vitamin D, without which it cannot absorb the calcium, so encourage children to be active, play sport, get plenty of fresh air and sunshine.

Pregnant and nursing mothers need to have a good store of calcium, and when you reach your thirties, keep up some sort of weight-bearing exercise to strengthen the bones.

The menopause is a crucial time. Consider the question of hormone replacement therapy (HRT), and take some extra calcium with vitamin D as a supplement.

A glass of milk, a tub of yogurt and 2oz/60g of cheese will provide the 1,000mg of calcium you need each day. Do eat the low-fat versions, and eat plenty of canned sardines (with the bones), lots of greens and dried fruit, nuts, beans, whole wheat bread, and plenty of watercress and parsley.

IODINE Essential for the proper working of the thyroid gland, which produces hormones that control many of the body's functions. It also gives some degree of protection against radiation damage to the thyroid. Lack of iodine causes lethargy, skin thickening, hair loss, growth problems, and goitre. Too much iodine may cause overactivity of the thyroid. Seaweed and seawater fish are the only dependable sources. But beware of taking too much of the kelp supplements. These can be high in iodine and may cause thyroid problems.

MANGANESE Needed for the formation of a number of enzymes, bone formation, muscle action, and fertility. A lack of manganese may cause bone and disk problems, as well as high blood sugar. It is found in all whole grain cereals, nuts, and tea. The safe maximum intake for adults is 1.4mg, for children 16µg per day.

PHOSPHORUS A vital mineral for bone formation, and as a constituent of cells. It is present in almost all foods, but foods rich in calcium are the best sources. Lack of phosphorus is rare and is only caused by certain antacid drugs.

POTASSIUM Essential for the proper functioning of all cells and nervous tissue. It is present in all foods except oils, fats, and sugars, but can be lost into the cooking water of vegetables, so use this to make soups, gravy, and stews. Pills that increase the passing of urine can cause a loss of this mineral, and this risk is higher in older people, who may eat less of the important foods. Most practitioners prescribe potassium alongside such diuretic drugs. Bananas are a great source.

BORON There is little scientific evidence about the need for this mineral. It is thought to be part of the bone-forming complex. Since it is not toxic in small doses, I advise it as an aid to combating osteoporosis.

TAKING MINERAL SUPPLEMENTS

If your diet is a good, varied mixture of the main food groups, you are not likely to need mineral pills, unless you have a particular health problem. There are certain situations when a supplement is indicated, however, so here is my selection of the best combination of quality and value for money: selenium with vitamins A, C and E; calcium with magnesium, boron and vitamin D; zinc with vitamin C; zinc with copper, for long-term use; iron as amino acid chelate. A mineral complex is best when combined with amino acids to make it more easily available for the body to use.

Read the labels carefully. Some products do not supply very much of the minerals you actually need. Do look carefully, and ask the store manager or pharmacist for help if you aren't sure. Some calcium supplements, for example, supply only 360mg of the 1,250mg of calcium you need if you are breastfeeding.

At these levels there is no risk of deficiency and no risk of undesirable side effects. Exceeding these safe doses would not necessarily cause side effects, but the UK Department of Health maintains that there is no evidence of any benefit being derived from higher doses.

Medicines and Drugs

Many of the drugs prescribed by general practitioners, and medicines bought over the counter, can have damaging effects on our stores of vitamins and minerals. So it is important to understand when there may be a need for extra supplements to compensate for these losses.

Apart from those included in the following list, you should be aware that everyday substances can also be a problem. Both nicotine and alcohol, for example, have a bad influence on your vitamin levels.

CHEMICAL ROBBERY

ANTACIDS can interfere with the absorption of vitamin A and B-complex vitamins, as well as the minerals calcium, magnesium, iron, and phosphorus.

ANTIBACTERIALS – isoniazid, the standard drug for the treatment of tuberculosis, causes pyridoxine deficiency. Supplements are usually given – if not, ask your doctor, especially as treatment may last for a year or more, and certainly no less than six to nine months.

ANTIBIOTICS generally interfere with the B-complex vitamins and with vitamin K, partly because they destroy some of the natural bacteria in the gut, which are involved in vitamin B synthesis.

ANTICANCER drugs, such as methotrexate, interfere with folic-acid absorption and may cause gastrointestinal bleeding and diarrhea. Patients being treated with methotrexate should not self-medicate with over-the-counter preparations containing folic acid, as this may interfere with the effectiveness of the drug.

ANTICOAGULANTS, including warfarin, aspirin, and all their relatives, affect vitamin K absorption.

ANTICONVULSANTS interfere with the body's absorption of vitamins B_6, D, and K, as well as folic acid. These drugs are normally taken for very extended periods of time, as in the treatment of epilepsy. Phenytoin (which is also used to treat irregular heartbeat) interferes with the absorption of calcium.

ANTIINFLAMMATORIES – sulfasalazine produces folic-acid loss. According to C.H. Smith and W.R. Bidlack in the *Journal of the American Dietetic Association*, "Even though folacin deficiency is common in moderate to severe inflammatory bowel disease, folacin absorption appears to be further diminished by the use of the anti-inflammatory agent sulfasalazine. Patients need to be encouraged to eat a varied and adequate diet rather than using folacin supplements."

ANTIMALARIALS can also act against folic acid and the long-term use of pyrimethamine (Daraprim, Fansidar, Maloprem) may cause megaloblastic anemia.

ANTIULCER drugs reduce the stomach's production of acid and can cause poor absorption of vitamin B_{12}.

CHOLESTEROL-LOWERING drugs – cholestyramine produces malabsorption of iron, beta-carotene, vitamins A, D, and K, and folic acid, when used for long periods of time.

DIURETICS deprive the body of vitamin B-complex, potassium, magnesium, and zinc.

HIGH-BLOOD-PRESSURE DRUGS, such as hydralazine, lower the level of vitamin B_6 in the body.

LAXATIVES, by speeding up the bowel function, cause many nutrients, both vitamins and minerals, to be lost, especially calcium and phosphorus. Long-term laxative abuse, such as that seen in eating disorders, is a common cause of drug-induced malnutrition. Vitamin D can be severely affected by the regular use of laxatives and this is of great importance to women at risk of osteoporosis, as vitamin D is essential for the absorption of calcium. Linseeds and linseed extracts have become a popular form of laxative in recent years, but unfortunately they have an adverse effect on the fat-soluble vitamins A, D, and E, leaching them out of the body.

ORAL CONTRACEPTIVE agents – the contraceptive pill is a major factor in nutritional status. It adversely affects folic acid, vitamins C, B_1, $_2$, $_6$ and $_{12}$ and vitamin E.

SLEEPING PILLS and antidepressants – barbiturate-type sleeping pills affect the uptake of vitamin D. Anti-depressants interfere with the chemical process of B_2 absorption and with the uptake of the minerals zinc and magnesium.

TRANQUILIZERS – stelazine is detrimental to vitamin B_{12} absorption.

HEALTH WARNING

Chemical robbery is insidious. It creeps up without warning and can have a very negative impact on your health – the last thing you need if you are taking some form of medicine for an existing illness.

Forewarned is forearmed. These are the most common culprits, so if you need to use them, at least take the right steps to keep you on the path to a speedy recovery.

Additives

The majority of people can eat almost any food without suffering ill-effects. But the substances that manufacturers add to some foods to improve shelf-life or appearance can exacerbate certain conditions and even cause a number of illnesses. Babies and young children are particularly vulnerable. For this reason it is important to be familiar with additives and to read the labels on packaged foods before buying them. The following list gives the most common additives.

ADDITIVES

Ammonium Chloride (also known as Sal Ammoniac)

Ammonium Polyphosphates

Benzoic Acid

Brilliant Blue FCF (also known as FD&C Blue No.1)

Butylated Hydroxyanisole (also known as BHA)

Butylated Hydroxytoluene (also known as BHT)

Calcium Benzoate

Calcium Disodium Ethylene Diamine Tetra-Acetate (also known as Calcium Disodium EDTA)

Calcium Polyphosphates

Calcium Propionate (also known as Calcium Propanoate)

Caramel

Carbon Dioxide

Carrageenan (also known as Irish Moss and as Carrageen)

Chlorine

Cochineal (also known as Carminic acid)

Diphenyl (also known as Biphenyl, and as Phenyl Benzene) (permitted on citrus fruit skins and in a small group of foods at low levels as a flavoring)

Dodecyl Gallate (permitted only in margarine)

Erythrosine (also known as FD&C Red No.3)

Ethyl 4-hydroxybenzoate (also known as Ethyl Para-hydroxybenzoate, and as Ethyl Paraben)

Ethyl 4-hydroxybenzoate, Sodium salt (also known as Sodium Ethyl Para-hydroxybenzoate)

Gum Arabic (also known as Gum Arabia, Acacia Gum, and Gum Senegal)

Indigo Carmine (also known as Indigotine and as FD&C Blue No.2)

Lactic Acid (also known as DL Lactic Acid)

Mannitol

Methyl 4-hydroxybenzoate (also known as Methyl Para-hydroxybenzoate, and as Methylparaben)

Methyl 4-hydroxybenzoate, Sodium Salt (also known as Sodium Methyl para-hydroxybenzoate)

Monopotassium Glutamate (also known as MPG and as Mono-Potassium Glutamate)

Monosodium Glutamate (also known as MSG)

Octyl Gallate (permitted only in margarine)

Polyoxyethelane (20) Sorbitan Monostearate (also known as Polysorbate 60, and as Tween 60)

Polyoxyethelane (20) Sorbitan Tristearate (also known as Polysorbate 65, and as Tween 65)

Potassium Acetate (permitted only as a synthetic flavoring, and not as a preservative)

Potassium Benzoate (permitted only to treat malt and as a residue in beer)

Potassium Bromate

Potassium Chloride

Potassium Metabisulfite

Potassium Nitrate

Potassium Nitrite

Propionic Acid (also known as Propanoic Acid)

Propyl 4-hydroxybenzoate (also known as Propylparaben)

Propyl 4-hydroxybenzoate Sodium (also known as Sodium Propyl Para-hydroxybenzoate)

Sodium Acetate

Sodium Aluminum Phosphate

Sodium Benzoate

Sodium 5'-Inosinate (also known as Disodium Inosinate)

Sodium Guanylate (also known as Guanosine 5' (Disodium Phosphate))

Sodium Hydrogen Sulfite (also known as Sodium Bisulfite)

Sodium Lactate

Sodium Metabisulfite

Sodium Nitrate

Sodium and Potassium Diphosphates – Disodium Dihydrogen Diphosphate, Trisodium Diphosphate, Tetrasodium Diphosphate, and Tetrapotassium Diphosphate

Sodium and Potassium Polyphosphates

Sodium and Potassium Triphosphates – Pentasodium Triphosphate and Pentapotassium Triphosphate

Sodium Nitrite

Sodium Propionate (also known as Sodium Propanoate)

Sodium Sulfate

Sodium Sulfite

Sorbic Acid

Sulfur Dioxide

Sunset Yellow FCF (also known as FD&C Yellow No.6)

Tartrazine (also known as FD&C Yellow No.5)

Babies should avoid the following additives: Potassium Nitrite, Sodium Nitrite, Sodium Nitrate, Potassium Nitrate, Sodium Acetate, Lactic Acid, Octyl Gallate, Dodecyl Gallate, Butylated Hydroxyanisole, Butylated Hydroxytoluene, Sodium Sulfate, Sodium Aluminum Phosphate, Monosodium Glutamate, Monopotassium Gluatamate, Sodium Guanylate, Sodium 5'-Inosinate, Sodium 5'-Ribonucleotides; they should not eat Sodium Lactate in large quantities.

Young children should avoid the following additives: Sodium Nitrite, Sodium Nitrate, Potassium Nitrate, Octyl Gallete, Dodecyl Gallate, Butylated Hydroxyanisole, Butylated Hydroxytoluene, Monosodium Glutamate, Sodium Guanylate, Sodium 5'-Inosinate, Sodium 5'-Ribonucleotides; they should not eat the following in large quantities: Sodium Benzoate, Potassium Benzoate, Calcium Benzoate, Ethyl 4-hydroxybenzoate, Ethyl 4-hydroxybenzoate, Sodium salt, Propyl 4-hydroxybenzoate, Propyl 4-hydroxybenzoate Sodium salt, Sodium Acetate, Sodium Lactate.

Further Reading

(All books on this list have been published in the UK, unless otherwise noted)

Aromatherapy

Aromatherapy by Christine Wildwood (Element Books, 1991)

Aromatherapy for Pregnancy and Childbirth by Margaret Fawcett (Element Books, 1993)

Arthritis and Rheumatism

Arthritis & Rheumatism: A Comprehensive Guide to Effective Treatment by Pat Young (Element Books, 1995)

Asthma

Asthma: A Comprehensive Guide to Effective Treatment by Roy Ridgway (Element Books)

Cancer

Cancer – A Positive Approach by Hilary Thomas and Karol Sikora (Thorsons, UK/USA, 1995)

Cancer and Complementary Therapies (BACUP, 1994)

Cancer and Nutrition by Rosy Daniel and Sandra Goodman (Bristol Cancer Help Centre, 1994)

Cancer Care ed. Jill David (Chapman & Hall, UK/USA, 1995)

Complementary Care and Cancer (CancerLink, 1993)

Understanding Cancer ed. Edith Rudinger (Consumers' Association, 1986)

Colds and Flu

The Natural Way Colds and Flu by Penny Davenport (Element Books, 1995)

Diabetes

Diabetes: A Comprehensive Guide to Effective Treatment by Catherine Steven (Element Books, 1995)

The Fitness Book for People with Diabetes by W. Guyton Hornsby, Jr. (American Diabetes Association, 1994)

Eating Disorders

Anorexia and Bulimia by Julia Buckroyd (Element Books, UK/USA, 1996)

Eczema

Eczema: A Comprehensive Guide to Effective Treatment by Sheena Meredith (Element Books)

General

A–Z of Natural Healthcare by Belinda Grant (Optima, 1993)

The Alternative Dictionary of Symptoms and Cures by Dr. Caroline Shreeve (Century, 1987)

Better Health through Natural Healing by Ross Tratler (McGraw-Hill, USA, 1987)

Choices in Healing by Michael Lerner (MIT Press, USA/UK, 1994)

The Complete Natural Health Consultant by Michael van Straten (Ebury, 1987)

The Complete Relaxation Book by James Hewitt (Rider, 1987)

The Doctor's Book of Home Remedies ed. Debora Tkac (Rodale Press, USA, 1994)

Encyclopaedia of Natural Medicine by Michael Murray and Joseph Pizzorno (Macdonald Optima, 1990)

The Family Medical Adviser (Reader's Digest, 1983)

The Fountain of Health: An A–Z of Traditional Chinese Medicine by Dr. Charles Windrige/Dr. Wu Xiaochun (Mainstream Publishing, 1994)

Gentle Medicine by Angela Smyth (Thorsons, 1994)

Guide to Complementary Medicine and Therapies by Anne Woodham (Health Education Authority, 1994)

The Handbook of Complementary Medicine by Stephen Fulder (Oxford Medical Publications, 1988)

The Healing Foods Cookbook by Jane Sen (Thorsons, 1996)

How to Live Longer and Feel Better by Linus Pauling (W. H. Freeman, USA, 1986)

Italy for the Gourmet Traveller by Fred Plotkin (Kyle Cathie, 1997)

Maximum Immunity by Michael Wiener (Gateway Books, 1986)

Medicine and Culture by Lynn Payer (Gollancz, 1990)

The Nervous System by Peter Nathan (Whurr Publishers, 1997)

Reader's Digest Family Guide to Alternative Medicine, ed. Dr. Patrick Pietroni (The Reader's Digest Association, UK/USA/South Africa/Australia, 1991)

The Roman Cookery of Apicius translated by John Edwards (Rider, 1989)

Seeds of Change, Five Plants that Transformed Mankind by Henry Hobhouse (Macmillan, 1992)

You Can Heal Your Life by Louise Hay (Eden Grove, USA, 1988)

Headaches and Migraines

Headaches by Dr. John Lockie with Karen Sullivan (Bloomsbury, 1992)

Migraine: A Comprehensive Guide to Effective Treatment by Eileen Herzberg (Element Books, 1994)

Heart Problems

Conquering Heart Disease by Richard Brown (Arterial Health Foundation, 1990)

Forty Something Forever: A Consumer's Guide to Chelation Therapy and Other Heartsavers by Arline and Harold Brecher (Healthsavers Press, USA, 1992)

Healing the Heart by Elizabeth Wilde McCormick (Optima, 1992)

Herbs

The Complete Herb Book by Jekka McVicar (Kyle Cathie, 1994)

The Complete Illustrated Holistic Herbal by David Hoffman (Element Books, UK/USA, 1996)

Dr Stuart's Encyclopedia of Herbs and Herbalism by Dr Malcolm Stuart (Egerton International, 1994)

The Family Medical Herbal by Kitty Campion (Dorling Kindersley, 1988)

Herbs for Common Ailments by Anne McIntyre (Gaia, 1992)

The Herb Society's Complete Medicinal Herbal by Penelope Ody (Dorling Kindersley, 1993)

The Home Herbal by Barbara Griggs (Pan Books, 1995)

The Illustrated Herbal Handbook for Everyone by Juliette de Bairacli Levy (Faber, 1991)

The New Green Pharmacy by Barbara Griggs (Vermillion, 1997)

Homeopathy

The Woman's Guide to Homeopathy by Dr Andrew Lockie and Dr Nicola Geddes (Hamish Hamilton, 1992)

IBS

Food Allergy and Intolerance by Jonathan Brostoff and Stephen Challacombe (Balliere Tindall, 1987)

IBS – A Complete Guide to Relief from Irritable Bowel Syndrome by Christine Dancey and Susan Backhouse (Robinson, 1997)

Mental and Emotional

Anxiety, Phobias & Panic Attacks by Elaine Sheehan (Element Books, UK, 1996)

Coping with Depression by Ivy Blackburn (Chambers, 1987)

Depression by Sue Breton (Element Books, 1996)

Healing and the Mind by Bill Moyers (Doubleday, USA, 1993)

Mind, Body and Immunity. How To Enhance Your Body's Natural Defences by Rachel Charles (Cedar, 1993)

Mind-Body Medicine: How to Use Your Mind for Better Health ed. by Daniel Goleman and Joel Gurin (Consumer Reports Books, USA, 1993)

Mind, Stress and Health by Richard Totman (Souvenir Press, 1990)

Stress: An Owner's Manual by Arthur Rowshan (Element Books, 1993)

Stressmanship by Dr. Audrey Livingstone Booth (Severn House, 1985)

MS

Coping with MS by Cynthia Benz (Macdonald-Optima, 1988)

Living with MS by Elizabeth Forsythe (Faber, 1979)

Maximizing Your Health in MS by D. Frankel and R. Buxbaum (National MS Society, USA, 1982)

MS Special Diet Cookbook by Geraldine Fitzgerald and Fenella Briscoe (Harper/Collins, 1989)

Multiple Sclerosis: A Comprehensive Guide To Effective Treatment by Richard Thomas (Element Books, 1995)

Multiple Sclerosis – The Facts by W.B. Matthews (OUP, 1993)

Multiple Sclerosis: A Guide for Patients and Their Families by L. C. Scheinberg (National MS Society, USA)

Multiple Sclerosis: The Self-Help Guide by Judy Graham (Thorsons, 1992)

Nutrition and Diet

The Amino Revolution by Robert Erdmann & Meirion Jones (Century, 1987)

The Complete Guide to Vitamins and Minerals by Leonard Mervyn (Thorsons, 1986)

The Food Tolerance Diet Book, by Elizabeth Workman, Dr. Virginia Jones, Dr. John Hunter (Dunitz, 1986)

Foods that Harm, Foods that Heal (Reader's Digest, 1996)

Food: Your Miracle Medicine by Jean Carper (Simon & Schuster, 1993)

The Healing Foods by Patricia Hausmann & Judith Benn Hurley (MJF Books, USA, 1989)

Healing Nutrients by Patrick Quillen (Contemporary Books, USA/Beaverbooks, Can, 1987, Penguin, 1989)

Healing through Nutrition by Dr Melvyn Werbach (Thorsons, 1995)

Minerals: What They Are and Why We Need Them by Miriam Polunin (Thorsons, 1979)

Nutritional Medicine by Stephen Davies and Alan Stewart (Pan Books, 1987)

Prescription for Nutritional Healing by James & Phyllis Balch (Avery Press, USA, 1990)

Superfoods: Superfoods Diet Book and Superfast Foods by Michael van Straten and Barbara Griggs (Dorling Kindersley, 1994)

200 New Food Combining Recipes by Inge Dries (Element Books)

The Vitamin Bible by Earl Mindell (Arrow, 1993)

Vitamin C, The Common Cold and Flu by Linus Pauling (Berkeley, USA, 1970)

Vitamin C: The Master Nutrient by Sandra Goodman (Keats, USA, 1991)

You are What you Eat by Kirsten Hartvig and Dr Nick Rowley (Piatkus, 1996)

PMS

Beat PMT through Diet by Maryon Stewart (Ebury Press, 1988)

Coping with Periods by Diana Saunders (Chambers, 1985)

Seeing Red: The Politics of Premenstrual Tension by S. Laws, V. Hey and A. Eagan (Hutchinson, 1986)

Self Help with PMS by Michelle Harrison (MacDonald, 1990)

Psoriasis

Beat Psoriasis, by Sandra Gibbons (Thorsons, 1992)

Diets to Help Psoriasis, by Harry Clements (Thorsons, 1981)

Useful Addresses

Ayurveda

NORTH AMERICA

American Association of Ayurvedic Medicine
PO Box 598
South Lancaster
Massachusetts 01561
USA
Tel: 1 800 843 8332
Fax: 1 201 777 1197

Canadian Association of Ayurvedic Medicine
PO Box 541
Station B
Ottawa
Ontario K1P 5P8
Canada
Tel: 1 613 837 5737

Bach flower remedies

AUSTRALIA

Martin & Pleasance
137 Swan Street
Richmond
Victoria 3121
Tel: 61 39 427 7422

EUROPE

Dr. Edward Bach Centre
Mount Vernon
Sotwell
Wallingford
Oxon OX10 0PZ
Great Britain
Tel: 44 1491 834678
Fax: 44 1491 825022

NORTH AMERICA

Nelson Bach USA Ltd
Wilmington Technology Park
100 Research Drive
Wilmington
Massachusetts 01887-4406
USA
Tel: 1 508 988 3833

Food Science

EUROPE

Pesticides Trust
Eurolink Centre
49 Effra Road
London SW2 1BZ
Great Britain
Tel. 44 171 274 8895

Soil Association
86 Colston Street
Bristol BS1 5BB
Great Britain
Tel: 44 117 929 0661
Fax: 44 117 925 2504

NORTH AMERICA

The Organic Foods Production Association
of North America
PO Box 1078
Greenfield
Massachusetts 01302
USA
Tel: 1 413 774 7511
Fax: 1 413 774 6432

Pesticide Action Network
North American Regional Center
116 New Montgomery Street
No. 810
San Francisco
California 94105
USA
Tel: 1 415 541 9140
Fax 1 415 541 9253

Herbalism

AUSTRALIA

National Herbalists Association of Australia
Suite 305
BST House
3 Smail Street
Broadway
New South Wales 2007
Tel: 61 2 211 6437
Fax: 61 2 211 6452

NORTH AMERICA

American Herbalists Guild
PO Box 1683
Soquel
California 95073
USA

Hydrotherapy

NORTH AMERICA

Aquatic Exercise Association
PO Box 1609
Nokomis
Florida 34274
USA
Tel: 1 813 486 8600

Naturopathy

AUSTRALIA

Australian Natural Therapists Association
(ANTA)
PO Box 308
Melrose Park
South Australia 5039
Tel. 61 8 371 3222
Fax: 61 8 297 0003

Federation of Natural and Traditional
Therapists (FNTT)
238 Ballarat Road
Footscray
Victoria 3011
Tel: 61 3 9318 3057

EUROPE

British College of Naturopathy and
Osteopathy
Frazer House
6 Netherhall Gardens
London NW3 5RR
Great Britain
Tel: 44 171 435 6464
Fax: 44 171 431 3630

General Council and Register of Naturopaths
Goswell House
2 Goswell Road
Street
Somerset BA16 0JG
Great Britain
Tel: 44 1458 840072
Fax: 44 1458 840075

NORTH AMERICA

American Association of Naturopathic
Physicians
PO Box 20386
Seattle
Washington 98102
USA
Tel: 1 206 323 7610

American Naturopathic Medical Association
PO Box 19221
Las Vegas
Nevada 89132
USA
Tel: 1 702 796 9067

Canadian Naturopathic Association
205, 1234 17th Avenue South West
PO Box 4143
Station C
Calgary
Alberta
Canada
Tel: 1 413 244 4487

Nutrition

EUROPE

British Nutrition Foundation
High Holborn House
52–4 High Holborn
London WC1V 6RQ
Great Britain
Tel: 44 171 404 6504

Vegetarian Society
Parkdale
Dunham Road
Altrincham
Cheshire WA14 4QG
Great Britain
Tel: 44 161 928 0793
Fax: 44 161 926 9182

NORTH AMERICA

American Association of Nutrition
Consultants
1641 East Sunset Road, Apt B-117
Las Vegas
Nevada 89119
USA
Tel: 1 709 361 1132

American Dietetics Association
216 West Jackson Boulevard
Apt 800
Chicago
Illinois 60606–6995
USA
Tel: 1 800 877 1600
Fax: 1 312 899 1979

International Association of Profesional
Natural Hygienists (fasting)
204 Stambaugh Building
Youngstown
Ohio 44503
USA
Tel: 1 216 746 5000
Fax. 1 216 746 1836

National Nutritional Foods Association
150 East Paularino Avenue
Apt 285
Costa Mesa
California 92626
USA
Tel: 1 714 966 6632
Fax: 1 714 641 7005

North American Vegetarian Society
PO Box 72
Dolgeville
New York NY 13329
USA
Tel: 1 518 568 7970

Support Groups

AUSTRALIA

Anorexia Bulimia Nervosa Association
(ABNA)
35 Fullarton Road
Kent Town
South Australia 5067
Tel: 61 8 362 6772

Australian Multiple Sclerosis Society
Private Bag Q1000
QVB PO Sydney
New South Wales 2000
Tel: 61 2 287 2929
Fax: 61 2 287 2987

Australia Professional Society on
Alcohol/Drugs
Centre for Drug and Alcohol Studies
Royal Prince Alfred Hospital
Camperdown
Sydney
New South Wales 2050

Diabetes Australia
National Office
5/7 Phipps Place
Deakin
Australian Capital Territory 26000
Tel: 61 6 285 3277

ME/Chronic Fatigue Syndrome Society of
New South Wales
Royal South Sydney Community Health
Complex
Joynton Avenue
Zetland
New South Wales 2017
Tel: 61 2 9439 6026
Fax: 61 2 9392 8160
E-mail: mesoc@zip.com.au

National Epilepsy Association
PO Box 224
Parramatta
New South Wales 2150
Tel: 61 2 891 6118
Fax: 61 2 891 6137

National Heart Foundation of Australia
343 Riley Street
Surrey Hills
New South Wales
Tel: 61 2 211 5188
Fax: 61 2 281 9835

Skin and Psoriasis Foundation of Victoria
PO Box 228
Collins Street
PO 3000
Melbourne 671962
Victoria

EUROPE

Alcohol Concern
Waterbridge House
32–6 Loman Street
London SE1 0EE
Great Britain
Tel: 44 171 928 7377

Alcoholics Anonymous
PO Box 1
Stonebow House
Stonebow
York YO1 2NJ
Great Britain
Tel: 44 1904 644026

Alzheimer's Disease Society
Gordon House
10 Greencoat Place
London SW1P 1PH
Great Britain
Tel: 44 171 306 0606
Fax: 44 171 306 0808

Useful Addresses

Anaphylaxis Campaign
PO Box 149
Fleet
Hampshire GU13 9XU
Great Britain

Arthritic Association
First Floor Suite
2 Hyde Gardens
Eastbourne
East Sussex BN21 4PN
Great Britain
Tel: 44 1323 416550/44 171 491 0233
Fax: 44 1323 639793
(Helpline: 44 800 289 170)

British Allergy Foundation
Deepdene House
30 Bellegrove Road
Welling
Kent DA16 3BY
Great Britain
Tel: 44 181 303 8525
Fax: 44 181 303 8792
(Helpline: 44 181 303 8583

British Association of Dermatologists
19 Fitzroy Square
London W1P 5HQ
Great Britain
Tel: 44 171 383 0266
Fax: 44 171 388 5263

British Diabetic Association
10 Queen Anne Street
London W1M 0BD
Great Britain
Tel: 44 171 323 1531
Fax: 44 171 637 3644

British Epilepsy Association
40 Hanover Square
Leeds LS3 1BE
Great Britain
Tel: 44 113 243 9393
Fax: 44 113 242 8804
(Helpline: 44 800 30 90 30)

British Heart Foundation
14 Fitzhardinge Street
London W1H 4DH
Great Britain
Tel: 44 171 935 0185
Fax: 44 171 486 5820

Cancer Research Campaign
10 Cambridge Terrace
London NW1 4JL
Great Britain
Tel: 44 171 224 1333

The Coeliac Society
PO Box 220
High Wycombe
Bucks HP11 2HY
Great Britain
Tel: 44 1494 437278
Fax: 44 1494 474349

Eating Disorders Association
Sackville Place
44 Magdalen Street
Norwich NR3 1JU
Great Britain
Helpline: 44 1603 621414
Fax: 44 1603 664915
Website: www.gurney.org.uk/eda/

Hyperactive Children's Support Group
71 Whyke Lane
Chichester
West Sussex PO19 2LD
Great Britain
Tel: 44 1903 725182

Imperial Cancer Research Fund
PO Box 123
Lincoln's Inn Fields
London WC2A 3PX
Great Britain
Tel: 44 171 242 0200

International Diabetes Federation
40 rue Washington
B-1050 Brussels
Belgium
Tel: 32 2 647 4414
Fax: 32 2 640 8565

Multiple Sclerosis Society
25 Effie Road
London SW6 1EE
Great Britain
Tel: 44 171 371 8000
Fax: 44 171 736 9861

ME (Myalgic Encephalomyelitis) Association
Stanhope House
High Street
Stanford-le-Hope
Essex SS17 0HA
Great Britain
Tel: 44 1375 642466
Fax: 44 1375 360256
(Helpline: 44 1375 361013)

National Association for Colitis and Crohn's Disease
98a London Road
St Albans
Herts AL1 1NX
Great Britain
Tel: 44 1717 844296

National Asthma Campaign
Providence House
Providence Place
London N1 0NT
Great Britain
Tel: 44 171 971 0444

Psoriasis Association
MIlton House
7 Milton Street
Northampton NN2 7JG
Great Britain
Tel: 44 1604 711129
Fax: 44 1604 792994

Raynaud's and Scleroderma Association
112 Crewe Road
Alsager
Cheshire ST7 2JA
Great Britain
Tel: 44 1270 872776

NORTH AMERICA

Alzheimer's Association
919 North Michigan Avenue
Apt 1000
Chicago
Illinois 60611
USA
Tel: 1 800 272 3900
Fax: 1 312 335 1110

American Anorexia and Bulimia Association
293 Central Park West
Suite 1R
New York NY10024
USA
Tel: 1 212 501 8351

American Association of Dermatology
930 North Maucham road
PO Box 4014
Schaumburg
Illinois 60168-4014
USA
Tel: 1 708 330 0230

American Diabetes Association
1660 Duke Street
Alexandria
Virginia 22314
USA
Tel: 1 800 232 3472

American Heart Association
7320 Greenville Avenue
Dallas
Texas 75231
USA

American Sleep Disorders Association
604 Second Street South West
Rochester
Minnesota 55900
USA
Tel: 1 507 287 6006

Cancer Control Society
2043 North Berendo Street
Los Angeles
California 90027
USA
Tel: 1 213 663 7801

Chronic Fatigue and Immune Dysfunction Syndrome (CFIDS) Association of America
PO Box 220398
Charlotte
North Carolina 2822-0398
USA
Tel: 1 800 442 3437
Fax: 1 704 365 9755
Internet: http://www.cfids.org
E-mail: info@cfids.org

Eating Disorders Awareness and Prevention
603 Steward Street
Suite 8013
Seattle
Washington 98101
USA
Tel: 1 206 382 3587

Epilepsy Foundation of America
4351 Garden City Drive
Landover
Maryland 20785
USA
Tel: 1 301 459 3700
Fax: 1 301 577 2684

National Multiple Sclerosis Society of the
USA
733 Third Avenue
New York NY10017-3288
USA
Tel: 1 212 986 3240
Fax: 1 212 986 7981

National Psoriasis Foundation
Suite 200
6415 South West Canyon Court
Portland
Oregon 97221
USA
Tel: 1 503 297 1545

National Wellness Institute
1045 Clark Street
Suite 210
PO Box 827
Stevens Point
Wisconsin 54481-0827
USA
Tel: 1 715 342 2969
Fax: 1 715 342 2979

Over Eaters Anonymous
PO Box 44020
Rio Rancho
New Mexico 87174-4020
USA
Tel: 1 505 891 2664

Substance Abuse and Mental Health Services
Administration
5600 Fishers Lane
Room 16-105
Rochville
Maryland 20857
USA

Index

Page numbers in **bold** indicate the main entry on a subject.

Index

Index